The Practical Muse

The Practical Muse

Pragmatist Poetics
in Hulme, Pound, and Stevens

Patricia Rae

Lewisburg
Bucknell University Press
London: Associated University Presses

Associated University Presses
440 Forsgate Drive
Cranbury, NJ 08512

Associated University Presses
16 Barter Street
London WC1A 2AH, England

Associated University Presses
P.O. Box 338, Port Credit
Mississauga, Ontario
Canada L5G 4L8

The paper used in this publication meets the requirements of the American National Standard for Permanence of Paper for Printed Library Materials Z39.48–1984.

Library of Congress Cataloging-in-Publication data

Rae Patricia, 1956–
    The practical muse : pragmatist poetics in Hulme, Pound, and Stevens / Patricia Rae.
        p.   cm.
    Includes bibliographical references and index.
    ISBN 0-8387-5352-3 (alk. paper)
    1. American Poetry—20th century—History and criticism.
    2. Pragmatism in literature. 3. Stevens, Wallace, 1879–1955—Criticism and interpretation. 4. Pound, Ezra, 1885–1972—Criticism and interpretation. 5. Hulme, T. E. (Thomas Ernest), 1883–1917.
    6. Modernism (Literature)—United States. 7. James, William, 1842–1910—Influence. 8. Poetics. I. Title.
    PS310.P66R34   1997
    811'.5209384—dc21   97-11896
                                                                              CIP

For my mother, Marion Rae, and in memory of my father,
John McQueen Rae
Fortitudine

Contents

Abbreviations

Works frequently cited are identified throughout the text and notes by the following abbreviations:

CP   Wallace Stevens. *The Collected Poems of Wallace Stevens*. New York: Knopf, 1954.

CSP   Ezra Pound. *Collected Shorter Poems*. London: Faber and Faber, 1952.

CW   T. E. Hulme. *The Collected Writings of T. E. Hulme*. Edited by Karen Csengeri. Oxford: Oxford University Press, 1994.

ERE   William James. *Essays in Radical Empiricism*. Edited by Frederick H. Burkhardt, Fredson Bowers, and Ignas K. Skrupselis. Cambridge: Harvard University Press, 1976.

GB   Ezra Pound. *Gaudier-Brzeska*. New York: New Directions, 1970.

LE   Ezra Pound. *Literary Essays of Ezra Pound*. Edited by T. S. Eliot. London: Faber and Faber, 1960.

MT   William James. *The Meaning of Truth*. Edited by Frederick H. Burkhardt, Fredson Bowers, and Ignas K. Skrupskelis. Cambridge: Harvard University Press, 1979.

NA   Wallace Stevens. *The Necessary Angel*. London: Faber and Faber, 1960.

OP   Wallace Stevens. *Opus Posthumous*. Edited by Milton J. Bates. Revised, enlarged, and corrected edition. New York: Knopf, 1989.

P   William James. *Pragmatism*. Edited by Frederick H. Burkhardt, Fredson Bowers, and Ignas K. Skrupskelis. Cambridge: Harvard University Press, 1975.

PP 1, 2   William James. *Principles of Psychology*. 2 vols. New York: Henry Holt, 1890; reprint Dover, 1950.

PU   William James. *A Pluralistic Universe*. Edited by Fredson Bowersand Ignas K. Skrupselis. Cambridge: Harvard University Press, 1977.

SP   Ezra Pound. *Selected Prose: 1909–1965.* Edited by William Cookson. London: Faber and Faber, 1960.

VRE   William James. *The Varieties of Religious Experience.* Harmondsworth: Penguin, 1982.

WB   William James. *The Will to Believe.* Edited by Frederick H. Burkhardt, Fredson Bowers, and Ignas K. Skrupskelis. Cambridge: Harvard University Press, 1979.

Preface

THIS study investigates the intersection of William James's pragmatism and the poetics of three modernist writers: T. E. Hulme, Ezra Pound, and Wallace Stevens. In doing so it follows in the wake of several comparative studies of pragmatism and modernist poetry.[1] It also aims to correct two tendencies in recent scholarship on the subject: a tendency to reduce literary pragmatism to a matter of *style* and a tendency to align it with the neopragmatism of Richard Rorty (the latter encouraged by Rorty's own description of pragmatism as the "philosophical counterpart" of modernist writing).[2] Literary modernism's pragmatist use of language, it argues, can be traced back to a pragmatist redescription of creative inspiration: an eschewal of metaphysical arguments about the *origins* of inspiration for thoughts about its *effects* or a decision to recast the traditional, "mystical" muse as a "practical" one. James provides an analogue for this double set of concerns: the set of recommendations he sets out in *Pragmatism* (1907) can be traced back to his pragmatist redescription of religious inspiration in *The Varieties of Religious Experience* (1902). When we explore the parallel between his work and that of the poets, a gap opens up between their Jamesian pragmatism and the Rortyan pragmatism generally ascribed to them.

In essence this study argues that James and the three poets are much more "optimistic" than Rorty, in James's sense of the word,[3] that is, more hopeful about the existence of God, the potential accuracy of seemingly mystical "revelations," possible correspondences between provisional "truths" and reality, and the advantage to be gained by subjecting those "truths" to an empirical test. Within the radical skepticism of Rorty's pragmatism, his ideal citizens are dogmatically "pessimistic," that is, atheistic and resistant both to theory-hope and to a faith in verification procedures. Denying any possibility of order in the world, hence of any match between reality and human truths, his "liberal ironists" make and unmake their "fictions" as Nietzsche did, feeling no sense of duty to "the facts." In Rorty's view Jamesian pragmatism commits itself to such a program when it rejects metaphysical standards and makes "satisfaction" the only measure of "truth"; modernist writing fulfils such a program in its aestheticism and antimimeticism, in being "the kind of literature which prides itself on its autonomy and novelty rather than its truthfulness to experience."[4] But he is wrong about James, and, if Hulme, Pound, and Stevens may be viewed as a representative sample, about modernism. James and the poets acknowledge that the existence of God and divine revelation are uncertainties, not certain illusions. Though they are committed to the pragmatist principle of identifying the truthfulness of a proposition with the "satisfaction" it brings, they also retain a commitment to verification-processes, for they assume that *no proposition will satisfy* that does not attend to the best evidence of "reality" available. A qualified optimism about theory-making and an attendant responsibility to "the facts," however mediated, is for them both an ethical and a political imperative. To put it another way, their preferred mode of expression is not the "fiction" but the "hypothesis."

After introducing the basic principles of Jamesian pragmatism, the study divides into two parts: an account of the early modernist poetics devised by Hulme and Pound in London, in Part One, and a more detailed investigation of Stevens's poetics, originating during James's tenure at Harvard, in Part Two. The individual chapters on Hulme and Pound, and the two chapters on Stevens, all trace the correlation (what I call, after James, a "reflex-action"[5]) between the poets' theories of creative inspiration and their poetic practice. They propose reasons and sources for their debt to James. They point to the Jamesian pragmatist character of the poets' work, finally, to illuminate certain central critical questions about Hulme's Romanticism or Classicism; about Pound's relationship to Hulme, and his allegiance to science or to religion; about Stevens's questionable representations of female muses and his poetry's aestheticism or worldliness.

The reconstruction of Hulme's Imagist poetics in Chapter 1 challenges the prevailing critical view of his work as an unrewarding tangle of "fallacies and contradictions."[6] It also shows that Hulme's description of an intuitionist and organicist creative process is not, as many have claimed, inconsistent with his expressed hostility to "romanticism." As I demonstrate, by "romanticism" Hulme means only a tendency to exaggerate the cognitive capacities of human beings. Thus, his "romanticism" includes both science's exaggerated claims for the analytical intellect, which have led to mechanism and determinism, and the grandiose claims made for intuition in Idealist aesthetics. His Jamesian account of inspiration is, then, wholly consistent with his "new classical" poetics in that it acknowledges the unique promise of intuition, without making definitive claims about its power. The major sources for Hulme's understanding of the creative process and its product were three French writers whose work overlapped with James's: the empirical psychologist Théodule Ribot and the philosophers Henri Bergson and Jules de Gaultier. As I explain, Ribot and Bergson provided Hulme with an alternative to the inspiring "Idea" in the form of a psychological entity called the *conception idéale*: a cluster of images and ideas, of unknown origin, appearing before the consciousness and demanding to be expressed. Gaultier offered a pragmatic rationale for articulating that "inside idea" and made some suggestions about the provisional language appropriate to the task. Hulme's notes also suggest that Imagism's central technique—the juxtaposition of concrete, analogous images—may have been inspired by James's own remarks on analogy in *A Pluralistic Universe* (1909). James celebrates the kind of analogy that highlights both similarity and difference, the trope that, like the hypothesis, both starts a generalization and keeps it pressed against experience. Hulme conceives analogy in the same way; it calls attention to some regular shadow in the world while focusing the reader's eye on the unassimilated details lying around what Hulme, after James, called the "fringe" of consciousness. Using James's own readings of analogy in *A Pluralistic Universe* as a hermeneutic model, we can appreciate Hulme's Imagist poems as the perfect expressions of "bracketed" moments of illumination. In inviting one to consider analogies between the moon and the stars and everyday objects, these poems encourage one to reconsider the grand metaphysical claims often attached to the celestial bodies. But they only *suggest* this demystification; they also invite the reader to look hard at the objects under discussion and to debate whether the similarities are overshadowed by the differences. The reader is drawn into an ongoing process of hypothesis-testing, in which an ordered world is a possibility under constant review.

Appreciating Hulme's debt to James makes it possible to explain and to clarify the parallels between Hulme's ideas and Ezra Pound's—parallels too often discounted by Pound's critics as they are by Pound himself. Chapter 2 explores Pound's early Vorticist poetics together with the Vorticist poetry and sculpture of Wyndham Lewis and Henri Gaudier-Brzeska to demonstrate how closely they resemble both Hulme's poetics and each other. Pound encountered James's ideas in London at the meetings of G. R. S. Mead's Quest Society, a forum for the study of religion and science which he attended faithfully from 1911 to 1913. Many of the essays in the society's journal, *The Quest*, were directly influenced by James, and these serve as an illuminating discursive context for the accounts of inspiration in Pound's Vorticist manifestos. Pound's Vorticist poet, overwhelmed by sudden noetic experiences whose origins remain unknown, is like James's mystic. Pound's "Image," the complex of feelings and ideas that presents itself in inspired moments, is a version of Ribot's and Bergson's *conception idéale*. Like James and Hulme, Pound felt that a faithful translation of this cluster required repudiating Symbolist techniques, with their presumptions about the world's identities, and embracing a more tentative trope, called by Pound the "interpretive metaphor." Pound emphasizes the hypothetical character of this metaphor by distinguishing it from the merely "ornamental" or "untrue" metaphor; as a hypothesis it invites the reader to an endless process of "discovery." This chapter concludes by showing that Vorticist painting and sculpture are designed to provoke the same kind of truth-seeking response. The works of Lewis and Gaudier-Brzeska initiate a process of abstraction by assimilating all things to geometric forms, but they also preserve references to the flux, thus inviting the viewer to question the adequacy of the simplifications. In other words, they are not the autotelic structures, or examples of "pure form," they have generally been seen to be; like their poetic equivalents, they retain a mimetic purpose.

The two chapters in Part Two focus on the two sides of the creative "reflex-action" in Wallace Stevens. Chapter 3 examines the affinities between Stevens's account of poetic inspiration and the accounts given by James and by his student (and subsequently Stevens's mentor) George Santayana. The exact nature of Stevens's debts to both philosophers is, as I show, relevant to recent discussions about Stevens and gender, particularly to Frank Lentricchia's view of Stevens as overanxious to reconcile poetry with manhood. Stevens's descriptions of the creative process corroborate Lentricchia's portrait. His circumspection regarding metaphysical discourse and mystical experience (both gendered feminine) was motivated by a fear of effeminacy: a discomfort with the passivity of the mystic and a sense that defending metaphysical truth-claims was a frivolous activity unbefitting a man. On the other hand, the strange figures Stevens offers as alternatives to the "mystic muse"—his nameless, faceless, usually female "companions of the conscience"[7]—may have been too readily taken to reflect misogyny or antifeminist values. Critics of Stevens's female figures have been understandably offended by their anonymity and by their apparent subservience to male desire. But when we fully appreciate their function within Stevens's theory of inspiration—that is, *as muses* corresponding to the divinities that James brackets in *The Varieties of Religious Experience*—we can also see that these figures are the means by which Stevens renounces and undercuts patriarchal authority. An account of creation that begins in an effort to avoid effeminacy culminates in an endorsement of what Stevens viewed as "feminine" values. If James contributed to Stevens's perception that metaphysical ways of thinking are unmanly, he may also have inspired his recognition that preserving his "virility" in one way means giving it up for "femininity" in another. For throughout his work, James personifies pragmatism as a woman, dedicated to "unstiffening" the rigid theories and subverting the binary oppositions of philosophy.

In demonstrating that Stevens's muse closely resembles James's divinity, chapter 3 also emphasizes her difference from the one George Santayana describes in *Interpretations of Poetry and Religion* (1900). Santayana upholds the Nietszchean view of gods and their communications as *nothing but* the projections of desire—as fantasies situated entirely within the self—but Stevens shares James's view that they may, indeed, be objective; his "necessary angels" float on the threshold between the subject and the outer world, their status, and the authority of their utterances, remaining undecided. Chapter 4 develops this argument, challenging a widely accepted view about Stevens's affinity with Santayana by showing that Stevens remains committed to the Jamesian point of view: it rejects the poetics of "fiction" usually attributed to him and describes his poetics of "hypothesis." Stevens has two methods of calling attention to the uncertain provenance and status of the insights accompanying inspiration. The first exploits what Bachelard has called the "poetics of space." Eschewing Idealist representations of intuitive moments as flights into "Infinity," he places his vatic figures within ironically circumscribed spaces—jars, crystals, and mirrors, and huts and houses—or in spaces midway between the earth and the sky. These "epochal" settings, as Husserl might call them, are tantamount to phenomenological brackets; they reduce the vatic moments that occur within them to facts of experience while suspending judgment about their ultimate significance. Corresponding to these qualifying landscapes are multifarious grammatical devices whereby Stevens suspends judgment about his poetic assertions: the use of modal auxiliaries and corrective tags, the juxtaposition of opposing statements, and the Imagist practice of arresting theories at the stage of a suggestive analogy or simile. Both Stevens's figurative landscapes and his grammar convey a qualified optimism about theory's potential. His figures for theory are houses whose walls *may* match the contours of the world, even if that match cannot be confirmed; his grammatical qualifiers cast doubt on hypothetical flights but also entertain the possibility of their truthfulness. Most important Stevens always leaves room for verifying theories against experience.

My discussion of Stevens's poetics of "hypothesis" is intended to show that the popular view of him as a poet of "fictions" is an important and damaging simplification. From his early reputation as an aesthete, to the New Critical celebration of his autotelic poetry, to his canonization as deconstructionist, even to recent discussions of his pragmatism by David M. LaGuardia and Thomas Grey, most commentators have ignored Stevens's qualified hope for mystical illumination and for the provisional utterances it inspires.[8] There has been a tendency to presume that in admitting doubt Stevens completely renounces faith and with it all accountability to "reality." This is, significantly, the same tendency that characterized critical reception of James's pragmatism. As chapter 4 also shows, Stevens himself anticipates and refutes these assumptions, using the same arguments as James directed against his critics, in *The Meaning of Truth* (1909). Though it has generally gone unnoticed, Stevens is fully as careful to place statements of skeptical doctrine under epochal suspension as he is to qualify statements expressing mystical hope. He also develops a version of what Gerald Myers has called James's "ethics of optimism,"[9] pointing out the perversity of choosing to be epistemologically and ontologically pessimistic where optimistic choices are just as viable. That he has generally been

credited with the complacent and conservative politics of a fictionalist is
the great irony of Stevens's reception, for he articulates a powerful critique
of fiction-making on political grounds. Like James and many opponents of
Rorty, including Cornel West and Clifford Geertz, Stevens sees an analogy
between the fiction-maker and the colonizer—both of them indulgers of
desire, cruelly indifferent to the "facts" of the worlds they describe. My
account of Stevens, then, suggests that he would have approved both of
neo-Jamesian criticisms of Rortyan neopragmatism and of recent efforts,
most notably by Alan Filreis and James Longenbach, to examine his poetry's engagement with the "actual world."[10]

The poetics of Hulme, Pound, and Stevens blend many attributes their
critics consider incompatible; like James's pragmatism they are both
"tender-minded" and "tough-minded," both "intellectualistic" and "sensa-
tionalistic," both "religious" and "irreligious," both "dogmatical" and
"sceptical" (P 13). In showing how their work reconciles these qualities,
this study aims throughout, and more pointedly in its fifth and final chapter,
to challenge criticism that presumes the poets' bifurcation. Binary thinking
has been responsible, for example, for the perception of a "contradiction"
in Hulme's work between his Bergsonian attack on romantic Idealism and
his absolutist ethics and politics. To explain this contradiction, his critics
have found it necessary to posit an ideological about-face midway through
his career, in which he repudiates Bergson's skepticism and embraces dogmatic thinkers on the political right. In fact, a Jamesian paradigm enables
us to see that his political ethics balance skepticism and dogmatism in the
same way his poetics do; the moral values he advocates are hypotheses,
worthy of being entertained both for the comfort they provide and for the
possibility of divine provenance. Similarly, Pound's critics have debated
whether he is a materialist or a mystic, a believer or a doubter in universal
order, when the truth is that he is something of both—someone who regarded the designs in his poetry as representing "not necessarily belief in a
permanent world" but "a belief in that direction."[11] When we appreciate
these complexities and relocate Pound, like Stevens, in a middle ground, it
becomes possible to close the extreme and implausible "gap" that Marjorie
Perloff has described as unbridgeable between the two poets:[12] the gap
between one poet preoccupied with reality, and another with the mind,
between one dedicated to the hard facts of history, the other with the
escapes enabled by imagination—the abyss, in short, between a "tough-
minded" poet and a "tender-minded" one.

In sum, then, the three case studies that follow aim to demonstrate the
usefulness of three major aspects of Jamesian pragmatism for modernist
poetics: its redescription of mystical experience in the language of empirical
psychology; its specifications for the hypothetical modes of expression appropriate for representing the knowledge gained in such experience; and

its careful preservation of both "tough" and "tender" attitudes within a
single complex. The "reflex-action" from inspiration to expression could
equally well have been traced through the work of other modernist writers,
in particular, those, like Frost, Eliot, and Stein, who came into James's
orbit at Harvard. It is in part a decision to sacrifice breadth of coverage
for depth of exploration that has led me to exclude these writers. But it is
also my hope that the less predictable choices of Hulme and the young
Pound will point to the international nature of James's influence, to the
role played by his ideas in the definition of modernist poetry in London as
well as Boston—a role usually granted only to the philosophies of Nietzsche
and Bergson. What follows is not meant as a comprehensive view of modernist poetics but as a proposal for reconsidering modernist writers, on
both sides of the Atlantic, in the light of an underestimated philosopher.
If I may myself conclude in a hypothesis, James's intense concern with
redescribing both sides of the creative process, and his inclusive attitude
toward faith in an era of doubt, may make his pragmatism—not Rorty's—
the best candidate for modernism's "philosophical counterpart."

Acknowledgments

I would like to thank the Social Sciences Research Council of Canada, the Faculty Research Grant Committee of the University of Victoria, and the Advisory Research Council and Office of Research Services at Queen's University for the funding that made this research possible. I am grateful also to the editors at Associated University Presses and to the staffs of the Bodleian Library and Corpus Christi College, Oxford; the Houghton Library at Harvard University; and the Stauffer Library at Queen's University. At the Stauffer Library, special thanks to Bonnie Cuddon for her unfailing expertise and good will and for finding me a place to work when I needed one.

My greatest debt among scholars is to Sanford Schwartz, whose fine work on literary modernism and continental philosophy first suggested to me that a special space could be carved out for James. He has generously lent his support to the project at various stages. I am also grateful to Frank Lentricchia, for an inspiring seminar at the School of Criticism and Theory in the summer of 1985; to Carlos Prado, for endorsing the project while disagreeing about Rorty; and to Eleanor Cook, for reading and commenting wisely upon an earlier version of the manuscript and for giving me the chance to present some of my thoughts on Stevens at the MLA convention in 1994. Holly Laird and Lars Engel provided a wonderful opportunity for scholars of pragmatism with their symposium at the University of Tulsa in the spring of 1993.

At Queen's, Karen Donnelly transcribed a large section of the manuscript at a crucial moment and Steve Cain and Ella Ophir were invaluable research assistants. The friendship of my colleagues has sustained me through the long process of seeing this project to completion; I am especially grateful to Les Monkman, Elizabeth Hanson, Paul Stevens, Sylvia Söderlind, Maggie Berg, Mel Wiebe, Lola Cuddy, and Laurene Snider for their wise counsel and support. Over the years, I have also benefited immeasurably from the intellectual companionship of Alan and Julia Thomas, Deirdre Coleman, Martha Bremser, Marwan El Sabban, Fadia Homaidan, William Abbott, Elspeth Garman, John Barnett, Lynn Tarzwell, Daphne Dumont, Julia McArthur, and Kathy G. Hleuka Soles.

But my deepest appreciation is reserved for my family. My mother, my late father, and my brother John have been endlessly supportive. T. S. Rae has been constant in his affection. My husband, Mark Jones, has been the best of critics and the best of friends, a paradigm of Jamesian tough– and tender–mindedness. This project would never have been completed without them.

*   *   *

Earlier versions of parts of chapter 1 have appeared as "T.E. Hulme's French Sources: A Reconsideration," *Comparative Literature* 41 (1989), 68–99, and "Imagism and *Bovarysme,*" *Southern Review* 21 (1988), 26–42. Chapter 2 has been published in a shorter form as "From Mystical Gaze to Pragmatic Game: Representations of Truth in Vorticist Art," *ELH* (1989): 689–720. I am grateful to the editors of these journals for permission to reprint.

I wish also to acknowledge the following, from which citations in this book are taken:

Collected Poems by Wallace Stevens. Copyright © 1954 by Wallace Stevens. Used by permission of Alfred A. Knopf, Inc. and Faber and Faber, Ltd.

Collected Shorter Poems by Ezra Pound. Copyright © 1952 by Ezra Pound. Used by permission of Faber and Faber, Ltd. and New Directions Publishing.

The Collected Writings of T. E. Hulme by T. E. Hulme. Edited by Karen Csengeri. Copyright © 1994 by Karen Csengeri. Used by permission of Oxford University Press.

Gaudier-Brzeska by Ezra Pound. Copyright © 1970 by Ezra Pound. Used by permission of New Directions Publishing.

Guide to Kulchur by Ezra Pound. Copyright © 1970 by Ezra Pound. Used by permission of New Directions Publishing.

Letters of Wallace Stevens by Wallace Stevens. Edited by Holly Stevens. Copyright © 1966 by Holly Stevens. Used by permission of Alfred A. Knopf, Inc. and Faber and Faber, Ltd.

The Necessary Angel by Wallace Stevens. Copyright © 1960 by Wallace Stevens. Reprinted by permission of Alfred A. Knopf, Inc. and Faber and Faber, Ltd.

The Practical Muse

Introduction: Inspiration, Reflex-action, and Pragmatism

> The germinal question concerning things brought for the first
> time before consciousness is not the theoretic "What is that?"
> but the practical "Who goes there?" or rather, as Horwicz has
> admirably put it, "What is to be done?"
> —William James, "The Sentiment of Rationality," WB

WILLIAM James's first aspiration was to be an artist. Why he gave up art
for science is unclear; it may have been because of his father's promptings
or his own perception that his artistic efforts were never to be anything
but mediocre.[1] The decision led him first to studies in physiology and medi-
cine, then to a distinguished career in psychology, with a special interest in
the psychology of religious experience, and, finally, in the last eight years
of his life, to the project of articulating and defending "pragmatism." But
James's interest in art never entirely disappeared. His writings about religious inspiration reveal a lingering fascination with creative inspiration,
and his pragmatism is as much a theory about how to paint, sculpt, and
write as it is a program for making and testing truth.

James's aesthetic theory is worth reconstructing, because it indirectly
shaped the theory and practice of several modernist poets. Reconstructing
the theory and appreciating its full significance for these poets necessitates
an understanding of James's positions on several major issues not overtly
connected with art. It also requires an effort to see the vital connection
between James's description of the religious consciousness and his pragmatism: an effort running counter to the prevailing tendency among James
scholars to compartmentalize his various interests.[2]

REINTEGRATING JAMES: A CAREER AS REFLEX-ACTION

That James's pragmatism and his work in the psychology of religion are
integrally related is suggested by a model for human consciousness popular
in James's time and central to his thought: the "reflex-action theory of

mind."[3] This conception of mental activity informs *The Principles of Psychology* (1890) and James's two major works on the psychology of religion, *The Will to Believe* (1897) and *The Varieties of Religious Experience* (1902). It is also crucial to his account of truth-making in *Pragmatism* (1907) and *The Meaning of Truth* (1909). Reintegrating the two sides of James's work becomes easier both when we note the pervasiveness of the "reflex-action" theory within it and when we appreciate how appropriate the model is for describing James's *corpus* as a whole.

James discusses the reflex-action theory of consciousness in detail in *The Principles of Psychology* and in two important essays reprinted in *The Will to Believe:* "The Sentiment of Rationality" (1879) and "Reflex-action and Theism" (1881).[4] The theory derives, he tells us, from a physiological principle first entertained by Descartes and established in the eighteenth century by the physiologists La Mattric and Cabanis: the principle that "the acts we perform are always the results of outward discharges from the nervous centres, and that these outward discharges are themselves the result of impressions from the external world."[5] For James and his contemporaries, this insight has led to the recognition that our mental states are an inseparable part of a continuum beginning with impressions and culminating in actions. Cognition is the second stage in a *"triad, neither of whose elements has any independent existence,"* a "cross-section . . . of what in its totality is a motor phenomenon."[6] The sequence of events in every cognitive experience is as follows:

> Any mind, constructed on the triadic-reflex pattern, must first get its *impression* from the object which it confronts; then *define* what that object is, and decide what *active measures* its presence demands; and finally *react. The stage of reaction depends on the stage of definition,* and these, of course, on the nature of the impressing object.[7]

This view of the close relationship between thought and action was to be important for James's pragmatism, because it committed him to acknowledging the *interestedness* of all theories or "definitions"; it pointed to the fact that all theorizing is contaminated by an awareness of how theories will "out" in action.[8] But it is also fascinating because it perfectly describes the sequence of James's interests, as he moved from the psychology of religion to pragmatism. It would not be inappropriate to describe James's career as a reflex-act writ large. On this view, *The Will to Believe* and *Varieties of Religious Experience* represent what we might call its "stage of definition." In these works James makes an effort to define a very common "impression" experienced by human beings, that is, the sense that an apparently transcendent and omniscient presence "knocks on our mental door and asks to be let in." He debates the wisdom of defining this impression in metaphysical terms, as a manifestation of "God" or of an eternal "Idea,"[9] and, deciding that such a definition would be unacceptable, proposes an alternative. The specifications for truth-making he sets out in *Pragmatism* and *The Meaning of Truth,* then, are the "active measures" corresponding to this act of "definition." More specifically, they are measures reflecting a decision to *withhold judgment* about the apparently divine being that intrudes on the consciousness and shares its secrets.[10]

The definition James ends up giving to seemingly mystical moments, or experiences of "inspiration,"[11] owes everything to the discourse of what was known in his time as the "new psychology." James's own *Principles of Psychology* was one of the first comprehensive introductions to the principles, techniques, and early results of this new science of mind. In her study of the importance of this "new psychology" for modernist literature, Judith Ryan has carefully distinguished two branches of the science—"empiricist" and "experimental" psychologies—and suggested that it is to the first of these alone that modernism is indebted.[12] But in view of James's vital work on "inspiration," and comparable work by other psychologist-philosophers such as Théodule Ribot and Henri Bergson, Ryan's distinction is far too restrictive. "Empiricist" and "experimental" psychologies differed in their techniques; the first relied on introspection, whereas the second collected physiological evidence of the mind's activities. But what they shared was important: a commitment to describing the mental experience of individuals without resorting to "metaphysical" speculation about its fundamental nature or first causes. "The mind all psychologists study," James insists, without discriminating between the experimentalist and the intuitionalist, "is the mind of distinct individuals inhabiting definite portions of a real space and of a real time. *With any other sort of mind,* absolute Intelligence, Mind unattached to a particular body, or Mind not subject to the course of time, [he] *has nothing to do*" (PP 1: 183; italics mine).

In committing himself to giving a purely "empirical"(VRE 52) account of revelatory experiences, as he does in *The Varieties of Religious Experience,* James rejects the temptation to attribute them to the intervention of some transcendent Being—Plato's Over-Soul, Schopenhauer's Will, Hegel's *Geist,* or the Judaeo-Christian God. In *The Principles of Psychology,* he calls such a Being the *"perfect object of belief"* (PP 2: 944): nothing could be more satisfying than to claim contact with it. But attributing the experience of illumination to such a principle would amount to making a statement about the experience's primary cause, which would violate James's commitment to the discourse of psychology. Instead he chooses to define the impression in phenomenological terms: the source becomes a presence that is *felt* or something that one *"considers* divine," but its real nature is always "bracketed."[13] For a single, genuinely mystical God, in other words,

James substitutes an indefinite number of beings that *function like* God; their identity, their origin inside or outside the consciousness, he deems irrelevant. Among his few specifications for such divinities is their *appearance* of otherness, their quality of *seeming* to come from outside the self.[14] It is this apparent independence from the beholder's desires that seems to authorize the propositions they whisper in his ear:

> [Mystical states] are states of insight into depths of truth unplumbed by the discursive intellect. They are illuminations, revelations, full of significance and importance, all inarticulate though they remain; and as a rule they carry with them a curious sense of authority for after-time.[15]

"Mystical" moments, then, are experiences of conviction, in which one feels that one's insights are absolutely true. Here it must be emphasized that James's emphasis is on the *feeling* of truthfulness rather than the *fact*. Being unable to claim definitively that the apparently autonomous divinity *is* what it *seems,* he must translate truth-claims into claims about the "sentiment" of a proposition's "rationality."[16] He is also obliged to concede that there may be as many divinities and apparently truthful propositions as there are self-proclaimed "mystics": disavowing all certain knowledge of first principles leads inexorably to pluralism (VRE 525).

If this new description of religious experience constitutes the significant act of "definition" in James's career, what are the "active measures" he devises in response to it? I propose that these "measures" are the specifications he develops for how people should handle the insights they enjoy in their moments of "illumination." James does not formulate this advice completely until *Pragmatism,* but he anticipates it in the writings on religion, where he addresses the problem of how people should deal with the conclusion to which their "mystical" experiences seem to point: that God exists.[17] James knows that his obligation to problematize the status of the divinity makes a final judgment about that proposition impossible. To decide definitively for or against it would be to violate the "opaque limit" (WB 30, 33) he places on a psychologist's understanding. Yet he also senses that *some* courageous position on the matter has to be taken. The decision, he realizes, is a "momentous" one, tantamount to the decision we face when lost in a blinding snowstorm: we may make the wrong choice—follow the wrong path—but "If we stand still we shall be frozen to death" (WB 30, 33).[18] His solution, which he calls "empirical theism,"[19] is a middle course between gnosticism and agnosticism. On the one hand, combining respect for testimonies about divine "visitations" with an acute awareness of the benefits of faith, he recommends that we should allow ourselves to accept the proposition about God's existence—to venture off faithfully into the snowstorm. But we must temper that belief with a certain amount of skepticism. That is to say, we must treat the proposition about God's existence as a "hypothesis" (VRE 428): a provisional truth whose authority will always rest on its continued compatibility with empirical evidence. The proposition, James says, will retain its credibility only if, when "you proceed to act upon your theory," it is "reversed by nothing that later turns up as your action's fruit," that is, if it "harmonize[s] so well with the entire drift of experience that the latter will, as it were, adopt it."[20]

The program James outlined for dealing with the proposition about God's existence inspired a whole new tradition in "empirical" theology; the American writers James Leuba, W. E. Hocking, and D. C. Mackintosh, and many contributors to the English journal *The Quest*, took up the task of justifying the proposition "in the same way as science justifies its hypotheses, that is to say, by reference to experience."[21] More importantly as I have suggested, the program served as a prototype for pragmatism—the program James devised for dealing with *any* proposition that invites belief. In its narrowest sense, the "pragmatic method" is one of reconciling philosophical disputes by asking whether the points on which opposing factions disagree make any significant difference in the world. In its more general sense, however, and the one that concerns me here, pragmatism is a *theory of truth*: a definition of what makes a theory valid. Succinctly put, the pragmatist view is that "*the true is the name of whatever proves itself to be good in the way of belief.*" There are many moments in life, James suggests, when we face decisions about whether or not to accept propositions that are as "momentous" as the proposition about God. Having no right to accept theories uncritically, as "revelations" from some transcendental Power (P 94), we must nonetheless make up our minds about them. In his estimation, the best thing to do in such circumstances is openly to indulge the interest that is bound to infect our theorizing anyway and to give our faith to the proposition that promises to be most useful to us. The "true" theory, in other words, is the one that "will carry us prosperously from any one part of our experience to any other part, linking things satisfactorily, working securely, simplifying, saving labor." (P 32). James illustrates his point by adapting his example from *The Will to Believe*: "If I am lost in the woods and starved, and find what looks like a cow-path," the "true" proposition must be that there is "a human habitation at the end of it," for believing in such a proposition, and heading down the path, may be the only means of salvation (P 42, 94, 34, 98). In short, with pragmatism *every* proposition must be regarded with the same calculated self-interest as the proposition about God. We must be constantly making Pascalian wagers.

Singling out self-interest as a criterion for truthfulness was one of the most contentious moves of James's career. His critics objected that such a position encouraged a complete lack of discipline in epistemological matters and that it was bound to lead many a dreamer to disaster; as James summarizes it, referring to the English philosopher whose work he regarded as compatible with his own, "A favorite formula for describing Mr. Schiller's doctrines and mine is that we are persons who think that by saying whatever you find it pleasant to say and calling it truth you fulfil every pragmatistic requirement." But as subsequent chapters will show, James's statement that truthfulness is coextensive with satisfactoriness does not mean his pragmatist is simply to believe everything he wants to believe. In both *Pragmatism* and *The Meaning of Truth,* James emphasizes that the "satisfaction" that makes a proposition true comes from much more than the indulgence of a longing: it is also dependent on seeing that proposition adequately corroborated by subsequent experience. "Following our mental image of a house along the cow-path," he says, "we actually come to see the house; we get the image's full verification. *Such simply and fully verified leadings are certainly the originals and prototypes of the truth-process.*" Just as empirical theism mediates between gnosticism and agnosticism, pragmatism "harmonizes" a "tender-minded" optimism about the truthfulness of propositions with a "tough-minded" concern that experience bears them out.[22]

The appropriate reaction to feelings of certainty, then, was for James an activity of fluctuating between faith and doubt, of making assertions and unmaking them, as "facts" demand. Recognizing that his ideal thinker respects "the coercions of the world of sense about him"[23] is vital if we are to appreciate how he and his poetic successors differ from other late nineteenth- and early twentieth-century philosophers whose programs for theory-making were predicated on uncertainty—particularly Friedrich Nietzsche, Jules de Gaultier, and the young George Santayana. Because I shall be emphasizing the empiricist responsibilities of Jamesian pragmatism throughout, I should clarify at the outset that James's commitment to testing theory against "fact" is not symptomatic of his falling back on a simple "correspondence" or "copy" theory of truth.[24] Two aspects of his theory, in particular, prevent such a lapse. First, James does not view the process of checking and revising with unadulterated confidence, but with what is best described as a cautious "epistemological optimism." He begins from the premise that the objectivity of the "facts" to be heeded cannot be definitively established. He maintains, however, that in the absence of such certainty we have as much reason to consider them right as we do to consider them wrong and to respect most those theories that best account for them. To do otherwise is both perverse and, as he explains in closely related writings on colonialism, ethically unacceptable.[25] Second, the reality James envisions the pragmatist testing his theories against is not immutable but in constant change, and the theories themselves play a role in its transformation. Instead of passively reflecting reality, the theory-maker helps to *bring about* a certain version of reality by imagining it. James gives a succinct summary of the process in *Pragmatism:*

> In the realm of truth-processes facts come independently and determine our beliefs provisionally. But these beliefs make us act, and as fast as they do so, they bring into sight or into existence new facts which redetermine the beliefs accordingly. So the whole coil and ball of truth, as it rolls up, is the product of a double influence. Truths emerge from facts; but they dip forward into facts again and add to them; which facts again create or reveal new truth (the word is indifferent) and so on indefinitely. (P 108)

James's conception of truth's "coil and ball" leads him to endorse an "ontological optimism" similar in rationale to his epistemological attitude. Where there is no compelling evidence to the contrary, his ideal thinker will always choose the happier theory over the sad one, knowing that his choice may be a self-fulfilling prophecy.

James appears to have been aware of the relevance of pragmatism for poetry. He includes verbal expressions among "reflex-actions," observing that "the current of life which *runs in* at our eyes or ears is meant to *run out* at our hands, feet, *or lips.*"[26] He also suggests that psychology's redefinition of the mystical moment has profound consequences for traditional notions of what constitutes poetic "genius," specifically for the conception of creative inspiration as something "divine, miraculous, and God-given."[27] The poet who feels inspired is for him no different from anyone who experiences moments of profound conviction: he must resist attributing his insight, unequivocally, to God. And the "active measures" the poet is to take, like those of any pragmatist, must respect this limitation without sacrificing either the epistemological or ontological benefits of faith. In "Reflex-action and Theism," James singles out the sculptor as someone who cannot "bid [his] . . . interests be passive," just because he can no longer testify confidently that he has been divinely inspired. The artist must express himself one way or another, and his choice is one "between operating to poor or to rich results."[28] James represents the poet's responsibilities in much the same way: his communications are not revelations of timeless Truth, but practical faith-acts taken in a moment of crisis. The poet's assertions will serve as "helps" to guide him and his audience through the intimidating "forest" of the here and now:

> They are, if I may use a simile, so many spots, or blazes,—blazes made by the axe of the human intellect on the trees of the otherwise trackless forest of human experience. They give you somewhere to go from. They give you a direction and a place to reach. They do not give you the integral forest with all its sunlit glories and its moonlit witcheries and wonders. Ferny dells, and mossy waterfalls, and secret magic nooks escape you, owned only by the wild things to whom the

region is a home. Happy they without the need of blazes! But to us the blazes give a sort of ownership. We can now use the forest, wend across it with companions, and enjoy its quality. It is no longer a place merely to get lost in and never return.[29]

James uses his topographical metaphor to remind us of the transcendental realm with which the poet can no longer claim certain contact: the forest he will explicate will not be an "integral" or "essential" one, normally hidden behind the phenomenal veil, but only the pressing world of immediate "experience." This is not to say that the poet has no chance of reaching the "essential" forest. Later in the same passage, James likens the trail he blazes to a path that *may* one day terminate in the "final valley" of absolute truth, so long as he adapts the blazes to overcome empirical obstacle after empirical obstacle. But for the present, it is "using" and "enjoying" the forest, and not "getting lost" in it, that counts. It is significant that James depicts the trail-blazing poet traveling "with companions," because he repeatedly reminds the pragmatist that the process of making and unmaking truths should be a community effort.[30] Moreover, because the poet's own instructions can only be "inconclusive,"[31] they are never coercive: he lets his companions know that they are free to follow or ignore them as they choose. As James says elsewhere of his own efforts at communication, "the most any one [sic] can do is to confess as candidly as he can the grounds for the faith that is in him and leave his example to work on others as it may."[32]

Hulme, Pound, and Stevens shared James's views both about the poet's epistemological predicament and about the use of words that was its appropriate resolution. To demonstrate the parallel between their work and his, I shall organize my investigations into their theory and practice on the reflex-action model, examining first how they interpret the "impressions" that initiate the activity and then the "active measures" they devise in response to it. The model suits their work because all three poets subscribe to an *expressive* poetics, in the widest sense of that term; they describe an activity in which the poet experiences what seems like a divine revelation, and then articulates the insights communicated. That is to say, they envision some "current" passing into the poet from what appears to be some other world, and passing out of him through his "lips." This model also enables us to appreciate the relationship between these poets' accounts of inspiration and the expressive measures they recommend and practice. It becomes clear that these are as mutually dependent as the "acts of definition" and "active measures" in all reflex activities, as interconnected as their parallel discussions in James.

"Mumbling About the Infinite": The "Mystical" Poetics of Symbolism

Like many modernist poets, Hulme, Pound, and Stevens shared a desire to rewrite an account of the poetic process they found intolerable. Their target—in some respects chimerical—was an account they associated with the German Idealist philosophers and ultimately with Plato, one they saw at work in English Romanticism, French Symbolism, American Transcendentalism, as well as in the work of "late Romantic" poets like Swinburne, Yeats, E. C. Stedman, and G. E. Woodberry. What these philosophers and poets had in common, in their eyes, was an essentially "mystical" account of the creative process and its product: a view of inspiration as an experience of achieving contact with a higher power and of poetry as a vehicle for the divine wisdom thus attained. So far as Hulme, Pound, and Stevens were concerned, the German Idealist account of art was in all important respects identical to the one Plato espouses in the *Ion* and the *Phaedrus:* they equated the state of renunciation Kant calls "disinterestedness" and its variations in other German Idealist writers, with the act of self-annihilation Plato called "divine madness."[33] The German Idealists themselves would have objected to such an interpretation; a comprehensive reading of their documents on art reveals that they backed off from attributing moments of disinterested insight to the intervention of superhuman powers and from viewing poetry as a vehicle for absolute truth.[34] But if the later poets got German Idealist theory wrong, some of the responsibility must rest with the Romantic and Symbolist writers who appealed to its authority; Symbolist manifestos, in particular, regularly assimilated Kant, Fichte, Schelling, Schopenhauer, and Hegel to Plato.[35] And if intermediaries like Baudelaire and Mallarmé themselves failed to note the ways the German Idealists undermined the overt mysticism in their work, this is itself understandable, because of the difficulty of the writings and because some of their more accessible and memorable passages contain no hint of such restraint.

Although the scope of this study precludes a detailed account of the Symbolists and their German sources, it is impossible to appreciate Hulme's, Pound's, and Stevens's affinity with James without some understanding of the mystical account of inspiration they, like James, were reacting against. To this end I would like to digress briefly and sketch the main features of the Symbolist aesthetic as I believe the poets perceived it. Here it will become apparent that some of the Symbolist poets, at least, also follow the reflex-action model, correlating their recommendations for expression with their definitions of inspiration. In interpreting inspiration as revelation, these poets appear prepared to accept the absolute authority of the poet's insights. They then endorse stylistic principles that reflect that authority, and, further, that challenge the reader to a very different interpretive process from the one posed by James's "blazes." If the modernist poets rewrite Symbolism's account of inspiration, their pragmatic style is a more generous alternative to its authoritarian grammar.

The account of creative experience in Schopenhauer's *Die Welt als Wille und Vorstellung* (1819) provides a perfect illustration of the German Idealist assimilation of Plato. As A. G. Lehmann has noted, Schopenhauer's description of what the poet undergoes reads like a "renovated theory of Platonic Ideas."[36] The poet suspends his analytical intellect, penetrates the phenomenal "veil," and apprehends the essences, or "Ideas," that lie behind it: the best, most reliable manifestations of a transcendental force called the Will. "The apprehended Idea is the true and only source of every genuine work of art."[37] Schopenhauer makes a careful distinction between the kind of creative process inspired by this "Idea" and the kind that begins with a "concept":

> The *concept* is abstract, discursive . . . attainable and intelligible only to him who has the faculty of reason, communicable by words without further assistance, entirely exhausted by its definition. The *Idea* on the other hand . . . is absolutely perceptive, individual, and, although representing an infinite number of particular things, is yet thoroughly definite. . . the *concept* is like a dead receptacle in which whatever has been put actually lies side by side, but out of which no more can be taken out (by analytical judgments) than has been put in (by synthetical reflection). The *Idea*, on the other hand, develops, in him who has grasped it, representations that are new as regards the concept of the same name; it is like a living organism, developing itself and endowed with generative force, which brings forth what was not previously put into it.[38]

Here Schopenhauer renovates Plato's account of inspiration to emphasize that the wisdom embodied in the apprehended "Ideas" is ineffable. In this respect, as in others, the poet's experience fulfils the criteria James set out in *The Varieties of Religious Experience* for mystical experience ("no adequate account" of the content of such experiences, he says there, "can be given in words"); Schopenhauer's model may have been Kant, who had attributed the same quality to "aesthetical ideas" in *The Critique of Judgment*.[39] Schopenhauer also follows Kant in specifying that the process the "Ideas" inspire is the heuristic one typical of organisms. When an Idea floats before his mind, the poet "is not conscious *in abstracto* of the intention and aim of his work"; he works "unconsciously, indeed instinctively," discovering new ideas and formal features as he goes. The result is a poem that itself resembles an organism—something whose full meaning will always elude analysis.[40]

Ironically, Schopenhauer identifies the poetry resulting from the apprehension of Ideas as allegory, dismissing "symbolism" as an inferior,
concept-driven art.[41] Like the English Romantics, the French Symbolists
inverted these terms, making symbolism the art that resists analysis, and
allegory the art that succumbs to it. Albert Mockel provides a classic example of how Schopenhauer's account of the creative process was used to
describe the genesis of verse, hence to elevate it:

> L'allégorie, comme le symbole, exprime l'abstrait par le concret. Symbole et
> allégorie sont également fondés sur l'analogie, et tous deux contiennent une
> image développée.
>   Mais je voudrais appeler l'allégorie l'oeuvre de l'esprit humain ou l'analogie
> est artificielle et extrinsèque, et j'appelerai symbole celle où l'analogie apparaît
> naturelle et intrinsèque.
>   L'allégorie serait la représentation explicite ou analytique, par une image, d'une
> idée abstraite PRÉCONÇUE.
>   Au contraire le symbole suppose la RECHERCHE INTUITIVE des divers élé-
> ments idéaux épars dans les Formes.[42]

> [Allegory, like symbol, expresses the abstract by means of the concrete. Symbol
> and allegory are equally based on analogy and both contained a developed image.
>   Allegory would be the explicit or analytical representation, by way of an image,
> of a preconceived abstract idea.
>   Symbol on the other hand presupposes the intuitive search for the various
> scattered ideal elements in the Forms.]

Although it would be wrong to suggest that all the French Symbolists pro-
fessed a kind of "absolute" idealism (some, like Remy de Gourmont, espoused a "subjective" idealism, in which the highest mind the poet
contacted was his own), Mockel's comments situate him within a line of
writers who did: a line running from Baudelaire, to Mallarmé and Rimbaud, to a later generation including not just Mockel but also Moréas
and Gide. Influenced both by the discourse of German Idealism and by its
permutations in Coleridge and Carlyle, these writers represent the poet as
"l'homme chargé de voir divinement" and inspiration as an experience of
piercing phenomenal veils, doors and windowpanes—with the glorious result of apprehending the objective, authoritative, and generative "Idées."
For Baudelaire, Mallarmé, and Rimbaud, the revealed Idea also functions
as the nexus of a divinely ordained network of synaesthetic relations. The
best-known account of the universal "correspondences" is Baudelaire's
poem of that name, which depicts the network of divine relations glimmer-
ing through "des forêts de symboles."[43] The poet's intuitive "moment," in
other words, is one in which he is suddenly aware of objective analogies
or equivalencies in the world, and the mysterious "symbol"—sometimes

in the world's text, sometimes in the text the poet constructs—is the aperture of the revelation. When Mallarmé writes about the experience of apprehending the objective relations in things, he imagines himself as a spider at the center of a web of divinely ordained connections.[44] Rimbaud attributes the phenomenon to an eruption from a universal consciousness, a subconscious mind whose contents originate "là-bas."[45]

Not surprisingly, the mystical discourse the Symbolists employ to describe poetic inspiration also governs their descriptions of inspiration's product. Typically, they describe the poem as a vehicle for the Idea: an icon whose words would become transparent, enabling the reader to share in the poet's divine illumination.[46] Although it would be wrong to represent Symbolist techniques as monolithic, it is not unreasonable to say that many formal features in their work reflect the mystical definitions they give to inspiration. At the simplest level, that of diction, their verse contains numerous claims about the poet's apprehension of the Infinite: of "les Cieux inconnus" or "les splendeurs situées derrière le tombeau."[47] In a more sophisticated technique, perfected by Mallarmé, it calls attention to the ephemerality of phenomena by evoking material objects indirectly, through synecdoche or negation.[48] Perhaps most significantly the Symbolists attempt to communicate the ineffable insights of inspiration—those that exceed discursive description—by organizing images into suggestive, nondiscursive arrangements. The key feature of those arrangements is that they have no clear rationale: the images chosen bear no obvious resemblance to one another, and the poets refrain from explaining what their connection might be. Rimbaud's "Le Bateau ivre," in its presentation of a kaleidoscopic series of apparently random images, is a classic example of this policy, as are a number of the prose poems in *Les Illuminations*.[49] In the drafts of Mallarmé's poems, too, we see a very deliberate effort to excise logical connectives and other explanatory material. The same clusters of images occur in poem after poem, accruing significance, not by any overt attribution of meaning but simply by their repeated association.[50] Mallarmé's refusal ever to explain his point directly can be attributed to his confidence that the choice of images he has made reflects poetry's transcendental origins. For him, as for many of his fellow Symbolists, the analogies simply reflect relations that "existent déjà dans le sein de la Beauté." They are examples of what Baudelaire calls "l'universelle analogie."[51]

There is a direct correlation between the Symbolists' supernaturalist claims for verse and the relatively few concessions their poetry makes to its audience. Baudelaire voices a sentiment as old as Aquinas when he suggests that the obscurity of poetry is not an intrinsic property, but a function of its readers' inadequacy: "tout est hiéroglyphique, et nous savons que les symboles ne sont obscurs que d'une manière relative, c'est-à-dire selon la pureté, la bonne volonté ou la clairvoyance des âmes."[52] [all is hieroglyphic, and we know that symbols are only obscure in a relative way, that is according to the purity, the good will and the clairvoyance of souls.] The young Yeats, profoundly influenced by Symbolism in both theory and practice, says essentially the same thing in pronouncing that symbol, unlike allegory, requires only "right instinct," not "right knowledge," for its understanding.[53] This attitude is evident not just in the method of juxtaposing apparently unrelated images, but also in the images—or "symbols"—themselves, and the interpretive challenges they pose. It is typical of Symbolist poetry that a contextualist reading renders a literal interpretation of its images impossible. The windows in Mallarmé's "Les Fenêtres" and the roses in Yeats's series of "Rose" poems simply could not be literal windows and roses, given the functions ascribed to them by their context. Seeking their significance then becomes a matter of guesswork: What other objects, for which windows and roses stand, might be capable of performing these functions? The reader is put into the position of having to divine the submerged tenor in what Northrop Frye would have called an "anagogic" metaphor: one in which claims about resemblance have ceded to absolute identification. Because the symbol is deemed by its authors to have "intrinsic" rather than "extrinsic" significance, it is regarded as being a *certain* communicator of its signified. No evidence or justification is needed for equivalencies that are divinely ordained. Understanding requires only that the reader be as clairvoyant as the poet.[54]

These, then, are the essentials of the "mystical" poetics the poets challenged. Hulme, Pound, and Stevens reacted to Symbolist claims about poetry's connection with "God" or the "Absolute" or the "Infinite" with all the suspicion appropriate to psychology and pragmatism: for them, as for James, these metaphysical terms were merely "power-bringing word[s] or name[s]"(P 31) serving to aggrandize poetry and the poet. Hulme exemplifies this visceral distaste for metaphysical discourse in his 1909 "Lecture on Modern Poetry," when he dismisses the "attempt[s] to explain technique" by "mumbl[ing] of the infinite" as so much "hocus-pocus."[55] A fuller statement of the position occurs in a notebook entry from about the same period:

> The literary man deliberately perpetrates a hypocrisy, in that he fits together his own isolated moments of ecstasy . . . and presents them as a picture of a higher life, thereby giving old maids a sense of superiority to other people and giving mandarins the opportunity to talk of "ideals." Then makes attempt to justify himself by inventing the soul and saying that occasionally the lower world gets glimpses of this, and that inferentially he is the medium. As a matter of fact being certain moments of ecstasy perhaps brought on by drink.[56]

The reasons for Hulme's, Pound's, and Stevens's contempt for Symbolist "hypocrisy" are in each case too complex to be reduced to easy generalizations, but collectively their manifestos suggest that this feeling was at least partially inspired by class and gender considerations. Hulme and Stevens, in particular, reveal a discomfort with representations of poetry that emphasize its "nobility," where an "ennobled" poetry is one claiming to transcend the demands and complexities of experience.[57] They share a need to represent poetry-making as good, honest, hard work: a laborious, painstaking activity and something of genuine use in the world.[58] In this they are very similar to James, who disparages Josiah Royce's philosophy of the Absolute as a "noble" philosophy "in the bad sense": one that ignores the "real world of sweat and dirt" (P 40). Closely related to this anxiety about work is the threat these poets felt Idealism posed to their manhood. Hulme's association of Idealist hypocrisy with "old maids" is consistent with many diatribes in his work against its "femininity"; all the talk about the "Infinite" was to him a lot of "moaning" and "whining"—something associated with "sentimentality rather than . . . virile thought." Stevens articulates his distress at feminizing conceptions of poetry in his essay "The Figure of the Youth as Virile Poet," where he points to the kind of "metaphysical" thinking characteristic of Idealism as a time-wasting activity that hardly "befits a man" and poses an alternative.[59] Although the concern among male modernist poets with expunging "feminine" values from poetry has been widely acknowledged,[60] recognizing their association of femininity with mysticism enables us to see something new: the attitudes favorable to feminist interests behind the façade of modernist *machismo*. In renouncing what James called the "feminine-mystical mind"(WB 224), the three male poets also give up the claims to privileged, absolute insight that might be used to authorize a patriarchal dogmatism. In Stevens's case, in particular, the virile gestures dismissing one kind of literary "femininity" mark the surreptitious return of other "feminine" values in his poetics: tentativeness, subversiveness, and alterability.

Whatever their reasons, Hulme, Pound, and Stevens were all devoted to changing the language in which the poetic process and its product was described, and the new language provided by empirical psychology was perfectly suited to the task. It must be emphasized that the poets' hostility to Idealist accounts of creation did not mean throwing them out lock, stock, and barrel. They endorse the anti-intellectualist aspects of those accounts— their claims about poetry's beginnings in an intuitive moment, about the heuristic process by which its intuitions are realized, and about the poem's resistance to analysis. What they reject is the *significance* transcendentalist discourse attributes to these phenomena. An acceptance of the intuitive and organic aspects of Idealist poetics is what led Frank Kermode in the 1950s, and a host of literary historians after him, to dismiss as nonsense modernist claims to be breaking with romanticism.[61] But although the modernists share a great deal with the romantics, it is no longer possible to argue, as

Kermode did, that their resistance to the mystical elements in romantic and Symbolist discourse was merely superficial, that "Hulme's artist," for example, is *simply* "the Romantic voyant expressed in terms more agreeable to a man who disliked some kinds of philosophical language," or that the "Hulmian Image, precise, orderly, anti-discursive, the product of intuition" is *nothing but* "the Symbol of the French poets given a new philosophical suit."[62] Recent theories of discourse have demonstrated the inseparability of meaning and politics from language. As the reflex-action model suggests, different choices at the "stage of definition" have different consequences for action—and in the modernist redescription of Idealist poetics, this was definitely the case.

A Practical Muse and a Pragmatist Poetry

The new psychology enabled Hulme, Pound, and Stevens to redescribe the moment of "illumination" or "epiphany" with which the creative activity begins. The result was what Judith Ryan, borrowing from the Austrian novelist Robert Musil, has described as "daylight mysticism": an account that rewrites "knowing" as "*feeling that* one knows," Truth as a psychological datum, the otherworldly light of revelation as the light of common day.[63] The key sources for the "daylight mysticism" found in Pound and Hulme were, in addition to James, Théodule Ribot and Henri Bergson. Ribot was the closest counterpart to James in France, a psychologist in his own right and a major publicist for psychology generally. Bergson is best known to critics of modernism as a philosopher of time, evolution, and free will, but he derived his positions on all these issues from recent work in psychology, especially Ribot's.[64] In their accounts of art, both Ribot and Bergson campaigned against the "Idealist" account of creative activity found in Symbolism, seeking to preserve its anti–intellectualism and organicism while exorcising the metaphysical principles to which it appeals. Most fascinating is the alternative description each offers for that mystical catalyst for creation, the "Idea." Ribot defines a "conception idéale" that functions in exactly the same way as Schopenhauer's and the Symbolists' Idea: it grips the attention, alerts the poet to likenesses or analogies, and governs a heuristic process of articulation. But he disengages this construct from metaphysics, describing it as a cluster of associated images and ideas springing up from the unconscious mind, where the origin of that mind is left undecided.[65] Worried that his account of creative intuition will be equated with Schopenhauer's, Bergson adapts the concept of the *conception idéale;* in his account it becomes "une certaine image intermédiaire entre la simplicité de l'intuition concrète et la complexité des abstractions qui la traduisent, image fuyante et évanouissante, qui hante, inaperçue peut-être, l'esprit du philosophe. . . ." ["a certain intermediary image between the simplicity of the concrete intuition and the complexity of the abstractions that translate it, a receding and vanishing image, which haunts, unperceived perhaps, the mind of the philosopher. . . ."] In its position as an "intermediary" and in its function as an arbiter of expression (Bergson represents it as a "fantôme qui nous hante pendant que nous tournons autour de la doctrine et auquel il faut s'adresser pour obtenir le signe décisif"), ["a phantom that haunts us while we turn about the doctrine and to which we must go in order to obtain the decisive signal"] the *conception idéale* is not just a demystified version of the "Idea" but also a neutralized version of Plato's mystical Muse.[66] It has a counterpart in the "divinities" James substituted for God in *The Varieties of Religious Experience*: objects of prayerful communion who communicate what *seems* like timeless wisdom yet who occupy no *certain* place in a transcendental world.

Recognizing the genesis and constitution of the *conception idéale* is essential to noticing an important, previously unseen parallel between Hulme, Pound, and Stevens: all three displace the Symbolists' "Idea" with the same kind of psychologized catalyst for creativity. Versions of the *conception idéale* appear over and over again in their manifestos, central elements in their attempts to speak of verse "in a plain way." Hulme writes of an "inside image" or "idea" that "precedes [the poet's] writing and makes it firm"; in elaborating this concept, he alludes directly to Bergson's *L'Évolution créatrice*.[67] In Pound's manifestos, the *conception idéale* appears as the "Image": the "PRIMARY FORM" that "PRESENTS ITSELF TO THE VIVID CONSCIOUSNESS" of the creating poet. Here, as in Ribot and Bergson, it is a cluster of associated images and ideas, erupting from the unconscious mind and generating new images and ideas in the process of being articulated. In Stevens, finally, the *conception idéale* appears both as "the first idea" and as the "companion of the conscience," who whispers words of wisdom in the poet's ear; Stevens shrinks from attributing the "first idea" to any "voluminous master folded in his fire" and renounces the right to call his interior paramour a "mystic muse." In sum, all of these entities function like the Symbolists' Idea and the Platonic Muse: they convince the poet of something and guide him through a process of articulation that is also a process of discovery. But all of them are without the "metaphysical baggage" carried by their Idealist counterparts.[68]

The substitution of *conceptions idéales* for Ideas was much more than merely the cosmetic change that Kermode, for one, suggests. In bracketing the source of inspiration, Hulme, Pound, and Stevens are making an important point about the status of poetic knowledge. Contrary to what many commentators have suggested, this is not a claim that the poet's insights are purely subjective—the projections of desire and nothing more. Rather these insights occupy what phenomenologists would call an "epochal" space:[69] whether they originate wholly "below" the mind, in desire, is as impossible to determine as whether they originate "Beyond" the mind, in God. All that can be known for certain is that they are a *genuine part* of the poet's mental experience. As Pound says of the "Image," or as any phenomenologist might say of the contents of consciousness, it is "real" simply, and only, "because we know it directly."[70]

Aided, then, by the French psychologists, as well as by James himself, Hulme, Pound, and Stevens reduced inspiration to what it was in *The Varieties of Religious Experience:* a sudden insight, accompanied by a feeling of certainty, whose cognitive value could not be known for certain. This important move is the first thing that made theirs a "pragmatist" poetics; the second is in the programs they devise for responding to the redefined "impression." That the three theorists are committed to the central principle of the reflex action model—the principle that one's "active measures" should appropriately reflect the "stage of definition"—is suggested by the fact that each of them is a champion of "sincerity." However limited they suspect the poet's insights might be, none of them is going to make him into a rhetorician or have him lie to protect his vocation.[71] This being the case, they face a major dilemma: If the poet's insights can only ever be inconclusive, on what grounds should he ever make any assertions at all? What right does he have to consider his insight of any interest to others? Should he not, at the least, follow the route taken by Impressionist poets and painters and refrain from venturing any generalization from his experience, aiming to record (as best as language enables him) only the unprocessed data of sense?[72] What prevents Hulme, Pound, and Stevens from discouraging any form of real assertion—from consigning the poet to the torpor of skepticism—is their very Jamesian recognition that the decision to throw one's weight behind a generalization is a "momentous" one. In their own ways, they all imagine the poet lost in the woods (or in what Hulme called the "cindery" expanse of the world).[73] They all know that believing in theories is a source of comfort in what otherwise seems like chaos and that avoiding such a practice altogether will be to condemn oneself to fear, confusion, and stasis forever. To use a term proposed by Kermode, each of their hypothetical poets lives in a moment of *kairos:* a "decisive moment" where what Stevens called "dithering" (CP 452) is indefensible.[74]

Believing that uncertainty should not stand in the way of assertion, Hulme, Pound, and Stevens all recommend provisional modes of expression comparable to the ones proposed by James. That is, they all encourage the poet to assert himself, but they also urge him to indicate that his propositions are contingent on empirical testing. As I shall show, the cornerstone of all three poetics is a particular form of metaphor: one preserving the tension between the pragmatist's obligation to generalize and his duty to attend to the "real world of sweat and dirt." This is the device that Pound called the "interpretive metaphor."[75] Recognizing how this trope fulfils James's specifications for pragmatism enables us to see clearly how it differs from the Symbol. In essence it is a method of simple juxtaposition (what Frye called a "literal" metaphor) or, at its most coercive, a simile (for Frye, a "descriptive" metaphor).[76] What distinguishes this trope from the Symbol[77] is its preservation of *both* the phenomenal images between which a likeness has been perceived (the Symbol submerges one of the terms, assuming their interchangeability). In Sanford Schwartz's terms, it is a trope that embodies a "dialectic of form and flux": "a form that unifies sensory particulars without losing sight of the differences between them."[78] Wielding this kind of metaphor, the pragmatist poet claims much less authority for the insight he communicates than do his transcendentalist counterparts. Instead of assuming a divinely ordained identity, he simply calls attention to an analogy. Instead of submerging one of the metaphor's terms and challenging the reader to intuit connections he believes are objective, he simply takes the first step in a process of *making* connections, preserving all the evidence for and against generalization. Thus, he gives the reader an opportunity *to judge for herself* whether or not the incipient theory will hold up, whether or not the similarities are sufficient to prevail over the differences. In effect he adopts the kind of generous communicative practice James recommended for the pragmatist, presenting "as candidly as he can the grounds for the faith that is in him and leaving an example to work on others as it may."

The "interpretive metaphor," in other words, like other, closely related devices we shall see in pragmatist poetry, is to play the role of a "blaze" in the forest. For Hulme the poem is a provisional "map," tracing a path through the cinders; for Pound it is an "equation" for building helpful "bridges and devices"; for Stevens it is a "hypothesis," intended "to help people to live their lives" (CP 516; NA 30).[79] It is a proposition, moreover, whose usefulness *doesn't preclude its truthfulness,* so long as its readers subject it to their own processes of testing and revising. As I hope to show, pragmatist poetry—in respecting both the limitations and the potential of a "practical muse"—also makes pragmatists of its interpreters.

PART ONE

1

Pragmatism and Imagism: The "New Classical" Poetics of T. E. Hulme

What I mean by classical in verse, then, is this. That even in the most imaginative flights there is always a holding back, a reservation. The classical poet never forgets this finiteness, this limit of man. He remembers always that he is mixed up with earth. He may jump, but he always returns back; he never flies away into the circumambient gas.

The truth is that there are no ultimate principles, upon which the whole of knowledge can be built once and for ever as upon a rock. But there are an infinity of analogues, which help us along, and give us a feeling of power over the chaos when we perceive them.

— T. E. Hulme, "Romanticism and Classicism" and "Cinders," CW

CRITICS of modernist literature have not been flattering to T. E. Hulme. Though Hulme has been characterized as the most dynamic thinker in the circle of "Imagist" poets that met regularly in London in 1909, a circle known to Ezra Pound before he defined his own "Imagisme," his prose writings have been dismissed as hopelessly inconsistent, even blatantly contradictory. Some of this reputation can be attributed to Pound, who, though he praised Hulme's poetry and appended five of Hulme's poems to his own volume *Ripostes* (1909), would never countenance suggestions that his own early poetics were indebted to Hulme's. Pound's critics have tended to take his dismissal at face value.[1] But the main occasion of such criticism has been Hulme's claim, echoed by T. S. Eliot, to be breaking with the "romantic" tradition in poetry. By most accounts, the "new classicism" he advocates resembles the tradition it claims to reject. Critics have also charged Hulme with inconsistency in his apparent allegiance both to epistemological relativism and to ethical absolutism: in his advocacy of Henri Bergson and of the right-wing thinkers Pierre Lasserre, Charles Maurras, and Georges Sorel.

45

Hulme's writings deserve a more sympathetic judgment. They do, indeed, anticipate key elements of Pound's poetics, and they are consistent on the whole. In this chapter I aim to demonstrate that consistency—especially by foregrounding elements of Hulme's thought that I shall later be locating in Pound's. Specifically, I emphasize three projects that both Hulme and Pound shared with, and perhaps drew from, James: the projects to redescribe seemingly mystical moments in a language stripped of mysticism, to justify translating those diminished insights into words, and, finally, to specify the provisionality of language suited to such a task. As in my consideration of James, I shall propose that the three projects are intimately connected, like the three stages in what James called "reflex-action."

Admittedly, organizing Hulme's comments according to this paradigm imposes an artificial order on them, but the recuperation is justified by a couple of special considerations. First, many of Hulme's most fascinating remarks on poetry exist only in the form of rudimentary notes, left behind when he died in the trenches in 1917, at the age of thirty-four. Herbert Read, his first editor, suggested that these notes were intended for a book concerned with both "the Psychology of Literature" and with "Expression and Style."[2] A plan for the book was found in Hulme's papers at the time of his death, and its subtitles suggest that he intended to produce a coherent account of the first of these three subjects, at least.[3] My effort to order them constitutes a speculative reconstruction of the account of poetry that would have emerged in that book, had it been completed. Second, the fragmentary nature of these writings has always necessitated speculative reconstruction; mine is in this respect only an alternative to readings that have, I believe, underestimated Hulme's intentions and so his importance. Specifically, my decision to correlate an account of Hulme's thoughts on the psychology of literary creation with his dicta on the other topics responds to the efforts of two critics, Michael Levenson and Karen Csengeri, to explain apparent contradictions in Hulme's thought by relegating them to discrete stages in his career. That policy, it seems to me, actually *creates* the contradictions it purports to explain. Csengeri, for example, argues that Hulme's support for Bergson represents a discrete stage in his career, which bears no relation to his early poetic experiments and is fundamentally at odds with the moral absolutism he took up in the last two years of his life.[4] The Jamesian reflex-action model shows that it is not necessary to temporalize these aspects of Hulme's thought to make them cohere. The importance of reconciling these aspects of Hulme's thought will appear most fully in my final chapter, which considers the supposed gap between Hulme's Bergsonian nominalism and his moral absolutism. There I shall argue that the two positions are legitimate, even essential partners in a pragmatist outlook: Hulme's versions of the "tough-mindedness" and the "tender-mindedness" that James hoped pragmatism would bring together.[5]

A word on the sources for Hulme's Jamesian ideas. The following discussion fathers some of these on three French psychologists and philosophers, Henri Bergson, Théodule Ribot, and Jules de Gaultier. This is not to suggest that Hulme did not have firsthand knowledge of James. His first publication was a 1909 review of A *Pluralistic Universe,* and his notes and essays allude, explicitly and implicitly, to most of James's other major works.[6] But he knew the French writers equally well (and Bergson much better), and all three of them cite James frequently and agreed with him on key issues. Ribot and Bergson alerted Hulme to the possibility of a "daylight mysticism" in offering him the terms for rewriting inspiration in a scientific way. Gaultier, the philosopher of "bovarysm," called himself a pragmatist and espoused a view of truth-making similar to, though more pessimistic than, James's. He appears to have contributed significantly to Hulme's pragmatist theory of language—to his program for articulating the insights inspiration brings, once the poet's moment of illumination has been stripped of "the light that never was on land or sea."[7]

ROMANTICISM AND CLASSICISM REVISITED

The principal essays that have led critics to question Hulme's repudiation of romanticism are "Romanticism and Classicism" (1911–12) and "Bergson's Theory of Art" (1911–12). In the first of these, it has been asserted, Hulme adopts two strikingly incompatible positions. He begins the essay by renouncing the art and politics of "romanticism" and vowing to further the cause of a new "classicism." He concludes it, however, by endorsing Coleridge's conception of the ideal poem as an organic unity. Murray Krieger charges that Hulme's "uncompromising prejudice against romanticism" is "betrayed" by his invocation of "romantic and Coleridgean concepts." Alun Jones, likewise, enlists Hulme in a company of early twentieth-century writers who have "relied on the theory of romanticism, particularly as conceived by Coleridge, to support what they consider to be an essentially classical position."[8] For several commentators the key is Hulme's enthusiastic endorsement of Bergson's claims for the faculty of "intuition," claims that seem at odds with the "new classicism's" goal of combating epistemological hubris. As Krieger puts it, no account of Hulme's anti-romanticism can explain how he, "in his 'Romanticism and Classicism,' can deny to the poet the possibility of moving beyond the world about him and yet, in his 'Bergson's Theory of Art,' . . . import the term 'intuition' to allow precisely for this possibility."[9]

In short at least in the two central essays in *Speculations,* too many of Hulme's weapons against romanticism appear to have been stolen from the enemy. But we must ask whether the causes Hulme was championing and

opposing were in fact as the critics have defined them. In "A Tory Philosophy" (1912), a series of articles not reproduced in either *Speculations* or
Samuel Hynes's collection *Further Speculations* (1955) and hence largely
neglected,[10] Hulme emphasizes that in pitting the forces of a new "classicism" against those of an old "romanticism" he is not using the terms
loosely. He proposes to stipulate his own definitions for the terms, and he
is convinced, perhaps too optimistically, that his stipulations will be
respected:

> It seems to me that in the history of such words there are three stages. In the
> first and earliest stage a word has a definite and precise meaning. You are certainly
> justified in using it, then. After this there comes a period when the word has
> about a dozen meanings. At this stage it is dangerous, and should be left alone.
> But, finally, you get to the state when it had [*sic*] three hundred meanings. It has
> then once again become useful and innocuous, for no one will have any precon-
> ceived notion of what it means, and will attentively wait to see exactly the shade
> of meaning, and the sense, which you yourself intend to give it. Their minds are
> in the receptive state; they are prepared to receive once again an accurate impres-
> sion from a word. Now the words "classic" and "romantic" have, after their
> long history from their first use by Goethe, at last reached this stage; and as I
> am prepared to give precise and accurate definitions, I think I am justified in
> using them.[11]

The critics who have accused Hulme of inconsistencies in his theory of
"romanticism" and "classicism" have been unaware of or have failed to
respect this statement of purpose. They have assumed that he applied the
terms in the widest sense[12] and have assessed his arguments in the light of
their own, preconceived definitions. Frank Kermode, whose *Romantic Image* remains one of the most eloquent and influential arguments for the
continuity between Hulme's work and both English Romanticism and
French Symbolism, is quite clear about what he himself means when he
uses the term "Romantic," and his understanding is typical:

> I here use "Romantic" in a restricted sense, as applicable to the literature of one
> epoch, beginning in the late years of the eighteenth century and not yet finished,
> and as referring to the high valuation placed during this period upon the image-
> making powers of the mind at the expense of its rational powers, and to the
> substitution of organicist for mechanistic modes of thinking about works of art.[13]

Kermode and others have perceived Hulme's new "classicism" as bogus
because it promotes a creative activity ruled by the powers of intuition
rather than reason, an activity whose product is organic rather than mechanical. If we respect the "precise and limited"[14] definition of "romanticism" to which Hulme actually subscribed, however, we can see how

intuitionism and organicism can be perfectly consistent with a battle for "classicism."

Hulme stipulates his definition of "romanticism" repeatedly: in "Romanticism and Classicism," in "A Tory Philosophy," and in a series of articles contributed to the 1915 New Age, published under the title "A Notebook."[15] Crucial to the better known account (in the first of these pieces) is a point made more clearly in the others: that "romanticism" is less a coherent set of philosophical principles than a fundamental attitude that may shape such principles. Like Husserl, whom he cites, and I. A. Richards, who followed his lead,[16] Hulme is primarily interested in defining romanticism as a weltanschauung: a "particular view of the relation of man to existence." For him, the "romantic" weltanschauung is essentially a profound optimism concerning human potential in the cosmos: a conviction "that man, the individual, is an infinite reservoir of possibilities." In Hulme's view this optimism is unjustified because it fails to honor the distinction between "human and divine things" determined in perpetuum by Adam's Fall; it introduces into human life "the *Perfection* that properly belongs to the non-human."[17] He claims that "romantic" overconfidence has prevailed in Western society since the Renaissance, shaping several seemingly unconnected philosophical positions and social practices: the Rousseauvian belief in humanity's essential goodness, ethical relativism, social liberalism, self-indulgent expressions of feeling in poetry, and the naturalist tradition in painting.[18] Most importantly, it has informed two types of epistemological arrogance, worth isolating because Hulme's counters to them are the basis of his "new classical" poetics.

The first type of epistemological hubris Hulme targets is the one that has sustained a metaphysical conception of poetry. Throughout his writings he disparages writers who have characterized poetic inspiration as a "divine act," in which the mind merges with a transcendental Spirit, taking on its knowledge.[19] This "bad metaphysic of art" is an inability to talk about the existence of beauty "without the infinite being in some way or other dragged in."[20] Hulme detects this failing in a wide range of writers, beginning with the German Idealists:

> Particularly in Germany, the land where theories of aesthetics were first created, the romantic aesthetes collated all beauty to an impression of the infinite involved in the identification of our being in absolute spirit. In the least element of beauty we have a total intuition of the whole world.[21]

This "bad metaphysic," Hulme insists, informed the English romanticism of Coleridge, Byron, and Shelley, and the French romanticism of Lamartine and Hugo.[22] From reading Tancrède de Visan's *L'Attitude du lyrisme contemporain* (1911) and the journalism of his fellow Imagist F. S. Flint, Hulme had also learned to be suspicious of the "metaphysical baggage" attending French Symbolist poetry and theory and of the mystical aesthetic of Schopenhauer, which was often echoed in Symbolist manifestos.[23] He expresses impatience with Schopenhauer's definition of inspiration as "the pure contemplation of the Idea in a moment of emancipation from the Will,"[24] and with the Symbolist tradition as it emerges in Yeats:

> W. B. Yeats attempts to ennoble his craft by strenuously believing in supernatural world, race-memory, magic, and saying that symbols can recall these where prose couldn't. This an attempt to bring in an infinity again.[25]

Although conceding that these revelation-claims may make emotive sense—they "may convey the kind of excitement" that art produces—Hulme insists that referentially they are unacceptable: they "in no way fit the actual process that the artist goes through."[26] Ultimately, such claims serve only to aggrandize the poet, by crediting him with knowledge unattainable in a postlapsarian world.

The second "romantic" claim Hulme opposes also has implications for poetry, though it is found primarily among students of "biology, psychology, and history." This is the hubristic assumption about human knowledge that he believes underlies determinism and mechanism. Hulme rails against the "nightmare" of these philosophies frequently in his notebooks and articles but addresses their roots in two closely related pieces: "Notes on Bergson" (1911) and "A Notebook" (1915–16). In the latter he explains that the problem can be traced to another failure to honor the distinction between things "human" and "divine." More specifically, it can be traced to the failure of human scientists to respect the "chasms" between their own fields of study, where knowledge must always be incomplete, and others where it can be absolute. He gives the following diagram of these realms:

> In order to simplify matters, it may be useful here to give the exposition a kind of geometrical character. Let us assume that reality is divided into three regions separated from one another by absolute divisions, by real discontinuities. (1) The inorganic world, of mathematical and physical science, (2) the organic world, dealt with by biology, psychology and history, and (3) the world of ethical and religious values. Imagine these three regions as the three zones marked out on a flat surface by two concentric circles. The outer zone is the world of physics, the inner that of religion and ethics, the intermediate one that of life. The outer and inner regions have certain characteristics in common. They have both an *absolute* character, and knowledge about them can legitimately be called absolute knowledge. The intermediate region of life is, on the other hand, essentially relative: it is dealt with by *loose* sciences like biology, psychology and history. A muddy mixed zone then lies between the two absolutes. To make the image a more faithful representation one would have to imagine the extreme zones partaking

of the perfection of geometrical figures, while the middle zone was covered with some confused muddy substance.[27]

Simply put, human sciences have overestimated their power to explain the "muddy" complexities of the organic world. They have maintained that human thought and action can be "calculate[d] with unfailing certainty."[28] And the cost of their arrogance has been a loss of belief in human freedom, in the possibility of unpredictable actions and willful alterations of behavior. A break with "romanticism," then, in Hulme's sense of it, will mean a break with something usually considered its opposite, particularly by students of English Romanticism: a mechanistic conception of consciousness.

When we appreciate the centrality of these two forms of epistemological *hubris* in the "romanticism" against which Hulme argues, it becomes possible to establish what a "classical" theory of poetic activity would have to entail. Two principles seem unavoidable. First, it would refrain from crediting either the poet or his product with contact with any transcendental realm; it would eschew the aggrandizing mysticism of Symbolist aesthetics.[29] Second, it would provide an alternative to mechanistic models of mind—models according to which any creative activity would be entirely predictable. A "classical" theory could, in sum, resemble the German Idealist account of the unpredictable, organic imagination predicated by Coleridge and Mallarmé, that is, the view that Kermode and others, in assessing Hulme, have insisted on calling "romantic." Where it would have to differ from those theories, if Hulme is to remain constant to his ideals, is in the significance it attaches to such an imagination. It would require a discourse stripped of the metaphysical claims that aggrandize and authorize the poet.

DAYLIGHT SYMBOLISM: RIBOT, BERGSON, AND THE *CONCEPTION IDÉALE*

Hulme's references to the creative activity reveal a "new classical" theory perfectly in line with his argument against what he calls romanticism. His account of creative activity recalls English Romantic and French Symbolist ones in beginning with a moment of intuitive insight and continuing with a process of articulation that is organic and unpredictable. In contrast to those accounts, however, he scrupulously limits the range of the inspiring vision and avoids attributing the process of articulation to the intervention of any transcendental spirit. Hulme's poet apprehends only the "small dry things" of the phenomenal world; he is enlightened by "the light of ordinary day, never the light that never was on land or sea."[30] His efforts to articulate this vision in words are guided by forces in his own, psychic *experience* references to the participation of an unfolding *Geist* are out of bounds.

As I have suggested, Hulme's "classical" redescription of the creative process owes a great deal to the work of two contemporary French philosopher/psychologists, Théodule Ribot and Henri Bergson. Hulme's work on Bergson is extensive and well known. Twenty-odd articles and lectures between 1909 and 1912, and a translation of the "Introduction à la métaphysique" (1903; published in 1912 as *An Introduction to Metaphysics*), made him Bergson's chief publicist in England. His fascination with Ribot was less public but arguably just as important to his views on imagination and language.[31] Now that Hulme's conception of "romanticism" has been made clear, the appeal both thinkers had for him is easy to understand, for they, too, sought to describe a creative activity that defied determinism in a language that eschewed metaphysics.

Théodule Ribot, psychologist, philosopher, educator, and founder of the prestigious *Revue philosophique,* was France's leading publicist of the foundling study of experimental psychology. Like James he devoted a great deal of energy to defining the boundaries of psychological discourse. In *La Psychologie anglaise contemporaine* (1870), he declared that the new science was to resist all attempts to establish the *causes premières* of mental phenomena and to concentrate solely on the observation and analysis of verifiable facts. Like the physical, biological, and chemical sciences before it, that is, psychology was to recoil from the elusive realm of metaphysics, "ce mystérieux au-delà qui dans toute science l'entoure et la presse" and to focus instead on the accessible realm of *les phénomènes.*[32] It was to conceive consciousness as a stream, bounded by a mysterious world it would be foolish, because futile, to say anything about:

> L'ensemble des connaissances humaines ressemble ainsi à un grand fleuve coulant à pleins bords, sous un ciel resplendissant de lumière, mais dont on ignore la source et l'embouchure, qui naît et meurt dans les nuages. Les esprits audacieux n'ont jamais pu ni eclaircir ce mystère ni l'oublier. Il y a toujours quelques intrépides pour se lancer resolument dans cette region inaccessible, d'ou ils reviennent aveugles, saisis de vertige, et racontant des choses si étranges que le monde les tient pour hallucinés.[33]

> [The entire collection of human knowledge resembles a great river flowing full between its banks, under a sky glowing with light, but whose source and mouth are unknown, which springs and dies in the clouds. Bold spirits have never been able either to solve this mystery or to forget it. There are always some sufficiently intrepid to throw themselves resolutely into this inaccessible region, whence they return blinded, giddy, and relating such strange things that the world holds them to be hallucinations.]

For Ribot renouncing discussion of the world beyond the stream meant demystifying—or more properly, "neutralizing"[34]—the discourse in which mind was described. Now mental events had to be represented as functions of the intellectual, emotional, and unconscious factors in the human psyche; they could no longer be attributed to *causes occultes*.[35] Late in his career, with *Essai sur l'imagination créatrice* (1900), Ribot brought these new restrictions to the project of describing artistic creation. As Albert Baron the English translator of the *Essai* observed and, as Hulme, who probably read that translation, would have appreciated, Ribot was a "Prometheus" among writers on aesthetics, dedicated to bringing the creative imagination down from its long-standing place in the heavens to a new place on earth.[36]

Ribot's neutralization of creative inspiration in the *Essai* was the culmination of an earlier inquiry into the psychology of religious experience, *La Psychologie des sentiments* (1896). In that study Ribot had anticipated several of James's strategies in *Varieties of Religious Experience* (and, indeed, called for a study of its kind). Primary among these was his effort to redescribe moments of profound, intuitive *knowing* as moments of intense, noetic *feeling*. Claims about divine revelation became manifestations of the *sentiment religieux*, whose *légitimité* he declared himself incompetent to judge. Moments like those enjoyed by fetishists, in which *l'infini* seems to reveal itself through common objects, became instances not of certain transcendence but only of profound feelings of longing for a higher world. In reconceiving religious experience as feeling, moreover, Ribot also represents it as a reflex-action, a series of three vitally related events. Alluding directly to James's work, he identifies the parts of this triad as

(1) un état intellectuel, perception ou idée, comme point de départ (une mauvaise nouvelle, une apparition terrifiante, une injure reçue); (2) un état affectif, l'émotion, tristesse, colère, peur; (3) les états organiques et les mouvements résultants de cette émotion. Mais le second moment, l'emotion ainsi conçue n'est plus qu'une entité et une pure hypothèse.[37]

[(1) an intellectual state, perception, or idea, as a starting-point (*e.g.*, a piece of bad news, a terrifying apparition, an injury received); (2) a state of feeling—the emotion; sorrow, anger, fear; (3) the organic states and movements resulting from this emotion. But the second point—the emotion conceived as such—is only an abstract entity, a mere hypothesis.]

In seemingly mystical moments, then, we are investing thoughts or apparitions with feeling and tending toward some kind of action. But if mystical experience has a distinguishing feature from other emotional experiences, all of which can be broken down in this way, it is the *intensity* of the feeling attached to the vision or message. That feeling is so strong that it renders the vision *maîtresse*, the "pivot et . . . [le] centre unique d'association"

(328); it gives it a hold over us that is "absolue" and "tyrannique."[38]
Ribot's commitment to psychological discourse does not allow him to suggest that this intensity is misplaced; he never asserts that the apparitions are
delusions or their messages false. But in invoking the reflex-action model, he
implies that they are not disinterested, a move that casts the authority of
their accompanying visions into doubt.[39]

In the *Essai sur l'imagination créatrice*, Ribot uses the same model to
redescribe the visionary moments at the beginning of the creative process.
Creative inspiration, he explains, is also part of a triadic reflex-action: it
involves the apprehension of a haunting idea, an emotional response to
that idea, and an ensuing act. The ensuing act—the actual construction
of the artwork—is the objectification of the idea; it results in the artist's
deliverance from the idea's tyrannical hold: "La représentation intense doit
s'objectiver, c'est-à-dire d'intérieure devenir extérieure, elle y parvient de
deux manières: par un acte réel, c'est le lot du commun des hommes, par
la création d'une oeuvre d'art qui débarrasse de l'obsession, c'est le propre
des artistes." [The intense representation must objectify itself, that is, from
being interior it must become exterior. It manages to do this in two ways:
by a real act, this is the way of common men, by the creation of a work
of art that relieves him of the obsession, this is the way of artists.] Along
with his redescription of knowledge as feeling, the most significant feature
of Ribot's account of artistic creation is his description of the inspiring idea
itself, the *conception idéale*. This entity is a cluster of images, or ideas
derived from images, and is the product of two activities: one of dissociation, by which its constituent images or ideas are separated from percepts,
and one of association, by which these fragments are drawn together. The
first of these two stages is governed by affective, rather than intellectual,
factors. The fragments of perceptual experience that survive in the memory
are invariably those which in the original experience aroused some strong
emotion: those "qui nous touchent en quelque manière, sous une forme
agréable ou pénible." [that touch us in some way, in a pleasant or painful
form.] The associative activity that follows may be controlled by either
intellect or emotion. Images may be clustered together because they evoke
similar emotions when first perceived or out of a rational recognition that
they share certain objective attributes, processes Ribot attributes to *l'imagination diffluente* and *l'imagination plastique*, respectively.[40]

In defining the *conception idéale* in these terms, Ribot is offering an
alternative to the mystical *Idée* that figured so largely in Symbolist accounts
of creativity. Ironically, early in his career he had written a book on Schopenhauer that served to disseminate the philosopher's ideas in Symbolist
circles.[41] Now his goal is to replace Schopenhauer's eternal Idea with something originating not *beyond* experience but *within* it:

Rien de moins justifié que la conception d'un archetype fixe (survivance non déguisée des Idées platoniciennes), illuminant l'inventeur qui le réproduit comme il peut. L'idéal n'est pas; il se fait dans l'inventeur et par lui; sa vie est un devenir.[42]

[Nothing less justified than the notion of a fixed archetype (an undisguised relic of Platonic ideas), illuminating the inventor who reproduces it as best he can. The ideal is not; it comes into being in the inventor and by him; its life is a becoming.]

The *conception idéale* resembles Schopenhauer's Idea in a number of ways. First, it appears suddenly in the creator's mind, at a moment when his analytical intellect is suspended.[43] Second, in at least some of its manifestations (those Ribot calls instances of "imagination intuitive"), it governs a heuristic process, in which the *idéal* is a *unité* continually giving rise to new images and ideas; its development, Ribot says, "est organique et on peut le comparer au processus embryologique qui fait sortir de l'ovule féconde un être vivant." [is organic and can be compared to the embryological process that brings forth a living being from a fertile egg.][44] But again if Ribot's account of its workings parallels Schopenhauer's (or Mallarmé's) in the *experiences* he associates with it, it differs in the *origin* he is prepared to attribute to it. He explains both its sudden appearance and its uncharted development by saying it springs from, and is fed by, the subconscious mind. Invoking the subconscious would be insufficient in itself to distinguish his account from Symbolist ones; Mallarmé, Rimbaud, and others appeal to a *universal* unconscious manifesting itself in individual minds. But Ribot avoids committing himself to the view that the subconscious has "une origine surnaturelle." He is equally reluctant to tie the subconscious to the material subject, to declare it "une activité purement physiologique."[45] Following the rules of psychological discourse, he resists *all* speculation about the ultimate nature of the other space from which inspiration springs: both that which would exalt it, by rendering it universal, and that which would diminish it, by tying it to the individual.[46]

The *conception idéale* enables Ribot to give a scientific account of those moments, so central to Symbolist accounts of art, in which objects of sense, both in nature and in the poem itself, become revelatory *symboles*. If a natural object (or poetic image) seems suddenly charged with associations, he observes, or if its synaesthetic correspondences become apparent, it is unnecessary to attribute that phenomenon to the appearance of the "[I]déal dans le sensible," the manifestation of "[l'I]dée cachée dans tout phénomène du événement matériel." Rather the enlightened poet (or reader) can be said to experience a cluster of empirical data—"une association de perception à perception, de perception à image ou d'image à image"—and to be overwhelmed by a sense of the authenticity of these connections, a sense that they are "réels et révélateurs." They are in the grip of what the psychology of feeling describes as *l'imagination mystique*:

> L'imagination mystique suppose une croyance inconditionnelle et permanente. Les mystiques sont des croyants au sens complet; ils ont la foi. Ce caractère leur est propre et il a son origine dans l'intensité de l'état affectif qui suscite et soutient cette forme de l'invention.

> [The mystic imagination presupposes an unconditional and permanent belief. Mystics are believers in the total sense; they have faith. This attribute is proper to them and it has its origin in the intensity of the affective state that incites and sustains this form of invention.]

There are points in Ribot's account of Symbolism when he forgets his obligation to remain neutral, claiming that the connections perceived by the mystic are *purement subjective,* or that objects become symbols only "au gré de [la] fantaisie."[47] But on the whole, his discussion has the same effect as his discussion of religious experience in *La Psychologie des sentiments:* it respects these revelatory experiences as facts but *suspends judgment* about what they ultimately mean.

The affinity between Ribot's psychological account of creative activity and the work of Henri Bergson will not be immediately obvious. What could an endeavor like Ribot's possibly share with one dedicated to asserting the spiritual, not material, status of mind; the free, not determined, nature of human consciousness; the organic, not mechanical, nature of natural evolution? The answer lies in the writers' agreement about a procedure for metaphysical inquiry that would give it a new legitimacy. In spite of his resolution to keep metaphysical questions out of psychology, Ribot by no means entirely denied the value of such questions. Indeed he maintained that to ban them altogether would be to enervate human thought.[48] When he established the *Revue philosophique,* he announced that the journal would be quite willing to include essays on metaphysical subjects. His proviso was that the philosopher should base his speculations entirely on the facts of experience uncovered by science; the *Revue,* for its part, would work to keep philosophers informed of the results being produced by empiricist and experimental psychology.[49] Bergson, Ribot's colleague at the Collège de France and a frequent contributor to the *Revue,* shared his conviction that the theories of metaphysics should be derived from empirical findings. In his "Introduction à la métaphysique" (1903), he announced that if metaphysics has any hope of working at all, "elle ne peut être qu'un effort pour remonter la pente naturelle du travail de la pensée, pour se placer tout de suite . . . dans la chose qu'on étudie, enfin pour aller de la réalité aux concepts et non plus des concepts à la réalité." [it can only be an effort to re-ascend the slope natural to the work of thought, to place oneself immediately . . . in the thing one is studying, in short, to go from reality to concepts and not from concepts to reality.][50] Bergson's own "metaphysical" assertions, such as those about the essentially unpredictable nature of mind and evolution, were inferences from the latest data of the psychological sciences, including, not infrequently, those of Ribot.[51]

Bergson's empirical approach to metaphysical questions was applauded by many thinkers who felt the need to reconcile antideterminism with science. Among these were French literary critics, like Tancrède de Visan, who approved of the Symbolist's account of a mysterious, heuristic creative activity but disapproved of the indiscriminate, mystical language they used to describe it. In his history of the Symbolist movement, which Hulme read and reviewed[52] and which may have helped to define his own "new classical" project, Visan praised Bergson's work for legitimizing the Symbolist aesthetic through "une métaphysique positive": that is, by giving a purely scientific description of its elements and nesting these within a metaphysic rooted firmly in empirical observation.[53] Although Bergson never gives any systematic account of the creative process, it is possible to reconstruct one from remarks in *Essai sur les données immédiates de la conscience* (1889), *Matière et mémoire* (1896), *Le Rire* (1900), "Introduction à la métaphysique" (1903), *L'Évolution créatrice* (1907), and *La Pensée et le mouvant* (1903–23).[54] Such a reconstruction reveals the accuracy of Visan's characterization of Bergson as the scientist of Symbolism.[55]

The first feature Bergson's account of the creative process shares with that of the Symbolists is its assertion that the activity begins with a moment of "intuition," in which the artist apprehends a reality of which he is not normally aware.[56] Unlike Schopenhauer, Mallarmé, or Baudelaire, however, and contrary to the view of many critics who have written of Bergson's impact on Hulme, Bergson does not represent that higher reality as a transcendental Spirit.[57] Where the Symbolists have the artist penetrating a veil of particulars to grasp universal Ideas, he defines quite different boundaries for the event. The interface his artist penetrates is simply the framework of concepts that normally obscures the complex individuality of objects; he apprehends the very realm the Symbolist artist transcends. While acknowledging the analogy between the two kinds of intuitive apprehension, Bergson is adamant that the end-point of his artist's vision is the temporal flux, or *la durée*:

Parce qu'un Schelling, un Schopenhauer et d'autres ont déjà fait appel à l'intuition, parce qu'ils ont plus ou moins opposé l'intuition à l'intelligence, on pouvait croire que nous appliquions la même méthode. Comme si leur intuition n'était pas une recherche immédiate de l'éternel. Comme s'il ne s'agissait pas au con-

traire, selon nous, de retrouver d'abord la durée vraie. . . . Ils n'ont pas vu que
le temps intellectualisé est espace, que l'intelligence travaille sur le fantôme de la
durée, mais non pas sur la durée même, que l'élimination du temps est l'acte
habituel, normal, banal, de notre entendement, que la relativité de notre connaissance de l'esprit vient précisément de là, et que des lors, pour passer de l'intellection à la vision, du rélatif à l'absolu, il n'y a pas à sortir du temps (nous en
sommes déjà sortis); il faut, au contraire, se replacer dans la durée et ressaisir la
réalité dans la mobilité qui en est l'essence.[58]

[Because a Schelling, a Schopenhauer and others have already called upon intuition, because they have more or less set up intuition in opposition to intelligence,
one might think that I was using the same method. But of course, their intuition
was an immediate search for the eternal. Whereas, on the contrary, for me it
was a question, above all, of finding true duration. . . . They did not see that
intellectualized time is space, that the intelligence works upon the phantom of
duration, not on duration itself, that the elimination of time is the habitual,
normal, commonplace act of our understanding, that the relativity of our knowledge of the mind is a direct result of this fact, and that hence, to pass from
intellection to vision, from the relative to the absolute, is not a question of getting
outside of time (we are already there); on the contrary, one must get back into
duration and recapture reality in the very mobility which is its essence.]

Bergson's artist may share with Schopenhauer's a mind that refrains from
analysis, and a sense, accordingly, of identification with the object before
him, but the range of his vision is retracted.[59] Occasionally Bergson's vocabulary suggests that he is willing to grant the artist access to a realm of
transcendental universals; in "Introduction à la métaphysique," for example, he describes the intuitive moment as one of apprehending something
absolu, or *parfait,* or *infini.*[60] But as Hulme understood, we must not take
Bergson's occasional use of "words like infinite" in a "much bigger sense
than is really intended."[61] When he characterizes the poet's understanding
as "infinite," he means only that he seems to grasp a reality so complex it
would take forever to reconstruct it discursively:

Toute analyse est . . . une traduction, un développement en symboles, une
représentation prise de points de vue successifs d'où l'on note autant de contacts
entre l'objet nouveau, qu'on étudie, et d'autres, que l'on croit déjà connaître.
Dans son désir éternellement inassouvi d'embrasser l'objet autour duquel elle est
condamné a tourner, l'analyse multiplie sans fin les points de vue pour compléter
la représentation toujours incomplète, varie sans relâche les symboles pour par-
faire la traduction toujours imparfaite. Elle se continue donc à l'infini. Mais
l'intuition . . . est un acte simple.[62]

[All analysis . . . a translation, a development into symbols, a representation
taken from successive points of view from which are noted a corresponding

number of contacts between the new object under consideration and others believed to be already known. In its eternally unsatisfied desire to embrace the object around which it is condemned to turn, analysis multipleis endlessly the points of view in order to complete the ever incomplete representation, varies interminably the symbols with the hope of perfecting the always imperfect translation. It is analysis ad infinitum. But intuition, if it is possible, is a simple act.]

In sum Bergson's poet contacts a timely realm, "infinite" only in the sense of being ineffable.

Another term Bergson provides for the infinitely complex reality the poet apprehends is *moi fondamentale*. He applies the term to the flux of unique, interpenetrated states at the heart of consciousness: a torrent of thoughts and feelings and images, each of which contains the one that precedes it and announces the one that follows. Supported by experimental evidence, the concept facilitates the aspect of his *métaphysique positive* so important to Hulme: the point that the consciousness is essentially unpredictable, free. As Bergson explains in the *Essai sur les données immédiates de la conscience,* the interpenetrated consciousness is not as amenable to reduction by deterministic laws as the atomistic one posited by John Stuart Mill and other associationist psychologists. An aggregate of discrete psychic states, like Mill's, invites speculation about the causal relations holding between its parts: a state of "anger," for example, can seem to be the consequence of a particular sequence of other states; or where a number of states coexist, the strongest of these can be said to dominate the others and thus to determine all a person's thoughts, feelings, and actions. It is tempting to believe that sufficient observation of such situations will result in the discovery of general laws. But what can be made to work for this atomistic view of consciousness does not work for the interpenetrated flux of the *moi fondamentale*. Where every state is permeated by the memory of all those which preceded it, Bergson argues, every new state that emerges will be unpredictable *because it is unique;* predictions about the eruption of "anger" in a person's consciousness will be meaningless, because no anger will be the same as any that has happened before. Equally, where the whole of the self is deemed to permeate every state, it makes no sense to speak of how a self can be dominated by any one state; it must always be regarded as self-determining, free.[63]

Despite the care he devotes to arguing for the essential freedom of the consciousness, Bergson does not contend that it is available to everyone or to anyone all of the time. Indeed, he argues that most people willingly conceive their own selves as atomistic, accepting certain sequences of feelings and actions as socially appropriate. The *moi superficiel* eventually becomes not just the only self of which they are aware but the only one controlling their actions, and they are transformed into just the sort of automatons the associationists describe.[64] It is only the artist who recovers this freedom, in his moments of intuition. When he penetrates the conceptual "veil," he transcends conventional conceptions of psychological life and with them any predictable behavior.[65] Bergson emphasizes the enormous effort required in sustaining such freedom, particularly as the poet seeks to express himself in language. People in contact only with their superficial selves, he says, use "[l]e langage réflexe"; they express themselves *automatiquement* or *machinalement,* exchanging "réponses toutes faites."[66] The poet, by contrast, agonizes, bending language to express what he really thinks and feels. Doing so is the very condition of his liberty.

Bergson describes the effort involved in translating the *moi fondamentale* into language in "L'Effort intellectuel," an essay published in Ribot's *Revue philosophique* in 1902 and important to Hulme. In the course of that discussion, he adds another element to his revision of the Symbolist aesthetic: his own version of Ribot's *conception idéale.*[67] The poetic process begins, Bergson says, with the sudden appearance in the fundamental self of an *idéal* or *schéma*: a mental sketch, "dont les éléments s'entrepénétrent," which the poet is to translate into "une représentation imagée dont les parties se juxtaposent."[68] Noting Ribot's distinction between the organic activity of translating this *unité* into *détails,* and a mechanical one in which one builds up a *unité* out of *détails,*[69] he claims the first of these for the poet. Poetic creation is an intuitive process, in which the original schema grows and develops through the effort of finding images into which to translate it. Like the creative experience of the Symbolist poet, that is, it is a struggle in which there is "une adaptation réciproque de la forme et de la matière."[70]

The *conception idéale* plays a significant role in Bergson's subsequent discussions of the creative activity. In a lecture delivered to the Bologna Congress in 1911, for example, which Hulme heard, he described it as a process guided by "une certaine image intermédiaire entre la simplicité de l'intuition concrète et la complexité des abstractions qui la traduisent, image fuyante et évanouissante, qui hante, inaperçue peut-être, l'esprit." [a certain intermediary image between the simplicity of the concrete intuition and the complexity of the abstractions which translate it, a receding and vanishing image, which haunts, unperceived perhaps, the mind . . .][71] But the most complete account of the "schema," and undoubtedly the one that had the greatest impact on Hulme, is found in *L'Évolution créatrice* (1907). There Bergson takes the boldest step of all in his *métaphysique positive,* suggesting that the artist's experience might be a model for global evolution. The evolutionary process, he argues, might be the manifestion of a spirit analogous to the *moi fondamentale,* which he calls *l'élan vital*: a process in which a cluster of interpenetrated potentialities analogous to the *conception idéale* is individuated into organisms, just as the *idéale* is individuated into various *strophes distinctes* and *vers distincts*. The struggle between these potentialities and matter, then, like the poet's struggle with "la matérialité du langage," may give rise to an unpredictable series of organisms and, ultimately, species.[72] In a moment of metaphoric insight that was to fascinate Hulme, Bergson likens the *élan vital* to a rocket, pressing through fragments of matter and lighting them up into organisms. Matter falls back from the movement of the impulse, like "les débris qui retombent des fusées éteintes."[73] It consists of what Arthur Mitchell, in his 1911 translation of *L'Évolution créatrice*, calls "cinders": ashes left behind when the rocket of life has passed, to be reorganized by impulses yet to come.[74]

Ribot's and Bergson's accounts of creative activity, then, fulfill the two central requirements of Hulme's "classical" aesthetic: they succeed in describing the process without making dogmatic predictions and represent its organicism without spilling the mystical into the realm of the human. In his plan for a book on aesthetics,[75] Hulme gives both writers a central place and indicates his intention of celebrating the scientific redescription of creation made possible by their "new psychology."[76] What does survive of his thoughts on the subject reveals how much he depends on both of them in formulating the theory of a neutralized—or "daylight"—Symbolism: Imagism.

One sign of Hulme's debt to Ribot and Bergson is his habit of interpreting claims about the apprehension of the "infinite" as expressions of intense feeling. For him romantic art always voices "the *emotions* that are grouped around the word infinite." The "escapes to the infinite" claimed by the platonic lover are the products of a "*sentimental* illusion." Although Hulme concedes that such transcendentalist claims are expressively appropriate, he refuses to admit that they are mimetically accurate. The statement that art involves the revelation of the "infinite in the finite," he asserts, may "convey the kind of *excitement*" involved in art's creation and reception, but it is unacceptable as a description of the "*actual process*" the artist goes through.[77] In distinguishing the feeling of infinity from the fact, Hulme executes a key move in his "new classical" aesthetic, showing that it is possible to credit moments of seemingly profound and unexpected insight without claiming undue authority for them. Two concepts borrowed from Ribot and Bergson enable him to develop this scientific redescription of creative intuition: inspiration begins with the apprehension of the *moi fondamentale,* and it proceeds by the guiding light of the *conception idéale.* Understanding the role of each enables us to see clearly that Hulme's account of the creative activity is not the "romantic Platonism" it has been said to be.[78][79]

Hulme endorses Bergson's concept of the *moi fondamentale* in "The Philosophy of Intensive Manifolds" (1911) and "Bergson's Theory of Art"

(1911–12). "Intensive manifold" is Hulme's own term for the kind of reality the "fundamental self" represents: "an absolute interpenetration—a complex thing which yet cannot be said to have parts because the parts run into each other, forming a continuous whole, and whose parts cannot even be conceived as existing separately." For Hulme, the useful thing about the conception of an interpenetrated reality is that it enables us to see how something "indescribable" may yet be knowable, and how extraordinary knowledge may nonetheless be "finite." Bergson's "fundamental self," in which "each state fades away into and interpenetrates the next state," resists description because ordinary language divides and atomizes. The faculty Bergson calls "intuition" eschews such categories and can therefore grasp its complexity. The complexity thus grasped is "infinite" only in the sense that its parts cannot be atomized; otherwise it is "finite," part of "nature," something absolutely "individual."[80] Hulme is especially taken with the possibilities such a "fundamental self" offers for redescribing creative inspiration. In representing the self as something attainable by an act of penetrating a conceptual veil, he says, and in crediting the artist with apprehending it, Bergson provides a version of Schopenhauer's mystical aesthetic moment *without the mysticism*:

> In essence, of course, his theory is exactly the same as Schopenhauer's. That is, they both want to convey over the same feeling about art. But Schopenhauer demands such a cumbrous machinery in order to get that feeling out. Art is the pure contemplation of the Idea in a moment of emancipation from the Will. To state a quite simple thing he has to invent two very extraordinary ones. In Bergson it is an actual contact with reality in a man who is emancipated from the ways of perception engendered by action, but the action is written with a small "a," not a large one.[81]

Like Schopenhauer's mystic, that is, Bergson's poet eschews action-oriented analysis for contemplative intuition, but his prize is a fuller understanding of his own complex self, nothing higher.

If Hulme sees the potential of the *moi fondamentale* for neutralizing Symbolist aesthetics, he appears to be fascinated by the same potential in the *conception idéale*. His notes on the creative activity contain several references to an "inside image" or "visual signification" or "idea" appearing suddenly before the poet's consciousness and demanding objectification in language.[82] Like Ribot he views this construct as a complex of images, dissociated from experience because they aroused some strong feeling and associated with one another because they are analogical.[83] And he uses it to describe the same aspects of the creative experience Schopenhauer and the Symbolists attributed to the mystical *Idée*. In one note, for example, he specifies that the analogous images "add something to each, and give a sense of wonder, a *sense of* being united in another mystic world."[84] His description of the authoritative feeling accompanying the images' appearance recalls Ribot's account of the role of the *idéale* in *l'imagination mystique,* in that it validates the perception of synaesthesic relations as psychological phenomenon but not as metaphysical fact. Hulme's complex is also involved in a process where content and form are inseparable—the same phenomenon the Symbolists credit to symbol, as opposed to allegory, and attribute to divine revelation. Its unsought analogues communicate an insight that "has no existence" apart from them, an insight that develops and changes as it is concretized:

> You may start writing a poem in an endeavour to express an idea which is present in your mind in a very hazy shape. The effort to express that idea in verse, the struggle with language, forces the idea as it were back on itself and brings out the original idea in a clearer shape. Before it was only confused. The idea has grown and developed because of the obstacles it had to meet.[85]

By itself, he notes, the construct "is nothing"; what matters is the "holding on" to it, "through the absolutely transforming influence of putting it into definiteness." True creative effort always leads to "accidental discovery": "Just as musician in striking notes on piano comes across what he wants, the painter on the canvas, so the poet not only gets the phrases he wants, but even from the words gets a *new* image."[86]

If Hulme understood the value of the *moi fondamentale* and *conception idéale* for neutralizing Symbolist accounts of creative inspiration, he also understood their usefulness in freeing imagination from determinism. In "The Philosophy of Intensive Manifolds," after outlining the first of these concepts, he explains in detail how a self thus conceived resists reduction to deterministic law.[87] He also endorses Bergson's view of the poet as one who, in regaining contact with this self, regains his freedom. Thinking, perhaps, of Bergson's argument in "L'Effort intellectuel" (an essay he singles out for discussion in his proposed book[88]), he conceives the poet's task as an extraordinarily difficult one, but one whose difficulty signifies the poet's release from the "determined and automatic" activities of the superficial self. Unlike people in touch only with their superficial selves, who express themselves in "determined and automatic" words (or in "reflex speech"), the poet agonizes to bend language to capture the "individual curves" of his states of mind.[89] His struggle is what ensures his activity's unpredictable course.[90] Hulme writes that Bergson's success in dealing with the "nightmare of determinism" is his "principal achievement" and notes with approval how he uses the creative activity of the poet as a model for evolution in *L'Évolution créatrice.* Among his notes on the poetic activity are several in which he brings those claims for evolution back to art: he characterizes writing, for example, as a "cindery thing done, not a pure thought made manifest in some counter-like way," and he describes works of art as "organised pieces of cinders."[91] The poet's difficult task of "moving from the ideal to the matter,"[92] in other words, is analogous to the struggle of the *élan vital* to make organisms: its products cannot be predicted.

Borrowing from the new psychology of Ribot and Bergson, then, Hulme sketches an account of the creative process perfectly in keeping with the ideals of a "new classicism": one that resists the hubristic claims both of mysticism and of determinism. Understanding his borrowings from the new psychology should enable us to appreciate not only the coherence of his account of the creative imagination but also his affinity with James, who led the new psychology in seeking a way to describe moments of enlightenment without "metaphysical baggage" and in arguing for the freedom of the will.[93] When we consider the implications of Hulme's scientific redescription of inspiration for style, we will see that this affinity extends much further. Hulme follows the same line of reasoning as James to justify a mode of expression structurally identical to the pragmatist's provisional truth.

THE PRAGMATIC TURN: JULES DE GAULTIER AND *LE BOVARYSME*

Hulme's efforts to psychologize the moment of "inspiration" are linked to his recommendations for style by the same rationale that links James's psychology of mysticism to his pragmatism. At the center of James's philosophical reflex-action, we have seen there is a double decision: a recognition, first, that no definitive decision can be made about the nature of knowledge attained in mystical inspiration, and, second, that because this is the case, the reaction to it must be calculated on the basis of *effects*. We see this double decision in "The Will to Believe" and *Varieties of Religious Experience,* when James likens the dilemma of the man with intimations of God to that of a man lost in a forest or a snowstorm. It will be impossible for such a man to know whether his intimations are accurate, James says, but it will also be wise for him to allow the possibility, because that is the only course that has a chance of leading him where he needs to go. In *Pragmatism,* James describes this resolution as one of "looking *away*" from debates about knowledge in the highest sense, and "looking . . . *towards* last things, fruits, consequences, facts" (P 32; my italics). Hulme's notes indicate that he, too, made this pragmatic "turn" and that it inflected his prescriptions for "new classical" poetry.

Hulme would have encountered a version of the pragmatic turn both in James and in the work of F. C. S. Schiller, the English humanist with whom James expressed a deep affinity.[94] The account of it to which he appears to have given closest attention, however, was that of another French thinker with whom he had some personal contact—Jules de Gaultier. The author of several books[95] and of many articles on contemporary psychology and philosophy, Gaultier was France's most enthusiastic publicist for American pragmatism. He described his own position as "essentiellement pragmatiste."[96] Gaultier's most detailed exposition of the pragmatic turn is found in a work predating James's *Pragmatism* by five years: *Le Bovarysme* (1902). Although the program for proposition-making he sets out there differs from James's in one key aspect, it is the result of the same carefully considered decision to abandon traditional truth-questions for ones about "fruits" and "consequences."

Gaultier's decision to shift his attention from truth to consequences was provoked by his interest in the psychological illness suffered by Flaubert's Emma Bovary. Madame Bovary imagines herself a great lady being offered the gift of absolute love. But she is in reality just the wife of a modest country doctor being pursued by a common seducer; in the end her vulgar lover fails to play the role her fiction demands, and her life is ruined. For Gaultier this "tragique voyageur muni d'une fausse carte" exemplifies a tendency common to all human beings, which he calls "le bovarysme": a tendency, in essence, "à se concevoir différents d'euxmêmes."[97] Central to the syndrome, as he describes it, is a construct similar to Ribot's *conception idéale*: a compelling "image" or "notion" or "image-notion" commanding powerful feelings of belief.[98] In some people the false conceptions of self may not be *floraisons naturelles* but ideals acquired through education— flowers clipped from other peoples' gardens. In the case of the *homme de génie,* they may be highly original. But whether borrowed or home-grown, these image-notions have an extraordinary hold over a person's mind; they are the means "dont il se fortifie et se défend."[99]

Gaultier catalogs a great number of common bovaric illusions—the property in some cases not just of individuals but of whole societies—and also identifies the needs they serve. Madame Bovary, he says, is just one victim of the image-notion of romantic love, whose origins may be traced to an instinctive need for procreation.[100] Napoleon Bonaparte, who clothed himself in the purple of the Caesars, was obsessed with a vision of himself within a grand tradition of heroic leaders, an illusion springing from a need to convince himself and others of his greatness. Among the illusions cherished by whole societies, Gaultier says, are two springing from the need to believe we control our own destinies: the idea of the freedom of the will and of the unity of the self. A widespread need to alleviate feelings of frustration and discontent inspires the common illusion that human happiness is attainable. But of all the false ideas that Gaultier detects at work in human experience, the most pervasive is the view that humans are capable of attaining absolute knowledge. This false conception, he says, stems from a need for certitude and has manifested itself in the confident claims of scientists, metaphysicians, and theologians alike. Hoping that their pursuits will enable them both to improve their material existence and to uncover truths not contingent on that existence, these thinkers busy themselves in the analysis of data, the construction of totalizing systems, and the formulation of dogma. Where they go wrong, in Gaultier's view, is in forgetting that there is no idea that is not the product of "une série d'expériences humaines," no notion "réligieuse, morale ou rationalle" that has not originated in the needs of a particular social group.[101]

Gaultier's study is on the verge of becoming a depressing catalog of illusions when he makes his pragmatic turn. First he decides to abandon metaphysical questions about truth and falsity. Following the same line of reasoning James was to use in his *Essays in Radical Empiricism*[102] (many of which predate *Pragmatism* and provide its rationale), he notes that his own argument has depended on the Cartesian distinction between mind and reality. The problem with that distinction, he now recognizes, is that it makes it impossible ever to know whether, in any particular case, the gap between subject and object is closed—whether one *really* knows what one *thinks* one knows. Where it is impossible to identify the true, the idea of the false loses all meaning: hence there ceases to be any ground for talking about bovaric "illusions." Gaultier therefore proposes a way of defining and evaluating such notions that does not depend on any transcendental assurance but that relies solely on *la vie phénoménale*.[103] From this new, phenomenalist point of view, bovaric image-notions are not categorically untrue, but only expectations *experience does not fulfill;* bovarysm is redefined as "la faculté départie à l'homme de se concevoir autre qu'il n'est *en tant que l'homme est impuissant à réaliser cette conception différente qu'il se forme de lui-même.*" [the faculty given man to conceive himself other than he is *in so far as man is unable to realize this different conception that he forms of himself.*][104] And the value of these notions is no longer a matter of their truthfulness but of their consequences for human life. "Délivré de la croyance en une vérité objective," Gaultier resolves, he will now evaluate image-notions solely on the basis of "leur efficacité à procurer les fins où l'on voit que l'activité humaine aboutit." [Liberated from the belief in an objective truth . . . their effectiveness in procuring the ends to which human activity is seen to converge.][105]

Gaultier's turn toward ends enables him to see the bovaric notions he has been criticizing in a new, much more positive light. He can now see, for example, that dreams of romantic love have aided the propagation of the species and that napoleonic notions of personal greatness have inspired many to accomplish much more than they would have done otherwise. Of some value now, too, for the pleasure they give, are two features of the metaphysical approach to truth from which Gaultier has turned away: the

Cartesian bifurcation of reality and the "croyance en une vérité objective." Gaultier likens the division of reality into subject and object to the creation of a theater in which the individual can enjoy the role of curious spectator, forgetting that he may be the author of what he sees. Although the goal of knowing and understanding the play is ultimately unattainable, the quest for it is the source of some of the greatest pleasures found in human life: the "joie de curiosité," the "passion d'apprécier, de juger, de comparer, de classer," the "épanouissement et . . . exubérance de la faculté de connaître." The tenacity of the notion that *une vérité objective* is attainable, moreover, ensures that the pleasure of the truth-game persists, even when theory after theory proves inadequate to account for what is observed: "Par le vertu de cette illusion métaphysique," Gaultier observes, "l'élan humain est assuré d'une ardeur toujours renaissante."[106]

The final section of *Le Bovarysme,* along with a related essay of 1901, "De la Nature des vérités," presents both a description of life in the phenomenal theater, and a prescription for responding to the image-notions appearing on its stage. Central to Gaultier's specifications are two contrary psychological tendencies, which he calls the *principe d'arrêt* and the *principe de mouvement.*[107] Broadly these are the tendencies to believe and to doubt: to affirm the objective existence of things and to question it,[108] to arrest the phenomenal flux in categories and to release it. For Gaultier there are profound dangers in indulging the first of these tendencies without the second—in allowing the compelling image-notions to reign unchecked.[109] The only acceptable approach is to allow *both* impulses to play: to indulge our faith in these notions but to be prepared to abandon them when they can be seen no longer to serve *l'utilité humaine.*[110] We should treat our comforting conceptions, Gaultier says, as *ressorts tendus*: curves bent to fit the contours of reality yet always on the verge of springing apart.[111]

Gaultier resolves the problem of bovaric self-deception, then, by acknowledging its beneficial effects and by allowing it to proceed so long as these benefits continue. The long-term effect of his policy will be an approach to reality like James's pragmatism, in which version after version of the truth is entertained and discarded. It is important to note one crucial respect, however, in which Gaultier's program differs from James's. The broad criterion for a theory's survival he identifies in *Le Bovarysme*—*l'utilité humaine*—masks a disagreement with James on what *constitutes* utility. For James the pragmatic "turn" means turning toward not just "fruits" and "consequences" *but also facts*: no notion can be useful, in his view, if it contradicts empirical evidence. Gaultier's turn toward consequences is a turn *away* from facts, a decision to support cases, like Emma Bovary's, where there is a clear discrepancy between notion and experience. In other writings Gaultier specifies that the primary concern of the provisional theory-maker is simply to satisfy *le sentiment esthétique*; he may justify any theory "as a phenomenon of beauty," regardless of whether experience bears out its claims.[112] As Hulme summarizes his attitude, all that really matters is that a philosophy paint "a good picture."[113]

Hulme wrote an article in praise of Gaultier's philosophy in 1909, and shortly afterward spent two days with the philosopher en route to the Philosophical Congress in Bologna, a meeting that left him marveling at the "consistency with which [Gaultier's] philosophy is all worked out."[114] It is unclear when he first read *Le Bovarysme,* but notes dated from as 1906 show that he shared many of Gaultier's preoccupations.[115] Like the philosopher he was fascinated by the phenomenon of false self-conception: by the wrongheaded belief in a unified "ego" or "personality," the "sentimental" illusions of the lover, the sense of the self as hero. His argument against romanticism was effectively an attack on a form of bovarysm: a "false conception of the character of human activities" according to which human nature is good and anything is possible.[116] Like Gaultier, Hulme discredits flattering self-conceptions by exposing their interestedness,[117] but moves beyond disillusionment to recognize the value of their effects. He characterizes this pragmatic turn thus:

> There may be an attitude which sees that most things are illusions, that experience is merely the gradual process of disillusionment, that the new as well as the old ideals turn out to be partial, non-continuous or infinite, but then in face of this decides that certain illusions or moods are pleasurable and exhilarating, and deliberately and knowingly encourages them. A judicious choice of illusions, leading to activities planned and carried out, is the only means of happiness, *e.g.* the exhilaration of regarding life as a procession or a war.[118]

Hulme is particularly cognizant of the benefits of conceiving the self as a hero. "Disillusionment," he writes, "comes when it is recognised that all heroic actions can be reduced to the simple laws of egoism." "But wonder can even then be found in the fact that there *are* such *different* and *clear-cut* laws and egoisms and that they have been created out of the chaos." There is a vital place for "the long note of the bugle . . . which moves all the world bodily out of the cinders and the mud."[119] His preoccupation with the benefits of bovarysm in war suggests that some of the notes may be dated as late as 1915. As I shall explain in my final chapter, a section of his 1915 series "A Notebook," not reprinted in *Speculations,* reveals that the endorsement of an absolutist ethics is motivated by pragmatic concerns, specifically by a sense of the utility of such a stance in wartime. Appreciating that fact will enable us to counter critical efforts to view Hulme's ethics as incompatible with his relativism.

If Hulme shares Gaultier's view that unrealistic ideals can be useful, he also shares his conviction that they must be held only provisionally, subject to revision and change. His notes reveal a fascination with temporary experiences of certainty: the moment in the library when one "seems to have definite clear cut moments, but not afterwards," the joyful sense of comprehension after an evening in a bar, which subsides as alcohol passes through the bloodstream. Where there is a "melancholy spirit," where the mind is "like a great desert lifeless," the sound of march music in the street "passes like [a] wave over that desert, unifies it, but then goes."[120] Such experiences seem to Hulme to be exemplary, in that they prevent any idea from reigning unchecked, or being hypostatized—something he, like Gaultier, sees as the source of unnecessary conflict and debate.[121] The "philosophic faculty," he writes, is generally "the easiest moving thing in nature," changing direction like a weathercock in the wind; we must make a deliberate effort to ensure that it retains this mobility, to be "sceptical of the first enthusiasm that a new idea gives."[122]

Hulme's views appear to diverge from Gaultier's only on the point where Gaultier's diverge from James's. Although he is not unaware of the aesthetic pleasures of theory-making,[123] Hulme appears to share James's commitment to heeding empirical evidence. He repeatedly expresses his disapproval of abstract ways of thinking that put men "in danger of forgetting that the world does really exist."[124] "Philosophical syntheses," he notes, "are seen to be meaningless as soon as we get into a bus with a dirty baby and a crowd." Hulme's most forceful statements about the importance of checking ideas against experience rely on the metaphor he derives from Bergson's *L'Evolution créatrice:* the vision of material reality as a chaos of "cinders." The "definite cinder," he says, must serve as a "criterion of nearly all judgment, philosophic and aesthetic." Or as he puts using another favorite figure, likening theories to protective "huts":

> All heroes, great men, go to the outside, away from the Room, and wrestle with cinders. . . .
> A house built is then a symbol, a Roman Viaduct; but the walk there and the dirt—this must jump right into the mind also.[125]

Hulme imagines the ongoing process of truth-making as one in which the desire for comfort is counterbalanced by the courage to face empirical reality. The responsible philosopher seeks the solace abstractions offer but is also brave enough to confront the complex, cindery world they shut out, the "real world of sweat and dirt."[126]

Hulme's understanding of the pragmatic value of theories and his commitment to empirical testing are mirrored in his program for the "new classical" poet. In denying the poet access to an authoritative "Idea" and granting him only an insight into the *conception idéale,* Hulme diminishes

his authority significantly, but he also has much to say about the comfort
the poet's insights may provide despite their limitations. The "Bard," he
says, has as much potential as any rousing "Band" for making temporary
sense of the chaos; he is capable of creating "ideals" that perform graceful
gymnastics on the phenomenal "stage."[127] All that is necessary is that he
write in a way that will call attention to the provisionality of his propositions, holding them accountable to experience. This pragmatist imperative
is what underlies the well-known passage from "Romanticism and Classicism" where Hulme contrasts the classical poet's attitude toward his utterances with the overweening confidence of the romantic poet. If the latter
expresses his insights enthusiastically, confident of their metaphysical foundation, the classical poet is wary of the enthusiasm his ideas give and
communicates that wariness:

> In the classical attitude you never seem to swing right along to the infinite
> nothing. If you say an extravagant thing which does exceed the limits inside to
> which you know man to be fastened, yet there is always conveyed in some way
> at the end an impression of yourself standing outside it, and not quite believing
> it, or consciously putting it forward as a flourish.[128]

Where Hulme's romantic poet allows only the first of Gaultier's two tendencies, the *principe d'arrêt,* his classical poet tempers it with the *principe
de mouvement.* He allows himself the satisfaction of theoretical flight and
checks that satisfaction, touching the ground:

> The romantic, because he thinks man infinite, must always be talking about
> the infinite. . . . What I mean by classical in verse . . . is this. That even in the most
> imaginative flights there is always a holding back, a reservation. The classical poet
> never forgets this finiteness, this limit of man. He remembers always that he is
> mixed up with earth. He may jump, but he always returns back; he never flies
> away into the circumambient gas.[129]

The classical poet's journey earthward invites two interpretations. It may
be that he is to acknowledge in his poetry the material conditions that have
shaped his insight and limit its authority. The "earth" with which he is
"mixed up" and to which he calls attention may be what Hulme describes
elsewhere as the "circumstances and prejudices of . . . class, experience,
capacity and body" informing his speculations.[130] Or it may be that in
forcing himself to return to earth he is simply taking to heart the duty
central to Jamesian pragmatism: the obligation to check his theories against
"cinders" of the material world. The latter interpretation is supported by
a comment later in the "Romanticism and Classicism" essay, where Hulme
observes that the "ultimate reality" with which the poet must concern
himself is the "hurly-burly" of life, the "struggle."[131] It is also corroborated

by many recommendations Hulme makes in his notebooks and essays concerning the language and structure of poetic utterances, instructions he was to follow to the letter in his own poetic experiments.

THE LINE AND THE FRINGE: THE PRAGMATIC FUNCTION OF RESEMBLANCE

Hulme indicates how the classical poet's descendental movement translates into style in a note entitled "*Analysis of the attitude of a man reading an argument.*" Describing an "algebraic" use of language, in which words are manipulated without thought for their material signifieds, he writes approvingly of efforts to demand greater accountability from language:

> (i) Compare in algebra, the real things are replaced by symbols. These symbols are manipulated according to certain laws which are independent of their meaning.
> N.B. At a certain point in the proof we cease to think of x as having a meaning and look upon it as a mere counter to be manipulated.
> (ii) An analogous phenomenon happens in reasoning in language. We replace meaning (i.e. *vision*) by words. These words fall into well-known patterns, i.e. into certain well-known phrases which we accept without thinking of their meaning, just as we do the x in algebra.
> *But* there is a constant movement above and below the line of meaning (representation). And this is used in dialectical argument. At any stage we can ask the opponent to show his hand, that is to turn all his *words* into visions, in realities we can see.[132]

Here the poet's descendental movement is one of translating "*words* into visions." As he puts it elsewhere, "In prose, as in algebra, concrete things are embodied in signs or counters which are moved about according to rules, without being visualized at all in the process"; prose's function is "to pass to conclusions without thinking." Poetry, on the other hand, "is not a counter language, but a visual concrete one": it "endeavours to arrest you, and to make you continuously see a physical thing, to prevent you gliding through an abstract process."[133] Hulme's sense that the poet must keep on eye on what his words signify is in keeping with his commitment to a free and unpredictable creative process. Hulme was aware of Bergson's connection of the manipulation of abstract *chiffres* and the automatic *langage réflexe* of the superficial self and of his suggestion that mechanistic behavior can be broken only by efforts to resist such complacent communications.[134] He would have encountered the same connection in James who, in *Pragmatism*, represents the pragmatist's "turn away from abstraction" and "towards facts" as a challenge to automatism in thought and speech. James's famous metaphor for the effort is an economic one:

> Truth lives . . . for the most part on a credit system. Our thoughts and beliefs "pass," so long as nothing challenges them, just as bank-notes pass so long as nobody refuses them. But this all points to direct face-to-face verifications somewhere, without which the fabric of truth collapses like a financial system with no cash-basis whatever. . . . beliefs verified concretely by somebody are the posts of the whole superstructure. (P 126–27)

For James abstract language resembles paper money—something easy to handle but of no intrinsic worth. The pragmatist will not allow the exchange of bank notes to proceed unimpeded but demands to know the real commodities these translate into—their cash value. Hulme may be thinking of James when he employs a similar metaphor. Where prose manipulates "worn-out coin[s]," he writes, poetry deals in real goods: its expression is "from *Real to Real* with all the intermediate forms keeping their *real* value."[135]

A Jamesian commitment to heeding empirical realities, then, informs the most basic stylistic feature of Hulme's new classical poetics: its concrete diction. His poet is to deal not with general words but with particular ones, not with vaguely suggestive phrases but with terms evoking the "small, dry things" of the material world.[136] The affinity between Hulme's program for expression and James's is most fully apparent, however, in a second essential element in his program: his insistence that the concrete words be selected and arranged so as to highlight the similarities in things. The poet "expresses his emotion at the sight of the vision he sees, his wonder and ecstasy" in "new analogies."[137] For Hulme analogies are perfect vehicles for the poet's cognitive feelings because their epistemological claims are modest yet also potentially useful. In a chaos that eludes final comprehension, they are a means of gaining temporary power:

> The truth is that there are no ultimate principles, upon which the whole of knowledge can be built once and for ever as upon a rock. But there are an infinity of analogues, which help us along, and give us a feeling of power over the chaos when we perceive them.[138]

Analogies, Hulme notes, can lead to "activities planned and carried out," as anyone will know who has ever experienced "the exhilaration of regarding life as a procession or a war."[139] In noting the practical value of analogies (and indeed the "pragmatic criterion"[140] by which they are to be judged) Hulme may have in mind a lengthy discussion of the subject in James's *A Pluralistic Universe,* the book he reviewed for the *New Age* in 1909.[141] James also discusses the "colossal usefulness" of our perceptions of "sameness of kind" in *Pragmatism*: "Once we know that whatever is of a kind is also of that kind's kind, we can travel through the universe as if with seven-league boots" (P 88). Another possible source for Hulme's insight into the usefulness of analogies is a passage in Ribot's *L'Évolution des idées générales* where the psychologist contrasts counterreasoning (*la pensée symbolique*) with analogical reasoning (the *logique des images*). Ribot notes that poets, in being drawn to the *logique des images,* resemble animals who base all their activities on perceptions of analogy. A cat, once burned, will halt before things that smoke; a horse, perceiving the analogy between a gully and a water-trough, will walk to the gully looking for something to drink. The criterion for animal reasoning is purely *pratique*: "Elle réussit ou elle échoue: ce qui la juge, c'est le succès ou l'insuccès."[142] Hulme's notes include several references to animal reasoning, contrasting it with abstract metaphysical speculation and representing it as an ideal worth emulating: "We must judge the world from the status of animals," he writes, "leaving out 'Truth,' etc."[143]

That the poetic analogy matches Hulme's specifications for fair theory-making is apparent also in his account of how it will affect its reader. The trope, in highlighting the "regular shadows" in things, is a gesture in the direction of a theory, the beginning of a flight into generalization. But in preserving the particular objects to which the incipient theory applies, it ensures that the flight into abstraction is *arrested* at an early stage, that it remains accountable to the earth. Hulme conceives the analogy as a kind of "visual chord," offering harmony in its patterning, yet preserving difference through its concreteness. It elicits the kind of awareness Hulme recommends in a note depicting the resistance the empirical world will offer to any burgeoning analogy:

All these sudden insights (*e.g.* the great analogy of a woman compared to the world in Brussels)—all of these start a line, which seems about to unify the world logically. But the line stops. There is no unity. All logic and life are made up of tangled ends like that.

Always think of the fringe and the cold walks, of the lines that lead nowhere.[144]

In the "cindery world" Hulme depicts, the underlying pattern suggested by the analogies is always belied by experience. Elsewhere he makes it clear that the disruption may come from the differences between things categorized together; only a Humpty-Dumpty, he observes, would make the mistake of viewing any two things as exactly alike. The scrupulous thinker, then, will want not only to keep his eye on the regular "line" the analogy marks but also to remain aware of the *fringe of cinders* that escapes that ecstatic recognition.[145] He will not rest in his appreciation for the theory until he also understands where it no longer applies. It is just this balance

of theoretical comprehension and empirical awareness that the concrete
analogy invites.

Hulme's vision of analogy's theoretical line and its concrete fringe may
be the strongest evidence we have of a direct link between James and his
poetic theory. Both figures emerge in James's work, with similar signifi-
cances. The first appears in James's own argument in praise of the kind of
analogy that "insists on the differences as well as the resemblances" between things—an argument to which he returns more than once and which
may serve to explain the predominance of metaphor in his own writing
(PU 75).[146] In a passage in *A Pluralistic Universe,* he praises the use of this
type of analogy in the work of the early nineteenth-century pantheist and
pluralist Gustav Theodor Fechner. He traces Fechner's use of the device to
his perception of the world as a place in which "every line of sameness
actually started and followed up would eventually give out, and cease to
be traceable any farther." As James explains further, according to Fechner,

> it is hard to trace a straight line of sameness, causation, or whatever it may be,
> through a series of . . . objects without swerving into some "respect" where the
> relation, as pursued originally, no longer holds: the objects have so many "as-
> pects" that we are constantly deflected from our original direction, and find, we
> know not why, that we are following something different from what we have
> started with. Thus a cat is in a sense the same as a mousetrap, and a mousetrap
> the same as a birdcage; but in no valuable or easily intelligible sense is a cat the
> same as a birdcage. . . . In every series of real terms, not only do the terms
> themselves and their associates and environments change, but we change, and
> their meaning for us changes, so that new kinds of sameness and types of causa-
> tion continually come into view and appeal to our interest. Our earlier lines,
> having grown irrelevant, are then dropped. (PU 151–52)

In calling attention to the differences that disrupt similarities, James says
Fechner encourages his readers not only to dismantle incipient categories,
but also to remain open to "new kinds of sameness." He is launched into
an ongoing process of making, unmaking, and remaking identical in its
dynamics to the process undertaken by the empirically minded pragmatist.
James's term for the awareness of new relations Fechner encourages—for
"the influence of a faint brain-process upon our thought, as it makes it
aware of relations and objects but dimly perceived"—is the fringe of consciousness (PP 1: 249). In his note about the line and the fringe, then,
Hulme appears to be compounding two of James's metaphors to endorse
a Jamesian view about the only acceptable way to make sense of a "pluralistic universe."[147]

Although his poetic output was very small, the fine little verses Hulme
did produce fulfilled his own specifications for a new "classical" poetry. In

reading them, we are alerted to strong, clear analogies between concrete things. In "Above the Dock" and "Autumn," for example, the perfect circle of the moon echoes the curve of a balloon, its red surface the ruddy visage of a farmer, and stars the bright faces of a crowd of children:

Above the Dock

Above the quiet dock in mid night,
Tangled in the tall mast's corded height,
Hangs the moon. What seemed so far away
Is but a child's balloon, forgotten after play.

Autumn

A touch of cold in the Autumn night—
I walked abroad,
And saw the ruddy moon lean over a hedge
Like a red-faced farmer.
I did not stop to speak, but nodded,
And round about were the wistful stars
With white faces like town children.[148]

Like the analogies Ribot attributes to an *imagination plastique,* the ones in these poems are readily discernible: clear lines of order in the flux.[149] In his best known poem, "The Embankment," Hulme relies on such striking analogies and writes about the comfort they bring:

The Embankment

(The fantasia of a fallen gentleman on a cold, bitter night.)

Once, in a finesse of fiddles found I ecstasy,
In the flash of gold heels on the hard pavement.
Now see I
That warmth's the very stuff of poesy.
Oh, God, make small
The old star-eaten blanket of the sky,
That I may fold it round me and in comfort lie.[150]

Once the speaker of the poem found "poesy" in the unarrested flux of experience: the "finesse of fiddles" and the "flash of gold heels." Now he finds it in analogies that stabilize the flux: analogies like that between the starry sky on a bitterly cold night and a moth-bitten blanket, tattered but warm. "The Embankment" is typical of Hulme's poems in its self-reflexiveness. Several foreground the affinities between objects a "romantic" poet, in Hulme's sense, might characterize as apertures onto the Infinite—the moon, the stars, the sea—and much humbler, more mundane objects. The effect of such linkages, as Geoffrey Hartman has observed, may be one of "descendental transformation": things potentially associated with the divine become aligned instead with the earth. And when the objects of contemplation are thus demystified, so, too, by implication, is the act of contemplation itself; Hartman has rightly associated the practice with poets, including Hulme, dedicated to countering the "vatic overestimation of poetry."[151]

If Hulme's poems continue his efforts to demystify poetic inspiration as well as fulfilling its concomitant recommendations about style, their style plays a key role in refining their message and in keeping it consistent with the approach to the subject Hulme found in contemporary psychology. As in Ribot and Bergson, the demystifications of inspiration in Hulme's poems are not thoroughgoing. If we read the descendental analogies according to Hulme's instructions in the note about the line and the fringe, the theories born from them are only provisional, subject to questioning and revising. The transcendental and mundane objects in poems like "Above the Dock" and "Autumn" may seem sufficiently alike to be categorized together, but their differences are also free to "jump right into the mind," disrupting our sense of their identity and the ensuing generalizations.[152] The moon's balloonlike roundness, or the frayed edges of the stars, may not be sufficient to offset the sense of mystery stirred by their remoteness and haunting light. The particulars preserved in these "solid images" may inspire us to question our first insight, perhaps even to reconsider the possibility of their mystical connections. We may even feel provoked to consider the celestial properties of the objects of earth. Hulme dramatizes something like the process of reading these analogies in the experience of "Susan Ann," the protagonist in a poem proleptic of Wallace Stevens:

Susan Ann and Immortality

Her head hung down
Gazed at earth, finally keen,
As the rabbit at the stoat,
Till the earth was sky,
Sky that was green,
And brown clouds passed
Like chestnut leaves along the ground.[153]

Susan Ann views her surroundings with the eyes of a rabbit, looking for an analogy to help her on her way, and perceives an affinity between earth and sky. But any descendental thoughts this vision may inspire are counterbalanced by ascendental ones; whenever Susan Ann reads the "sky" as "green," she also sees the "earth" as "sky." Like the comminglings of sea and sky we shall see in Stevens, Hulme's represents an equivocal position about the status of poetic vision. They don't so much demystify it as neutralize it.[154]

Hulme's analogical poetry, then, is the perfect counterpart to his scientific redescription of the intuitive moment with which the poetic process begins. It suggests that we must be skeptical about what it means to be inspired by the moon and stars, wary of making claims about our capacity ever to see beyond the phenomenal veil and conscious of the desire for comfort that motivates the quest for order. But it also withholds final judgment about such moments. As we shall see, the match between a psychological account of inspiration and a similarly equivocal poetry is something developed more fully, and in some ways more consistently, by Ezra Pound.

2
The "Image" and the Chess-Game: Ezra Pound's Vorticist Art

Ezra Pound's proudest contribution to the Vorticist journal *Blast,* and the only poem that he was ever to identify as "pure vorticism,"[1] was a "Dogmatic Statement on the Game and Play of Chess." The images in this poem, brightly colored combatants in a fierce battle, are nouns transformed into verbs, chess pieces metaphorically identified with the Roman letters that trace their actions. These brilliant pawn-Y's, bishop-X's and knight-L's strike, cleave and loop one another, breaking rank and reforming, until an assault on a king renders one army victorious. The black-and-white design of the empty chessboard then predominates, but only for a moment. Harnessed energy leaks, the captured escape, and the vanquished arise from their ashes to propose a "renewing of contest."[2]

Pound subtitled his poem "Theme for a Series of Pictures," and this has led critics to observe that its dynamic images and abrupt rhythms mirror many those of Vorticist painting. Beyond this, the parallel suggests that Pound's chess game may be read as an allegory for the mental processes that both of these arts seem to embody and encourage. Many of Pound's contemporaries, including Hulme and Ernest Fenollosa, frequently used chess or checkers as a metaphor for abstract reasoning.[3] The pieces, by their nature representative "types," performed functions similar to those of the words or concepts substituted, in such reasoning, for particulars. The rules of chess, in which certain pieces are capable of certain moves, seemed analogous to the rigorous laws of logic. And the game's object— to reduce variety to simplicity, the different to the same—strikingly resembled the goal of any theoretician. In short chess was an apt image for what James, in his seminal article "The Sentiment of Rationality" (1879), had called the "philosophic passion *par excellence*" (WB 58): the urge to resolve the muddy chaos of phenomena to the clean, geometric grid of abstract theory. In Pound's Vorticist chess game, however, this "theoretic need" does not reign unchecked but seems to be endlessly challenged and subverted. The pieces on the grid are not dead counters, enabling the abstract thinker to remain disengaged from the object of his calculations, but are "living in form"; their vitality is integral to their identity.[4] The patterns they make are inherently unstable, like theories that form and dissolve even as they are made. The "renewing of contest" proposed at the end of the poem betrays the irony of Pound's subtitle: this resolution is no "Dogmatic Statement" but a solution to be challenged. In Jamesian terms the passion for abstraction depicted in Pound's poem is counterbalanced by its "sister passion," the "passion for distinguishing": the preference for "incoherence" over order, for the "concrete fulness" of things over any "absolute datum" (WB 59, 63) that subsumes their differences. "A Game of Chess" is a poem about the cooperation of two antagonistic tendencies of mind. As such it is a model of what I shall call the "tensional" aesthetic of Vorticism.[5]

Historians of the Vorticist movement have struggled to discern strategies common to its poetry and its painting and sculpture. More often than not, they have concluded that the poets and artists of *Blast* were unified only by the nominal leadership of Wyndham Lewis and not by any rigorous common philosophy.[6] But there are strategies in common between the literary branch of Vorticism that Pound called "Imagisme" and the Vorticist visual art advertised by Lewis.[7] Pound explicitly sought a "psychological or philosophical definition" of Imagiste poetry; he hoped that Imagisme would be remembered as a doctrine about the creation of poetry as well as its criticism.[8] Lewis, too, was interested in describing the creative process as well as its product. Both of their accounts of creativity are in the tradition of expressionist aesthetics, most recently embodied in the theoretical writings of Post-Impressionist painters like Whistler and Kandinsky.[9] Like these painters, Pound and Lewis aimed primarily, not at the imitation of nature but at "sincere self-expression." They upheld a "musical conception of form," a commitment to expressing complex states of mind in appropriate "arrangements," whether of language or of form and color.[10] This expressionist agenda entailed what I have been calling the reflex-action model of the creative process: the design of the work of art reflected the artist's assessment of his state of mind. More specifically Pound and Lewis sought forms that would reflect their conceptions of the *epistemological significance* of states of inspiration.

Pound's descriptions of the Imagiste poet's moments of inspiration have led some critics to classify Vorticism as a mystical or Symbolist aesthetic. This view has gathered some support from recent studies documenting Pound's associations with spiritualists during his years in London (1909–16).[11] In a study of Pound's friendship with Yeats, James Longenbach claims that Pound supposed the "Imagiste" to be inspired by an "Image" with supernatural origins. The Imagiste poem, Longenbach writes, "is an attempt to embody the *transcendental* Image in words."[12] Longenbach's "mystical" conception of Vorticism, supported by Leon Surette and Andrzej Sosnowski, among many others, is diametrically opposed to another tradition in Pound criticism that characterizes him as a Nietzschean skeptic.[13] In what follows I shall argue that Pound's (and Lewis's) attitude toward inspiration is neither dogmatic mysticism nor dogmatic skepticism but something *in between:* the *neutral* attitude of a psychologist. Central to my argument is the contention that Pound's "Image" is a close relative of the construct that Hulme called the "inside idea," Ribot and Bergson the *conception idéale:* a psychological concept whose origins are bracketed. I shall contend not only that this construct is a neutralized version of the Symbolist "Idea" but that its neutrality explains the key differences between Imagiste and Symbolist style. The trope Pound recommends to the Imagiste—the "interpretive metaphor"—presents *only as a possibility* the transcendental relations that the Symbolist symbol takes for granted. The similarities between Pound's and Hulme's accounts of the creative reflexaction are striking, despite Pound's disavowal of any close connection.

Like my account of Hulme's Imagist poetics, my account of Vorticism maps correlations with the work of James. The affinity between Pound and James has until recently gone largely unnoticed. Walter Sutton has proposed a convincing analogy between the structure of *The Cantos* and that of James's "pluralistic universe," arguing that both reflect the same position about the kind of coherence it is possible to claim in modern times. In a study dedicated largely to exploring Pound's affinities with Emerson and bringing Frank Lentricchia's reading of James to Pound, Cary Wolfe has ably demonstrated Pound's and James's shared dedication to individualism, the language and conventions of private property, and the project of reinstating "virility" in American culture.[14] Because a comprehensive study of *The Cantos* is beyond the scope of my study, I shall defer to Sutton's, and focus my attention almost exclusively on Pound's early poetry and manifestos. Among other things this exercise should demonstrate that Sutton is wrong to dissociate the early poetics from the late.[15]

Although we have no evidence that Pound read James, the years 1909–16 saw him associating with many who had. He met with Hulme and the Imagists during 1909, the year Hulme reviewed *A Pluralistic Universe,* and renewed his acquaintance with Hulme in 1911, attending his Tuesday evenings in Frith St., Soho. He spent the winter of 1913–14 living with Yeats, while Yeats incorporated insights from *The Varieties of Religious Experience* into an essay on Swedenborg. (Yeats would also have had stories to tell of a personal meeting with James, in which the two men debated the possibility of a universal human memory.[16]) Another opportunity for absorbing James's ideas would have been the weekly meetings of the Quest Society, which Pound attended faithfully between 1911 and 1913, along with Hulme, Lewis, Yeats, Rebecca West, Arthur Symons, John Masefield, and other literary figures. Founded by Pound's good friend G. R. S. Mead in 1897, the Society was dedicated to inquiry into religious and other supranormal experiences. Pound presented his important essay "Psychology and Troubadours" there and published it in the Society's journal, *The Quest*, in October 1912. Leon Surette has observed that this essay, in focusing on elements of pagan mysticism in *Provencale* poetry, was typical of writings in the journal.[17] But although Surette uses this to suggest that Pound's views match the *dogmatic* spiritualism of many of *The Quest*'s contributors, I would argue that they reflect the more *qualified* spiritualism of contributors writing in the spirit of James.

To clarify the immediate discursive context for Pound's Jamesian tenets, then, I preface my account of his Vorticist aesthetic with a brief survey of Jamesian writings in *The Quest*.

JAMES AND *THE QUEST*

James's interest in religious experience extended to an active sympathy for spiritualism and the occult. As vice president and then president of the American Branch of the Society for Psychical Research,[18] he encouraged the Society's members to talk about psychic and necromantic experiences in the discourse of empirical psychology. On the face of it, such discourse would seem to have been incompatible with the spiritualist project; James himself wrote that psychology was to avoid claims about contact with the world beyond appearances.[19] But in his view, claims about the apprehension and intervention of the supernatural would only ever become respectable if spiritualists first offered precise records of these experiences while avoiding metaphysical claims. In a statement of purpose for the Society written in 1885, he wrote:

> I take it the urgent thing ... is to ascertain in a manner so thorough as to constitute evidence that will be accepted by outsiders, just what the phenomenal conditions of certain concrete phenomenal occurences are. Not till that is done, can spiritualistic or anti-spiritualistic activities be even mooted. I'm sure that the more we can steer clear of theories at first, the better.[20]

Or as he put it five years later, writing to Thomas Davidson, "The only Society worth lifting one's finger for must be one for *investigation of cases,* not for theoretic discussion—for *facts,* and not yet for *philosophy.*"[21] James contributed to this program by editing the work of the Society's members and by collecting records of occult experiences. On reading drafts of one of F. W. H. Myers's books on visionary experience, for example, he advised Myers to tone down his "transmundane enthusiasm," which he thought likely to put off the unconverted reader. His own use of psychological discourse is evident in descriptions like the following, from an extended study of the visions of a Boston medium, Mrs. Piper:

In the trances of this medium, I cannot resist the conviction that knowledge appears which she has never gained by the ordinary waking use of her eyes and ears and wits. *What the source of this knowledge may be I know not, and have not the glimmer of an explanatory suggestion to make; but from admitting the fact of such knowledge I can see no escape.*[22]

As in any scientific investigation, it is not the *cause* of phenomena but the *effect* that counts.

The vital thing to notice about the cautious language James uses to discuss psychic phenomena is that it only *avoids* supernaturalist claims; it does not discount them. To adopt a dogmatically skeptical position toward such claims, as scientists at the time were in the habit of doing—to dismiss spiritualism as so much "dingy twaddle"—would be to lapse into another brand of metaphysics and not to be a true scientist at all.[23] Though he was never to express outright belief in the supernatural origin of occult phenomena, James came, on the whole, to be far more sympathetic to the faith of the spiritualists than to the skepticism of their detractors. His leanings toward faith came after years of data collection. For example, in his final report on Mrs. Piper, in 1909, he concludes that "when I connect the Piper case with all the other cases I know of automatic writing and mediumship, and with the whole record of spirit-possession in human history, the notion that such an immense current of experience, complex in so many ways, should spell out absolutely nothing but the word 'humbug,' acquires a character of unlikeliness."[24] Similarly, assessing what the Society for Psychical Research has accomplished, twenty-four years after he set out its scientific program, he sees its spiritualist thesis largely corroborated:

How often has "Science" killed off all spook philosophy, and laid ghosts and raps and "telepathy" away underground as so much popular delusion. Yet never before were these things offered us so voluminously, and never in such authentic-seeming shape or such good credentials. The tide seems steadily to be rising, in spite of all the expedients of scientific orthodoxy. It is hard not to suspect that here may be something different from a mere chapter in human gullibility.[25]

The project of renouncing the world of the spirit to legitimize it is replicated in James's most important work on spiritual matters, *The Varieties of Religious Experience.* There he catalogs hundreds of instances of "mystical" moments—moments he defines as those when human beings, their wills in abeyance, seem suddenly to apprehend ineffable "truths"—without making claims about their origins.[26] Although he observes that "mystical" experiences are characterized by "convincingness," that they are "absolutely authoritative over the individuals to whom they come," he resists authorizing them by attributing them to a divine cause; the moment of enchantment, he writes, might be "a gift of God's grace," or it might be a "gift of our organism" (VRE 72, 422, 47). Like Ribot, he explains the sudden appearance of mystical visions by saying they spring from the "unconscious" mind: a *liminal* space, neither human nor divine, neither dependent on the body nor free of it.[27] After all his careful efforts to avoid talk of origins, however, and when all the data is scrupulously laid out, James again finds himself compelled to give more credence to spiritualist than to materialist explanations. "The whole drift of my education," James concludes, "persuade[s] me that the world of our present consciousness is only one out of many worlds of consciousness that exist, and that those other worlds must contain experiences which have a meaning for our life also; and that although in the main their experiences and those of this world keep discrete, yet the two become continuous at certain points, and higher energies filter in" (VRE 519).

James's careful balance between scientific caution and spiritualist hope was shared by many, if not all, members of the Quest Society. Appreciating this fact about the Society helps us to avoid two false assumptions common in discussions of its importance for Pound: the assumption, first, that it stood for a dogmatic spiritualism, and, second, that this position was incompatible with a respect for science.[28] If contributors to *The Quest* were united in anything, it was only in their *refusal to dismiss the possibility* of a spirit world. At one extreme, certainly, there were people like G. R. S. Mead, Evelyn Underhill, and A. H. Ward who were firm believers. But there were also a great number of empiricists—Émile Boutroux, Rev. F. Aveling, Prof. Karl Joel, Rev. Walter Walsh, Rev. W. F. Cobb, and W. R. Boyce Gibson, to name a few—who shared a Jamesian commitment to documenting "mystical" experience, reserving judgment about its ultimate significance. Several of these writers commented on the error of assuming that religious hope and a dedication to scientific method are mutually exclusive. Rev. Walsh, for example, argues that a religion that eschews science "will never command the allegiance of men who are at once intelligent and good."[29] Rev. Aveling offers to explain why the notion of the mutual incompatibility of religion and science has become so entrenched. The problem, as he sees it, is a misunderstanding of empirical psychology:

[P]sychological materialism finds an apparent though not a real support in the method of empirical psychology. The fact that the science *neglects* the soul systematically, as being beyond its scope, makes it appear similar to the materialistic philosophy which *denies* the existence of the soul. Materialism profits by the apparent resemblance, and seems in consequence to be more scientific than spiritualism.[30]

Like his fellow empiricists in *The Quest*, Aveling understands what James took pains to emphasize: the aim of psychology was only to *evade* transcendental entities like the "soul," not to discount them. Rightly understood, the discourse of psychology could give spiritualism much needed respectability.[31]

One manifestation of psychological discourse in The Quest, and another important link with James, is the frequent classification of intuitive experiences as instances of *feeling* rather than *knowing*. Echoing James's move in "The Sentiment of Rationality,"[32] several contributors to The Quest emphasize that the "emotional assurance" experienced by the mystic is not to be confused with knowledge. "Intuition and Knowledge," writes W. R. Boyce Gibson, are "*vitally* distinct," not merely the "convex [and] concave side of one and the same curve."[33] Two writers use the distinction to distinguish legitimate forms of intuitionism from illegitimate ones. For Émile Boutroux, the English Romantic poets were guilty of confusing mystical feeling with knowledge. Gibson criticizes Bergson's account of intuition, which sometimes gives "the impression that the mere intuition of duration is in itself a metaphysical accomplishment."[34] Boutroux's point is in keeping with a general tendency among empirical theologians in this period to regard the English Romantics as dogmatic, or unself-conscious mystics—a view we have seen is central to Hulme's argument against them.[35] Gibson's claim about Bergson is corroborated by the many critics of modernism who have questioned modernism's repudiation of romanticism on the grounds of its affiliation with Bergson.[36]

If the empiricists in The Quest were careful to resist knowledge-claims, they were also wary of attributing sudden, intuitive insights to the intervention of supernatural beings, whether these be pagan gods, the Judaeo-Christian God, the ghosts of the dead, or mystic muses. Such beings, in their view, are simply *facts of inner experience*: "real" to those who experience them but otherwise impossible to affirm or deny. Several contributors preserve the liminality of such beings by saying they spring from the subconscious or subliminal mind. J. Arthur Hill, James H. Hyslop, and Émile Boutroux share James's view that such a move enables discussion about visitations from "beyond," without commitment to origins. Like him, too, they take pains to emphasize that relegating mystical visitors to the subconscious is not tantamount to dismissing them as illusions. As Hill points out, "the difficulty is, that we do not know where the farther frontiers lie, of this subliminal or transmarginal field. Inspiration may come either from or *through* this field; and we have no criterion to decide which it is." Boutroux points to several psychologists, including Ribot, who have explained the liminal nature of the subconscious, and he singles out James's *Varieties of Religious Experience* as a text that successfully exploits this ambiguity for spiritualism.[37]

The scientific discussions of mystical experience in The Quest included a subset that would have been of special interest to Pound and to which his own "Psychology and Troubadours" belonged: discussions of the moment of sudden, intuitive insight at the beginning of the creative experience. While dogmatic mystics like Underhill, Ward, and H. Stanley Redgrove were keeping alive what Hulme calls a "romantic" account of creativity, arguing that the artist enjoys an "intuition of the Real shining through the veil of sense" or that he "mediate[s] between the transcendental and his fellow men," the empiricists were trying to give a scientific account of the same activity.[38] At the heart of the empiricists' efforts to neutralize a mystical account of creativity was the move central to Hulme's efforts to do the same: an attempt to substitute a *conception idéale* for an inspiring "Idea." Ward's and Underhill's accounts, like Symbolist ones, had the artist apprehending a prelinguistic complex of divine origin.[39] When Boutroux and Hill discuss the "scheme" to which the artist gives "definition and expression," however, they are more cautious about its origin. For them the construct originates in the "subliminal self," a liminal space whose contents are neither subjective nor objective. "Is this subliminal self a faculty that enables us to enter into relation with supernatural beings, a faculty that is analogous, *mutatis mutandis*, to our senses and our capacity for objective experience? At present it is impossible to say."[40]

The empiricists of *The Quest* followed up their redescription of the inspiring "Idea" with recommendations about the form that would give it adequate expression—a form appropriately different from the one proposed by its dogmatic spiritualists. Underhill completes her account of the divinely inspired artist by claiming that "symbolism" is the only adequate mode of expression. Her enthusiasm for Symbolist methods is shared by Redgrove, who defines "all genuine art" as "the manipulation of the symbols of nature and experience so that their spiritual meaning may be blazoned forth."[41] The empiricists, however, propose another mode of expression, more compatible with their more equivocal attitude toward inspiration. But before turning to their recommendations, which have much in common with the stylistic tenets of Imagisme, I would like to return to the question of Pound's mysticism, particularly his seemingly esoteric "Doctrine of the 'Image.'"[42]

POUND'S MYSTICISM: "REAL" GODS AND THE "IMAGE"

It is not difficult to see why recent critics of Vorticism have been prepared to view it as a "mystical" aesthetic. Many of Pound's remarks suggest that he imagines the creative experience to begin with a moment of divine revelation. In his *Quest* article on the troubadours, for example, he celebrates those moments when a person may suddenly feel "his immortality upon him," when he is struck by a "vision unsought," a "vision gained without machination." These are the moments, he says, when the "gods" appear, and they are moments of absolute conviction: Persephone and De- meter, Laurel and Artemis, "are intelligible, vital, essential . . . to those people to whom they occur." A few years after noting the "delightful psy- chic experience" of the troubadours, Pound describes the unsought vision inspiring the Imagiste poet. It begins with the appearance in conscious- nessness of a "primary pigment" called the "IMAGE"—an event marked by all the properties of "mystical" experience, if we are to take James's definition of such experiences in *Varieties of Religious Experience* as norma- tive.[43] Like the object in any mystical vision, the Image is intuited, emerging when action, will, and intellect are suspended. Like the insights accom- panying mystical experiences, too, the ones accompanying it seem ineffable: it is "the word beyond formulated language."[44] Apprehending the Image, moreover, means feeling elevated above the habitual constraints of time and of space (Ret. 4); Pound captures its seeming transcendence by comparing it to an equation of analytic geometry—such as $(x-a)^2 + (y-b)^2 = r^2$:

> It is the circle. It is not a particular circle, it is any circle and all circles. It is nothing that is not a circle. It is the circle free of space and time limits. It is the universal, existing in perfection, in freedom from space and time.[45]

In defining the Image as a universal, Pound comes close to calling it an Idea and affirming its status as a vehicle of timeless knowledge. And he grants it much the same function in the creative process as the Idea has in the accounts of Schopenhauer and the Symbolists and of Underhill and Ward. Like that entity, and unlike the "dead concepts" initiating allegory, it gener- ates a potentially infinite number of unforetold versions of itself in the poet's mind. The Image is a "VORTEX, from which, and through which, and into which, ideas are constantly rushing."[46]

But if Pound's descriptions of the appearance of the gods and of the Image suggest that he affirms the divine nature of inspiration, other aspects of these accounts absolve them of such "transmundane enthusiasm." In fact Pound respects the discursive limits legislated by James for psychologi- cal science. Pound writes explicitly about the difference between the scien- tist and the metaphysician in two essays of 1912 and 1913, "The Wisdom of Poetry" and "The Serious Artist"; the scientist, he says, is on the watch for "unassailable data," which it is the metaphysician's responsibility to judge. His own accounts of mystical experience scrupulously follow the example of the scientist, carefully acknowledging such experience as "scien- tific fact" but resisting speculation about whether it is as epistemologically significant as it seems. Numerous comments about intuitive and visionary experiences, both during the Vorticist period and subsequently, reflect this caution. One example from his later work is a description of Swedenborg's visions in *Guide to Kulchur:*

> At least two kinds of statement are found in philosophers. Spinoza writes:
>
> The intellectual love of things consists in the understanding of their perfections.
>
> Swedenborg, if you permit him to be called a philosopher, writes: I saw three angels, they had hats on their heads.
>
> Both carry conviction. *One may be a bit in the dark as to what constituted Swedenborg's optic impressions but one does not doubt that he had such impressions.*[47]

Like James in his representation of Mrs. Piper, Pound acknowledges the reality of Swedenborg's vision for Swedenborg while witholding judgment about its cause. And precisely the same caution marks his descriptions of divine visions, in early writings like "Psychology and Troubadours." The gods, he notes, are *"real for those who experience them"*; they are part of a "delightful psychic *experience"*; beyond that there is nothing to say.[48]

The Image, too, is firmly situated within the jurisdiction of empirical psychology. Pound acknowledges only the sense of freedom from time and space limits it evokes, not the fact. He views it as real only in the sense that it is *experienced:*

> An *[I]mage,* in our sense, is real because we know it directly. If it have an age-old traditional meaning this may serve as proof to the professional student of symbology that we have stood in the deathless light, or that we have walked in some arbour of his traditional paradiso, but that is not our affair.[49]

Here Pound is bringing a psychologist's discipline to the claims for poetic inspiration made by the Symbolists, especially to the claim that the poet's unsought vision has significance owing to its transcendental origin. "Image" is his term for what Ribot and Bergson called the *conception idéale,* Hulme the "inside idea," and Boutroux the "scheme": a "cluster of fused ideas," associated by the force of "emotion," appearing in the consciousness and demanding "adequate expression" in words.[50] Conceding his debt to the "new psychology" and to the work of the British psychologist Bernard Hart, in particular, he describes his Image as "that which presents an intellectual and emotional complex in an instant of time."[51] Hart had explained the connection between the Image and subconscious "complexes" in an essay contributed to Hugo Münsterberg's *Subconscious Phenomena* (1910)—a volume reviewed in *The Quest* in 1911:

The subconscious (*unbewusstsein*) is regarded as a sea of unconscious ideas and emotions, upon whose surface plays the phenomenal consciousness of which we are personally aware.

These unconscious ideas are agglomerated into groups with accompanying affects, the systems thus formed being termed "complexes." These complexes are regarded as possessing both potential and kinetic energy, and thus are capable of influencing the flow of phenomenal consciousness according to certain definite laws. The nature of their influence is dependent upon the relation they have to each other and to the normally dominating or ego complex. The complex may either cause the direct introduction into consciousness of its constituent ideas and affect, or its influence may be distorted and indirect. The indirect effects may be of the most various types—symbolisms, word forgetting, disturbance of the association processes, etc. *A single idea or image in consciousness may be conditioned (constellated) by a multiplicity of unconscious complexes.*[52]

If it is this account Pound has in mind in saying the Image "presents" a "complex," he is shifting the origin of symbolism-effects from the "deathless light" to the liminal twilight zone of the subconscious.

Pound's mysticism, in short, belongs with that of the empiricists in the Quest Society, not the dogmatists. He respects revelatory experiences as a fact of experience but systematically and self-consciously reserves judgment about their divine origins. As he was to summarize his position in the 1921 manifesto, "Axiomata":

If the consciousness receives or has received such effects from the theos, or from something not the theos yet which the consciousness has been incapable of understanding or classifying either as theos or a-theos, it is incapable of reducing these sensations to coherent sequence of cause and effect. . . . As the consciousness observes the results of the senses, it observes also the mirage of the senses, or what may be a mirage of the senses, or an affect from the theos, the non-comprehensible.[53]

It would not be quite accurate, however, simply to say that Pound is equivocal about revelatory experiences. Like James he also moves beyond his scientific detachment to express a cautious *optimism* about their theistic origins. Kevin Oderman has detected such an attitude in "Psychology and Troubadours," when Pound, debating whether to give a "visionary interpretation" to Arnaut Daniel's experiences, concedes that "in none of these things singly is there any specific *proof*."[54] As Oderman rightly observes, the word "singly" betrays Pound's leanings toward belief; it "suggests . . . that together the items in [Pound's] catalogue of considerations do amount to a kind of proof, while avoiding the responsibility of calling it a proof."[55] Pound's position, in other words, comes close to James's assertion that, though there is no "knock-down" evidence of the spiritualist hypothesis, the "general drift of his experience" would seem to corroborate it. Much the same attitude is conveyed by the 1914 poem "Coitus":

> The gilded phaloi of the crocuses
> are thrusting at the spring air.
> Here is there nought of dead gods
> But a procession of festival,
> A procession, O Giulio Romano,
> Fit for your spirit to dwell in.
> Dione, your nights are upon us.[56]

The speaker here is not sure his profound "sense-of" the spirit inhabiting the crocuses is evidence of live gods, but he does know there is "naught" in it to support the hypothesis of "dead" ones. Rather than perversely denying the evidence of his experience, then, he is prepared to imagine that he owes his vision to Dione, mother of Aphrodite, rather than to the heat of his own imagination.

The cautious respect for spiritualism in "Coitus" and "Psychology and Troubadours" is evident throughout Pound's accounts of mystical experience, including those concerning the Vorticist poet and the "Image" it is his duty to "render." And Pound's recommendations about how to go about "rendering" are likewise informed by this attitude. To appreciate how this is so, it is necessary to turn again to parallel recommendations made by James and his followers in *The Quest*.

PROVISIONAL SYMBOLISM: THE ANALOGY AS HYPOTHESIS

That the Quest Society was concerned not just with the status of mystical visions but also with how they should be communicated is apparent from the statement of purpose with which G. R. S. Mead launched its journal in 1909. The goal of the Society, he writes, is to explore "the two great complementary courses which must be followed by every individual soul": the "throwing of the mind outwards to things beyond" and the effort "to *create,* to *express* that which this extension of consciousness has awakened within its deepest nature."[57] Evelyn Underhill and H. Stanley Redgrove may have had this twofold obligation in mind when they extolled "symbolist" techniques for communicating cosmic insights. Predictably when the empiricists of *The Quest* discussed poetic expression, they proposed alternative measures reflecting their reluctance to characterize the poet's insights as "first-hand communications from the Transcendent Order" but without discounting that possibility altogether.[58]

The expression on which several of the empiricists settled as an alternative to Symbolism was the "hypothesis": a proposition that advertises its own provisionality, inviting its reader to accept it only on the condition it meet a series of empirical tests.[59] As G. R. S. Mead makes clear in a 1913 essay summarizing Hans Vaihinger's *The Philosophy of "As If"*, the hypothesis is not to be confused with the "fiction." It differs from that more playful trope in *preserving the possibility of its own truthfulness*—a possibility reflected in the verification process it demands:

> Hypothesis always looks to reality—i.e. the mental representation or concept contained in it, claims or hopes to be found congruous with a percept that will one day be given; it submits itself to the test of reality and demands final verification, that is, it wants to be substantiated as true, as actually a real expression of the real (144); an hypothesis looks for a definite fixation. The fiction, on the contrary, is merely an auxiliary representation, or image, a scaffolding that should be taken down later on (148); it can demand only justification. Thus the hypothesis remains, the fiction falls away. The former builds up a construct of real substantial knowledge, the latter is only a methodological or formal means. The hypothesis is a result of thought, the fiction a means or method of thought. The intent of the hypothesis is to discover, that of the fiction to invent (149).[60]

In essence the fiction is the utterance of the dogmatic skeptic, who has no doubt that what he says is a lie. The hypothesis, on the other hand, is the provisional offering of the thinker who is cautiously optimistic about the truth of what he has to say: the perfect expression, then, for the Jamesian spiritualist.

The champions of hypothesis in *The Quest* would have found powerful support for their position in the chapter on "Mysticism" in *The Varieties of Religious Experience*.[61] In a passage vital to understanding the link between James's phenomenology of religion and his pragmatism, James weighs the expressive options open to people who believe they have received mystical enlightenment. Acknowledging that the insights are "absolutely authoritative" over those who experience them and that it is tempting, therefore, to represent them as dogma, he reminds his reader that there are insufficient grounds to "make it a duty for those who stand outside of them to accept [them] . . . uncritically" (VRE 422). He suggests that a more equitable relation between speaker and listener is called for, in which the listener is invited to test and, if necessary, dispute the propositions. Notably James also observes that it is the speaker's right to offer the propositions as if they *might* be true; there is no reason to deny "the possibility of other orders of truth" they represent (VRE 423). On balance, then, the most sensible decision is to represent them as "hypotheses":

> Mystical states indeed wield no authority due simply to their being mystical states. But the higher ones among them point in directions to which the religious

sentiments even of non-mystical men incline. They tell of the supremacy of the ideal, of vastness, of union, of safety and of rest. They offer us *hypotheses,* hypotheses which we may voluntarily ignore, but which as thinkers we cannot possibly upset. The supernaturalism and optimism to which they would persuade us may, interpreted in one way or another, be after all the truest of insights into the meaning of this life. (VRE 428)

If James believes the hypothesis to be the fairest way of representing mystical insights, he is also convinced that this form will be the most readily received. This conviction stems from a belief in two conflicting, yet fundamental, human needs, evident in his earliest essays on psychology and also in *Pragmatism.* Every human being, in his view, knows two impulses, which he calls the "passion for simplification" and the "passion for distinguishing,"[62] that is, the impulse to believe in divine order and to doubt it, or to find an authoritative account of the world, and to find details such an account fails to explain. Neither impulse can satisfactorily function without the other: every person weary of the world's "concrete clash and dust and pettiness," James observes, will be comforted by the idea of timeless laws. But confronted with any dogmatic proposition, they will feel a need to turn to what lies outside or "beyond" it: "Our mind is so wedded to the process of seeing an other beside every item of its experience, that when the notion of an absolute datum is presented to it, it goes through its usual procedure and remains pointing at the void beyond, as if in that lay further matter for contemplation."[63] The only satisfactory method of formulating theories about the world, therefore, will be to choose a form that *balances* philosophic and empiricist desires—such as the hypothesis.[64]

James's appreciation for communications achieving "a compromise between an abstract monotony and a concrete heterogeneity" (WB 60) also underlies his support for another mode of hypothesis, which I have discussed briefly in connection with Hulme and which is more important still for Pound. This is the kind of "analogy" that James finds in the work of Gustav Fechner. In *A Pluralistic Universe,* we will recall, James praises Fechner's analogies *because they function like hypotheses:* they offer both provisional abstractions and an empirical field against which those abstractions might be tested. At the same time as these analogies suggest the similarity between two things, that is, they invite the reader to look closely at their properties and to consider how they differ. The perception of difference then leads one to investigate the other, perhaps more appropriate, "relations" that lie invitingly around the "fringe." James describes this process as one in which the beginnings of "conceptual knowledge" are continually being offset by "direct acquaintance" with the particulars involved (PU 112) and offers several sample readings of analogy to illustrate the point. Contemplating the analogy sometimes noted between the earth

and an animal, for example, he agrees that both "develop organically" or
"from within." Having observed this, however, he looks more closely at
these things and notices where the likeness ends:

> Long ago the earth was called an animal; but a planet is a higher class of being
> than either man or animal; not only quantitatively greater, like a vaster and
> more awkward whale or elephant, but a being whose enormous size requires an
> altogether different plan of life. Our animal organization comes from our inferi-
> ority. Our need of moving to and fro, of stretching our limbs and bending our
> bodies, shows only our defect. What are our legs but crutches, by means of
> which, with restless efforts, we go hunting after the things we have not inside of
> ourselves. But the earth is no such cripple; why should she who already possesses
> within herself the things we so painfully pursue, have limbs analogous to ours?
> Shall she mimic a small part of herself? What need has she of arms, with nothing
> to reach for? of a neck, with no head to carry? (PU 74)

The anatomical differences between earth and animal lead James to cast
his mind outside the emerging category, in search of a "higher class of
being" that will better accommodate the earth. He makes it clear, moreover, that any new relations uncovered in that quest will be subject to the
same kind of scrutiny, that the process of "dipping" theory into fact will
go on indefinitely.

James's praise for Fechner's use of analogy is part of a larger attempt to
substitute a "pluralistic" metaphysics for a "monistic" one, and it is possible, therefore, that he conceives the analogy as an alternative to certain
forms of Symbolist practice. I am thinking here of the kind of Symbolism
sustained by a faith both in fixed categories and, more extremely, in "correspondences": the Symbolism of a Swedenborg or an Emerson, or of French
Symbolist successors like Baudelaire and Mallarmé.[65] For these writers
every natural object belongs to a certain type and is sufficiently wedded
with other objects in its category to serve as their proxies; the poet can
rely on natural images to serve as windows onto a vast unity, fixed for
eternity in the mind of God. By contrast in the provisional account of the
universe James proposes in *A Pluralistic Universe* (and to some extent in
Pragmatism), there can be no certainty about the existence of the "*one
Knower*" (P 71) and therefore no certainty about either the category to
which any particular belongs or its synaesthetic correspondences. If the
monistic universe is one in which every particular "arrives with all its
carriers supporting it," James's alternative is one in which it can easily
"take up or drop another thing" without "losing its identity" (PU 145–46);
indeed it demands such treatment if it is to be interpreted responsibly. But
in demanding the constant disruption of identities, alliances, and significa-
tions, James does not mean to suggest that he envisions a world definitively
devoid of any kind of order or interrelation. His vision is one in which

"things are 'with' one another in many ways" (PU 145); he even admits that "some day . . . even total union, with one knower, one origin, and a universe consolidated in every conceivable way, may turn out to be the most acceptable of all hypotheses." "How much of union there may be," he insists, is a question that . . . *can only be decided empirically*" (my italics), through an ongoing quest that respects every detail "not 'overcome'" (P 78–79) by the proposed patterns. The tentative analogy—unlike the dogmatic symbol—will provoke such a quest, as we feel the "rush of our thought forward through its fringes" (PU 128).

I have already suggested that Hulme understood the affinity between analogy and hypothesis and that his own poems respond to James's proposed hermeneutics. A fuller case can be made for the affinity between hypothesis and the trope Pound recommended to the Imagiste: the "interpretive metaphor."

Rendering the "Image": The "Interpretive Metaphor"

Pound's specifications for Imagiste style reflect his wish that the poet, too, be a scientist—or empirical psychologist—in representing his states of consciousness. Like a psychologist the Imagiste will record his cognitive experiences without speculating about what they finally mean; the job of assessing them belongs to the philosopher.[66] At the heart of his restraint will be a refusal to speculate about the origins of his inspiring insights: "As Dante writes of the sunlight coming through the clouds from a hidden source and illuminating part of a field . . . so [is the poet] on the alert for colour perceptions of a subtler sort, *neither affirming them to be 'astral' or 'spiritual' nor denying the formulae of theosophy*." More specifically, it is his task to "render the *[I]mage*," whether that complex is "perceived or conceived," "subjective or objective."[67]

One manifestation of such a commitment is Pound's own habit, in both early and late poetry, of equivocating about the ontological status of "ghosts" and "gods." From early "visionary" poems like "Coitus" to the late *Cantos,* he presents the appearance of such beings as undeniable fact, emphasizing at the same time that nothing can be known for sure about their origins. "The Flame," for example, a poem first published in 1911 and closely related in subject matter to "Psychology and Troubadours," announces unequivocally that "there are many gods whom we have seen." That these visions represent a merging of soul with eternity, however, he will propose only provisionally—as a hypothesis:

> *If* I have merged my soul, or utterly
> Am solved and bound in, through aught here on earth,

There canst thou find me, O thou anxious thou,
Who call'st about my gates for some lost me. . . .

(CSP 65)[68]

Similarly, the "ghosts" who appear in *The Cantos* (a work James Longenbach has placed in the genre of "dialogues with the dead") are typically of uncertain provenance. Witness the passage Daniel Pearlman has called the "visionary climax" of *The Pisan Cantos*—perhaps of *The Cantos* as a whole;[69]

Ed ascoltando al leggier mormorio
    there came new subtlety of eyes into my tent,
whether of spirit or hypostasis,
    but what the blindfold hides
or at carneval

                        nor any pair showed anger

    Saw but the eyes and stance between the eyes,
colour, diastasis,
        careless or unaware it had not the
whole tent's room
nor was place for the full *Eidos*
interpass, penetrate
        casting but shade beyond the other lights
            sky's clear
            night's sea
            green of the mountain pool
            shone from the unmasked eyes in half-mask's space.[70]

As Albert Gelpi has observed, this is the "fullest revelation of divinity" Pound allows in *The Cantos*.[71] But for all that, it is not assuredly a revelation either of "hypostasis" or of the "full *Eidos*." The eyes are suspended in a "half-mask's space": the liminal space of phenomenological reduction, where everything essential about them is left undecided. In his practice of suspending gods and ghosts in enclosed spaces, Pound strongly resembles Wallace Stevens, whose liminal divinities I shall be discussing in detail. The "[t]re donne intorno alla mia mente" in Canto 78 are relatives of Stevens's many interior paramours: sufficiently objective to encourage communion but not so objective that they escape construction by their perceivers' desires.[72]

The part of Pound's scientific poetics that most concerns us here is what he calls the interpretive or absolute metaphor, or, in his second use of the term, the "Image."[73] This figure fulfils a scientific program, the essential task of the Vorticist poet being to represent a cluster of associated percepts, ideas, and emotions whose origins remain unknown. Not knowing the origin of this "Image" means not knowing the degree to which its contents can be trusted; perhaps the relations it presents are a sign from the "theos," perhaps only the "mirage" of desire. Faced with this uncertainty, the Vorticist poet must choose a form that neither overestimates nor underestimates the insight: one that neither affirms its truthfulness nor rules it out. In several manifestos Pound indicates that the alternative to "dogma" is metaphor. ("I ask the reader to regard what follows," he writes, "not as dogma, but as a metaphor which I find convenient to express certain relations."[74]) The "interpretive" kind of metaphor is more specialized: a figure that avoids dogma but that also preserves the possibility of its own truthfulness. It is the form Pound attributes in "Psychology and Troubadours," like James in *The Varieties of Religious Experience,* to the best forms of religion: a "working hypothesis."[75]

More than just desire to match expression to insight attracted Pound to hypothetical forms of expression. Hypotheses are not just provisional propositions but practical ones—as in "working hypotheses"—and it becomes clear that Pound makes what I have called the "pragmatic turn." In several passages he pointedly turns from questions of origin to questions of effect. In "Axiomata" he likens unexplained revelations to "bullets" or the symptoms of an unidentified "bacillus"; there may be "no knowledge" about their "ultimate nature," but it is of vital importance to respond usefully to their "superficial effects."[76] He regards such revelations, that is, as the equivalent of what James called "practical truths": things not to understand but to *act on,* with an eye to doing some good (ERE 13). He passes this agenda on to the poet through numerous comments characterizing poetry not just as science but as *applied* science: a practice of fashioning helpful "devices." Poems, he writes, should be like "engines," making whatever light inspiration brings accessible to readers, so they may put it to use; they are to be "sources" of energy, whatever their own "ultimate sources" may be.[77]

Another factor contributing to Pound's attraction to hypothesis is his Jamesian sense that neither the impulse to simplify the world through theory, nor the counterimpulse to attend to empirical particulars, can prevail on its own. On the one hand, he knows that holding theories rigidly, without checking them against particulars, will lead to mental "atrophy." On the other hand, he views representations that make no effort to simplify the flux—like Impressionist or Futurist paintings—as "flaccid," or unmanly.[78] His commitment to an aesthetic that balances the two tendencies is something he was later to affirm in *ABC of Reading,* in a passage employing the same economic analogy James uses in *Pragmatism.* For James the pragmatist may employ abstractions, or bank notes, only so long as he remains mindful of their cash value (P 32). For Pound's poet "any general statement is like a cheque drawn on a bank. Its value depends on what is there to meet it. . . . An abstract or general statement is GOOD if it be ultimately found to correspond with the facts."[79]

For scientific, practical, and psychological reasons, then, Pound champions a form of metaphor that compromises between abstraction and heterogeneity. It is to seek the same balance Ernest Fenollosa detected in the Chinese ideogram: a construct preserving evidence of the particulars threatened by the growing abstraction, like a "blood-stained battle-flag."[80] Providing an example of such a metaphor, in "Vorticism," Pound calls attention first to its function of highlighting similarities:

> Victor Plarr tells me that once, when he was walking over snow with a Japanese naval officer, they came to a place where a cat had crossed the path, and the officer said, "Stop, I am making a poem." Which poem was, roughly, as follows:—
>
> > "The footsteps of the cat upon the snow:
> > (are like) plum-blossoms."
>
> The words "are like" would not occur in the original, but I add them for clarity.[81]

Like the biological "slides" to which he was to compare poetic analogies in *ABC of Reading,* the images of footprints and blossoms invite "continual COMPARISON of one . . . specimen with another."[82] But he also makes it clear that poetic images are to elicit perceptions of difference as well as similarity; the capacity to recognize that "things hitherto deemed identical or similar are dissimilar," he observes in "I Gather the Limbs of Osiris," is vital to intellectual advancement.[83]

The central device in Pound's Vorticist poetry, in sum, was to invite a very particular kind of reading: one in which, as Paul Ricoeur would put it, "the movement toward the genus is arrested by the resistance of the difference."[84] In the terms Hulme borrowed from James to describe Imagist analogies, it is one in which we follow a line of similarity until it stops and then take up other relations presenting themselves around the "fringe" of consciousness. James's reading of Fechner's analogy between earth and animal, then, provides an apt model for reading Imagiste poems like "In a Station of the Metro":

> The apparition of these faces in the crowd;
> Petals on a wet, black bough.
>
> (CSP 119)

In calling attention to an analogy between the ghostlike faces that emerge in the dark of a subway station and the pink-white petals crowding on a branch in the spring rain, the poem directs the reader toward a generalization about the mutual beauty and fragility of person and blossom. Presently, however, our satisfaction in that thought is disrupted—perhaps by the uncomfortable parallel between the tree branch and the transit station from which faces and petals seem to spring. We may feel compelled to object that the similarities between these long, black, thin backdrops are more than countered by their differences. The faces bear no organic relation to their setting as do the petals to the bough. They do not spring from it, but it from them. The subway station is something the people behind these faces have constructed, something they have built to take shelter from the rain these petals accept with complete passivity. With the refined insight brought by this recognition of difference, we are compelled to seek a new, more exact analogy—an analogy, of course, that will elicit its own objections and be mentally dismantled in favor of one that seems still more fitting. The poem trips off an open-ended quest for temporary insights, momentary satisfactions, incipient categories that dissolve almost as soon as they are conceived. The reader's mind is no still center, but a whirling vortex, in which hopeful, centripetal gestures toward truth are as soon undone by a centrifugal motion. The process is the same one to which the historical particulars juxtaposed in *The Cantos* invite their readers. Asked to determine what makes events from different historical periods similar and different, the reader of *The Cantos* engages in an ongoing quest to establish what endures in human experiences and what changes.

It is thus that the "Image" (in the second sense of the term) functions as a generator, charging its reader with new ideas, new variations on her initial insight. Because I have suggested that it shares this capacity with the symbol, it is also important to note the differences between their effects. The symbol I am thinking of, again, is the apparent conduit of "les splendeurs situées derrière le tombeau": an image, or group of images, made "transparentes et révélatrices" by being placed in such illogical circumstances that the reader is forced to look "beyond" it in search of its *correspondances*.[85] Poems like Mallarmé's meditation on the "ptyx," or Yeats's homages to the "Rose," reflect their authors' confidence in a fixed system of equivalencies.[86] There is to be no debate with the reader about these identities; the poet simply assumes them and proceeds from there to make their synaesthetic or synechdochical substitutions. The Imagiste, by contrast, assumes nothing. Instead of expecting the reader to intuit the world's identities, he asks her only to observe and to test apparent similarities that may—or may not—reflect divine order. It is significant that Pound, despite his admiration for many aspects of Symbolist practice, disparages those aspects of its style that reflect a dogmatic mysticism: synaesthetic substitutions, anagogic metaphors ("we do NOT say that one thing *is* another"), the creation of contexts demanding exclusive attention to the "symbolic function" of images.[87] All these differences with Symbolism might be traced to Pound's Jamesian wariness of translating feeling into knowledge, experienced relations into essential categories.

Pound's repudiation of Symbolism does not mean, however, that he wishes the Imagiste to engage in unrestrained figurative play. Because he is committed to a practice in which the possibility of permanent relations is not assumed *but not denied either,* he insists that the poet hold his analogies up to some standard of objectivity. An "interpretive" metaphor, he says, is not an "ornamental" or "untrue" one. It articulates ideas as well as feelings—it "interprets" the world—and in doing so it must seem plausible to the reader:

> An art is vital only so long as it is interpretive, so long, that is, as it manifests something which the artist perceives at greater intensity and more intimately than his public. If he be the seeing one among the sightless, *they will attend him only so long as his statements seem, or are proven true.* If he forsake this honour of interpreting, if he speak for the pleasure of hearing his own voice, though they may listen for a while to the babble and to the sound of the painted words, there comes, after a little, a murmur, a slight stirring, and then that condition which we see about us, and which is cried out upon as the "divorce of art and life."[88]

In distinguishing between true and false metaphors and championing the former, Pound may have been influenced by Mead's account of Vaihinger in *The Quest,* which extends the hypothesis/fiction dichotomy to metaphor: "[A] clear distinction must be drawn between true and substantive analogies, which it is the business of semi-fictions, or of hypotheses, and of the objective method of induction to discover, and fully fictitious analogies, which are purely the business of the subjective method."[89] Of course the instruction to distinguish objective from merely subjective relations begs the question of how such a distinction can be made and how such a project can be reconciled with the poet's other obligation to avoid the objective/subjective binary. Yet Pound clearly believes that disciplining association with reference to the "facts" is both plausible and necessary.[90] In this he shares in the most controversial aspect of Jamesian pragmatism: the desire to make *the best possible effort* at explaining the world accurately, *just in case* accurate explanations are possible.

Pound viewed the "interpretive metaphor," then, with the same kind of mild optimism with which James regarded the pragmatic truth. It was a useful construct, offered in uncertainty, but having some chance of corresponding to an ordered world. We hear this qualified epistemological hope in "Vorticism," when Pound, having rejected an overconfident symbolism, goes on to describe his Imagisme as "symbolism in its profounder sense": "*not necessarily* belief in a permanent world" but "*a belief in that direc-*

tion." We also encounter it in "The Wisdom of Poetry," in a passage under-scoring the Jamesian insight that usefulness and potential truthfulness are not incompatible:

> Is the formula nothing, or is it cabala and the sign of unintelligible magic? The engineer, understanding and translating to the many, builds for the uninitiated bridges and devices. He speaks their language. For the initiated the signs are a door into eternity and into the boundless ether.[91]

The best poem, in Pound's view, will be the one that helps readers to get on with their lives and offers what may be genuine insights into eternity to those prepared to see them. In striving to do both, it is, in theory at least, much less elitist than many observers of the influence of mystical thought on Pound's work would contend.[92] Its aim is not so much to separate the sheep from the goats, by challenging its audience to participate in an assured revelation, but to offer help to everyone, by enabling them to participate in a process of testing and revising propositions that *might* one day lead them into light.

SUGGESTIONS OF FINALITY: VORTICIST PAINTING AND SCULPTURE

With the notable exception of Reed Dasenbrock, commentators on Vorticist painting and sculpture have regarded its distinctive feature as "its use of total abstraction."[93] This aspect of the artists' practice has been characterized as an effort to "invoke a reality beyond the senses"—an effort to exchange the phenomenal flux for eternal patterns and categories.[94] The problem with this reading, however, is the same one with conflations of Imagisme and Symbolism: it takes into account only one of the two tendencies that balance and correct each other in Vorticist art, privileging its "religious" or "theoretic" impulse at the cost of its very real "sister passion" for particulars.

Like many artists and art theorists in his time, Lewis identified abstraction in art with claims to mystical knowledge.[95] And one of the most notable features of his "Review of Contemporary Art" in *Blast II* is his hostility to *pure* abstraction. One painter guilty of such an extreme, in his estimation, is Wassily Kandinsky: "the only PURELY abstract painter in Europe." Kandinsky's manifestos (one of which was excerpted in *Blast*) had celebrated the artist's capacity for unmediated insight into the spirit world. He imagined his own paintings functioning like Symbolist poems, communicating states of mind through forms and colors tied to them by fixed correspondences. For Lewis, Kandinsky's theory is badly in need of renovation—or exorcism:

Kandinsky, docile to the intuitive fluctuations of his soul, and anxious to render his hand and mind elastic and receptive, follows this unreal entity into its cloud-world, out of the material and solid universe.

He allows the Bach-like will that resides in each good artist to be made war on by the slovenly and wandering Spirit. He allows the rigid chambers of his Brain to become a mystic house haunted by an automatic and puerile Spook, that leaves a delicate trail like a snail.

The Blavatskyish soul is another Spook that needs laying, if it gets a vogue, just as Michael Angelo does.[96]

If, as James says, "the absence of definite sensible images" is the "*sine qua non* of a contemplation of the divine higher truths" (VRE 54), we might interpret Lewis's anxiety before Kandinsky's painting as dismay at its failure to acknowledge its own arbitrariness. Like Pound a few months earlier, Lewis detects in Kandinsky's claims to be "passive and medium-like" an unwillingness to acknowledge any contribution by his own "Will and consciousness" to what he takes to be eternal truths.[97] Like Pound, too, he is suspicious of the dogmatic synaesthetic grammar this blindness entails, that is, Kandinsky's reliance on "spiritual values and musical analogies."[98]

But if Lewis bars Vorticism from representing universals, he does not insist it render uncomprehended phenomenal chaos. If he recoils from Kandinsky's Expressionism[99] or Picasso's most abstract experiments with Cubism, he does not wholeheartedly embrace the skepticism of Impressionism and Futurism. As Lewis knew, the Impressionists had worked from a highly subjectivist epistemology, regarding the artist's insights as nothing more than the "response of a unique sensibility to a moment." Their ideology was dogmatically relativist and pluralistic. Having no access to transcendental realities, the Impressionist was obliged to preserve every accident, every irregularity, in nature; for Renoir and Monet to reduce any part of the shimmering panorama of sense-data to regularity, as the Cubists were to do, would have been too coercive an interpretation. But Lewis cannot accept such programmatic passivity. If the Cubist speaks too categorically, the Impressionist (and his successor, the Futurist) is so tentative he might as well not speak at all; his paintings are "an absurd and gloomy waste of time."[100]

Lewis's objection to Impressionism is motivated in part by a recognition of the practical value of simplifying the flux. Because they "do not sufficiently dominate the contents of their pictures," the Impressionists and Futurists remain completely "subjugated" to Nature. They are effeminate "chicken-men," where "the Vorticist is not the Slave of Commotion, but it's [*sic*] Master."[101] In insisting on the importance of subjecting the world to some kind of interpretation, Lewis enacts his own subtle but unmistakable version of the pragmatic turn, justifying a course of action by appealing, not to truth but to consequences.

In sum, Lewis cannot countenance the unchecked operation in art of either the "philosophic tendency" or its opposite, the "passion for distinguishing." And his desire for the balance leads him, as it does Pound, to champion a kind of art that compromises between abstract monotony and concrete heterogeneity. "The finest Art," Lewis maintains, "is not pure Abstraction, nor is it unorganized life." "We must constantly strive to ENRICH abstraction till it is almost plain life, or rather to get deeply enough immersed in material life to experience the shaping power amongst its vibrations."[102] Vorticist painting or sculpture is to elicit the same combination of comfort and discomfort evoked by the poem that suggests a similarity between dissimilar things. It is to reassure the viewer with suggestions of general categories, approximating living things to geometric abstractions, but that identification is never to be complete. If it suggests an object's likeness to one generic shape, it will make an alternative category equally visible. Like the Imagiste's concrete analogy, it "must catch . . . clearness and . . . logic *in the midst of contradictions:* not settle down and snooze on an acquired, easily possessed and mastered, satisfying shape."[103]

The last point on which Lewis's aesthetic accords with Pound's is in its qualified optimism about the existence of universal order and the possibility that the work of art might provide a glimpse into it. Lewis concedes that such order *might* be visible, if we "could see with larger eyes." He even concedes that Kandinsky's mystical correspondences are "feasible." Though he rejects the kind of art that presumes mystical correspondences and that depends on their apprehension for their effect, he won't deny that the viewer of Vorticist art might *experience* such correspondences.[104] In short Lewis's Vorticism disallows only dogmatic mysticism, not gestures "in the direction of" a permanent world: "[G]od-like lines are not for us, but, rather, a powerful but remote *suggestion of finality,* or an elementary organization of a dark insect swarming, like the passing of a cloud's shadow or the path of a wind."[105]

Lewis's vision of a tensional art is borne out in the sculptures and paintings produced by members of the Vorticist circle, which included Lewis himself, William Roberts, Helen Saunders, Frederick Etchells, David Bomberg, and Edward Wadsworth. Most of the works reproduced in the issues of *Blast,* or exhibited under the Vorticist banner, maintain a tense balance between abstraction and representation, geometric categories and irregular phenomena. Emblematic of these, in the way it "bur[ies] EUCLID deep in the living flesh," is Gaudier-Brzeska's magnificent sculpture, "Red Stone Dancer" (1913). As Pound was to note in his book on Gaudier-Brzeska, in this sculpture the bare triangles and circle labled on the face and breast are made "fully incarnate" by the moving body flowing into them.[106] If the viewer's eye gravitates to one of these abstractions, as if to what James called an "absolute datum," the sculpture invites it simultaneously to concentrate on the fringe, to consider the dancer's unique motion-in-time. The dancer's head plays a special role in the sculpture's simultaneous efforts to assert and to subvert abstraction. As an imperfect triangle, whose sides bulge into curved or "organic" lines, it is an "animated" abstraction, subverted by the demands of life.[107] It also answers Lewis's call for double categorization, in being not simply a triangle or a sphere but a form demanding "interplay" between these categories: a "spherical triangle."[108]

The Vorticist *corpus* contains many figures like the "Red Stone Dancer," aspiring to transcend their vitality and become universal. Lewis's paintings "Centauress" (1912) and "Enemy of the Stars" (1913), for example, along with William Roberts's "Religion" (1913–14), not only embody but seem to narrate such an aspiration: their highly abstract, yet just recognizably human, figures both approach the condition of pure abstraction and strain unsuccessfully heavenward. Bomberg's "Mud Bath" (1914) alludes in its title to the cindery world from which its discernibly human figures spring. Some Vorticist works achieve the same balance in landscapes. In Etchells's "Dieppe" (1913), houses, chimneys, and bridges, refined of many of their accidental characteristics, retain the energy of the busy port-town by appearing to whirl around the picture's center. The landscape sustains a palpable tension between the tendencies to move out of and into life. Finally the tension between abstraction and life can also be discerned in many paintings that seem on the surface to fail Lewis's specifications, because they seem totally devoid of representative content. Etchells's perfectly abstract "Progression" achieves the tension with a degenerating grid, suggesting a conflict between the forces of order and of chaos. Similarly in Bomberg's "Ju-Jitsu" (1913), a grid of black-and-white squares is disrupted by a chaotic array of colorful, diagonal forms—forms abstracted from human bodies.[109] The illusion here is of a chessboard, whose bare perfection fails to prevail entirely over the bloody bodies of its chess pieces. It reminds us, of course, of Pound's poem about the chessboard, with its message that no abstract resolution is final, that every black-and-white solution requires a colorful new contest.[110]

The expressive arrangements of the Vorticist poet and artist, then, are similar both in rationale and constitution to the hypotheses James envisions for the seeming mystic and, ultimately, for the pragmatist. They reflect the conviction that it is hubristic to assume contact with transcendental truths. They are also informed, however, by the recognition that moments in which such contact seems to be achieved are an undeniable part of our experience and that it would be foolish to deny ourselves the hope they inspire. James, Pound, and Lewis are caught between their discomfort with dogmatism and their inability to be entirely skeptical about intuitions that may be more affirmed than denied by the stream of experience. To be chronically distrustful of our quasi-mystical moments, as James points out to a friend who has challenged him to give up his faith, and as Pound would no doubt have replied to anyone who wished to deny the poet his passion to articulate the Image, would be to assert "a dogmatic disbelief in any extant consciousness higher than that of the . . . human mind, and this in the teeth of the extraordinary vivacity of man's psychological commerce with something ideal that *feels as if it* were also actual."[111] The pragmatic truth, the poetic Image, and the Vorticist painting, accordingly, are energetic assertions that, although not claiming to be windows on eternity, do not extinguish all hope of celestial fire either. They respond to our religious needs, our philosophic passions, by providing hypotheses, exploratory analogies, hints of a universal geometry. At the same time, however, they very deliberately preserve the context in which these insights arise, assaulting our peripheral vision with reminders of the phenomenal life that would be sacrificed to the pattern. The truths they posit seem inherently unstable, liable to revert to chaos at every moment, as our sister passion for distinguishing reasserts itself and focuses on the details that resist assimilation. By holding each of the two tendencies in check, these constructs fulfill their intended function of expressing not the simple fact of truth attained, but the complex *feeling of* attaining it, not the dead relic of a truth said-and-done but the electricity of the *consciousness of* a truth coming-into-being. The truths of pragmatism and the poems and paintings of Vorticism actively pursue the condition Heidegger, the heir of Husserl's and James's phenomenologies, was to envision for art: they are designed to be the fields for the "fighting of the battle in which the unconcealedness of beings . . . or truth, is won," the loci for truth's "*becoming and happening.*"[112] And in offering their audiences simultaneously both the light of unconcealedness and the dark of concealment, both the theoretical objects to inspire belief and the phenomenal evidence to elicit doubt, they invite them to take their place at the table where the chess game of truth-making is played. Their challenge is perpetual, and if James's understanding of our restive psychic life is right, it is irresistible.

PART TWO

3

Effacing the Muse:
Inspiration and Virility in Wallace Stevens

W ALLACE Stevens's sensitivity to the language in which theorists of poetry discuss their subject is apparent from the opening pages of his collection of essays, *The Necessary Angel*. Stevens is discussing his readerly response to Plato's figure of the soul in the *Phaedrus*. The figure identifies the soul's two potential dispositions with two winged horses: the soul's noble part, "perfect and fully winged," "soars upward and is the ruler of the universe"; its imperfect part "loses her feathers, and drooping in her flight at last settles on the solid ground." Stevens's response to the passage travels, like the winged animals depicted there, in two contrary directions. At first he is thoroughly caught up in the figure and experiences an enthusiasm very like the noble soul's ascent into the heavens. Suddenly, however, he finds himself drooping in his flight, settling, like the lesser soul, on the ground. The explanation he gives for his sudden loss of enthusiasm has to do with a distinction between what I. A. Richards (whose work he consulted before writing the essay) would call the "scientific" and the "emotive" aspects of Plato's figure. Stevens's engagement with the figure breaks, he tells us, when he recognizes that it fails to "adhere to what is real," that is, when he remembers that the soul to which it refers "no longer exists." He concludes that, although Plato's figure may appeal to the emotions, we "cannot yield ourselves" to "this gorgeous nonsense."[1]

Plato's figure is the progenitor of a long tradition of writings depicting poetic inspiration as transcendental flight, and Stevens's account of it cannot fail to recall T. E. Hulme: the difference between the emotive power of a statement and its referential validity is precisely the distinction Hulme used to dismantle Schopenhauer.[2] Stevens's special discomfort with the references to the "soul" matches the frustration Hulme expresses with late romantic aestheticians at the beginning of the "Lecture on Modern Poetry." Stevens's affinity with Hulme is most striking, however, in his account of an experience of an ascent arrested and turned into a fall. For in defining the "new classical" attitude, Hulme traces precisely the same trajectory. Whereas Hulme's "romantic" attitude, we recall, "is always flying, flying over abysses, flying up into the eternal gases," in the case of the "new classicist," "there is always a *holding back, a reservation.* . . . He remembers always that he is mixed up with earth. He may jump, but *he always returns back;* he never flies away into the circumambient gas."[3] Stevens is our best example of the "new classicism," modern poetry's subtlest practitioner of the arrested flight. The sudden self-consciousness that deflates his enthusiasm for Plato's image is characteristic, whether he is describing how poetry happens, prescribing the principles for poetic style, or practicing his own poetic art. And in his case, no less than in Hulme's and Pound's, the reflex-action model of poetics holds firm: his hostility to extravagant claims for inspiration informs other claims that, in matters of style, the practicing poet "cannot be a charioteer traversing vacant space, however ethereal."[4]

The psychological experience Stevens describes, like those recorded by Hulme and Pound, is in many respects perfectly in keeping with the "revelation" theories of his Platonic and Idealist predecessors. That he thinks of the poet's moment of inspiration as both intuitive and seemingly revelatory is apparent in a 1937 essay in which he affirms the importance of the "irrational" element in poetry and draws an analogy between the poet's inspiring vision and the mystic's insight into some transcendental order.[5] Later essays, including "The Noble Rider and the Sound of Words" (1942) and "The Figure of the Youth as Virile Poet" (1943), reinforce the picture of a poet gifted with the power to glimpse truths that to others lie hidden behind a veil. We read of the "occasional ecstasy, or ecstatic freedom of the mind that is the poet's special privilege," of the feelings of "exaltation," "elevation," and "illumination" that accompany his urge to create.[6]

But if Stevens repeatedly affirms that the poet's initial *feeling* is one of *ecstasis,* he is just as consistent in objecting to the ecstatic *language* in which Platonist and other Idealist theorists of poetry have so often described it— language that credits the feeling with the highest epistemological value. He assures the reader of the essay on the irrational that he does not "for a moment mean to indulge in mystical rhetoric," that he has "no patience with that sort of thing."[7] In "The Figure of the Youth as Virile Poet," he banishes "the false conception of the imagination as some incalculable *vates*" within the poet (NA 61). One of his ways of demonstrating his commitment to demystifying the imagination is to stress that the analogy he draws between the poet and the mystic is just that, an analogy; it has none of the force of an absolute identification:

> It is certain that the experience of the poet is of no less a degree than the experience of the mystic and we may be certain that in the case of poets, the peers of saints, those experiences are of no less a degree than the experiences of the saints themselves. It is a question of the nature of the experience. It is not a question

of identifying or relating dissimilar figures; that is to say, it is not a question of making saints out of poets or poets out of saints. (NA 50–51)

The poet is like the bona fide saint, but the knowledge he attains in his moments of illumination is not to be confused with the revealed wisdom of God. What seems like knowledge is in fact only belief: the ecstatic moment is a moment of "triumph over the incredible," poetic truth "the truth of credible things" (NA 60, 53).[8] In a move that clarifies his affinity with Hulme, moreover, Stevens describes his efforts to check grandiose claims about poetic cognition as a reaction against romanticism. His conception of "romantic thought" is drawn from Cassirer's *An Essay on Man*. As Stevens summarizes it,

> In romantic thought the theory of poetic imagination had reached its climax. Imagination is no longer that special human activity which builds up the human world of art. It now has universal metaphysical value. Poetic imagination is the only clue to reality. Fichte's idealism is based upon his conception of "productive imagination." Schelling declared in his *System of Transcendental Idealism* that art is the consummation of philosophy. In nature, in morality, in history we are still living in the propylaeum of philosophical wisdom; in art we enter into the sanctuary itself. The true poem is not the work of the individual artist; it is the universe itself, the one work of art which is forever perfecting itself.[9]

Stevens understands that there is something "in the nature of the imagination itself" that makes claims about a poet's access to transcendental wisdom very compelling. After all the feeling of illumination the poet enjoys begs to be explained, and no account of it is more flattering than the claim for a visitation from God. But Stevens is determined not to yield to such a temptation. Carrying on the torch of the new classicism, he insists that no worthwhile discussion of poetics can begin until the imagination is "cleansed" of the romantic, or, to use his synonym for the outmoded attitudes, of the "metaphysical."[10]

Stevens's motivation in renouncing the language of metaphysics is subtly different from, though not incompatible with, Hulme's revulsion at its hubris. For Stevens the most pressing problem with romantic accounts of imagination is not their overestimation of the truth-value of poetry but their tendency to underestimate, and potentially to undermine, its usefulness. If Stevens recoils from equating the poet and the bona fide mystic, it is not because he knows for certain they are not the same—the question of the comparative truth-value of their insights is, as we shall see, a moot point. It is rather because he understands that every representation of imagination entails a set of recommendations concerning poetic practice, and he does not wish to condone a practice indifferent to the here and now by affirming the poet's communion with the timeless and eternal. Stevens's remarks on the French Symbolist poets are more sparing than one might wish, but they are sufficient to reveal his frustration with an aesthetic ideal of escaping from the "actual" world into a higher reality. Writing to Thomas McGreevy in 1949, Stevens records his sense that the poems of Baudelaire are "beginning to date" because they sacrifice so much of the actual for the splendors beyond the veil. A year later he suggests that the work of Rimbaud presents similar problems.[11] And in "The Effects of Analogy" (1948), he blames Valéry's sense that "his imagination is not wholly his own" but part of one "much larger," and his consequent efforts to "live . . . on the verge of consciousness," for the "marginal, subliminal" quality of his poetry.[12] If Stevens insists that poets avoid the transcendentalism of the French poets, or of any other romantics, he is equally concerned that they shun the *passive* pose these poets assume in relation to the things they contemplate. His general hope for the imagination is that it be "intrepid" and "vital" and that it have an *active* role in making the world a better place.[13]

POETRY AND MANHOOD

To put it another way—and so to engage with one of the most contentious issues in Stevens criticism in recent years—Stevens recoils from the picture of the "hieratic" poet because he is determined to salvage the kind of engagement with real experience that makes him a man.[14] The story of Stevens's lifelong struggle to assure himself that poetry need not be unmanly has been told most memorably by Frank Lentricchia. As Lentricchia tells it, Stevens's discomfort with the image of the poet as an unworldly contemplative stems from a desire to reconcile his avocation with the indoctrination undergone by most American males of his time—with countless lessons to the effect that his attention belonged with the "real" world, the world where a responsible man makes a living and a difference. Typical of the attitude is a gentle warning he received from his father when he was a young student at Harvard: "I am convinced from the Poetry (?) you wrote your Mother that the afflatus is not serious—and does not interfere with some real hard work."[15]

Like Hulme, who also expressed anxieties about poetry's threat to manhood, Stevens thought the two need not be incompatible, that the real problem lay only in a certain way of *thinking about* poetry:

Poetry and Manhood: those who say poetry is now the peculiar province of women say so because ideas about poetry are effeminate. Homer, Dante, Shakespeare, Milton, Keats, Browning, much of Tennyson—they are your man-poets. Silly verse is always the work of silly men.[16]

The "effeminate ideas" Stevens had in mind here were, according to Lentricchia, those of the "genteel" circle of critics that attained prominence in late nineteenth-century America, a circle that included E. C. Stedman, Henry Van Dyke, R. H. Stoddard, Richard Watson Gilder, and G. E. Woodberry.[17] As Lentricchia tells it, a characteristic project of these late romantic critics, and one Stevens found particularly offensive, was their representation of Keats as one who owed his best poetry to his renunciation of the very goals, both sexual and material, that every American male was expected to pursue. The "genteel" theorists' threat to masculinity may be seen, for instance, in Stedman's treatises on *Genius* and *The Nature and Elements of Poetry*, which are unabashedly platonist in celebrating the "divine power" of the poet and which equate inspiration with a liberation from desire. Stedman finds women better equipped than men to achieve this blessing, because femininity is, in his opinion, identical with disengagement and self-denial: "The revelations of the feminine heart," as he puts it, "are the more beautiful and welcome, because the typical woman is purer, more unselfish, more consecrated, than the typical man." The poetic faculty, he says, is the equivalent of "women's intuition," and the reasonable cost of this gift is the poet's retreat to a place equivalent to that of selfless womankind: a place on the sidelines of life. When Stevens scorns the passivity and "marginality" of Symbolist writing, or warns that to "dwell apart" in the imagination is to lose "the masculine nature" the poet should possess, he shares Stedman's assumptions about gender, though not his valuations.[18]

To describe the poet's experience of "illumination" without sacrificing his virility is, then, one of the central challenges Stevens assumes in his poetic theory. As I shall explain, some of the gestures he makes in attempting to solve it have been excoriated by feminist critics. I would like, however, to keep Stevens's hostility to "metaphysics" separate from his fear of "femininity" until later. For there is much of interest in his account of inspiration apart from the gender issues involved. In what follows I would like to consider how Stevens's views on the matter compare both with those of James and with those of James's student—and Stevens's friend—George Santayana. Once we understand Stevens's position in relation to these two similar, but vitally distinct, ones, it will be possible to shed more light on the controversial moves with which he bears anxieties about his manhood.

Masculine Empiricisms at Harvard: James and Santayana

When Stevens indicates in "The Figure of the Youth as Virile Poet" that he wishes to eschew metaphysics, he specifies that he is motivated to do so by "all the reasons stated by William James."[19] James and his student George Santayana were two of the brightest lights at Harvard during Stevens's years there as an undergraduate (1897–1900), and both regularly make critics' lists of Stevens's most formative philosophical influences. Until recently, however, and despite the invocation of James in the "Virile Poet" essay, the lion's share of critical attention has gone to Santayana, largely because of the close personal association he enjoyed with the young poet, and because of the moving tribute Stevens wrote him much later in life, "To an Old Philosopher in Rome."[20] Milton Bates and Alan Filreis have even suggested that during the Harvard years Santayana served as the sympathetic "parent" Garrett Stevens was not, encouraging the young poet to pursue that impractical vocation of which his real father was so very suspicious.[21] Although there is no evidence that Stevens ever met James, his recollections of Harvard reveal that he was well aware of his presence, and familiar, at the very least, with his thoughts about the "will to believe." Stevens uses the phrase on several occasions, most notably in discussing the theme of "Notes Toward a Supreme Fiction."[22]

Establishing precisely what Stevens read and borrowed from the two philosophers is difficult, in part because, as Harold Bloom has noted, Stevens had a propensity for denying he owed anything to others.[23] Between his own very rare admissions and archival evidence, we know for certain only that he read, or heard excerpts from, three or four of Santayana's books, and, after their publication in 1920, James's letters.[24] Studies by Frank Doggett, Margaret Peterson, and David M. LaGuardia, which document a number of apparent allusions to James and Santayana, have done much to suggest that Stevens knew far more of the philosophers' work than he was prepared to acknowledge, and I hope, in part, to reinforce that impression here. My main purpose in considering James's and Santayana's work, however, is less to establish certain borrowings than it is to shed light on the ideas and projects Stevens shares with both, that is, his concerns with demystifying the moment of inspiration and with finding a mode of articulation that sufficiently acknowledges that demystification. In the end, too, it is to propose that Stevens's positions on both of these issues have more in common with James than with Santayana.

For James and Santayana had an uncertain relationship, and their philosophies, while similar in many respects, deserve to be distinguished carefully. That the two philosophers are often regarded as a single, collective influence on Stevens is unsurprising, given their own gracious assurances to one another in their correspondence that they shared a great deal of common ground.[25] Santayana confirmed his affinity with James in a "Brief History" of his opinions written long after his teacher was dead, in which he wrote that he had inherited the two most important aspects of James's philosophy: his impatience with "metaphysics" and "a sort of pragmatism." Yet every word of praise the two philosophers had for one another is mingled with reproach. In a letter to George Palmer, written shortly after the publication of Santayana's *Interpretations of Poetry and Religion* (1900), James expresses his admiration for the energy of Santayana's argument but abhors its substance, calling his philosophy a "perfection of rottenness." For his part Santayana recalls that his own "sort of pragmatism" was not enough to mitigate the "rude shock" of reading *Pragmatism:* quite simply he "could not stomach that way of speaking about truth."[26] The moment of inspiration and its means of expression are two issues on which James's and Santayana's views need clarification; an understanding of their similarities and differences on these issues will aid us in clarifying Stevens's position and its ramifications.

When he endorses all of James's "reasons" for rejecting metaphysics, Stevens does not clearly outline what these reasons were. The only point on which he is explicit is that James shared his anxiety about preserving his virility and that metaphysics struck him as a waste of time, a distraction from the sort of useful work that *"befits a man."*[27] Readers of *Pragmatism* will recall that James represents the man who spends his time debating fundamental, abstract principles as the "tender-minded" Bostonian, and the man who doesn't waste his time on such matters as the "Rocky-mountain tough" (P 13–14). In *The Will to Believe,* similarly, he contrasts the "feminine-mystical" mind (WB 224) with a tougher kind of mind that regards transcendentalist claims with extreme skepticism. We have already seen that the suspicion of metaphysics in *Pragmatism* is continuous with James's effort to establish psychology as an empirical science in *The Principles of Psychology.* Of greater relevance to Stevens, and therefore what I would like to focus on here, is the more elaborate justification for rejecting metaphysics outlined in James's *Essays on Radical Empiricism* (1912).[28] Here James outlines clearly the particular "time-wasting" dilemma the rejection of metaphysics enables him to avoid. And as it turns out, this is precisely the dilemma Stevens wrestles with in his early poetry—only to escape by the route James recommends.

As I have already noted, James first identified the problem rejecting metaphysics would solve in "The Sentiment of Rationality," when he observed that "to *know* is one thing," but "to know for certain *that* we know" quite another (WB 20). We are never satisfied, in other words, with feeling certain about something; we feel the need to ask the unanswerable question whether or not our certainty is justified. In the *Radical Empiricism* essays, James locates the origin of this need to second guess our feelings of certainty in the philosophical decision made by Descartes: the decision to divide the world into the two, discrete substances of mind and matter. Once one has divided the world thus, it is impossible to see how the abyss can ever be bridged, how subject and object can ever become one in an act of knowing. Even if we *feel* that we have leapt over the abyss, after a burst of Kantian "Reason" or Bergsonian "intuition," there is no way of confirming this feeling that does not itself involve the operation of the subjective consciousness; we are caught in our own subjectivity as in a web.

In the *Essays on Radical Empiricism,* James contends that the first step toward getting out of the irreconcilable problems posed by Cartesian metaphysics is recognizing that the bifurcation of experience into subject and object is a counterintuitive, even unnatural act. In what he calls "pure" or "immediate" experience—the life of consciousness as lived before we ever begin to reflect upon it—"there is no self-splitting of it into consciousness and what that consciousness is 'of'" (ERE 13). He captures the texture of this undivided experience with an analogy from the art world:

> That which is outside of us and that which is inside, that which has extension and that which does not, blend into one another in an indissoluble marriage. This reminds me of those circular panoramas in which real objects, rocks, plants, broken chariots, etc., which occupy the foreground, are so ingeniously tied in with the painted background depicting a battle or a spacious landscape, that one can no longer distinguish the objects from the painting. The seams and the joints are imperceptible.[29]

We can overcome Descartes' unresolvable epistemological problem, James suggests, simply by abandoning the perverse practice of dividing up what is naturally undivided. To forgo this activity and to choose instead to study "pure" experience (what he had earlier called the undifferentiated "stream of our consciousness" (PP I 236)) is what James has in mind when he calls on his reader to embrace a "radical empiricism." If we go back to what we are given naturally, James suggests, we will eliminate the need to second guess our apparent insights into truth, the need to assure ourselves that what we see, or what we feel we know, corresponds to some transexperiential reality. What "streams" before our eyes will be sufficient "'truth,' practical truth, *something to act on,* at its own movement" (ERE 13).[30]

As we have seen, this decision to restrict his concern to matters of pure experience governed James's treatment of the "certainties" enjoyed by would-be mystics in *The Varieties of Religious Experience.* In that treatise he subjects the "trance-like states of insight into truth" to which scores of believers have attested to a "purely empirical" study, translating truth-claims, which he cannot respect, into belief-claims, which he can (VRE 24, 52).[31] His practice here resembles Stevens's account of inspiration as much as it does Pound's. One aspect that is of particular relevance to Stevens, however, and that we haven't yet considered in detail, is its description of the seemingly animate being who inspires the mystic's timeless insights: on what James, prior to his commitment to the language of psychology, might have called "God." James's definition of this entity proves remarkably similar to Stevens's definition of the being behind the poet's moments of "illumination." Indeed one might say that Stevens's muse is James's God.

The general character of James's empirical account of divinity is apparent in his definition of "religion" in *The Varieties of Religious Experience:*

> Religion . . . as I now ask you arbitrarily to take it, shall mean for us *the feelings, acts and experiences of individual men in their solitude, so far as they apprehend themselves to stand in relation to whatever they may consider the divine.* (VRE 31)[32]

This definition reflects James's decision elsewhere in the text to break down immediate experience into what Husserl was to call the interdependent entities of *noesis* and *noema.* James described this as a "conscious field *plus* its object as felt or thought of *plus* an attitude towards the object *plus* the sense of a self to whom the attitude belongs" (VRE 499).[33] What matters in any experience of a "divinity"—what *makes* the thing experienced as a divinity—is the *attitude* with which one inevitably regards it, an attitude that concerns, first and foremost, the position this thing assumes in relation to the self. Supreme among the noetic qualities that make something "divine," in James's estimation, is that of seeming "other" or "more" than the worshipper (VRE 510–11).[34] To have an experience of sudden revelation or prayerful communion is to have a sense of sudden union with this being and, like Yeats's Leda, to "put on [its] knowledge" in the process.[35] It is the profound sense that the divinity is found, not projected—that it operates independently of the worshipper's needs and desires—that lends the quality of "convincingness" to the insights it communicates (VRE 72). And it is from this sense of convincingness that all the other noetic qualities of the godlike ensue: most notably that of seeming the source of complete happiness, peace, reassurance, and fulfillment (VRE 47, 49, 78–79).

At the same time as he identifies apparent alterity as an eidetic feature of the divinity, however, James is scrupulous about the restrictions demanded by his empiricism. He cannily avoids the questions a dualist would ask, that is, whether that otherness is real, or illusory, or whether the divinity is a product of desire or independent of it. This commitment is reflected in a number of equivocal comments in *The Varieties of Religious Experience* concerning the origin of the divinity, some of which I have already discussed.[36] Most significant among these for Stevens are James's efforts to account for the impression of otherness by saying that the divinity's *immediate* origin—the space from which it springs into consciousness—is the subliminal or subconscious mind (VRE 511–13). As I have explained, with this explanation he can credit testimonies about the divinity's otherness, without breaking his vow to leave subject and object blended. For in his view it is the character of the subconscious mind to be other than the conscious one, a space from which strange specters may arise unbidden. But it is also its character to be *itself* of unknown origin, perhaps constituted entirely by the personal experience of the subject, perhaps manifesting the operation of a greater Spirit. James figures the space from which the divinity springs as a "threshold" (VRE 243, 513): a location neither inside nor outside the desiring self.[37]

James recognized that situating the divinity in the subconscious mind would threaten orthodox believers. His remarks to such believers in *The Varieties of Religious Experience* and in the Pascalian essay "The Will to Believe" (1896) reveal the difficulty of sustaining the perfect neutrality required of radical empiricism and James's nuanced tendency toward affirmation. Having dutifully refused to claim any *certainty* about its ontological status, James still feels the need to speculate about whether it is more *likely* to be a product of desire or an objective reality. His need comes out of the recognition, not just that he must have some response for the faithful but also that taking a position about God is a "momentous" (WB 16–17, 30) decision in the life of an individual, one that, if negative, means the definitive loss of certain benefits and opportunities. His response, accordingly, turns out to be far more reassuring to the orthodox believer than it is discouraging:

> But if you, being orthodox Christians, ask me as a psychologist whether the reference of a phenomenon to a subliminal self does not exclude the notion of the direct presence of the Deity altogether, I have to say frankly that as a psychologist I do not see why it necessarily should. The lower manifestations of the Subliminal, indeed, fall within the resources of the personal subject: his ordinary sense-material, inattentively taken in and subconsciously remembered and combined, will account for all his usual automatisms. But just as our primary wide-awake consciousness throws open our sense to the touch of things material, so it is logically conceivable that *if there be* higher spiritual agencies that can directly touch us, the psychological condition of their doing so *might be* our possession of a subconscious region which alone should yield access to them. The hubbub of the waking life *might* close a door which in the dreamy Subliminal *might* remain ajar or open. (VRE 242; penultimate and final italics mine)

Although remaining faithful to his psychological discourse, James leans more toward endorsing the objectivity of the divinity than the opposite, taking pains to emphasize that uncertainty does as much to protect the possibility of God as to threaten it. Elsewhere in *The Varieties of Religious Experience* and throughout "The Will to Believe," he goes so far as to suggest that choosing the antitheistic position, when greater benefits seem to ensue from the theistic one and when we have "no philosophic excuse for calling the unseen or mystical world unreal" (VRE 516), is sheer perversity.[38]

If James's commitment to the language of psychology leads him to define a liminal divinity, it also results in his defining one whose identity remains a mystery and may, therefore, be infinitely variable. When he replaces God with the more indeterminate phrase "whatever they may consider the divine," he is saying that the divinity of the catalyst is not intrinsic to it but is a matter of *how it is apprehended*. The corollary of this view is that there is virtually no restriction on the kind of raw material (Husserl's ὕλη) that might be apprehended in this way. "*Any object*" of attention, so far as James is concerned, can constitute an object of religious faith:

All that the facts require is that the power should be both other and larger than our conscious selves. Anything larger will do, if only it be large enough to trust for the next step. It need not be infinite, it need not be solitary. It might conceivably even be only a larger and more godlike self, of which the present self would then be but the mutilated expression, and the universe might conceivably be a collection of such selves, of different degrees of inclusiveness, with no absolute unity realized in it at all. (VRE 525)[39]

James's willingness to entertain an unlimited number of divinities is, in part, just another way of avoiding an unmanly, time-wasting activity. He contrasts his practice with the fruitless attempts of "gnostics" like Cardinal Newman to determine the intrinsic qualities of a single, exclusive God (VRE 439–42).[40] His decision not to specify the precise character of the divinity is also inspired, however, by a "strange phenomenon" encountered in his study of religious experience. This is the syndrome, first identified by Kant, wherein "a mind [can believe] with all its strength in the real presence of a set of things of no one of which it can form any notion whatsoever" (VRE 55). "The sentiment of reality," James says, can "attach itself so strongly to our object of belief that our whole life is polarized through and through . . . by its sense of the existence of the thing believed in, and yet that thing, for purpose of definite description, can hardly be said to be present to our mind at all." He elaborates with a metaphor that would have appealed to the Pound of "Axiomata." Where the mind is so engrossed, he says,

it is as if a bar of iron, without touch or sight, with no representative faculty whatever, might nevertheless be strongly endowed with an inner capacity for magnetic feeling; and as if, through the various arousals of its magnetism by magnets coming and going in its neighbourhood, it might be consciously determined to different attitudes and tendencies. Such a bar of iron *could never give you an outward description of the agencies that had the power of stirring it so strongly;* yet of their presence, and of their significance for its life, it would be intensely aware through every fibre of its being. (VRE 55–56; my italics)

James compares the mystic with the lover who enjoys the effects of his beloved's presence without seeing her:

> Such is the human ontological imagination, and such is the convincingness of what it brings to birth. Unpicturable beings are realized, and realized with an intensity almost like that of an hallucination. They determine our vital attitude as decisively as the vital attitude of lovers is determined by the habitual sense, by which each is haunted, of the other being in the world. A lover has notoriously this sense of the continuous being of his idol, *even when his attention is addressed to other matters and he no longer represents her features.* (VRE 72; my italics)

For reasons both scientific and pragmatic, James depicts a divinity that is not just without an origin but *without a face.*

As I have already demonstrated, James's redefinition of the divinity in the language of psychology directly shapes his recommendations for how the mystic should articulate the insights gleaned from its appearance. The first of its essential features, its liminality, determines James's view that the mystic should employ hypothetical modes of expression. In pulling the divinity onto the threshold, James can no longer authorize the articulation of the insights as if they are God-given Truths. But just as he insists the mystic's uncertainty about the divinity does not mean he is to dismiss it as an illusion, so he insists that his uncertainty about the insights should not lead him to conclude they are falsehoods. In reserving the right to keep the "door" in the subconscious open for God, James allows the mystic (and later the pragmatist) to retain the option of regarding his tensional offerings as *"possibly really true* guides" to reality.[41] As he was to put it in *The Meaning of Truth:*

> *Total conflux of the mind with the reality* would be the absolute limit of truth, there could be no better or more satisfying knowledge than that.
>
> Such total conflux, it is needless to say, is *already explicitly provided for, as a possibility, in my account of the matter.* If an idea should ever lead us not only *towards,* or *up to,* or *against,* a reality, but so close that we and the reality should *melt together,* it would be made absolutely true, according to me, by that performance. (MT 87–88)

And, as we have seen, it is this possibility of truthfulness, this possibility of reaching a "point of termination" (MT 65–66), where theory and reality coincide, that leads James to identify the mystic's ideal utterances as *hypotheses* (VRE 428). They are not to be tossed off casually, as if they have no chance of being true anyway, but pressed strenuously against the onrushing stream of experience, continually revised, in the hope they and "reality" will one day match. Those insights will prove "most true" that "most successfully dip back into the finite stream of feeling and grow most easily confluent with some particular wave or wavelet" (ERE 49).

It is also vital to notice how the second essential feature of James's divinity, its anonymity, shapes his views about how the mystic is to present his utterances. The understanding that the noetic attitude that constructs divinities is indiscriminate, that it may attach itself to any object seemingly "other" than its worshipper, leads James to conclude that the mystic has *no right to be anything other than a pluralist*. For if, as he explains, there is nothing to privilege one hyletic kernal, apprehended-as-divine, over another, there is nothing to privilege the insights that ensue from one act of communion with one divinity over those that come from a like experience with another:

> The fact is that the mystical feeling of enlargement, union, and emancipation has no specific intellectual content whatever of its own. It is capable of forming matrimonial alliances with material furnished by the most diverse philosophies and theologies, provided only they can find a place in their framework for its peculiar emotional mood. We have no right, therefore, to invoke its prestige as distinctively in favor of any special belief, such as that in absolute idealism, or in the absolute monistic identity, or in the absolute goodness, of the world. (VRE 425–26)

The indeterminate "divinity" that James constructs in *The Varieties of Religious Experience* is vitally linked to his view that a mystic should share that insight with others but that he should remain respectful of contrary points of view. Mystics, he says, "have no right to claim that we ought to accept the deliverance of their peculiar experiences, if we are ourselves outsiders and feel no private call thereto. The utmost they can ever ask of us in this life is to admit they establish a presumption" (VRE 424). Despite the misguided appropriation of his work by strong men like Mussolini (who were attracted to James's account of truth for its emphasis on ends), James thought no feeling of conviction strong enough to justify an attempt to impose one's insights upon others. As his years of political activism attest, and as Stevens, who learned much from him, was undoubtedly aware, he was the staunchest of opponents of dogmatic forms of expression—the most fervent of anti-imperialists.[42]

Santayana shared James's strong belief that all accounts of mental experience should be purged of metaphysics. When James invites the reader to turn his back on metaphysics in *Pragmatism*, he formulates his appeal in territorial terms: "The earth of things, long thrown into shadow by the glories of the upper ether, must retain its rights" (P 62). Santayana uses the same spatial metaphor in the peroration to the opening chapter of his

Interpretations of Poetry and Religion (1900), suggesting that "Nature" is more worthy of concern than the vague extensity preferred by the "magician":

> When we compare the temple which we call Nature, built out of sights and sounds by memory and understanding, with all the wonderful worlds evocable by the magician's wand, may we not prefer the humbler and more lasting edifice, not only as a dwelling, but even as a house of prayer?[43]

Earlier in the same chapter, Santayana makes it clear that he also shares James's motivation for redirecting attention to the world at hand: a desire to bypass the agonizing epistemological problems that ensue from Cartesian dualism. His main concern in *Interpretations of Poetry and Religion* is to establish the considerable value of imagination in human life. The success of this effort will, he realizes, depend on his ability to overcome what has been the greatest source of suspicion toward imagination: a fear of the subjective interest that may "infect" it, making its constructions less than accurate mirrors of reality. Santayana equates this fear with what he calls "mysticism," a synonym for what James calls "metaphysics": technically "the surrender of a category of thought on account of the discovery of its relativity."[44] And, like James, he points out that this attitude is founded on a bifurcation of experience that is both unnatural and unnecessary: the very idea of an absolute reality "external" to our subjective constructions, he says, is itself merely a "human notion" and one to which it is totally unreasonable, therefore, to sacrifice all others. Mysticism strikes Santayana as an unnecessary position that debilitates its exponents, an "incurable disease."[45] In encouraging his audience to return their attention to the humbler edifice of empirical experience, he hopes to immunize them against this ailment and so to make a new evaluation of imagination possible—one concerned not with the accuracy of its correspondences but with the beneficence of its effects.

Santayana's commitment to a "radically empirical" approach to imagination is nowhere clearer than when he comes to discuss the artist's moment of illumination—a seemingly "mystical" moment in James's sense of the word.[46] His definition of the genus to which creative inspiration belongs, religious experience, closely resembles James's in its careful respect for the psychological reality if not for the ontological objectivity of the being whose truths are revealed:

> The gods sometimes appear, and when they do they bring us a foretaste of that sublime victory of mind over matter which we may never gain in experience but which may constantly be gained in thought. When natural phenomena are conceived as the manifestation of divine life, human life itself, by sympathy with that ideal projection of itself, enlarges its customary bounds, until it seems cap-

able of becoming the life of the universe. A god is a *conceived victory of mind over Nature*. A visible god is *the consciousness of such a victory momentarily attained*.[47]

Santayana's reduction of a "visible god" to the "consciousness of" contact with some universal principle demonstrates a Hulmean "new classical" dedication to avoiding claims about transcendental realities. The same concern is evident in Santayana's early treatise on aesthetics, *The Sense of Beauty* (1896), which refers specifically to the moments when the artist recognizes an "ideal" or has a glimpse of a "perfection" and is then inspired to translate it into art. Recalling the long platonic tradition that has explained these "vision[s] of unexampled beauty" as insights into the soul-world, Santayana acknowledges the value of such hyperbolic claims as "expressions" of feeling. But like Hulme and Stevens, he finds these claims inadequate as scientific "explanations." Although the platonists "have sometimes a strong sense of the *facts of consciousness*," their resolution of such experience into eternal Ideas does not "explain the phenomena or hit upon the actual law of things."[48] To eliminate such inaccuracies, Santayana proposes eliminating questions of cause altogether and simply focusing on the "actual feelings" of inspiration. Like James (who once remarked that a "permanently existing 'idea' . . . which makes its appearance before the footlights of consciousness at periodical intervals is as mythological an entity as the Jack of Spades" [PP 1 230]), he will describe the apparent apprehension of an Idea simply as "an emotion, an affectation of our volitional and appreciative measure." As in *Interpretations of Poetry and Religion,* he finds no reason to complicate matters by devising a realm beyond that of immediate experience: "An absolute perfection, independent of human nature and its variations, may interest the metaphysician; but the artist and the man will be satisfied with a perfection that is *inseparable from the consciousness* of mankind, since it is at once the natural vision of the imagination, and the rational goal of the will." The apprehension that inspires the artist is, in short, "an *affection of* the soul, a *consciousness of* joy and security, a pang, a dream, a pure pleasure. It is an *experience:* there is nothing more to be said about it" (SB 163; my italics).[49]

At the outset, then, there appears to be little to distinguish Santayana from James on the subject of inspiration. The moment of illumination remains a fact of uncertain provenance; the mystic or artist who feels compelled to articulate his insights has no means of confirming, and therefore no obligation to confirm, their authority.[50] Despite Santayana's overt commitment to empirical psychology, however, he fails to sustain the perfectly equivocal attitude toward the sources for inspiration that psychology requires, and he abandons neutrality by moving, not just in the direction opposite James, but much further—to a place outside of empiricism and back in "metaphysics."

The move that separates Santayana from James and that lies at the heart of all that offended James about Santayana's work is also one that makes his work offensive to orthodox believers in precisely the way that James's might be but is not. While James keeps his divinity poised on the threshold between self and other, remaining optimistic that it might have originated in a place beyond the open door, Santayana surreptitiously slips his divinity back inside the self and *slams the door shut*. He unequivocally denies that it is anything more than a subjective construction. In *The Sense of Beauty*, this betrayal of Santayana's commitment to avoid speculating about the ultimate causes of religious experience follows some devious observations about how perfectly the objects of worship fulfill their worshippers' desires. Santayana starts by dutifully admitting that the "ideal" objects of Christian worship—Christ, the Virgin Mary, the saints—"may have been exactly [the objective beings] our imagination pictures them to be," but he dwells at much greater length on how convenient these objects of faith have proven to be.[51] And from simply appreciating their usefulness, which would not have offended James in the slightest, he slips into affirming that these objects actually *have their origin* in the needs they fill, and ultimately they are *nothing but* the projections of desire, a position that James found completely unacceptable.[52] Thus Santayana's final characterization of the figure of Christ:

> The Christ men have loved and adored is an ideal of their own hearts, the construction of an ever-present personality, living and intimately understood, out of the fragments of story and doctrine connected with a name. This *subjective image* has inspired all the prayers, all the conversions, all the penances, charities and sacrifices, as well as half the art of the Christian world.[53]

Christ is to be celebrated as a profitable idea but only as a profitable idea. As Santayana expressed it in a letter to James, Christianity, like all religions, is "exquisite moonshine."[54]

What holds for Santayana's description of Christ, and other specifically religious ideals, also holds for his descriptions of the ideals inspiring the artist. He gives lip service to the possibility that these perfections really might be the preexistent universals that they seem:

> The Platonic idea of a tree may exist; how should I deny it? How should I deny that I might find myself outside the sky gazing at it, and feeling that I, with my mental vision, am beholding the plenitude of arboreal beauty, perceived in this world only as a vague essence haunting the multiplicity of finite trees?[55]

But then he asserts unequivocally that the artist is himself the *sole origina-tor* of these ideals: that they are the "residu[a] of experience," relative to "our partial nature," the products of a "subjective bias."[56] In the end as he boasts to James, Santayana is a thoroughgoing materialist as regards the insights that inspire art.[57] He breaks his obligation to equivocate and affirms their origin in the artist's idiosyncratic needs. And thus he lapses back into metaphysics, contending that the artist *doesn't* have contact with the transcendental perfections he thinks he does. In a move that would dismay his teacher, he indulges in what James, discussing religious faith in "The Sentiment of Rationality," describes disapprovingly as "dogmatic" skepticism.

But what are the implications for expression of Santayana's skeptical view of the source of inspiration? Once again the reflex-action model holds firm. Despite Santayana's claims in *The Sense of Beauty* that he does not intend to be hortatory in his discussion of aesthetics,[58] his remarks both there and in *Interpretations* reveal a strong preference for certain modes of expression above others. And in both cases, at least at first, his taste closely resembles James's. Inspired by a problematic divinity, the poet has no right to use dogmatic utterances but must employ expressions that seem on the brink of disintegration, expressions that are demonstrably open to questioning and revision. A poem appropriate to the divinity that has in-spired it will, for Santayana, make it apparent that its assertions, however compelling, always leave something in doubt:

> The nature of our materials—be they words, colours, or plastic matter—impose a limit and bias upon our expression. The reality of experience can never be quite rendered through these media. The greatest mastery of technique will there-fore come short of perfect adequacy and exhaustiveness; there must always re-main a penumbra and fringe of suggestion if the most explicit representation is to communicate a truth. When there is real profundity,—when the living core of things is most firmly grasped,—there will accordingly be a felt inadequacy of expression, and an appeal to the observer to piece out our imperfections with his thoughts.[59]

The clearest example Santayana gives in *The Sense of Beauty* of an art that attains this ideal is an architectural one. Rejecting the stable, uncluttered lines of classical Greek buildings, which testify to their own "perfection," he celebrates Gothic architecture instead: buildings whose stability at first sight seems "hopeless" and whose lines are cluttered with numerous unas-similable ornaments.[60] This preference recalls James's hostility to classical architecture, which he associates, in *Pragmatism*, with the dogmatic, un-bending utterances of rationalism (P 17–18). A discussion praising compa-rable values in poetry is found in *Interpretations of Poetry and Religion*, where Santayana praises as exemplary the flexible, playful utterances of

Emerson. Whereas overly "earnest" readers of Emerson, Santayana says, have detected in his work only the authoritative assertions of a confident transcendentalist, what he most admires about the philosopher is his assumption of something very like a "new classical" irony with regard to those assertions. For all Emerson's metaphysical talk about "Nature, Law, God, Benefit, or Beauty," Santayana contends that he was merely playing with the rhetoric of romanticism; in fact, he was always pointing to the inadequacy of his claims, discarding them almost as soon as making them.[61] Emerson was like "a young god making experiments in creation," perennially embarking "on a new and better plan."[62]

Santayana's taste for unstable modes of expression, then, clearly allies him with James. But the resemblance holds only up to a point. The equivocal expressions Santayana celebrates differ from James's in fundamental ways. The difference between the two forms of expression can be attributed to the different place each philosopher ascribes to the source for inspiration; it is a difference in the criteria each believes should guide the revision of the propositions. In James's case, as I've noted, the fact that the divinity might well fall beyond the threshold of subjectivity means that "inspired" insights may well be perfectly accurate representations of reality. As long as this possibility remains open, the inspired mystic or poet has an obligation to test his insights against the oncoming flux, in an effort to hasten the movement toward that point of "termination" where insight and reality might coincide. In other words James's truths disintegrate only when they fail to be empirically accurate. Santayana, on the other hand, ends up imprisoning his "ideals" (ancestors of what he later calls "essences")[63] within the subject, and for him, therefore, James's program of testing seems pointless drudgery. If the insights that strike us with all the force of certainty can never be absolutely true, he reasons, why should we labor to make them so? There are more realistic and more profitable goals for the mind's constructions:

> Mind was not created for the sake of discovering the absolute truth. The absolute truth has its own intangible reality, and scorns to be known. The function of the mind is rather to increase the wealth of the universe in the spiritual dimension, by adding appearance to substance . . . and by creating all those perspectives, and those emotions of wonder, adventure, curiosity and laughter which omniscience would exclude.[64]

Like Aristotle, whom he invokes, Santayana would have the poet forego the criterion of empirical accuracy in poetry, in favor of gratifying emotional and spiritual needs. If it is the function of the poet to be constantly "building new structures," the "guiding principle" in the construction and destruction of propositions is not a concern with fact but "a mood or a quality of sentiment": a concern with matching propositions "to the deeper innate cravings of the mind."[65] The poet will abandon old structures only to build new ones "nearer to the heart's desire." In being answerable only to his "heart," he enjoys much greater freedom than the provisional truth-maker envisioned by James. He is no more constrained in his practice than the daydreaming child, "who puffs himself out in his daydreams into an endless variety of heroes and lovers"; the "growth, variations, and exuberance of [his] fancy may be unlimited."[66]

It should now be clear why James and Santayana could both be so certain of their affinities and yet so conscious of their differences. In retreating from metaphysics, they trace parallel courses, but in their final assessments of the significance of inspired moments, in their prescriptions for the wielding of the insights gained there, they go very different ways. James's discomfort with Santayana's program can be inferred from his bewildered response, in *The Meaning of Truth,* to critics who represent his pragmatic attitude toward truth in terms perfectly appropriate to Santayana's. These critics "take James to mean . . . that whatever proves subjectively expedient in the way of our thinking is 'true' in the absolute and unrestricted sense of the word, *whether it corresponds to any objective state of things outside of our thought or not*" (MT 126; my italics). His objection reaffirms the firm commitment to empirical verification that Santayana repudiates:

> Having previously written that truth means "agreement with reality," and insisted that the chief part of the expediency of any one opinion is its agreement with the rest of acknowledged truth, I apprehended no exclusively subjectivistic reading of my meaning. My mind was so filled with the notion of objective reference that I never dreamed that my hearers would let go of it; and the very last accusation I expected was that in speaking of ideas and their satisfactions, I was denying realities outside. My only wonder now is that critics should have found so silly a personage as I must have seemed in their eyes, worthy of explicit refutation.[67]

That James recognized in Santayana the very views he was renouncing is apparent in a letter to George Palmer written shortly after the publication of *Interpretations of Poetry and Religion:* James admires the "splendid impertinence" with which Santayana espouses his theories but takes strong exception to his student's pessimism and materialism. Santayana's conviction that so much value could inhere in a realm independent of practical existence is, to his way of thinking, frivolous and irresponsible. Santayana, for his part, was well aware of James's disapproval. In a 1905 letter to James, he refers in passing to the "empirical reserve or abstension" with which James has greeted his dogmatic skepticism and the program for truth-making it inspires.[68]

In demonstrating how a significant disagreement in attitudes toward the catalyst for inspiration translates into a significant difference in recommendations for expression, the aesthetics of James and Santayana confirm the reflex-action model of poetics. Both for what they have in common, and, eventually, for what divides them, they will be important paradigms to keep in mind as we return to Stevens and his dilemma over how to remain a man and a poet, too.

STEVENS'S RADICAL EMPIRICISM: TWO PARABLES

Stevens's comments in essays like "The Noble Rider and the Sound of Words" and "The Figure of the Youth as Virile Poet" leave little doubt that he shared James's and Santayana's commitment to renouncing metaphysics. Two poems written much earlier chronicle the process of reasoning that led to that commitment and reveal the extent to which Stevens shared James's reasons for the shift. "The Comedian as the Letter C" (1923) and "Sea Surface Full of Clouds" (1924) tell stories of how traditional, metaphysical thinkers become radical empiricists. Both poems dramatize the types of questing and questioning that go with the Cartesian habit of dividing subject from object and then demanding "to know for certain *that* we know." Both comment on the futility of such endeavors and the frustrations they cause. In the end the protagonists of both poems abandon their efforts to achieve certainty and accept the humbler vocation of contemplating the realm of "pure experience." The spaces they eventually become resigned to inhabiting are prototypes for the space in which Stevens situates all his discussions of mental activity, in poetry and prose, for the rest of his career.

"The Comedian as the Letter C" is a parable about a poet's attempts to establish certain knowledge about himself and his world. When Stevens's poet-hero Crispin sails to America, he does so to transcend the "distortion of romance" (CP 30) that has obscured his vision and to apprehend things as they are. His quest for truth is to be directed both outward and inward: he is confident that he will uncover the "veritable ding-an-sich" in the form of a "starker, barer world" and in the form of a "starker, barer self" (CP 28–29). The self he will discover will be one stripped of the false aggrandizement that cloaked it in Europe. But it will be a self willing to confront the world as it truly is and so a self that is truly heroic.

As Jules de Gaultier might have predicted, however, Crispin's quests for the truth about his world and his self fail dismally. When the poet reaches the new world, after a bracing journey, his faith in his newfound clarity of vision fuels a series of enthusiastic enterprises, which founder as the clear-eyed self he imagines succumbs to illusion after satisfying illusion. Adventures in Yucatan and on a journey north to Carolina reveal him to be as susceptible to the habits of romanticizing both his environment and himself as never before. He himself comes to recognize this susceptibility, a weakness for the "moonlight" that enables him to evade the harsh realities exposed by the sun:

> Thus he conceived his voyaging to be
> An up and down between two elements,
> A fluctuating between sun and moon,
> A sally into gold and crimson forms,
> As on this voyage, out of goblinry,
> And then retirement like a turning back
> And sinking down to the indulgences
> That in the moonlight have their habitude.
>
> (CP 35)

Understanding his weakness and appreciating "how much / Of what he saw he never saw at all" (CP 36), at first simply inspires Crispin to renew his devotion to experiencing an unmediated reality. This leads him to his most ambitious enterprise yet: a plan to establish a colony, encompassing the whole of North and South American continents, on his new principles, which are not just materialist but democratic and apparently socialist.[69] Crucial to this venture, as he sees it, is the abandonment of all "mental moonlight," including the false ideals that inspire the dogmatic, authoritarian rule of European-style monarchies: "[E]xit lex, / Rex and principium," he declares, "exit the whole / Shebang" (CP 36–37). In place of such a system, he imagines a society that will allow all its constituents to voice the various points of view inspired by their particular environments: "The man in Georgia waking among pines / Should be pine-spokesman" (CP 38). In practice, however, his determination to allow the inhabitants of the new world to speak for themselves gives way to a greater desire to impose order, in the form of his own values, on them. He cannot tolerate the primitive ways of the "gross Indian" (CP 38), any more than he can the unmanaged fecundity of the wilderness. Instead of allowing this threatening other to assert itself, he responds by imposing the very kind of *lex* and *principium* he has vowed to abandon. In poetic terms he wills that the "Sierra scan" (CP 38). The ironic image of Crispin, as a quasi-militaristic ruler "not indifferent to smart detail" (CP 38), makes it clear, once again, that he has been harboring an illusion: he cannot abandon the dogmatism he has vowed to renounce.

The end of "The Comedian as the Letter C" sees Crispin give up his colony and indeed all his determined questing for truth. For many critics his decision to retire with his wife to a little cabin in the wilderness signals

a degeneration into "an 'indulgent fatalis[m]' and skepticism."[70] Finding
himself deluded again and again, Crispin is overwhelmed by the insight
that he will never be able to transcend the distortions introduced by desire,
and he simply gives up. But there is another reading of the state of mind
the poet enjoys in the privacy of his "Nice Shady Home" (CP 40). His
retirement is a retreat from the agonizing and finally fruitless efforts inspired by what James called "metaphysics" and Santayana "mysticism."
The "reproach / That first drove Crispin to his wandering" (CP 39) was
Cartesian doubt—the desire, not just to seem to know the truth, but to
know for certain that he knew it. Whether deriding the "mythology of
self" (CP 28) that characterized his life in Europe, or the idealizing "moonlight" that distorted his vision of America, or, in the last instance, the
desire-dependent dreams that interfered with his reception of a plurality of
American voices,

> He could not be content with counterfeit,
> With masquerade of thought, with hapless words
> That must belie the racking masquerade,
> With fictive flourishes that preordained
> His passion's permit, hang of coat, degree
> Of buttons, measure of his salt. Such trash
> Might help the blind, not him, serenely sly.
> It irked beyond his patience.
>
> (CP 39)

Crispin's retirement does not mark the abandonment of all hope of knowledge so much as it does the abandonment of all the anxieties involved in
metaphysical verification. It is a decision to accept "things within his actual
eye" for what they are, without agonizing about the "ding an sich" that
may be distorted in the process: a willingness to "stop short before a plum /
And be content" (CP 40), knowing that the essential fruit lies beyond his
grasp.

In exchanging the vast spaces of ocean and continent for a more "condign" (CP 42) space, Crispin ends up inhabiting the "humbler and more
lasting edifice" that James and Santayana both regarded (at least initially)
as the only appropriate space for intellectual speculation. And the life he
lives within it is far from marking Crispin's degeneration into the "great
American slob," as Richard Adams puts it.[71] It is a life of active assertion-
making, after the general style recommended by both of the Harvard philosophers. As husband and father, Crispin is still the author of numerous
pronouncements about the way things are or should be. What is noticeable
about the statements of doctrine he utters now, however, is that they are
not the rigid and far-flung laws he envisioned in his fantasy of colonization
but the flexible, ironic utterances of one who has abandoned confidence in

the purity of his insights without abandoning the exercise of his will. The exemplary utterance Stevens offers is an anecdote that turns out to be identical with the text of "Comedian" itself, an account of a life that may be "doctrinal" in "design" but not in "form." This "pronunciamento," we are told, is "disguised," this "strident" summary "muted"; each assertion it contains is qualified by "after-shining flicks" (CP 46).

The attitude assumed by the speaker at the end of the poem, a speaker who turns out to be Crispin himself, is a pragmatic willingness to gain whatever benefit there is in making sense of things, however temporary the construction. If the account of things he has just given turns out to be "false" (CP 45), this is not the cause for despair it has been in the past: the "relation" (equally, the act of telling and the connection that unifies it) will simply come "benignly" to its end (CP 46). In his acceptance of a radically empirical realm for his speculations and of flexible forms for their expression, Crispin defines, after James and Santayana, Stevens's own mature poetics. "The Comedian as the Letter C" is not, as Adams and others would have it, the despairing statement of a poet who would not publish another book of poetry for twelve years. It is the justification, the optimistic manifesto, and, as "disguised pronunciamento," the formal prototype for all that is to come.

Often dismissed as merely a formal experiment, devoid of any significant content,[72] "Sea Surface Full of Clouds" in fact communicates the same message as "Comedian" about the dubious practice of reaching irritably after certainty. Again it presents a speaker recollecting and questioning the nature of his own cognitive experiences, and again that speaker concludes that his concern with establishing the truthfulness of these perceptions is misguided and embraces a new, less ambitious and more accepting attitude toward them.

Like Crispin, the speaker in "Sea Surface" is a former sea-farer. The voyage he recollects, however, is no epic journey: it is a lazy sail, a holiday sail off the Mexican coast. In recording the perceptions he enjoyed on that journey along with the associations they called up in his mind, he establishes a fact about those experiences which aligns them with the "pure experiences" described in the *Essays on Radical Empiricism*.[73] This is the fact that, at least initially, the consciousness involved in perception and the objects it perceives are seamless, intermingled in an "indissoluble marriage." The poem's cantos record a series of days, each both like and unlike the others. In each case the speaker recalls how night or morning brought with it a calming of the sea, and how the morning light "made one think" of chocolate and umbrellas; the variants are the particular affective qualities attached by the imagination to the chocolate and the umbrellas, then to the ocean's green, and finally to the ocean itself. Several features of these descriptions reinforce the impression of seamlessness. The sunlight, on the one hand represented as the objective agent that set off his imaginings (it "made one think" (CP 99, 100, 101), is, on the other, represented as having been always already transformed by the consciousness: into "summer" (CP 98) or "jelly yellow" (CP 99) or a dozy "mallow morning" (CP 101).[74] Inner and outer worlds mingle further as we are told how the sea assumed the emotions of the speaker, becoming "perplexed," "tense," "tranced," "malic[ious]," and "indolen[t]" (CP 99–101). (Stevens indulges in the "pathetic fallacy" in defiance of Ruskin, but with the blessings of James and Santayana.[75]) This mingling of the attributes of sea and self, moreover, invites an allegorical reading of the sea *as* self.[76] If the sea represents the speaker's consciousness, the sky becomes the external world with which that consciousness interacts. And in his account of that interaction, Stevens resists attributing primacy; the sea doesn't just *reflect* the clouds, it is *full* of clouds: "The sea-clouds whitened far below the calm / And moved, as blooms move, in the swimming green / And in its watery radiance." Likewise the speaker reverses traditional wisdom on the source of the color of sea and sky. At least "sometimes" the sea did not reflect the color of the sky, but itself "poured brilliant iris on the glistening blue." The watery radiance and the glistening sky (CP 99) exchange roles as readily as they do qualities, putting in question which is the primary agent in the perceptual experience.[77]

Stevens's speaker gives a textbook example of "pure experience" and points to Jamesian doctrine in his allegory of sea and sky, but he also dramatizes the kind of anxious reaching after certainty that James believed did violence to that experience. In canto I he interrupts his description of the experience to ask precisely the kind of question that the undifferentiated environment would seem to resist: a question about the origins of his perceptions and, in effect, about their validity:

> Who, then, in that ambrosial latitude
> Out of the light evolved the moving blooms,
>
> Who, then, evolved the sea-blooms from the clouds
> Diffusing balm in that Pacific calm?
>
> (CP 99)

The descriptions in cantos II, III, and IV are disrupted in a similar way, as the speaker inquires into the identity of the subject who beheld or heard the imaginative visions that become increasingly complex and that sometimes assume the character of divine revelations ("blue heaven spread / Its crystalline pendentives on the sea" [CP 100]; the sea evokes the "Salt masks of beard" of Jehovah [CP 101]). In demanding to know where these apparently mystical insights originate, Stevens's speaker is asking for the certainty demanded by agnosticism and dismissed as an unfortunate requirement by James, that is, the reassurance that mystical knowledge *is* knowledge.[78]

The answers that the speaker provides for his own questions suggest, moreover, that he shares James's view that there can be no such reassurance. On one level his answers appear to dismiss the calming revelations as fantasies, the entirely subjective creations of *mon âme, ma vie, mon amour,* or *ma foi.* On closer examination, however, these answers seem to affirm that the speaker's visions may, in fact, have objective sources. For in constructing the speaker's answers, Stevens puts objective or potentially objective entities in apposition with his subjective ones. The speaker's creative *âme* is in apposition with his *enfant* (CP 99), and his *vie* with a *frère du ciel:* "*C'était mon enfant, mon bijou, mon âme . . . C'était mon frère du ciel, ma view, mon or*" (CP 99, 100). In the third reply, the word *amour* may just as well refer to the object that inspires love as to the feeling itself; and in the fourth, the *nonchalance divine* in apposition to *ma foi* may refer as easily to the indifference of an objective divinity as to the speaker's own easygoing faith in a divinity's benevolence. The speaker's answers, in other words, reassert the impossibility of establishing whether the visions are subjective or objective; they suggest that there is no way out of the dilemma introduced by the questioning.

That the speaker recognizes the impasse he has come to and the need for reconsidering the attitudes that have led him to it becomes clear in the poem's fifth canto, where his final question about the origin of his imaginative visions becomes a double entendre calling into question the act of questioning itself. On one level the speaker is simply inquiring again about the source of the visions he encountered "that November." This time he wants to know why the sea suddenly assumed the aspect of a conjurer, creating, and playfully juggling, the clouds. Again he attributes this vision to a source of uncertain provenance—a "bastard" spirit:

> What pistache one, ingenious and droll,
> Beheld the sovereign clouds as jugglery
> And the sea as turquoise-turbaned Sambo, neat
> At tossing saucers—cloudy-conjuring sea?
> *C'était mon esprit bâtard, l'ignominie.*

On another level, however, the passage appears to be a question, not about the originator of the imaginative visions but about the self that has been reflecting, at one remove, on that imaginer. We can see this by resurrecting the allegorical reading of the sea, the reading that transforms it from an object contemplated *by* the self into a figure *for* the self. When we read the "cloudy-conjuring sea" as an emblem for the self (or, as Dorothy Emerson has suggested, for the creative unconscious[79]) the speaker no longer seems to be asking about the origin of the visions. Rather, he seems to be asking a question about the credentials of the self that has been asking such questions: the self that has retroactively divided and introduced doubt into what began as a pure experience. From this vantage, the italicized answer to the question communicates a sudden disgust with the whole process of questioning the poem has documented. That self has no certain origin, hence no special authority in suggesting that the self is an illusionist: the bastard has been engaged in a futile, even "ignominious" activity.

When sea and sky join forces in the final lines of the poem, to swamp the final act of questioning, the tone is optimistic, even triumphant:

> The sovereign clouds came clustering. The conch
> Of loyal conjuration trumped. The wind
> Of green blooms turning crisped the motley hue
>
> To clearing opalescence. Then the sea
> And heaven rolled as one and from the two
> Came fresh transfigurings of freshest blue.
>
> (CP 102)

Coming in the wake of the speaker's recognition about the futility of the kind of questions he has been asking, this final, happy memory of how pure experience reasserted itself suggests a renewed commitment to that experience. The speaker seems to have happily assumed the stance of James's radical empiricist, perched on the edge of an advancing wave crest, and falling forward into the onrushing stream. The "fresh transfigurings of freshest blue" he encounters are the visions brought by a new morning, their origins now regarded as best left uninvestigated. (It is no coincidence that, in this final canto, the phrase repeatedly used to suggest a line of causation [the sun "made one think"] gives way to an ellipses, followed by simple statement of fact ["One thought . . ."] [CP 102].) It has become a commonplace in Stevens's criticism that the "blue" of these transfigurings is the color Stevens used throughout his career to denote imagination.[80] The important lesson of "Sea Surface" for students of the Stevensian imagination is that Stevens refuses to grant either that color, or the faculty with which it is associated, any certain origins in either heaven or earth, and he views the most acceptable response to that uncertainty as acquiescence. Imaginative visions are blue, and, as he was to put it many years later, for something "[t]o be blue, / There must be no questions" (CP 429).

STEVENS'S LIMINAL DIVINITIES

"The Comedian as the Letter C" and "Sea Surface Full of Clouds" demonstrate that Stevens shares James's and Santayana's commitment to a radically empirical approach to experiences of inspiration. The resemblance between the poet and the philosophers, however, goes deeper than this. Like James and Santayana, Stevens is preoccupied with using the principles of radical empiricism to revise traditional representations of inspiring divinities. The beings at issue here are the figures Stevens, in a 1951 address to the Poetry Society, was to call the "genius[es] of poetry" (OP 252). More particularly, they are his female muses: figures whose treatment in his prose and poetry has sparked a number of complaints from feminist critics of the "images of women" school. If we consider Stevens's muses primarily as figures for the source of inspiration, however, we see that many of their features may be attributed to a radically empirical discourse on creativity, and this makes it possible to recuperate Stevens, to some degree, for feminism. A representation of a muse is, among other things, a statement of the artist's claim to (or disclaimer of) authority. Many of Stevens's muses, and many of his most swaggering, willfully "virile" gestures toward them, seem offensive when considered purely as representations *of women*, but when taken specifically *as muses,* and read on a Jamesian model, they turn out to support what many feminist critics have championed as progressive and even "feminine" values—specifically they constitute renunciations of dogmatic authority.

As his essays show, Stevens conceives the moment of inspiration as both intuitive and ecstatic. The other feature of that experience to be noted is its status as an act of prayer—if, with James, we may understand prayer as encompassing "every kind of inward communion or conversation with [a] power recognized as divine" (VRE 464) and every kind of experience that involves an "active and mutual" intercourse between a subject and his or her object of worship (VRE 465). Stevens describes "poetic" experiences as those in which the consciousness becomes engaged with "something unreal": they entail the kind of concentration we engage in when we look at a photograph of someone who is absent, or "writ[e] a letter to a person at a distance" (OP 255).[81] Or as he puts it in his 1951 address to the Poetry Society:

> Individual poets, whatever their imperfections may be, are driven all their lives by that *inner companion of the conscience* which is, after all, the genius of poetry in their hearts and minds. I speak of a companion of the conscience because to every faithful poet the faithful poem is an act of conscience. (OP 253; my italics)

Stevens explains the feelings of illumination that inspire poets by attributing them to the presence before the consciousness of beings from whom wisdom seems to emanate: beings that, like those "companions" humans have found for centuries in the gods, are "assumed to be full of the secret of things" (OP 261). Like James he senses the "otherness" of these inspiring partners. "When the mind is like a hall is which thought is like a voice speaking," he notes, "the voice is always that of *someone else*" (OP 194; my italics). For him, as for a long line of male poets, the apparent alterity of these muses is captured by emphasizing their difference in sex. The muse-figures in his work are often glittering "brides," who share their wisdom with their male admirers in acts of sexual union.[82]

At the same time as he describes these prayerful acts of communication with divine others, however, Stevens makes numerous efforts to prevent "metaphysical" or "mystical" rhetoric from contaminating his descriptions. His position on the matter dividing James and Santayana is therefore a subject of interest, and something I shall address presently. For the moment, it can simply be said that many of his portraits of inspiring divinities meet the general specifications on which the two philosophers agree. Two major features of James's and Santayana's empirical procedures are found repeatedly in Stevens's portraits. First though they are represented as seeming to be other than the worshipper, Stevens's divinities are carefully denied any assured status as objective, mystical beings. His dedication to this principle is evident in the "credo" he writes for the ephebe in "The Figure of the Youth as Virile Poet":

No longer do I believe that there is a mystic muse, sister of the Minotaur. This is another of the monsters I had for nurse, whom I have wasted. I am myself a part of what is real, and it is my own speech and the strength of it, this only, that I hear or ever shall. (NA 60)

Stevens renounces the "mystic muse" and replaces it with a hybrid—the "sister of the Minotaur" to whom these remarks are directed (this phrase is not an appositive, as it is usually read, but a vocative). The "sister of the Minotaur" is a liminal being, both animal and divinity, both objective reality and subjective illusion. By representing her both as "half-beast" and somewhat "more than human" (NA 52), he suggests that her origins are just as possibly material as spiritual; in James's words she is just as possibly "an illusion of the senses" as "a gift of God's grace."[83] In addition to depriving his divinities of any certain origin, moreover, Stevens is consistently unconcerned with determining who or what these beings really are. What matters to him, as to James and Santayana both, is not the essential nature of these beings but the effect of communing with them. Typical of Stevens's thoughts on the matter are some comments made in response to Henri Brémond, who had written that the creation of "pure poetry" begins in an act of prayerful communion. Brémond had recommended this experience as a means of attaining contact with a real God. For Stevens, however, the value of the experience lies not in the special nature of the being that is *uncovered* but in the benefits that ensue from apprehending something that *seems as if it is* divine:

> If we descend a little from this height and apply the looser and broader definition of pure poetry, it is possible to say that, while it can lie in the temperament of very few of us to write poetry in order to find God, it is probably the purpose of each of us to write poetry to find *the good which, in the Platonic sense, is synonymous with God.* (OP 228; my italics.)

For "God," Stevens substitutes a noematic category that includes anything that performs the *function* of God: the function of seeming to give the poet an insight into "what is harmonious and orderly" in things (OP 228). (He effects a similar transformation at the end of "Sunday Morning," where he describes a ring of men directing their devotion to "the sun, / Not as a god, but *as a god might be*" [CP 70; my italics].) This shift from a concern with essences to a concern with effects, from an interest in the identity of the object of worship to an interest exclusively in what function such an object can perform, is what makes Stevens not just a radical empiricist as regards inspiration but also a pragmatist. His insistence that "it is the belief and not the god that counts" (OP 188) is his version of what I have been calling the "pragmatic turn."

Ambiguous, anonymous muses therefore abound in Stevens's poetry. We find another "sister of the Minotaur," for instance, in the hybrid of lean animal and heavenly goddess Stevens depicts in the "Apostrophe to Vincentine," a figure who floats in a middle space between earth and sky.[84] The "Angel Surrounded by Paysans" is a muse of this type; endowed neither with "ashen wing" nor "tepid aureole" (CP 496), only "half seen" (CP 497), and, hence, presumably, half imagined, this figure makes its brief appearance on a threshold:

> I am the angel of reality,
> Seen for a minute standing in the door.
>
> I have neither ashen wing nor wear of ore
> And live without a tepid aureole,
>
> Or stars that follow me, not to attend,
> But, of my being and its knowing, part.
>
> I am one of you and being one of you
> Is being and knowing what I am and know.

(CP 496)

Like James's decision to represent the subconscious dwelling place of the divinity as a threshold, Stevens's use of a doorway to frame his muse problematizes her alterity. She claims to be "of reality" but also to be "the necessary angel." Her liminality extends even to her gender. Glancing coquettishly over her shoulder before disappearing, she seems female, yet she is also, pointedly, "a *man* / Of the mind" (CP 497; my italics).[85]

Perhaps the most precise philosophical description of the muse in all of Stevens is found in a poem in *Transport to Summer* called "So-and-So Reclining on Her Couch." "So-and-So" belongs to a long tradition of nude figures who have served as muses. As Robert Graves has observed, male poets have often used a "woman divested of all garments or ornaments" as "the emblem of perfect truth"; her nudity [ensures] her freedom—like some transcendental Idea—from [the] accidental features that would "commit her to [a] particular position in time and space."[86] In Stevens's poem, however, the nude's ontological status, hence the authority of what she communicates, is under debate. The speaker of the poem begins by entertaining two opposing hypotheses, or projections, concerning the figure before him. Both projections amount to judgments about the muse's reality. "Projection A" paints the muse as an illusion, an "apparition" fulfilling the speaker's fantasies of seductive innocence. "Projection B" makes the muse into a genuinely transcendental reality—an essential Idea—whose authority, as such, is signified by a crown. Both of these hypotheses give way, however, to a third and "final" proposition about the muse's status, "Projection C":

> . . . She floats in the contention, the flux
> Between the thing as idea and
> The idea as thing. She is half who made her.
> This is the final Projection, C.
>
> (CP 295)

The theory the speaker settles on here is one designed to mediate between the skeptical and absolutist propositions that have gone before it. Here the figure "floats in the contention" between subjective construct ("the thing as idea") and objective category ("[t]he idea as thing"). This account is in keeping with the first description of her as she is radically experienced, a description that underscores her uncertain genealogy, her anonymity:

> She floats in air at the level of
> The eye, completely anonymous,
> Born, as she was, at twenty-one,
>
> Without lineage or language, only
> The curving of her hips, as motionless gesture,
> Eyes dripping blue, so much to learn.
>
> (CP 295)

Like James's indifference to the true identity of inspiring divinities, the speaker's lack of concern with who this muse is signals his renunciation of metaphysics for pragmatism. When he offers his "thanks" (CP 296) to her at the end of the poem, he is expressing his gratitude for her usefulness, for the fleeting *sense of* her otherness that has enabled him to commune with her and feel himself enlightened. Although he assigns a name to the muse as he leaves her (Mrs. Pappadopoulos), this act is indicative more of the confidence that he has gained from that experience than it is of any genuine interest in who she is. And in identifying her both as "Mrs." and as a variant of "Pappa," Stevens calls attention to the superficiality of this identification—she is identified by the patriarchal system rather than allowed to assert her identity herself. It is clearly the belief and not the goddess that counts.

If "So-and-So" evokes the tradition of painterly odalisques, she most closely resembles those of Henri Matisse, which also characteristically hover "at the level of / The eye" (CP 295), midway between (subjective) ground and (objective) sky.[87] Stevens's muses also resemble Matisse's, and more importantly James's, in being *faceless*—another feature underscoring their uncertain identity.[88] The speaker in "Yellow Afternoon" finds satisfaction, for example, in the murmurings of a woman whose face is a blank:

> Everything comes to him
> From the middle of his field. The odor
> Of earth penetrates more deeply than any word.
> There he touches his being. There as he is
> He is. The thought that he had found all this
> Among men, in a woman—she caught his breath—
> But he came back as one comes back from the sun
> To lie on one's bed in the dark, close to a face
> Without eyes or mouth, that looks at one and
>   speaks.
>
>   (CP 237)

This portrait (or nonportrait) that presents a void where a woman's features might be receives its most deliberate and explicit comment in "The Woman in Sunshine." Both poems corroborate James's bracketing of the lover with the mystic, for they assume the capacity to be aware, in "every fibre of [one's] being" (VRE 56), of the presence of someone of whom one can give no "outward description" at all:

> It is only that this warmth and movement are *like*
> The warmth and movement of a woman.
>
> *It is not that there is any image in the air*
> *Nor the beginning nor end of a form:*

> *It is empty.* But a woman in threadless gold
> Burns us with brushings of her dress
>
> And a dissociated abundance of being,
> More definite for what she is—
>
> Because she is disembodied,
> Bearing the odors of the summer fields,
>
> Confessing the taciturn and yet indifferent,
> Invisibly clear, the only love.
>
> (CP 445; my italics)

This woman's disembodiment is essential to her value for the speaker. Being nowhere she is everywhere; her unspecified expressions of love envelope him.

Stevens's muses, then, are faceless objects of worship, of untraceable origin, whose importance lies solely in the benefits they bring. Like the visions ultimately enjoyed by the speaker of "Sea Surface Full of Clouds," and like all the objects inhabiting "middle" spaces in Stevens's poetry,[89] they are simply to be appreciated, no questions asked. James H. Leuba, a psychologist of religion contemporary with James, captures Stevens's priorities when he describes the utilitarian role played by God in the lives of most believers. James cites Leuba in *The Varieties of Religious Experience*:

> "The truth of the matter can be put," says Leuba, "in this way: *God is not known, he is not understood; he is used*—sometimes as meat-purveyor, sometimes as moral support, sometimes as friend, sometimes as an object of love. If he proves himself useful, the religious consciousness asks for no more than that. *Does God really exist? How does he exist? Who is he?* are so many irrelevant questions." (VRE 506–7)

Stevens makes a strikingly similar point in describing the character of the gods, in "Two or Three Ideas":

> [T]he celestial atmosphere of these deities, their ultimate remote celestial residences are not matters of chance. Their fundamental glory is the fundamental glory of men and women, who . . . elevate it, *without too much searching of its identity.* (OP 261)

If Stevens's policy of allowing the muse to remain anonymous, of asking no "irrelevant questions" about her identity, reflects his understanding of how divinities function in human life, it also releases him from a time-consuming and ultimately futile investigation. It is a policy comparable, once again, to Crispin's decision, after a frustrating quest, to abandon his obsession with determining what is "counterfeit" and what is not. One of the poems that best captures what the "ask no questions" policy can mean in a man's life is "Le Monocle de Mon Oncle." At the beginning of this poem, the middle-aged protagonist finds himself in a state of paralysis about the mysticism of both inspiration and love, unable to decide which of two conflicting attitudes toward his muse he should heed. He is filled at once with a distrust of her genuineness (a skepticism that "bursts" her "watery syllable") and also with an overwhelming will to believe in her or "to make believe a starry *connaissance*" [CP 13]). In the following stanzas, where he turns to the example of history's many other poets and lovers, he finds that their trust in their muses has invariably been misplaced; figured as barbers they have sought to impose their vision of order on the world, and it has proved mere fashion—the "braids" of "Utamaro's beauties," "the mountainous coiffures of Bath." "Have all the barbers lived in vain," he asks, "that not one curl in nature has survived?" (CP 14).[90] But this disillusionment is displaced by the speaker's need to discover something that justifies such faith, to know that all acts of loving and believing have not been "for nothing" (CP 14). And by the end of the poem, he appears to have reached the Jamesian conclusion that the potential unreliability of muses—the possibility that they and their messages are constructed by the desires of those who apprehend them—is not enough to justify renouncing them, given the comfort and hope they bring. The mystical "star" he worshipped when young has turned out to have all the constancy of a "firefly" (CP 15) and the muse's truths have been only ephemeral, "fluttering" things, yet he is still prepared to entertain her, to continue his pursuit of "the origin and course of love" (CP 18). The reasoning behind the speaker's pragmatic acceptance makes the poem a powerful advertisement for pragmatism as the philosophy of midlife crisis. The speaker adopts this approach at that liminal point in life when experience has brought him a degree of skepticism but when enough time still remains that he feels an urgency to make the most of it. An unalloyed confidence in the muse is the privilege of "fiery boys" (CP 14); a willingness to entertain her because, and insofar as, she is useful, is the chastened but enduring "faith of forty" (CP 16).[91]

The famous apostrophe that opens "Notes Toward a Supreme Fiction" provides a final example of Stevens's propensity for effacing his muse:

> And for what, except for you, do I feel love?
> Do I press the extremest book of the wisest man
> Close to me, hidden in me day and night?
> In the uncertain light of single, certain truth,
> Equal in living changingness to the light
> In which I meet you, in which we sit at rest,

> For a moment in the central of our being,
> The vivid transparence that you bring is peace.
>
> (CP 380)

Readers who know "Notes" only by the text of the *Collected Poems* have tended to identify the muse addressed here with the friend to whom Stevens dedicates the poem: Henry Church. This reading depends on the dedication's appearing immediately after the title and before the apostrophe; it is more than slightly compromised by Stevens's wish (respected in *Transport to Summer* but not subsequently) that the dedication appear *before* the title, precisely to "*dissociate* [the apostrophe] from Mr. Church."[92] When we consider the opening of "Notes" in the context of Stevens's other apostrophes to the muse, however, it becomes apparent that the important thing is not the identity of the muse but the fact that it is given no clear identity at all. This being could be anyone or anything that seems other than the subject, so long as it seems at this moment to become one with him; addressed as "*you*" it moves to a place "in the central of *our* being." You is a pronoun without an antecendent, a blank place-holder: anyone. In this sense, the ambiguity that made it *possible* to identify the muse with Church is significant. To put it differently, this muse is a liminal creature, ungendered, neither fiction nor fact, the light in which it appears neither "uncertain" nor "certain." Thus, it reflects the advice the virile young ephebe receives in the opening cantos: like the "first idea" that inspires him (and like Pound's "Image" or Ribot's *conception idéale*), it is neither traced to the subject's "inventing mind as source" nor identified with a "voluminous master folded in his fire" (CP 381). The speaker's decision, finally, to embrace the muse is clearly the result of the same kind of world-weary pragmatism that motivates the speaker in "Monocle." From the muted declaration of love in the apostrophe's first line, we know that we are not in the presence of an unbridled passion; the speaker entertains his muse not out of some all-consuming devotion but because that figure is the *only* thing toward which he feels love. He makes it clear, furthermore, that he is not about to use superlatives to describe the wisdom this muse communicates—the implied answer to his second rhetorical question is negative. In the end he embraces the muse simply because he is conscious of the value of her (or his) effect: a perfect, even if only passing, "peace."

DOUBLE GESTURES: STEVENS AND SEXISM

Stevens's faceless muses have drawn harsh criticism from feminist critics. Writing in the tradition of Simone de Beauvoir, Sandra Gilbert and Susan Gubar have suggested that such figures, wherever they appear in poetry

written by men, are captives subjugated by the colonizing force of the penis/
pen.[93] For Gilbert and Gubar, these nameless women have been reduced to
"ciphers," vacancies defined only by the male desires they service; they
deserve to be met with the same indignation the eighteenth-century poet
Anne Finch expressed when contemplating all the women who have played
the role of subservient helpmates in male creative activity:

> Happy you three! happy the Race of Men!
> Born to inform or to correct the Pen
> To proffits pleasures freedom and command
> Whilst we beside you but as Cyphers stand
> T'increase your Numbers and to swell th'account
>
> Of your delights which from our charms amount
> That since the Fall (by our seducement wrought)
> Ours is the greater losse as ours the greater fault.[94]

Similarly though it is by no means her final judgment of Stevens, Jacqueline
Brogan notes the disturbing way in which women in Stevens's poetry become "empty ciphers for masculine rumination and scripting," figures con-
cealed "behind a phallocentric and concomitantly erotic perspective." And
in a brilliant analysis of "Peter Quince at the Clavier," Mary Nyquist
characterizes the figure of Susanna as a "floating signifier" for lascivious
elders and self-serving speaker alike. When Gilbert and Gubar consider
Stevens's case, they cite the dialogue between the virile young poet and the
"Sister of the Minotaur" as symptomatic of a concerted effort to recuperate
and retrench "the heavy fact of male literary authority."[95]

Read as female figures positioned in relation to male speakers, Stevens's
faceless women resemble pornographic mistresses, performing exactly as
their men desire. The relationship of domination and subordination typi-
fying these acts of communion is starkly captured by the speaker's fantasy
in the early poem "Two Figures in Dense Violet Light":

> Be the voice of night and Florida in my ear.
> Use dusky words and dusky images.
> Darken your speech.
>
> Speak, even, as if I did not hear you speaking,
> But spoke for you perfectly in my thoughts,
> Conceiving words,
>
> As the night conceives the sea-sounds in silence,
> And out of their droning sibilants makes
> A serenade.

(CP 86)

To read passages like this one as evidence of a thoroughgoing retrenchment of masculine authority, however, would be greatly to oversimplify their significance. In Foucauldian terms, it would be to acknowledge only one of the "orders of knowledge" to which they belong. For it mustn't be forgotten that Stevens's faceless figures are not just *women* but *muses:* representations of the source of poetic knowledge and measures of poetic authority. Mary Arensberg stresses their function in both discourses:

> Art and *eros* is a combination which has certainly contributed to the male (and female) poets' creation of an inner muse, but the paramour functions in the poetic process as *much more* than a therapeutic substitute for erotic desire or as a vehicle of sublimation. She is the ancient voice of the oracle . . . who helps her poet discover the hidden knowledge of the world or the invisible in the visible. She is . . . the inhabitant of the inner sanctums of the poet's mind, the sybil in her cave sending messages of instruction.[96]

If we accept that the role of these subjugated figures is not just to provide erotic satisfaction but also to communicate messages that the male poet then "relates" as poetry, their subjugation takes on a far more complex meaning. The poet's representation of the muse becomes a sign of his attitude toward his insights and, by the law of reflex-action, an indicator of *how* he intends to represent these communications to others. And the policy for expression corresponding to the anonymous, obedient muse is, paradoxically, one surprisingly congenial to feminist interests.

The essence of the feminist objection to Stevens's ciphered women is that they lack independence, that Stevens has them do and say nothing that is not designed to bring fulfillment to the men who apprehend them. When we read these figures as muses, however, Stevens's decision to represent them as the puppets of masculine desire turns out, paradoxically, to be *the means by which he renounces* the right to transcendental knowledge and dogmatism—a decision feminist critics must applaud. As we have seen in the case of James and Santayana, in the discourse on inspiring divinities, a poet's or mystic's confidence in his insights *depends entirely on the autonomy* of his divinity: if it functions independently of the recipient's desire, its communications are not contaminated by the falsifications of subjective interest and can be translated into dogma. If, on the other hand, the divinity whispers in a poet's ear only what he wants to hear, he loses the right to claim disinterestedness, and so to represent his insights as the pure Truth of God. In sum the kind of independence that Gilbert and Gubar miss in Stevens's muses would only function to reinforce the "male literary authority" they also wish to see undermined. As Nietzsche puts it, in the midst of his own debate about how to define a male poet's relationship to women, the right to use a dogmatic, philosophical language goes hand in hand with allowing the sybils who float before his consciousness to keep their distance:

When a man stands in the midst of his own noise, in the midst of his own surf of plans and projects, then he is apt also to see quiet, magical beings gliding past him and to long for their happiness and seclusion: *women*. He almost thinks that his better self dwells there among the women, and that in these quiet regions even the loudest surf turns into deathly quiet, and life itself into a dream about life. Yet! Yet! Noble enthusiast, even on the most beautiful sailboat there is a lot of noise, and unfortunately much small and petty noise. The magic and the most powerful effect of women is, [in order to speak the language of the philosophers], action at a distance, *actio in distans;* but this requires first of all and above all—*distance*.[97]

It might still be objected, of course, that Stevens should not portray women as muses at all, that whatever variations his female figures play on the theme still only serve to establish male identity. But Stevens is doing so self-consciously and self-critically. In "So-and-So Reclining on her Couch," particularly, he seems to be reflecting parodically on *all* muses, deconstructing the muse as category. There and elsewhere ("To the One of Fictive Music" is another example) he *dramatizes* how the female figure is constructed as muse, how she is distanced and authorized by "invisible gestures" (CP 295) to serve the patriarchal interests of men like Mr. Pappadapoulos.

Stevens's radically empirical conception of the muse, then, while having the appearance of a macho swagger and while designed to avoid the "unmanly" preoccupations of metaphysics, costs him the traditional male authority that goes with metaphysical assurance. To commune with such a muse, as Stevens does at the beginning of "Notes Toward a Supreme Fiction," is to concede that one will not write "the extremest book of the wisest man" (CP 380). Stevens makes it clear that he is conscious of the cost of his reconstruction of the muse in "The Figure of the Youth as Virile Poet," where he represents the virility of the youth as a *new kind* of virility, displacing the traditional virility exemplified by the authoritative father-figure. While the young poet flexes his muscles before the Sister of the Minotaur, or revels in the "manly" self-reliance that is attained by substituting radical empiricism for metaphysical questioning ("*I am myself a part of what is real and it is my own speech and the strength of it, this only, that I hear or ever shall*" [NA 63]), he breaks with tradition in becoming a pluralist: "*I am the truth, since I am part of what is real, but neither more nor less than those around me* (NA 63). The difference between the traditional masculinity the ephebe rejects, and the new masculinity he celebrates, is the difference between the two kinds of virility later portrayed in "Life on a Battleship": the virility espoused by the captain of the S. S. *Masculine,* who, holding himself in possession of the "final simplification," simply "asserts and fires the guns," and that espoused by one of his shipmen, who realizes that truth is a compilation of many stories, not one.[98]

The utterances that characterize the new virility will be as different from dogmatic, patriarchal speech as Crispin's "Disguised pronunciamento" is from the "lex, / Rex and principium" (CP 36–37) he attempted to impose on a continent: they are to be offered generously to others but not coercively; the new poet sustains no illusions about either their universality or their permanence. Stevens's clearest account of the new kind of poetic truth in the "Virile Poet" essay might be drawn directly from the description of tensional truth in James's *Pragmatism:* what the poet offers is simply an apparent "agreement with reality, brought about by the imagination of a man disposed to be strongly influenced by [his] imagination, which he believes, *for a time,* to be true" (NA 54; my italics).

In assessing the apparent misogyny in Stevens's representations of cipherlike muses, therefore, it seems important to acknowledge that these muses are the means by which he casts aside other patriarchal attitudes and practices. Effacing the muse means evading the "philosophico-theoretical domination," that is for many feminist critics coterminous with the operations of the phallus.[99] It means rejecting "everything finite, definite, structured," every theory "that erects itself as perfection."[100] If there is any doubt about the vital connection between Stevens's decision to curtail the muse's independence—to draw her in from the heavens to the threshold of the self—and his recognition of the provisionality of poetic truth, it should be dispelled by the words of the liminal muse in "Angel Surrounded by Paysans," who claims direct responsibility for making his perceptions more flexible:

> . . . I am the necessary angel of earth,
> Since, *in my sight,* you see the earth again,
>
> Cleared of its stiff and stubborn, man-locked set,
> And, in my hearing, you hear its tragic drone
>
> Rise liquidly in liquid lingerings,
> Like watery words awash; like meanings said
>
> By repetitions of half-meanings.
>
>   (CP 496–97; my italics)

Guided by his muse, the ephebe is forced to acknowledge the provisionality of all those categories with which he might interpret the world, and to open himself up to its elusive, chaotic flux.

In calling for a new virility in poetry, in other words, Stevens is simultaneously and surreptitiously endorsing what he (and his critics also) regard as feminine values. He is embracing the feminine principle portrayed in early poems like "Infanta Marina" and "The Paltry Nude Starts on a Spring

Voyage," a "discontent" with accepted positions and a desire to plunge into the "brine and bellowing / Of the high interiors of the sea" (CP 5); the power of the "light feminine" later described in "Of Hartford in a Purple Light," a light that suffuses the world with a purple glow, blurring the sharp boundaries made visible by "light masculine" (CP 226–27).[101] As Mary Doyle Springer has noted, the feminine principle Stevens celebrates in such poems is remarkably similar, both in its significance and in its representations, to the feminine principle Hélène Cixous has declared to be the driving force in *écriture féminine*.[102] For Cixous feminine writing involves renouncing dogmatism for pluralism, giving up phallogocentrism for the "gift of alterability": its spirit is exemplified by the image of a heterogeneous and changing sea.[103] Cixous also shares with Stevens a vision of subversive femininity as a bird, who evades the enclosing categories of masculine dogma. For Cixous,

> Flying is woman's gesture—flying in language and making it fly. . . . It's no accident: women take after birds and robbers just as robbers take after women and birds. They (*illes*) go by, fly the coop, take pleasure in . . . dislocating things and values, breaking them all up, emptying structures, and turning propriety upside down.[104]

For Stevens in the poetry of the new virility, "the masculine myths we used to make" will become "transparenc[ies] through which the swallow weaves" (CP 518), making a mockery of their absolutist pretensions.

Thus if Stevens's new poetics begins in a fear of femininity, a fear resulting from his engenderment as an American male, it ends up incorporating what Stevens perceives to be femininity of another kind. Condemned for its association with metaphysics, femininity slips back into favor as a corrective to traditional masculine ambitions to order the world. In his entirety the virile young poet is an androgynous figure, who, though exemplifying in some ways a swaggering masculinity, at the same time feels a subversive "woman . . . at the centre of [his] heart" (CP 323). In a poem written near the end of his life, "Farewell Without a Guitar," Stevens demonstrates the effect of the subversive, feminine principle on the figure he uses as a prototype for makers of masculine affirmations: the noble rider (NA 35). The scene is late autumn:

> Spring's bright paradise has come to this.
> Now the thousand-leaved green falls to the ground.
> Farewell, my days.
>
> The thousand-leaved red
> Comes to this thunder of light
> As its autumnal terminal—

A Spanish storm,
A wide, still Aragonese,
In which the horse walks home without a rider,

Head down. The reflections and repetitions,

The blows and buffets of fresh senses
Of the rider that was,

Are a final construction.
Like glass and sun, of male reality
And of that other and her desire.

                                    (OP 125; my italics)

Throughout Stevens, autumn is the season that signifies the end of belief—
the death of the optimistic "credences" of summer.[105] If the noble rider's
journey was a manly assertion, his horse's lonely return home is the effect
of the efforts of a female "other" to cast doubt on that assertion, to prevent
it from assuming a timeless, transcendental place in the "circumambient
gas."

As there were philosophical precedents for Stevens's suspicion of the
feminine, so there were precedents for his practice of welcoming it in a new
guise. One of these, interestingly enough, is found in James's *Pragmatism*.
Having displayed impatience with the "feminine-mystical" mind and extolled the virtues of the empirically minded "Rocky-Mountain tough,"
James takes the curious step of emphasizing pragmatism's likeness to a
woman. In terms anticipating Stevens's in "Angel Surrounded by Paysans,"
he writes that pragmatism

> "unstiffens" our theories. She has in fact no prejudices whatever, no obstructive
> dogmas, no rigid canons of what shall count as proof. She is completely genial.
> She will entertain any hypothesis, she will consider any evidence. . . . Her only
> test of probable truth is what works best in the way of leading us, what fits every
> part of life best and combines with the collectivity of experience's demands,
> nothing being omitted.[106]

Again we see the subversive element in the theory-making process, the
enemy of dogmatism, the open-minded, if demanding, champion of pluralism, represented as a feminine principle—as if the male pragmatist felt
the need to distinguish, once again, his "tough-minded," antimetaphysical
approach to the world from the old masculinity of the dogmatic patriarch.
A similarly unexpected, but explicable, reinsertion of feminine values into
the creative process can be found in Nietzsche. As Derrida has argued
in *Spurs*, Nietzsche's writings combine a virulent misogyny with several
"apparently feminist" propositions, not the least of which is a profound

assault on the truths that find expression in writing.[107] Nietzsche may deride the "feminine" passivity of mysticism, and even speak out passionately against a certain kind of "feminism," but he also appreciates, and aspires to incorporate into his own style, a skepticism he believes to be the quintessence of femininity.[108] The "feminine operation" on truth that Nietzsche celebrates is one that honors the epochal suspension demanded by radical empiricism and phenomenology: one that suspends all assertions "between the tenter-hooks of quotation marks."[109]

Derrida's discussion of Nietzsche is useful, not just in pointing out a precedent for Stevens's unexpected union of misogyny and feminine flexibility but also for providing a name for the kind of rhetorical gesture, common in Stevens, that weds such apparently incompatible attitudes: the "spurring" operation. As Derrida defines it, two features distinguish such an operation. It is an *apotropaic* gesture designed to intercept hostility, a "pointed object" like a quill, a prow, or a phallus, "surging ahead" to meet an anticipated enemy attack.[110] It is also what Derrida calls elsewhere a "*double* gesture," an ironic assertion communicating a message at odds with the one implied by its aggressive surface.[111] It is as spurring operations I would argue, that Stevens's most offensive displays of virility can be understood. Muscle-flexing gestures like the subjugation of the muse or the virile young poet's declaration of self-sufficiency are his way of satisfying the forces of his own engenderment, at the same time as he pursues work that is fundamentally at odds with them.[112]

Of the many examples that might be drawn from Stevens's work to demonstrate the double gestures implicit in his virile poses, none offers so fitting a conclusion to a discussion of Stevens's attitudes to gender and poetic inspiration as Canto X of "Le Monocle de Mon Oncle." This canto provides a wonderfully condensed summary of the moves by which Stevens retreats from the mystical model of inspiration. It begins by denying any access to what James and Pound, in similar moves, had called "the integral forest with all its . . . moonlight witcheries and wonders" and the "arbour" of a "traditional paradiso":[113]

> The fops of fancy in their poems leave
> Memorabilia of the mystic spouts,
> Spontaneously watering their gritty soils.
> I am a yeoman, as such fellows go,
> I know no magic trees, no balmy boughs,
> No silver-ruddy, gold-vermilion fruits.

Having dissociated himself from the foppish ways of those who have posed as passive conduits for mystic muses, the speaker goes on to boast of another kind of experience, one that affirms a kind of masculinity the "fops" lack. The grove of magic trees gives way to a single, unmistakeably phallic one:

> But, after all, I know a tree that bears
> A semblance to the thing I have in mind.
> It stands gigantic, with a certain tip
> To which all birds come sometime in their time.
> But when they go that tip still tips the tree.
>
> (CP 17)

This is the pose of self-reliance, the mask of a man boasting that his mighty penis will survive the departure of the many "birds" who are attracted to it. But from behind this portrait of swaggering machismo there glimmers a familiar pentimento. The "birds" here are not just the women—the lovers and muses—who find it impossible to resist the speaker's masculinity. As the case of the subversive "swallow" has attested, they are also examples of Stevens's favorite symbol for the restless, truth-seeking consciousness; like James in *The Principles of Psychology*, Stevens envisions the life of the mind as a "bird's life," an "alternation of flights and perchings" (PP 1: 236).[114] And in this context the speaker *identifies* with the birds. He is the one whose mind has chosen to visit this tree, instead of the mystical arbors favored by the "fops of fancy"; the tree, for its part, marks the spot where the mind relaxes into a sense of understanding, until it is overcome with doubt and flies on. The most significant thing we learn about the mind's resting-place, moreover, this perch that marks only a "semblance" to the speaker's ideal, is that whatever insight it offers the questing mind resists transport. The reality it represents remains just outside of the speaker's grasp. Having perhaps touched it he can neither appropriate it, nor translate it into any kind of dogma.[115]

As a seeker of truth, then, the speaker in Canto X of "Le Monocle" fails to achieve his highest goal. And however macho the pose he strikes, his virility, insofar as it is bound up with a sense of authority, is seriously undermined. His fate dovetails neatly with those of at least two of the many other questing birds to be found in Stevens's poetry, whose positions may be aligned with that of the virile young poet Stevens idealizes. The speaker of "Credences of Summer" orders his "cock bright," for example, to pause for a moment on a similar kind of perch:

> Fly low, cock bright, and stop on a bean pole. Let
> Your brown breast redden, while you wait for warmth . . .

The cock's breast "reddens" (in bird-code, becomes male),[116] as the questing mind warms into certainty. But whatever comprehending vision the bird attains from this "point of survey," it rapidly "falls apart" (CP

373, 377); the old perch must be abandoned in favor of a new destination, and the insight gleaned there cannot be transported. As Stevens depicts the course of another, complementary bird in "Esthétique du Mal,"

> The bird
> In the brightest landscape downwardly revolves
> *Disdaining* each astringent ripening,
> *Evading* the point of redness, not content
> To repose . . .

(CP 381; my italics)

As chapter 4 will show, the evasion of redness and rest demanded by a faceless muse is the cardinal principle of Stevens's poetics.

4

Stevens's Pragmatism: The Poetics of Hypothesis

STEVENS'S instructions to the ephebe in the "Noble Rider" and "Virile Poet" essays and elsewhere suggest that he is committed to the reflex-action model of expressionist theory. How the virile young poet is to express himself is a direct consequence of decisions made in the theoretical shadow-space between inspiration and creation—a direct reflection of Stevens's decision about how to figure the muse. It remains, however, to determine how true Stevens is to these prescriptions in his own poetry. Do his own poems consistently reflect the conception of a muse who "floats in the contention" between reality and illusion? Do the assertions he makes there dutifully observe the disavowal of metaphysics so central to his conception of the new masculinity?

The answer is yes and in a very precise way. First, Stevens develops a number of expressive strategies that place the authority of his utterances under suspension. Like Pound's "Serious Artist," he writes poems that advertise their status as records of states of consciousness only, as accounts of nothing more and nothing less than "that which appears as truth to a certain sort of mind under certain conditions."[1] Second, he fully appreciates the implications of the muse's liminality for preserving the possibility of genuine enlightenment. If he concedes that every proposition is an uncertainty, he also shares James's view that uncertainty is insufficient reason for giving up on the possibility of being right and its attendant responsibilities. Indeed, resisting epistemological and other pessimisms is for him, as for James, both an ethical and political imperative. The upshot of this is that Stevens is not the quintessential "fiction-maker" he is generally perceived to be, but a poet of "hypothesis"—a poet who believes, with James, Hulme, and Pound, that the poet's utterances should be accountable to the empirical world.

EPOCHAL SPACES

One of Stevens's most distinctive expressive strategies could have been inspired by a challenge issued by T. E. Hulme in one of his more cryptic "Cinders":

Space.
I. Admitted the pragmatic criterion of any analogy that makes for clearness.
II. Now *space* is essential to clearness. A developed notion, perhaps, but now essential.
III. The idealists analyse space into a mode of arranging sensations. But this gives us an unimaginable world existing all at a point.
IV. Why not try the reverse process and put all ideas (purely mental states) into terms of *space* (cf. landscape thinking)? (CW 19)

Like a true pragmatist, Hulme takes exception to Idealism's dogmatic reduction of the idea of space. Like a true pragmatist, too, he attempts to counter that reduction by attempting to establish the use to which that beleaguered idea might be put. And the suggestion he comes up with is one of interest, potentially, to any expressionist artist: Why not use representations of space as objective correlatives for states of consciousness? Hulme would have been gratified by the evidence for the efficacy of his suggestion collected in Bachelard's *Poetics of Space,* a compendium of "the human value[s]" poets have found in different "sorts of space."[2] He would also have been intrigued by the fundamental role played by "landscape thinking" in the poetry of Stevens, to which Bachelard's study provides a suggestive gloss. For there is no doubt that, in the words of the "Latest Freed Man," Stevens's poetic landscapes have "doctrinal" significance (CP 204). We are justified in reading the "simplified geography" (CP 334) of his verse, in all its variations, as a metaphor for changing states of mind.[3]

When he meditates on the combinations of land, sea, and sky that appear in his poetry, Stevens is adamant that these are not to be confused with real landscapes, immediately perceived. If Stevens knew nothing of Hulme's directive, he certainly knew, and evidently took to heart, the mandate Santayana delivered to poetry in *Interpretations of Poetry and Religion:*

The visible landscape is not a proper object for poetry. Its elements, and especially the emotional stimulation it gives, may be suggested or expressed in verse; but landscape is not thereby represented in its proper form; it appears only as an element and associate of moral unities. Painting, architecture, and gardening, with their art of stage setting, have the visible landscape for their object, and to these arts we may leave it. *But there is a sort of landscape larger than the visible, which escapes the synthesis of the eye; it is present to that topographical sense by which we always live in the consciousness that there is a sea, that there are mountains, that the sky is above us, even when we do not see it. . . . This cosmic landscape poetry alone can render,* and it is no small part of the art to awaken the sense of it at the right moment, so that the object that occupies the centre of vision may be seen in its true lights, coloured by its wider associations, and dignified by its felt affinities to things permanent or great.[4]

ιasizes that each of his poetic spaces is a "landscape *of the*
ι5), "less place than *thought of* place" (CP 433; my italics).
ιs the mind creates, rather than places that shape the mind,
ριaces meant to express the mind, rather than to mirror an outer
world. They are the equivalents, in poetry, of Cézanne's or Chagall's Post-
Impressionist landscapes.[5]

The expressive spaces a poet uses, of course, will depend on how he
interprets the states of mind that demand expressing. Optimistic writers
believing their epiphanic moments to be insights into Truth, for example,
have frequently reached for images of infinity. As Mircea Eliade explains,
"The regions above man's reach," "the starry places," have been habitually
"invested with the divine majesty of the *transcendent,* of *absolute reality.*"[6]
Given the apparent affinity between images of extensity and an extreme
degree of certainty, it is significant and appropriate that Stevens consistently
calls attention not to the boundless sweep of his poetic spaces but to their
boundaries, borderlines, and horizons. This practice is the first of several
expressive techniques that fulfill his commitment to qualifying, or suspending judgment about, feelings of conviction. Though it is perfectly in
keeping with Hulme's "new classical" values, this practice is less likely to
have been inspired by Hulme than by Santayana, whose *The Sense of
Beauty* was in many ways proleptic of Imagist manifestos. In this treatise,
Santayana's appeal to the reader to value the humble edifice of nature (also
eloquently articulated, as we have seen, in *Interpretations of Poetry and
Religion*) takes the form of a directive to artists to draw their expressive
materials exclusively from images of the empirical world—what Hulme
called the world of small, dry things. Santayana describes his mission as a
reaction against "romanticism": having subjected creative inspiration to a
phenomenological reduction, he disparages the romantic habit of expressing it with references to "infinite" perfections.[7]

Stevens expresses his commitment to renouncing the language of infini-
tude in a poem from *Ideas of Order* called "Academic Discourse at Ha-
vana"—a poem that might serve as an Imagist manifesto. The Symbolist
swans, it tells us, are dead, and gone with them are all the poet's aspirations
to be a seer of celestial mysteries:

> Grandmother and her basketful of pears
> Must be the crux for our compendia.
> That's world enough and more, if one includes
> Her daughters to the peached and ivory wench
> For whom the towers are built. *The burgher's breast,
> And not a delicate ether star-impaled,
> Must be the place for prodigy.* . . .

> (CP 143–44; my italics)

Stevens reiterates this view in "A Collect of Philosophy" when he expresses his sympathy with Victor Hugo's remark that "the stars are no longer mentionable in poetry" (OP 268). On the rare occasion when he admits the night-sky as a subject, he is careful to strip it of its traditional associations with timeless, mystical realities. Like Hulme, who sought to demystify the delicate ether by likening it to a moth-eaten blanket, Stevens subjects the stars to what Geoffrey Hartman has called "descendental" transformations.[8] Rejecting metaphors that suggest the stars' participation in a timeless, monistic Absolute—the figure, for example, of pendants hanging in strict formation around a "German chandelier" (CP 172)—he instead employs figures that emphasize the stars' autonomy, plurality, and containment within the world of time. Once conceived as bodies moving together "as one," the stars "disband" and start to fly "like insects of fire in a cavern of night" (CP 230).[9] Instead of symbolizing the souls of the dead, they are linked (in a simile uncannily similar to that in Hulme's "Autumn") with the faces of those who gaze at them and who construct their significance:

> Tonight the stars are like a crowd of faces
> Moving round the sky and singing
> And laughing, a crowd of men,
> Whose singing is a mode of laughter,
>
> Never angels, nothing of the dead,
> Faces to people night's brilliancy,
> Laughing and singing and being happy,
> Filling the imagination's need.
>
> (CP 218)[10]

In dualist conceptions of the world, which would divide it into "One part . . . man, the other god" (CP 218), the stars may play the role of fissures between the phenomenal and noumenal realms. Stevens's descendental transformations seek to *close* these fissures and to convert the night-sky from an interface between two realities into the horizon of a singular, self-sufficient one. Although he anticipates this position in "Sunday Morning," when he rejects the interpretation of the sky as a "dividing and indifferent blue" (CP 68), his clearest objection to the philosophy that makes the sky a veil and the star sites of its "penetration" is in a poem in *Transport to Summer* called "Crude Foyer." There he asserts that the "landscape of the mind / Is a landscape only of the eye": there is no nook beyond it in which, at the end of all questing, one might "sit and breathe / An innocence of an absolute." The only moment of peace a poet contemplating the sky will know is to be found in realizing that there is nothing to be sought beyond it, in accepting that the mystical *there* "turns out to be *here*" (CP 305; my italics).

But the landscape to which Stevens would confine his poet is not just a space below the arch of the sky. It is also a space above the ground, as detached from those metaphysical associations that cling to earth and sea as it is severed from the mysteries of heaven. As we have seen in "Sea Surface Full of Clouds," Stevens associates the lower stratum of space with the desiring, prejudicial self. Having concluded that the origin of imaginative insights is undecidable, he favors an ambiguous realm that mingles subjective sea and objective sky. Similar synthetic images appear on occasion in the later poetry.[11] Another one of Stevens's methods of communicating the sense that his intuitions are neither true nor false is to emphasize the *middleness* of his expressive landscapes. If ascending beyond the sky denotes a contact with absolute truth and descending below the ground a sinking into solipsism, hovering *in between* these "two poles" (CP 197) avoids what James called "the two opposite dangers of believing too little [and] of believing too much" (WB 7).[12] But the appeal of middle spaces is equalled by the difficulty of attaining them, as Stevens suggests in "The Ultimate Poem Is Abstract":

> It would be enough
> If we were ever, just once, at the middle, fixed
> In This Beautiful World Of Ours and not as now,
>
> Helplessly at the edge, enough to be
> Complete, because at the middle, if only in sense,
> And in that enormous sense, merely enjoy.
>
> (CP 430)

The major obstacle to reaching this middle state—as the parables of "Comedian" and "Sea Surface" foretell—is the impulse to divisive, metaphysical questioning. Stevens muses in "Like Decorations in a Nigger Cemetery":

> Under the mat of frost and over the mat of clouds.
> But in between lies the sphere of my fortune
> And the fortunes of frost and of clouds,
> All alike, except for the rules of the rabbis,
> Happy men, distinguishing frost and clouds.
>
> (CP 151)

The state of middleness is attainable only when we choose to adopt the habits of mind of rabbits, not rabbis—as Stevens affirms in his poem "A Rabbit as King of the Ghosts." Like Hulme who knew that looking at the world with the eyes of an animal meant "leaving out 'Truth', etc." (CW 14), Stevens knows that there is grounds for celebration in a rabbit's state of mind: a state that is all acceptance and no questioning, in which all consideration of the validity of what one believes ceases, "and nothing need be explained."[13] The self-centered creature in "A Rabbit as King of the Ghosts" imagines himself inhabiting a space that "touches all [the] edges" (CP 209) of the world, but, significantly, that stops short of penetrating them. Neither objective nor subjective, this "third world without knowledge" (CP 323) is the same space occupied by Stevens's "Latest Freed Man," the happy character who, "having just / Escaped from the truth," eschews what lies below or beyond his perceptual field, enjoying only the changing weather conditions that fill it. His contented consciousness dwells at the center of reality, simply enjoying its "color and mist" like some kind of "ox" (CP 204–5).

Stevens's middle spaces, then, are the correlatives of his decision to suspend his muses "in the contention" between reality and illusion. They are tropes for a consciousness whose every insight is subject to phenomenological reduction, the origin of these insights certainly being neither the voice of "earth" nor the voice of "ether" (CP 177). As the settings for the "outlines of being and its expressings" (CP 424), these spaces correspond to what James called the self-containing space of consciousness entertained by radical empiricism (ERE 99). They correspond, too, to the space Husserl, following James's lead, used to figure the consciousness:

Consciousness, considered in its "purity," must be reckoned as a *self-contained system of Being*, as a system of *Absolute Being*, into which nothing can penetrate, and from which nothing can escape; which has no spatio-temporal exterior, and can be inside no spatio-temporal system; which cannot experience causality from anything nor exert causality upon anything, it being presupposed that casuality [sic] bears the normal sense of natural causality as a relation of dependence between realities.[14]

As if to stress the lack of interaction between phenomenologically reduced experience and the outer world—the consequence of suspending judgment about their origins—Stevens frequently represents his middle spaces as being confined within glasses or jars. The bottle in "The Indigo Glass in the Grass" (OP 42–43), the glass standing "in the centre" between metaphysical "poles," in "The Glass of Water" (CP 198), the jar confining the birds in "Looking Across the Fields and Watching the Birds Fly" (CP 519), and many other similar vessels are containers that neutralize the significance of whatever takes place inside of them—specimen jars for the scientifically detached "Serious Artist."[15]

The dominant figure of containment in Stevens's poetry, however, is one that might have been inspired by James's and Husserl's successor, Heidegger. Husserl's student attached great significance to the etymological link between the word "to be" and the word "to dwell."[16] He represented the state in which one suspends all metaphysical questioning as a state of dwelling within a bounded space—within the walls of what he called the "house of Being."[17] There is no hard evidence that Stevens knew anything of Heidegger until after publishing *The Rock*, if even then, but the word dwelling plays a comparable role for him throughout his career.[18] Whether he is describing the condition of the "dweller in the dark cabin" in "Hymn from a Watermelon Pavilion" (CP 88), or of the scholar "separately dwelling" in "Somnambulisma" (CP 304), or of the speaker enjoying a "dwelling" with his "Interior Paramour" (CP 524), Stevens portrays these figures as occupying a "simple space" where all "[metaphysical] thinking [has been] blown away" (CP 153).[19] Cozy "homes" and "hermitages" abound in the poetry, all places whose inhabitants have let go of their anxiety to determine the ultimate validity of what they perceive and believe. The cabin Crispin retreats to is such a place; it is by relinquishing metaphysical thinking, with all of its hopes and disappointments, that he becomes "magister of a single room" (CP 42). The mental "Misericordia" Stevens imagines in "An Ordinary Evening in New Haven" (CP 485) is such a place; as Harold Bloom has observed, the one space in a monastery where strict rules are suspended is an apt image for a place of release "from the anxieties of seeking to determine the division between real and unreal."[20] Stevens's decision to describe one typical inhabitant of an epochal space as "The Latest *Freed* Man (CP 204) underscores the paradoxical nature of being confined within its boundaries: to be so enclosed is to be released from habits of thought that are far more confining. In Bachelard's terms, to find shelter in an epochal space is to return to "the bosom of the house" one enjoys in childhood, to be free once again from the anxieties introduced by "conscious metaphysics."[21] Or as Heidegger describes the condition: "To dwell, to be set at peace, means to remain at peace within the free, the preserve, the free sphere that safeguards each thing in its essence."[22]

Doxic Dramas

But what about what goes on *within* these confined spaces? Heidegger regarded the house of Being as a stage for the ongoing dramas of cognition, its boundary "not that at which something stops" so much as "that from which something begins its essential unfolding."[23] Stevens, similarly, treats his bounded spaces as "Theatre[s] / Of Trope" (CP 397), in which the correlatives of cognitive action—images of light, birds, and buildings—are in constant flux. The typical epochal space in Stevens's poetry is a "place of perpetual undulation" (CP 60). The light that fills it is constantly shifting; the birds that inhabit it cannot settle for long on their perches; and the buildings erected within it are constantly rising or falling into rubble.

Like comparable, unstable images in Heidegger, as well as in Santayana, James, and Husserl, these images are Stevens's means of capturing the "restless iteration" of thought (CP 60). Technically, that is, they capture changes in what James called the "psychic attitude" the mind adopts toward propositions (PP II, 917) or in what Husserl called the range of "doxic modalities":[24] the varying shades of belief and doubt a mind may direct toward whatever perceptual or conceptual matter is at hand. Stevens directs us to look for such motion in his poetry and to interpret it as signifying shifting attitudes in "The Irrational Element in Poetry," where he emphasizes that it is the "poetry of the subject," the "attitude" or "bearing" a writer assumes toward a particular subject-matter, that is "paramount" in his poetry (OP 226–27).[25]

Husserl outlines the range of doxic possibilities in *Ideas*. In any consciousness, he observes,

> The way of "*certain*" *belief* can pass over into that of *suggestion* or *presumption*, or into that of *question* and *doubt*; and, according to the line taken, that which appears . . . will adopt the *ontical modalities* of the "*possible*," the "*probable*," the "*questionable*," and the "*doubtful*" respectively.[26]

To trace the fluctuations of Stevens's recurring images is to encounter the full range of degrees of belief and doubt Husserl describes. It is to discover the fittedness, therefore, of these dramas to the demands of his liminal muse, who authorizes no stable conviction, only uncertainty. Perhaps most interestingly, it is to discover something about the *stubbornness* of Stevens's commitment to this muse and to the state of epochal suspension it demands. For at its most extreme, the need to believe can exert enormous pressure on the detached, avowedly uncommitted attitude of the "Serious Artist." It can tempt him to accept a metaphysical foundation for the perception or proposition he contemplates, to affirm its absolute truth, and so to violate the borders of the *epoche*. But in the majority of the analogous cases posed by Stevens's light, birds, and houses, the boundaries that reduce the perceptions, ensuring their uncertain status as knowledge, put up remarkable resistance to such pressure. In his use of space, Stevens remains faithful to his liminal muse.

The first significant indicator of Stevens's doxic attitudes is the light that fills his bounded spaces. In its general character, the kind of light he chooses is in keeping with specifications Hulme made for the new classicist. Inverting what he saw as the preferences of Wordsworth, Hulme dictated that the kind of light that should infiltrate poetry is "always the light of ordinary day, never the light that never was on land or sea" (CW 66).[27] Heidegger provides a compelling etymological explanation for Hulme's concern in *Being and Time*, when he points out that *phaino* (the root of the "phenomenon" in phenomenological reduction) means "to bring to the light of day."[28] If a space is to express a cognitive act that has been subjected to epochal suspension, it is only appropriate that it should reject images of light that imply divine sanction, images like Shelley's "white radiance of Eternity" or Yeats's "spiritual flame."[29] Stevens reveals his own commitment to restricting himself to the light of common day in "Sunday Morning," when he displays his company of virile empiricists performing their ritual dance in brilliant sunlight. The members of the audience in "The Man with the Blue Guitar" reinforce the point when they, in arguing for a phenomenological poetics, flex their collective muscle and proclaim that "we are men of sun / And men of day and never of pointed night" (CP 137).

But the daylight flooding Stevens's expressive spaces does more than simply reaffirm his rejection of the "unmanly" concerns of metaphysics; it is also a sensitive gauge of the degree of faith he is willing to attach to whatever subject is at hand. Once again, Husserl's adaptation of a Jamesian principle is useful for understanding the laws that govern Stevens's epochal spaces. Like James in *The Principles of Psychology* and *The Varieties of Religious Experience,* Husserl uses light as a figure for conscious awareness. In an elaborate development of the figure, he uses the image of an illuminating "ray" or "cone" to concretize an act of "attention": an experience of entertaining a proposition as a possibility. A proposition that falls into "half-shadow" and then "full darkness," accordingly, is one gradually fading from the mind's agenda, losing all plausibility.[30] As James described the phenomenon in the life of a mystic, "the believer alternates between warmth and coldness in his faith" as his "sense of the real presence of objects fluctuates" (VRE 64). Stevens, similarly, correlates the degrees of certainty that attend propositions with differing intensities of light and warmth, hitching doxic attitudes to the cycles of light and darkness, warmth and coolness, that mark the days and the seasons. In his scheme it is late summer that brings a feeling of cognitive satisfaction: "the brilliant mercy of a sure repose. . . . Things certain sustaining us in certainty" (CP 375). The "[c]redences of [s]ummer" (CP 372) correspond to a surge of intellectual activity, a riot of efforts to discover the resemblances in things.[31] When the season turns to winter, and the way of certain belief passes over into doubt, the cold is so extreme that none of these intellectual constructs— these brilliant products of "venereal soil" (CP 47)—survive. The light of attention goes out, lacking any ideas or propositions that need attending.

Stevens summarizes the course of the "seasons of belief" (CP 255) in a late portrait of that quintessential "symbol of the seeker," Ulysses:

> His mind presents the world
> And in his mind the world revolves.
> The revolutions through day and night,

Through wild spaces of other suns and moons,
Round summer and angular winter and winds,
Are matched by other revolutions
In which the world goes round and round
In the crystal atmospheres of the mind,
Light's comedies, dark's tragedies,
Like things produced by a climate, the world
Goes round in the climates of the mind
And bears its floraisons of imagery.

(OP 129)

In linking doxic modalities with the turning of the days and years, Stevens is able to emphasize a point that is crucial to his overall conception of truth-making: Faith dies but is always reborn, and the death of one idea is always followed by the birth of another. As surely as summer is lost, it comes again; as surely as one theory dies, and a feeling of belief with it, another theory, and a renewed faith, arise to take its place. Stevens equates the resurgence of theory-hope with the resurgence of a masculine will. In "Puella Parvula," for example, a poem that contains the most brutal of appeals to a subservient muse, we encounter a speaker longing for something new to believe after "every thread of summer" has been "unwoven." He finds an outlet for this desire by ordering a "wild bitch" to be "what he tells [her] to be" (CP 456), that is, to inspire him again with truths that answer his needs.

The lure of extreme certainty signified by the intense light and heat of late summer threatens Steven's commitment to equivocation. But he is vigilant in preventing his records of certainty from becoming claims for knowledge. His major effort to this end is to cast doubt on the *source* of the light and warmth that makes August the season of cognitive contentment. He consistently uses the sun to signify absolute reality or essential truth. In his heliotropic spaces, it is at the moment when the "furiously burning father-fire" is closest—summer's "perihelion" (CP 365, 490)—that cognitive desires "no longer move," bringing a sense of genuine revelation.[32] He avoids crediting such moments of illumination with mystical significance, however, by relentlessly suspending judgment about whether the perceived sun is actual or imagined. In other words, to avoid implying that a feeling of illumination amounts to a genuine illumination, he maintains a perspective on the sun identical to that recommended to the aspiring young poet in "Notes Toward a Supreme Fiction." As the ephebe's teacher puts it:

You must become an ignorant man again
And see the sun clearly with an ignorant eye
And see it clearly in the idea of it.

Never suppose an inventing mind as source
Of this idea nor for that mind compose
A voluminous master folded in his fire.

(CP 380–81; my italics)

Stevens uses a number of techniques to ensure that the origin of the summer sun and the authority of the truths believed in its presence remain unknown. One common device in this effort is that favorite figure of radical empiricists: personification. In at least two of his representations of high summer, the sun assumes the character of its perceiver, thus losing any appearance of pure objectivity. Like the satisfied man who enjoys its rays, the sun "inhales his proper air, and rests" (CP 373). Like a believer facing the inevitable onset of fall, winter, and spring, it becomes restless in its contentment, desiring "[i]n a consummate prime . . . [a] further consummation" (CP 318).[33] Stevens also dramatizes what it means to accept sunshine for its own sake, without regard for its origin, in his portrait of the "Latest Freed Man." Recovering from an illness and rising from his bed, the freed man finds his dwelling filled with sunlight. But he confounds the sun with the "strong man" he feels himself becoming; it is not clear to him whether the light and strength are things "he gives" or things that come shining into his room from the outside (CP 204–5). Most important is his recognition that the matter is not worth debating: he knows that what really counts is simply that the sun and the strength are indisputable experiences, what James called sufficient, practical realities:

It was how the sun came shining into his room:
To be without a description of to be,
For a moment on rising, at the edge of the bed, to be,
To have the ant of the self changed to an ox
With its organic boomings, to be changed
From a doctor into an ox, before standing up,
To know that the change and that the ox-like struggle
Comes from the strength that is the strength of the sun,
Whether it comes directly or from the sun.
It was how he was free. It was how his freedom came.

(CP 205)[34]

The effect of "The Latest Freed Man" is to demonstrate an epiphanic moment without claiming a mystical source for, and hence endorsing, the illumination. The reduction it achieves is best appreciated by comparing it to its Symbolist intertext, Mallarmé's "Les Fenêtres." Where Mallarmé makes the windows of a sickroom fissures for Truth, openings through which transcendental reality shoots its rays, Stevens obscures the source of the edifying light: it is simply there. And the certainty it inspires is simply there with it; the revelation it seems to bring can in no way be confirmed.

As I have been suggesting, Stevens also articulates a range of doxic attitudes through the actions of flocks of restless birds, winging their way up, down, and around his middle spaces. If we regard Stevens's lighted spaces as correlatives for states of consciousness, the birds correspond to the impulse to theorize that is part of these states. Stevens is quite explicit about the correspondence: the birds in "Sunday Morning" "test the reality" of things "by their sweet questionings" (CP 68); the blackbird in "Thirteen Ways of Looking at a Blackbird (in the most understated of its thirteen transformations) is "involved in what [one] know[s]" (CP 94).[35] There appears to be a consistent correspondence, moreover, between the place a bird occupies in its undulating flight pattern and particular degrees of belief and doubt. The reader might be inclined to interpret a bird's flight upward as an ascent into absolute knowledge, its descent into a crevice as a lapse into darkest ignorance. But this would be to use a code appropriate for poetic landscapes constructed on dualistic principles, where a flight of sufficient strength and duration leads a mind to truths beyond a phenomenal veil. In Stevens's self-sufficient space, where it is simply the *feeling* of certainty and not claims about its significance that counts, another code appears to assume priority: one that reverses the connotations of soaring and settling. As I have suggested, an illuminating intertext for Stevens's conception of cognitive flights is a passage from the most famous chapter of James's *Principles of Psychology* on "The Stream of Thought." Here James depicts the watery flux of consciousness as a sanctuary for the same kind of truth-seeking bird:

> As we take, in fact, a general view of the wonderful stream of our consciousness, what strikes us first is this different pace of its parts. Like a bird's life, it seems to be made of an alternation of flights and perchings. . . . The resting-places are usually occupied by sensorial imaginations of some sort, whose peculiarity is that they can be held before the mind for an indefinite time, and contemplated without changing; the places of flight are filled with thoughts of relations, static or dynamic, that for the most part obtain between the matters contemplated in the periods of comparative rest. (PP 1: 236)

For James's bird a state of rest signals a state of cognitive satisfaction, an enjoyment of that "ease, peace, [and] rest" that constitutes the sentiment of rationality.[36] A flight upward, on the other hand, signals the bird's dissatisfaction with what it has believed; it is a quest for a better account of things than any the bird has previously formulated. If the "main use of the transitive parts" of the bird's experience is "to lead us from one substantive conclusion to another," James says, "the main end of our thinking is at all times the attainment of some other substantive part than the one from which we have just been dislodged" (PP 1: 236). In this extended metaphor, the undulation from perch to flight and perch again signals the cooperation of what he calls the "philosophic" tendency to construct and enjoy a theory and its subversive opposite. His representation of the perennially restless bird communicates the same point as the discussion of those tendencies in "The Sentiment of Rationality": the process of constructing and dismantling theories in which they cooperate is inevitable and ongoing.

Stevens was certainly familiar with the concept of the stream of thought, and might well have been inspired by James's vision of the birds who inhabit it. In the poems "Somnambulisma" and "Dry Loaf," he situates his cognitive birds in a watery realm more appropriate for fish (a realm, like that in "Sea Surface Full of Clouds," that turns sky into sea). In James's words, the birds are "like fishes swimming in the sea of sense, bounded above by the superior element, but unable to breathe it pure or penetrate it" (P 64):

> On an old shore, the vulgar ocean rolls
> Noiselessly, noiselessly, resembling a thin bird,
> That thinks of settling, yet never settles, on a nest.
>
> The wings keep spreading and yet are never wings.
> The claws keep scratching on the shale, the shallow shale,
> The sounding shallow, until by water washed away.
> The generations of the bird are all
> By water washed away. They follow after.
> They follow, follow, follow, in water washed away.
>
> (CP 304)

Like the closely related pigeons in "Sunday Morning" and their counterparts in James, this "thin bird" is caught in an "ambiguous undulation" (CP 70), a relentless shift from belief into doubt and back again. If the experiences of the other birds in Stevens's poetry are any indication, its brief moment of contact with the shale signals what it did for James's: a fleeting sense of cognitive satisfaction. When the "cock bright" (CP 373) pauses on his bean pole in "Credences of Summer," for example, the sun warms him momentarily into feeling the rationality of an otherwise chaotic garden. When a dove alights on a column in "Description without Place," his sense of satisfaction is so strong that it promises to serve as a touchstone in the future: "a sense / To which we refer" subsequent experience (CP 343). The example of the other birds suggests, too, that the "thin bird's" restless departure from his perch indicates a sudden doubt about what it has briefly believed. Driven by a subversive, feminine principle, they abandon "masculine myth[s]" (CP 518) before these myths become rigid. They fly away on "bright, discursive wings," seeking new, more satisfactory "perfections" (CP 243, 318). The final tercet in the passage from "Somnambulisma" points to the significance of the perchings and flights over time. Here, as in "The Man with the Blue Guitar" and "Extracts from Addresses to the Academy of Fine Ideas," Stevens hypostatizes the "thin bird," transforming it from an intellectual impulse into the substantive product of such an impulse: a thought (CP 165, 254). When he represents it and the countless "generations" after it being relentlessly "washed away," he adds another to the host of vivid metaphors we have now seen for processes of ongoing, revisionary thinking.

The downs and ups of Stevens's birds, then, parallel in their significance the ebbs and flows of his "seasons of belief." This parallel continues in the strategies by which Stevens suspends judgment about their questing. He is careful, first of all, to describe rather than to explain the birds' flights. Like James in *The Varieties of Religious Experience,* he records moments of extraordinary conviction while refusing to say whether the conviction is justified. All he will say about even "One's grand flights," "One's tootings at the weddings of the soul," is that they "*Occur as they occur*" (CP 222; my italics). Often, too, he refuses to portray the bird actually reaching its perch, the "palm" that "rises up beyond the sea" or looms "at the end of the mind" (CP 344; OP 118). The birds in "Auroras of Autumn," for example, are "palm-eyed / And vanishing" (CP 416). Beckoning from the other side of the self-contained landscape, the tree-tip offers a resting place, like the "foyer" already discussed, where the birds *might* finally "sit and breathe / An innocence of an absolute" (CP 305). For the birds to reach such a spot would be for them to pierce the borders of the *epoche,* to reopen one of those fissures Stevens has worked so hard to close; in Hulme's terms it would be to fly away into the "circumambient gas." Accordingly however intense their "desire to be at the end of distances" (CP 527), Stevens ensures that the palm, like the "receding shores" in "Sunday Morning" (CP 519) remains forever beyond their reach. In spatial terms this means allowing the borders of the *epoche* to spin outward, so that no matter how far the birds fly or how high their point of survey, the boundary is always farther, higher. Stevens turns the specimen jar, that is, into something endlessly expandable, hence unbreakable: "A glass aswarm with things going as far as they can" (CP 519).[37]

The most frequent images Stevens uses to figure the doxic attitudes are architectural. The buildings relevant here are to be distinguished from the cosy "dwellings" with which Stevens, like Heidegger, figures Being. They are the equivalents, instead, of the thoughts the rational part of the mind constructs *within* these dwellings or of the constructs Heidegger imagined when he claimed that "thinking *builds upon* the house of Being."[38] Stevens envisions theoretical houses springing up within the larger tenements of consciousness, "houses . . . Sounding in transparent dwellings of the self"

(CP 466). These structures arise despite the longing, articulated in "Decorations in a Nigger Cemetary," "Evening Without Angels," and elsewhere, for a "simple space" in which thought will be "blown away" (CP 153). In "Evening Without Angels," Stevens suggests that the theoretical houses have their value, despite the challenge they pose to the peace of the *epoche:*

> Bare night is best. Bare earth is best. Bare, bare,
> *Except for our own houses,* huddled low
> Beneath the arches and their spangled air,
> Beneath the rhapsodies of fire and fire,
> Where the voice that is in us makes a true response,
> Where the voice that is great within us rises up,
> As we stand gazing at the rounded moon.
>
> (CP 137–38; my italics)

That there is reason to read these secondary houses as theoretical constructs is suggested by an early poem called "Architecture," where a speaker contemplates constructing a "chastel de . . . pensée" out of crudely analyzed "blocks" of sun (OP 37–38) and by an uncharacteristically direct passage in the late poem, "The Sail of Ulysses." Here Stevens uses a strikingly Heideggerian image of the structures that begin their "unfolding" within Ulysses' lighted mind, identifying them clearly as the products of an impulse to order the phenomenal chaos:

> This is the true creator, the wavor
> Waving purpling wands, the thinker
> Thinking gold thoughts in a golden mind,
> Loftily jingled, radiant,
> The joy of meaning in design
> Wrenched out of chaos . . . The quiet lamp
> For this creator is a lamp
> Enlarging like a nocturnal ray
> The space in which it stands, the shine
> Of darkness, creating from nothingness
> Such black constructions, such public shapes
> And murky masonry. . . .
>
> (OP 127)

Whether they take the form of stolid classical "capitols" (CP 403) or of the airy arches and naves of gothic cathedrals (CP 59, 140, 293) or of simple houses erected on tropical islands (CP 393), Stevens's secondary edifices protect their inhabitants—as theories do their theorists—from the "squirming facts" (CP 215) of experience. Like Hulme, who likened "groups of ideas" to "huts for men to live in," shelters where they might hide away from the world's "cindery" expanse (CW 12), Stevens describes his buildings as places of "refuge" (CP 373, 270) from a world of "sand" (CP 215), a world as multiplex and chaotic as a rubbish dump. In Stevens's case, the figure may be inspired by James or Santayana. Both philosophers acknowledge the architectural nature of theory, particularly its capacity to offer protection from a reality that was otherwise "muddy, bewildering, painful and perplexed" (P 17–18).[39]

A theory has the power of providing shelter from the "empirical sand-heap world" (James, WB 61), however, only so long as it inspires belief. And given what Stevens's undulating seasons and birds have indicated about the fickleness of doxic attitudes, it is not surprising that his theoretical buildings are anything but stable. Typical of Stevens's secondary edifices in their unsoundness are the dubious shelters of "Auroras of Autumn": the ambiguous "capitol" that "It may be, is emerging or has just / Collapsed" and the scholar's house that is threatened by "flames" (CP 416–17). Lacking any firm, metaphysical foundation, buttressed by nothing more certain than the ambiguous "blue" of radically empirical experience, they fall into dust. Stevens's picture of their disintegration in "The Public Square" calls to mind the collapsing grids found in Vorticist cityscapes:

> A slash of angular blacks
> Like a fractured edifice
> That was buttressed by blue slants
> In a coma of the moon.
>
> A slash and the edifice fell,
> Pylon and pier fell down.
> A mountain-blue cloud arose
> Like a thing in which they fell,
>
> Fell slowly as when at night
> A languid janitor bears
> his lantern through colonnades
> And the architecture swoons.
>
> (CP 109)

In keeping with his general tendency to harmonize his codes for doxic modalities, Stevens ties the life cycle of his theoretical shelters closely to the passage of the seasons. His buildings frequently achieve their greatest stability in the season of cognitive contentment, high summer. He refers to "the enclosures of hypotheses / On which men speculated in summer when they were half asleep" (CP 516), and he titles a set of brief, provisional assertions "Blue Buildings in the Summer Air" (CP 216). The corrosion and collapse of his houses correspond to the encroachment of doubt as summer turns into fall. Witness this striking passage from "Auroras of Autumn":

> Farewell to an idea . . . A cabin stands,
> Deserted, on a beach. It is white,
> As by a custom or according to
>
> An ancestral theme or as a consequence
> Of an infinite course. The flowers against the wall
> Are white, a little dried, a kind of mark
>
> Reminding, trying to remind, of a white
> That was different, something else, last year
> Or before, not the white of an aging afternoon,
>
> Whether fresher or duller, whether of winter cloud
> Or of winter sky, from horizon to horizon.
> The wind is blowing the sand across the floor.
>
> (CP 412)

In its prime the shelter Stevens describes here was a telling white: the purest, most comprehensive, most comforting of theories, "the accomplishment / Of an extremist in an exercise" (CP 412). But the encroachment of autumn means the speaker's reconception of that whiteness, his sudden perception that the theory is less than totally satisfactory. The pristine condition of the cabin is disrupted by the sand that blows across the floor like the grit of empirical experience the theory has failed to accommodate; the "idea" is on its way to becoming the kind of curious anachronism Stevens anticipates in "A Postcard from the Volcano": "A dirty house in a gutted world" (CP 159).[40]

That Stevens implicates empirical cinders in the demise of his theoretical structures will prove significant when we come to consider his affinities with James. For now it is worth noting simply that the provisional nature of Stevens's shelters has something to do with their failure to keep the world's complexity at bay and that Stevens considers this failure to be part of a cycle as inevitable as the turning of the seasons and the undulation of the birds. By correlating their erection and collapse with these natural and cyclical fluctuations, Stevens reinforces his support for James's view that the struggle between philosophic and skeptical tendencies is never-ending. And this does not simply mean that we must be discouraged about theories, depressed by the fact that every "structure of ideas" can "result only in disaster" (CP 326). It also means that there will be no giving up, that "[t]he cancellings, the negations are never final" (CP 414). As winter can't last forever, so Stevens has faith that an abandoned theory, a "hotel boarded and bare," need not serve as a "panorama of despair" (CP 135) but only as an inspiration to build anew. One of Stevens's most compelling visions of the ongoing process of theory-making is found in the late poem, "St.

Armorer's Church from the Outside," where he depicts the crumbling structure of an old church in the process of being overtaken by a new chapel arising within it. Like a "sacred syllable rising from sacked speech" (CP 530), the chapel constitutes "a new account of everything old" (CP 529); it is the product of a cognitive impulse that wills not just to discard discredited beliefs but to revise or reconstitute and thus revitalize them. Stevens captures the hope represented by this resurgence of architectural activity in terms strikingly reminiscent of Hulme's Bergsonian vision of the progress of the *élan vital*. Just as Hulme imagined that fiery impulse lighting dead ashes briefly into meaning, so Stevens pictures the chapel rising "from Terre Ensevelie, / *An ember yes among its cindery noes*" (CP 529; my italics).

Emphasizing the ephemerality of his edifices is one of Stevens's ways of stressing that the theories they represent remain subject to epochal qualification. These shelters may seem adequate to account for the world, he suggests, but eventually the grit will show; they will reveal themselves to be prejudicial and inadequate. To appreciate the extent to which Stevens resists endorsing theories metaphysically, however, we must concentrate on those instances when his metaphysical urge would seem greatest: those moments when the intellect offers what seem to be absolute and comprehensive accounts of the way things are. The resistance Stevens offers in such situations is closely related to his method of thwarting the aspirations of his relation-seeking birds—not a surprising thing, given that the impulse driving the birds is identical with the architectural one. To appreciate this resistance, it helps to note that Stevens often coordinates these codes and makes the buildings the perches where the birds find momentary satisfaction. In examining an experience of apparently unequivocal understanding, for example, in "To an Old Philosopher in Rome," he likens the state to attaining "the naked majesty, if you like, / Of bird-nest arches" (CP 510). In another passage, from "Architecture" (one that also underscores the virility expressed through theory-making), he suggests that the apex of the ideal theoretical building is identical with that most coveted nest, the tip of the palm:

> Let us build the building of light.
> Push up the towers
> To the cock-tops.
> These are the pointings of our edifice,
> Which, like a gorgeous palm,
> Shall tuft the commonplace.

> (OP 38)

Noting the equivalence between the roof of the building and the ultimate bird's nest helps us to understand Stevens's final mode of ensuring his fidelity to the *epoche*. Throughout his poetry Stevens represents theory-making as a quest to puncture the external boundary of the *epoche*, enabling the mind that nests there to pass beyond the prejudice born of time and place. In "Credences," for example, the "refuge that the end creates" resembles "the natural tower of all the world," a comprehensive "point of survey" (CP 373). The ideal "chastel de . . . [p]ensée" imagined in "Architecture" offers its inhabitants a panoramic view over "whole seasons" (OP 37), as if from a point in eternity. But Stevens is not so inconsistent as to allow the intellect to attain, under the guise of a builder, a destination it is denied when it masquerades as a bird. In the same way as he frustrates his birds' efforts to find a perch on the other side of the epochal boundary, he works to thwart the aspirations of the builders who would create such perches, who would push the buildings vertically, higher and higher, until they "[p]ierce . . . the sky" (OP 38). His policy on this matter is voiced by the irascible, antimetaphysical audience in "The Man with the Blue Guitar"; a poet, they contend, should never presume to represent his intellectual creation as a "structure of vaults" converging on "a point of light" (CP 167).[41]

To frustrate the vertical aspirations of the architectural impulse, Stevens does not so much limit its power, or belittle the height and breadth of its constructs, as expand the borders of the *epoche* and defer its destination. In "Extracts from Addresses to the Academy of Ideas," he anticipates Derrida, portraying the world this impulse inhabits as a space that will always already be constructed. No matter how hard it tries, in other words, it will find itself contained within a text, a "world of words to the end of it" (CP 345):

> Messieurs,
> It is an artificial world. The rose
> Of paper is of the nature of its world.
> The sea is so many written words; the sky
> Is blue, clear, cloudy, high, dark, wide and round;
> The mountains inscribe themselves upon the walls.
>
> (CP 252)

Stevens suggests that the borders of the *epoche* are *themselves* intellectual constructions and that the buildings rising up beneath them, no matter how high they extend, have no hope of encountering anything constitutionally different from themselves. Theory grows outward to meet not reality but more theory, all of it as "different from reality" (CP 344) as that which has gone before. In "Things of August," Stevens varies the metaphor by transforming the boundary of Being into an eggshell, which itself lies deep within another; the theoretical impulse that pushes against it, intent on shattering it, will succeed only to find itself trapped within another enclosure, and another, and another (CP 490).[42] As he describes the phenomenon elsewhere, "our nature is an illimitable space through which the intelligence moves without coming to an end" (NA 53).

The exemplary deferral of a destination in Stevens is the one found in his tribute to the dying Santayana, "To an Old Philosopher in Rome." It is difficult to imagine greater pressure being applied on the borders of the *epoche* than here, as Stevens imagines what Santayana must understand, now that he stands on "the threshold of heaven" (CP 508). At first his hope for the philosopher's insight at this penultimate moment seems unlimited. Santayana has realized the theoretical architect's dream: the "total grandeur of a total edifice" (CP 510). The threshold on which he stands appears to be the place where "[t]wo parallels become one" (CP 511), where a burgeoning conception of reality ("Rome") coincides with the comprehensive reality it has been aspiring toward ("that more merciful Rome / Beyond"). What the dying man sees, finally, appears to be something "beyond the eye, / Not of its sphere" (CP 508); the fissure closed with the collapse of dualism has apparently reopened. For all the strength of such statements, however, Stevens does much to qualify them and thus to admit that Santayana's apocalyptic vision attains no more certain status than a simple appearance of supreme rationality. To the claim that the dying man sees "beyond the eye," for example, he adds, "and yet not far beyond." If the constructed and real Romes seem to coincide, they are in fact alike "in the make of the mind" (CP 508)—a studiously noncommittal observation. Not to be overlooked, either, is the "as if" that infiltrates Stevens's claims about the convergence of construction and reality, conceding that there's no way to confirm what appears to be:

> It is *as if* in a human dignity
> Two parallels become one . . .
>
> (CP 508; my italics)

> He stops upon this threshold,
> *As if* the design of all his words takes form
> And frame from thinking and is realized.
>
> (CP 511; my italics)

In effect these qualifications draw another circle around the one on whose edge the philosopher rests, deferring the assurance that what seems like absolute knowledge is what it seems. For Santayana to know is one thing; for Stevens to know that he knows quite another. Hence Stevens's vision of Santayana's vision of the "Rome / Beyond" becomes just another "shape within the ancient circles of shapes" (CP 509)—just another text within a universe of textuality.

One of the most fascinating methods by which Stevens demonstrates the endlessly expandable borders of the *epoche*, both in "To an Old Philosopher" and elsewhere, is his use of images that evoke what Bachelard has called the feeling of "intimate immensity."[43] Described simply these are representations of a *limited* space that seems nonetheless to *contain infinity;* the implication is that even the kind of certainty demanding expression in images of infinite space remains subject to epochal qualification. Some realist philosophers of James's generation perceived an analogy between the epochal consciousness and a mirror; like the consciousness "mirror-space" presents the appearance of three dimensions—the third of potentially infinite depth—in a plane of two.[44] Bachelard also describes the kind of space that "accumulates its infinity within its own boundaries" (186), in which the "concrete" or "miniature" can "accumulate size," be "*vast* in its way" (215). Similarly, Stevens explicitly correlates the immensity experienced by the dying philosopher with the mundane boundedness experienced by his observers but without pronouncing either experience to be really veritable: "So that *we feel,* in this illumined large, / The veritable small" (CP 509; my italics). Thus though the poem sometimes seems to privilege its own veritable empirical vision over the philosopher's transcendent Vision, both remain bracketed within the "*sentiment* of rationality." Stevens therefore concludes with a both-and stance, with both visions being credited equally:

> It is a kind of total grandeur at the end,
> With every visible thing enlarged and yet
> No more than a bed, a chair and moving nuns,
> The immensest theatre, the pillared porch,
> The book and candle in your ambered room. . . .
>
>   (CP 510)

The same overlay of infinite and finite perceptions of space can be found in "The Latest Freed Man," where everything in the room he inhabits is, at the height of his certainty, "bulging and blazing and big in itself" (CP 205) and perhaps even in "On the Road Home," where a decision to abandon metaphysical thinking makes the "grapes seem [. . .] fatter" (CP 203). In all these cases, Stevens effects what Bachelard calls a "topoanalytical inversion," folding an infinite "outside" back into the limited "inside" of phenomenal reality (226).[45] A passage from "An Ordinary Evening at New Haven" makes his intention explicit. It is especially interesting for the way it identifies the move to contain infinity with the attempt to contain the intellectual will to go "roundabout" the containing walls, then "through" them:

>   We seek
> Nothing beyond reality. *Within it,*

Everything, the spirit's alchemicana
Included, the spirit that goes roundabout
And through included, not merely the visible,

The solid, but the movable, the moment,
The coming on of feasts and the habits of saints,
The pattern of the heavens and high, night air.

(CP 471–2; my italics)[46]

The doxic dramas Stevens stages within the "landscape of the mind," then, dutifully reflect the limitations posed by his liminal muse. They capture the perennial vacillation demanded by an oracle without an origin; they ensure that the absolute faith she inspires when at her most compelling never translates into dogma. Stevens summarizes what happens at the most intense moments in the life cycles of his lights, birds, and buildings in "Final Soliloquy of the Interior Paramour"—a poem that Harold Bloom mistakenly represents as a claim about absolute revelation.[47] These moments may *feel* like moments of perfect communion with a mystic muse. But even the "intensest rendezvous," and the wisdom communicated therein, remain confined within the space that leaves everything undecided, undecidable:

Here, now, we forget each other and ourselves.
We feel the obscurity of an order, a whole,
A knowledge, that which arranged the rendezvous.

Within its vital boundary, in the mind.

(CP 524; my italics)

FICTION OR HYPOTHESIS?

If Stevens's doxic dramas honor his commitment to remembering the provisionality of theories, it remains to establish whether his view of those theories' ultimate potential more closely resembles Santayana's or James's. Stevens is not perfectly neutral in entertaining the life cycle of intellectual and imaginative constructions. As with the two philosophers, his attempt to avoid judging the final truth of these structures cedes to speculation about what is probable. The disagreement between the two philosophers concerned whether or not theoretical or imaginative constructions might ever be inspired by a reliable "divinity." Although James was prepared to entertain the possibility that a divinity might speak from beyond the desiring self, Santayana firmly denied such an option, and the upshot was a significant difference in the constructions each deemed appropriate for communicating "inspired" insights.

For a lucid review of the difference between James's pragmatic hypothesis and Santayana's pleasurable fiction, we may turn once again to Hans Vaihinger, whose own version of the tensional assertion is sometimes cited as a model for Stevens's.[48] As Pound learned from G. R. S. Mead in *The Quest*, in *Philosophie des Als Ob* (1911)[49] Vaihinger asserts that hypotheses and fictions are distinguished by the earnestness and cynicism, respectively, that guide their construction and destruction. Whereas the hypothesis is something considered probable, the fiction is always "known to be false"; where the person uttering a hypothesis wishes it "to be an adequate expression of some reality still unknown," and so constructs it in a serious effort "to mirror this objective reality correctly," the one offering a fiction knows from the start "that it is an inadequate, subjective and pictorial manner of conception, whose coincidence with reality is, from the start, excluded and which cannot, therefore, be afterwards verified."[50] The hypothesis, in other words, seeks to coincide with objective reality and will fall apart when "the facts of experience" appear to contradict it. The fiction, on the other hand, needs not give the actual world so much as a passing glance and remains invulnerable to whatever challenge that world poses. It falls apart only when it has performed whatever function—emotional, aesthetic, practical—its user has in mind for it.[51]

Vaihinger emphasizes the importance of distinguishing between hypotheses and fictions because he is particularly concerned with protecting the rights of the latter. One of his major goals in *The Philosophy of "As If"* is to champion the use of tensional fictions similar, if not quite identical, to those of Santayana. In doing so he feels the need to defend them from critics who, mistaking them for hypotheses, have held them up to unfair expectations. The greatest injustice, in Vaihinger's opinion, has occurred when fictions have been subjected to tests of truth or falsehood. When people mistake the fictional notion of a divinity for a hypothesis, for example, they waste enormous amounts of time and energy in futile attempts at verifying it. The same is true of Kant's fictional concept of the thing-in-itself and of many fictional notions of the Absolute.[52] The potential value of these constructions, in other words, has too often been scuttled by readers who fail to recognize that the fiction-maker is not attempting to account for things as they really are. In Sir Philip Sidney's words Vaihinger proposes that the fiction-maker "never lies" because he "nothing affirms"; it should be apparent to those who encounter his assertions that truth is not a possibility, so not an issue.[53]

To Vaihinger's defense of the particular rights and freedoms of fictions, however (and similar arguments going back to Sidney's *Defense*), must be added an equally important warning about the danger of mistaking hypotheses for their more carefree counterparts. To mistake a hypothetical utterance for a dogmatically skeptical announcement is not to waste time but to squander opportunity. It is to insist that a door is closed, where the proprietor of the door wishes it to remain open. It is also to perceive that proprietor as an irresponsible solipsist, when he may in fact have a profound sense of duty to the claims of the actual world. This double underestimation was precisely what frustrated James about many hostile critical responses to his description of the tensional, pragmatic truth in *Pragmatism*. The source of the problem was James's refusal to make metaphysical claims for that construct—his insistence on keeping it under epochal suspension. This renunciation of certainty was enough to cause critics like Josiah Royce to object that the pragmatist must therefore be free to "play fast and loose" (MT 47) with his propositions. As James tells it, Royce could not fathom how he, in denying absolute certainty even to empirical perceptions, could leave his thinker with "any duty to think truly" (MT 46). But in regarding pragmatism with such suspicion, Royce and others ignored a crucial part of the pragmatic program: James's warning that rejecting a claim to *certainty* does not entail rejecting truth as a *possibility*.[54] They might have heeded the following words, for example, from "The Will to Believe":

> But please observe, now, that when as empiricists we give up the doctrine of objective certitude, we do not thereby give up the quest or hope of truth itself. We can still pin our faith on its existence, and still believe that we gain an even better position towards it by systematically continuing to roll up experiences and think. (WB 23–24)

In *The Meaning of Truth*, James emphasizes further that the radically empirical experience against which the pragmatist tests his propositions is not any less pressing for being of indeterminate objectivity. Indeed, he insists that it commands much more prudence than the avowedly objective, trans-empirical criteria to which Royce and other absolutists would turn instead, and that it is finally the only assurance of a theory's validity, even for them:

> The only *real* guarantee we have against licentious thinking is the circumpressure of experience itself, which gets us sick of concrete errors, whether there be a trans-empirical reality or not. How does the partisan of absolute reality know what this orders him to think? He cannot get direct sight of the absolute; and he has no means of guessing what it wants of him except by following the humanistic clues. (MT 47)

The error of James's detractors is, in other words, to regard anything less than the doxic modality of absolute *certainty* as a modality of absolute *doubt*. It is to interpret a refusal to claim *absolute* authority for one's perceptions as a denial of *any chance* of their authority. It is also to interpret an equivocation about the *possibility* of knowing as a claim that there is *nothing objective to be known*—epistemological modesty as subjective idealism—and thus to deny James's powerful respect both for the existence of a reality independent of perception and for the urgent claim that reality may make on us through the "circumpressure" of radical experience.[55] As the marxist critique of modernism makes clear, a willingness to regulate one's thinking in accordance with the "actual world" is a significant political decision. It marks the difference between a person who honors social responsibilities and one who retreats into a self-indulgent fetishism; between one who believes in the intransigence of social conditions and one who believes these to be infinitely malleable products of the mind; between one who respects the difference of others and one who constructs others entirely out of his or her own experience. In short, to mistake a hypothetical thinker as a fiction-maker, whether it be James or any one else, is to pave the way for the still greater injustice of uninformed judgments of his or her politics and ethics.

I emphasize the perils of mistaking hypotheses for fictions because a great number of Stevens's commentators have fallen into this trap. For the most part, critics have failed to recognize any distinction between the two types of tensional proposition; *all* provisional utterances, so far as they are concerned, are fictions. Where they have acknowledged a difference, they have been less than careful in their attempts to determine which of the two types of proposition Stevens in fact endorses, to establish whether he is, in epistemological matters, finally a pessimist or an optimist.[56] My own account of Stevens, particularly my account of how his expanding *epoche* thwarts the aspirations of relation-seeking birds and buildings, would seem to support the view that Stevens had a profoundly negative view of theory's potential. But although I would stand by my observation that Stevens represents even the most convincing theoretical accomplishment as being in doubt, I shall also argue that this is less than half of the story. If he resists claiming to know for certain that we can grasp the truth, he also resists claiming to know that we can't grasp it. This Jamesian resistance to skepticism is, moreover, on balance the more powerful force in the poetry, both in the theory of provisional utterances it articulates and in the particular provisional utterances it employs. That this is so will become apparent when we examine the evidence for Stevens's position on two matters vital to the dispute between James and Santayana. First we must examine Stevens's attitude toward the kind of "dogmatic disbelief" that James found so "impertinent" in the work of Santayana.[57] Second, we must take a closer look at the role he assigns to truth-making to the empirical world, both as *telos* and arbiter.

EPISTEMOLOGICAL OPTIMISM

Stevens's response to the kind of dogmatic skepticism Santayana exemplified is, at the very least, one of caution. In essence this is because he recognizes that claims about the inevitability of illusion are as foundationless as claims about absolute knowledge. He is as reluctant, therefore, as Heidegger was to accept a philosophy that violates the *epoche* from the bottom, simply "turning Platonism on its head."[58] A number of passages, taken from different points in his career, testify to his recognition that disillusion may turn out to be the "last illusion" (CP 468). As Milton Bates has noted, the portrait of the skeptic in *Harmonium*'s "Palace of the Babies" portrays disbelief as "a form of wilful ignorance" no less questionable than the unexamined faith it rejects.[59] Stevens also turns the tables on skepticism in *Ideas of Order,* when he observes that a theory about the inadequacy of a previous theory "proves nothing," being "Just one more truth, one more / Element in the immense disorder of truths" (CP 216). But his definitive statement of this position is found in "The Pure Good of Theory," from *Transport to Summer:*

> Yet to speak of the whole world as metaphor
> Is still to stick to the contents of the mind
>
> And the desire to believe in a metaphor.
> It is to stick to the nicer knowledge of
> Belief, *that what it believes in is not true.*
>
> (CP 332; my italics)

Here Stevens situates a radically skeptical philosophy ("the whole world as metaphor") firmly within the "contents of the mind"—within the qualifying boundaries, in other words, of the *epoche*. He subjects the theory of endless textuality that thwarts the aspirations of bird and architect to its own dismantling, describing it as just one more evasive metaphor in an ever-expanding field of such metaphors.[60] Stevens reinforces this epochal suspension of skepticism, moreover, by qualifying the statement summarizing the skeptical position ("what [belief] believes in is not true"). The dogmatic statement about the inevitability of illusion is merely the "nicer" knowledge of belief, the more satisfying of many potential theories about human cognition—satisfying perhaps because it absolves one of responsibility for knowing. The "of" that defines the relationship of this knowledge to "belief" is ambiguous, so as to undermine its credibility: skepticism is not indubitable knowledge about belief, but knowledge delivered by belief and so less than certain.

Stevens uses similar grammatical qualifiers in posing the Santayanan position in the opening lines of "Asides on the Oboe":

> The prologues are over. It is a question, now,
> Of final belief. So, *say that final belief*
> *Must be in a fiction*. It is time to choose.
>
> (CP 250; my italics)

Far from being an unequivocal assertion of the skeptical position, as Frank Kermode and others have implied, the statement that "final belief / Must be in a fiction" is preceded by a qualifier that renders it merely provisional.[61] "[S]ay that" every theory we believe in must be false, Stevens says: it is time to decide whether or not we should still be believers. A similar qualification follows another statement frequently cited in support of the view of Stevens as epistemological pessimist: "The squirming facts exceed the squamous mind," he writes, "*If one may say so*" (CP 215; my italics). Like many other grammatical qualifiers in Stevens's work, the ones in these examples function to ensure his loyalty to the liminal muse. In qualifying the skeptical position, their ultimate function is not to restrain the divinity from wandering freely beyond the threshold but rather to prevent her from sliding down into the realm of pure subjectivity. Stevens affirms this motive when he contemplates the fate of the inspiring "Fat girl" at the end of "Notes Toward a Supreme Fiction." Foreseeing acts of skeptical theorizing that would deny this muse *any* chance of autonomy by reducing her to a "fiction that results from feeling" (CP 406), he emphasizes that these theories about her subordination must themselves to be subjected to epochal suspension. To maintain that she is wholly subject to desire is to stop her independent "revolving." But there is no guarantee that she has lost her independence; the theory about that loss, no less than any theory, is confined to that familiar, transparent enclosure where everything remains in question: a jar made this time, not out of glass, but out of "crystal" (CP 407).[62]

Contrary to much of the criticism, then, Stevens is at least as vigilant of the dangers of believing too little as he is of believing too much. In geographical terms he is at least as reluctant to sink below sea-surface as he is to fly away to some space beyond the sky; he resists the path of the "white pigeon" in "Monocle," who "flutters to the ground, / Grown tired of flight" (CP 17). That he is more suspicious of the cynicism that would reduce all intellectual efforts to fictions than he is of the openness that would enable them to be hypotheses is also apparent in a series of ruminations in which he examines pessimism—both general and specifically epistemological—at very close range. As his portrait of the willful skeptic in "Palace of the Babies" implies, he shares James's awareness that insights into the nature of the world and humankind may have everything to do with the attitude of the thinker. And as he suggests in another poem from *Harmonium,* "Gubbinal," to come to dogmatically tragic conclusions, such as "The world is ugly / And the people are sad" (CP 85), is to be willfully perverse.

Stevens clarifies the nature of this perversity in a number of later passages that recall his attack on the divisive, Cartesian spirit in "Sea Surface Full of Clouds." He suggests that the fear that we perceive or understand falsely arises only *after* we have experienced faith in our perceptions and theories, and he dismisses this fear as counterintuitive. The most striking formulation of this is found in a passage from the "It Must Give Pleasure" section of "Notes," where the insight at stake has all the marks of a religious revelation:

> But the difficultest rigor is forthwith,
> On the image of what we see, to catch from that
> Irrational moment its unreasoning,
> As when the sun comes rising, when the sea
> Clears deeply, when the moon hangs on the wall
>
> Of heaven-haven. These are *not* things transformed.
> *Yet we are shaken by them as if they were.*
> *We reason about them with a later reason.*

(CP 398–99; my italics)

We have moments, in other words, when we seem to "see into the life of things" but attempt to explain away what we have come to understand. Some incorrigible impulse leads us to dismantle what at first seems indubitable, to make of "what we see clearly / And have seen, a place dependent on ourselves" (CP 401). Where the attack on the reflective spirit in "Sea Surface" served only to support a campaign for the necessity of suspending judgment about experiences of certainty, however, here the balance tips clearly toward epistemological optimism. What we lose when we reflect pessimistically on our insights may possibly be something genuinely untransformed, the unmediated truth that is the object of all our seeking.

Given all that Stevens implies about the provisionality of theories, we must of course be wary of making claims about his absolute commitment to any of the positions he himself articulates. His Jamesian attacks on epistemological pessimism are so frequent, however, that they seem to represent a dominant attitude. The regret he expresses in "Notes" for the perverse habit of rejecting compelling truths also emerges in "An Ordinary Evening in New Haven," as he summarizes the activities of a character he calls a *hidalgo* (a Spanish gentleman). As Harold Bloom has rightly noted, this figure represents the reflective component in a divided self—what Freud called the superego.[63] We learn in Canto XXV that in the *hidalgo*'s retrospective glances, "What was real turned into something most unreal" (CP 483); the speaker attempts in subsequent cantos, accordingly, to return to

a state of faith uncorrupted by reflection.[64] A final account of how the
mind may willfully interpret reality as illusion is found in a poem from
Parts of a World called "Phosphor Reading by His Own Light." Here the
particular reality denied by the reflective superego is the objective meaning
that a text may confer on its reader, the incontrovertible "greenness"[65] that
emanates from a page. Stevens accuses the skeptical "realist" of falsely
attributing that meaning to the constructive power of his own expectations:

> Look, realist, not knowing what you expect.
> The green falls on you as you look,
>
> Falls on and makes and gives, even a speech.
> And you think that that is what you expect . . .
>
> (CP 267)

In this case his attempt to counter epistemological pessimism amounts to
a proleptic warning to radical theorists of reader-response.

Stevens is not always as confident as he appears in these passages that
the theorist who emphasizes the constructive, and not the receptive, power
of the mind is completely mistaken. But he is invariably much more concerned to intercept precipitous claims about the inevitability of illusion
than to temper dreams about the possibility of attaining truth. Like James,
he senses that a pessimism about cognitive capacities is the dominant mood
of the age, and that it is important, therefore, to emphasize that a more
optimistic attitude is just as viable—that our insights might very well be
accurate representations of reality, even if we cannot be sure of them. To
be a "realist" about one's perceptions, as Phosphor and other scholars wish
to be, is not necessarily to sing a despairing tune; it is at least as respectable
to hold out hope that they might coincide with reality. Stevens makes the
point in his memorable epigram comparing the relative authorities of disso-
nant crow and mellifluous oriole:

> From oriole to crow, note the decline
> In music. Crow is realist. *But, then,*
> *Oriole, also, may be realist.*
>
> (CP 154; my italics)

The possibility that our "certainty" may in fact be sustained by "Things
certain," that "to seem" may actually be "to be," is also the dominant
theme of the two great poems of *Transport to Summer,* "Credences of
Summer" and "Description Without Place" (CP 375, 377, 339, 342).

Stevens's view of the attitude that distinguished Santayana from James
is, then, at the very least, that it must not be regarded as the *only* response
to a loss of certainty. In less balanced moments, it is a bafflement that

people choose to renounce the more attractive possibility, even a suspicion that the pessimistic choice is the evil or immoral one. Stevens's amazement at the popularity of the choice is captured most memorably in the closing canto from "Examination of the Hero in a Time of War." The sonnet begins with a familiar account of the decreation of theories that takes place as summer turns to fall. The particular proposition at stake in this case is a theory about the human capacity for heroism:

> Each false thing ends. The bouquet of summer
> Turns blue and on its empty table
> It is stale and the water is discolored.
> True autumn stands then in the doorway.
> After the hero, the familiar
> Man makes the hero artificial.
>
> (CP 280)

But Stevens follows this description with a question about our tendency to embrace the destructive wisdom of autumn, over all the hope offered by the formulations of summer:

> But was the summer false? The hero?
> How did we come to think that autumn
> Was the veritable season, that familiar
> Man was the veritable man?
>
> (CP 280–81)

The right option, clearly, is not to allow heroism's unfamiliarity to signify its impossibility. An even stronger suspicion of the skeptical option emerges in a poem that represents epistemological pessimism and optimism in terms borrowed from Genesis, "Auroras of Autumn." Here Stevens personifies the impulse to discredit our thoughts and perceptions as a "serpent" and equates disbelief with that creature's "poison" (CP 411). When we succumb to skepticism, he implies, we have succumbed to the serpent's temptation, and so "It leaps through us, through all our heavens leaps, / Extinguishing our planets, one by one" (CP 417). The final point of the poem is to reintroduce prelapsarian "innocence" as a viable attainment (CP 418–20), to suggest that the possibility of union with God-given truth is "not / Less real" (CP 418) than the theory that such wisdom has been irretrievably lost. "Examination of the Hero in a Time of War" ends the same way, with a recommendation that we reconsider that summer may "truly bear" (CP 281) the truth about human capacities it promises. Both poems mirror, in their structure and conclusion, a succinct poem called "Desire and the Object," where Stevens, after giving both pessimistic and optimistic views of cognition serious con-sideration, gives the final and most emphatic mention to the happier theory:

It could be that the sun shines
Because I desire it to shine *or else*
That I desire it to shine because it shines.

(OP 113; my italics)[66]

   Stevens engages in an effort to convince an already skeptical world that
there may be "a degree of perception at which what is real and what is
imagined are one" (OP 192). "Hypotheses," he writes, "though they may
appear to be very distant illuminations, could be the fires of fate" (NA 81).
These reminders that the truth may rest with our beliefs rather than with
our doubts match James's resurrection of the option of epistemological
optimism. In some of their incarnations, especially those written during the
Second World War, these propositions are also motivated by a Jamesian
perception about how beliefs may function as self-fulfilling prophecies. In
"Examination of the Hero" in particular, published in 1942, Stevens addresses an audience in need of inspiration if they are to rise to the challenges
of war. In encouraging them to reconsider a proposition about the human
capacity for heroism, he implies that that renewed belief may have the
power to *create* the reality it foretells. As he puts it in another discussion
of the subject, in the "soldier" coda to "Notes," it is often possible for the
"fictive hero"—by inspiring behaviour in his own image—to become the
"real" (CP 408).[67]

REALISM AND THE EMPIRICAL TEST

   If Stevens advocates the optimism of the hypothesis-maker, he also endorses what Vaihinger identified as the second, crucial characteristic of such
a theorist: a readiness to submit his fictions to the test of empirical reality.
Alan Filreis and James Longenbach have offered convincing evidence that
Stevens's critics have greatly underestimated Stevens's respect for the "actual world."[68] The tendency has been to interpret Stevens's enthusiasm for
the power of imagination as evidence of a fundamental subjective idealism.
But this approach throws away the baby with the bathwater: to acknowledge a faculty with the power of transforming objective reality is not necessarily to deny that reality any degree of independence. James's response to
"the slanderous charge that [the pragmatist] den[ies] real existence" (MT
8) was to emphasize that he remained an "epistemological realist" (MT
106) and that all his questing assumed a belief in "existent objects" (MT 6).
"[T]he existence of the object," he contends, "is the only reason" why
pragmatic truths are capable of working (MT 8).[69] As if he, too, was wary
of how his retreat from metaphysics would be interpreted, Stevens also

repeatedly affirms his belief in the existence of an objective reality. He summarizes the position in an account of Crispin's intellectual growth:

> He first, as realist, admitted that
> Whoever hunts a matinal continent
> May, after all, *stop short before a plum*
> *And be content and still be realist.*
> The words of things entangle and confuse.
> *The plum survives its poems.*
>
> (CP 40–41; my italics)

The word realist has a different sense in this passage from the one it sustains in Stevens's pithy vignette about the oriole and the crow. There to be a realist means to have an accurate sense of the nature of reality. Here it means to be a believer in a reality independent of the inadequate constructions that can be made of it, a world that is in some respects not "susceptible to metaphor" (OP 204). Stevens emphasizes his faith in such a world in several other poems celebrating the existence of "good, fat, guzzly fruit" (CP 41). We encounter a set of "pears," for example, whose most significant characteristic is that they "are not seen / As the observer wills" (CP 197), and a "pineapple" described as "the irreducible X / At the bottom of imagined artifice" (NA 83). In a wartime poem called "A Dish of Peaches in Russia," an exiled Russian identifies the plump fruit with the beloved village he has left behind him and with the undeniable "ferocities" (CP 224) now tearing it apart—realities no less true because they lie beyond his sight.

Stevens's respect for the existence of an objective reality is suggested by the determination of his relation-seeking birds and buildings. Were more of these birds to remain content with "the pleasures of merely circulating" (CP 149)—with a lazy wheeling that shows no impatience with epochal boundaries[70]—he might be said to be documenting Santayanan fiction-making: an essentially aimless practice in that it holds out no hope for any correlation of construct and reality. The fact that it is the aim of these birds, however, as of Stevens's architects and sailors, to shatter the *epoche* and attain certainty, suggests otherwise; their efforts presuppose some epistemological hope. Stevens's dramatization of the life cycles of birds and buildings implies, moreover, that the impulses engaged in an ongoing quest for truth are guided by empirical criteria. When an idea disintegrates in these dramas, it is not merely out of whim but because it fails to correspond to evidence from the actual world. It seems significant, for example, that the "generations" of birds in "Somnambulisma" are "*By water* washed away" (CP 304; my italics). This image appears to be an allusion to James's account of the dissolution of theory in the *Essays on Radical Empiricism*: it implies that theories dissolve in the face of significant resistance from the "stream" of experience, when experience poses a "collision" (as opposed

to a "confluence" [ERE 49]) with what they have counted "as truth or
fact" (ERE 34). More obviously Stevens frequently attributes the collapse
of his theoretical buildings to the force of an empirical world whose complexities they have failed to explain. We've seen that the disintegration of
the summer cabin in "Auroras" is signaled by the blowing of "sand" (CP
412) across its floor, as if its walls are beginning to fail in their effort to
hold at bay the myriad details of a cindery world. What remains on the
planter's property in "Notes Toward a Supreme Fiction," after the collapse
of his nice, cosy home, are "three scraggy trees weighted / With garbled
green" (CP 393): they have succumbed to what Stevens later describes as
"the barbarous green / Of . . . harsh reality."[71]

It is, in short, no accident that Stevens describes the theoretical buildings
of summer as "enclosures of hypotheses" (CP 516). Like the constructs of
James's pragmatist, they are not only erected in optimism but revised in
accordance with the "real world of sweat and dirt." Critics who see only
Stevens's appreciation for imagination think in unnecessarily binary terms.
Stevens sees the subjective force of imagination and the objective presence
of reality working together in mutual "interdependence" (NA 27); the latter exerts its force to keep the former's desires in check. "The poetry of a
work of imagination," he contends, should "constantly illustrate the fundamental and endless struggle with *fact*" (OP 242; my italics).

THE GRAMMAR OF HYPOTHESIS

If Stevens's representations of theoretical constructions are evidence that
he remains faithful to the idea of a liminal muse, we can find other proofs
of this loyalty in the diction and syntax of his poetry. As it is a rare light,
bird, or building in his doxic dramas that does not falter in its confidence,
so it is a rare assertion that Stevens does not qualify. And as the images of
theory-making preserve a Jamesian optimism about theory's potential, his
methods of qualification preserve the same kind of optimism about the
propositions they modify. In other words if Stevens *dramatizes* the life
cycles of hypotheses in his epochal landscapes, he also develops a sophisticated *grammar* for making hypothetical statements. His own poetic assertions, accordingly, are precisely what a virile poet's assertions were to be,
in response to the Sister of thĕ Minotaur: tentative, often temporary
"agreement[s] with reality" (NA 54), offered with some hope, if not confidence, that they might be true.

Of the many critics who have written about Stevens's language, Helen
Vendler has performed an especially valuable service in cataloging the terms
that serve as signposts for his "Qualified Assertions." These modal auxilia-

ries, which Stevens usually uses to modify potentially unconditional assertions in the present tense, cover the full range of the intentional (and
ontical) modalities Husserl outlines in the passage from *Ideas* I have quoted.
Vendler distinguishes possibility's "might," for example, from probability's
"would," and from doubtfulness's "suppose," "say that," "perhaps," and
"must."[72] To be complete, however, a catalog of Stevens's qualifying techniques must also acknowledge the temporal options he chooses from in
checking his assertions. The force of a modal auxiliary depends on where
it is placed.

Stevens's first option, in wielding his qualifiers, is to *stagger* affirmation
and doubt, to make a confident assertion and then to challenge it. We see
this in the passage where Stevens speculates about the insight of the dying
Santayana: the philosopher's vision reaches "beyond the eye, / Not of its
sphere, *and yet* not far beyond" (CP 508). It is the technique used in "Notes
Toward a Supreme Fiction," where he undermines the kind of sarcastic
paraphrase of Christian beliefs typical of unbelievers by appending the
cynical tag "Or so they said" (CP 400), and in "The Green Plant," when
he confidently declares the whole world unknowable, except for the unequivocal presence of some glaring green vegetation (CP 506). Poems like
"Notes" and "A World Without Peculiarity" offer extended sequences of
such fluctuation, in which propositions are asserted, undermined, and then
reasserted, with new vigor. These shifting patterns of faith and doubt are
the grammatical equivalent of the flickering lights, revolving seasons, undulating birds, and unstable buildings in Stevens's landscapes. They correspond to the sequences of making and unmaking Hulme linked to the ebb
and flow of music; Stevens himself alludes to this rhythm in "An Ordinary
Evening in New Haven," when he likens the "activities of the formulae of
statement" to "A philosopher practicing scales on his piano, / A woman
writing a note and tearing it up" (CP 488). In any sequential pattern of
qualification, the final proposition is the one with greatest weight. Paying
attention to what comes last is one of the ways of seeing which side of an
issue Stevens, never dogmatic, leans toward.

Stevens's second option, however, and by far his most frequent choice,
is to exchange the "restless iteration" (CP 60) of belief and doubt for
grammatical structures that render belief and doubt *simultaneous*. (He acknowledges his propensity for such utterances in observing that "[M]y
opinions generally change even while I am in the act of expressing them"
[165]).[73] Often this means introducing the qualifier first and allowing a
confident assertion to follow soon thereafter. Consider, for example, the
effect of the qualifier "There might be," in the following passage from
"Credences of Summer":

> *There might be,* too, a change immenser than
> A poet's metaphors in which being would

Come true, a point in the fire of music where
Dazzle yields to a clarity and we observe,

And observing is completing and we are content,
In a world that shrinks to an immediate whole,

That we do not need to understand, complete
Without secret arrangements of it in the mind.

(CP 341; my italics)

As Vendler notes, the distance between "There might be" and the present-tense assertion it modifies ("we observe") is sufficiently wide to give the latter maximum credibility. The qualifier's presence prior to the assertion, however, ensures that the claim posited is rendered uncertain from the start and that at the same time as it is asserted, it is undermined. If the other examples I have given offer a proposition and then a counterproposition, this is a "cry that contains its converse in itself" (CP 471). A similar structure can be found in another comment on Santayana's cognitive experience in the face of death, in "To an Old Philosopher in Rome":

It is *as if* in a human dignity
Two parallels become one. . . .

(CP 508; my italics)

Or in "Study of Images II," where Stevens likens the same kind of experience to a nuptial union:

As if, as if, as if the disparate halves
Of things were waiting in a betrothal known
To none, awaiting espousal to the sound

Of right joining, a music of ideas, the burning
And breeding and bearing birth of harmony,
The final relation, the marriage of the rest.

(CP 464–65; my italics)

In all three examples, the qualifier precedes assertions about the attainment of absolute truth. An admission of uncertainty frames an assertion about supreme certainty. These structures are the grammatical equivalent, in other words, of the images of containment in Stevens's landscapes, the images of epochal walls encircling the greatest achievements of lights, birds, and buildings. They are propositions that evoke, in their internal tension, the experience attributed to the dying Santayana, where "the extreme of the known" coincides with "the extreme / Of the unknown": instances where the reader, like Santayana, is called on to feel "The human end in the spirit's greatest reach" (CP 508).

If Stevens's grammatical practices correspond to his descriptions of truth-making, they have also been misunderstood in the same way. Like the expositors of his philosophy of truth, many critics of his language have regarded his endemic uncertainty as evidence of a thoroughgoing, Santayanan skepticism.[74] They have tended to regard his various methods of hedging (or "dithering") as certain proof that "his poems are about . . . the *impossibility* of knowing anything,"[75] instead of acknowledging the *possibility* of truthfulness left open by all modal auxiliaries short of simple negations. In doing so, too, they have ignored the crucial role played by empirical evidence in the disintegration of Stevens's tensional propositions: a role in keeping with that intrinsically optimistic "struggle with fact" (OP 242) James advocated and Santayana dismissed as pointless. Our ability to appreciate that Stevens practices the Jamesian kind of truth-making he preaches depends on a willingness to resist the kind of binary thinking James discouraged—the kind of thinking that insists that a philosopher be either a believer or a doubter, either a champion of reality or a champion of imagination. In examining Stevens's practice, in other words, we must be willing to take to heart Stevens's recognition that choosing between apparent opposites may be a matter of choosing not "Between / But of" (CP 403): his recognition that when confronted with a choice between reality and imagination, in particular, "it is not a choice of one over the other, but a matter of treating the two as equal and inseparable" (NA 24).

One example of the tendency to read Stevens as more of an epistemological pessimist than he actually is is Vendler's account of his use of the word "must"—an aberration in what is otherwise a remarkably sensitive cataloging of his terminology of qualification. Despite her choice of the word "hypothesis" as a general term for Stevens's qualified assertions, she denies to "must" propositions the element of hope that makes them genuinely hypothetical. Whenever Stevens's speakers use the term, she insists, they engage in an act of fiction-making, an act of asserting something they know in their hearts to be untrue. "Must," she says, "is not a word of faith, but a word of doubt, implying as it does an unbearable otherwise."[76] Her example is the following passage from "Notes":

> To discover winter and know it well, to find,
> Not to impose, not to have reasoned at all,
> Out of nothing to have come on major weather,
>
> It is possible, possible, possible. It must
> Be possible. It must be that in time
> The real will from its crude compoundings come. . . .
>
> (CP 404)

Although Vendler is correct in noting that these "must" propositions are motivated by desire, and even in her perception that this desire is motivated by a sense of an "unbearable otherwise," she goes too far in insisting that the speaker in this passage is convinced of the falsity of these propositions. The speaker may well be possessed by a "fevered" desire that the "real" will eventually reveal itself,[77] but this demonstrates *only* that the alternative seems unbearable. It is not by any means proof of his conviction that what he desires can never coincide with what is. Indeed, we have more reason to imagine, given Stevens's many admonitions against epistemological pessimism, that the speaker desires reality to shine *because he knows it shines.* As James warned, it is essential that we not mistake someone who has renounced "the doctrine of objective certitude" (in this case by prefacing his assertion with an optative qualifier) for someone who has "give[n] up" all "hope of truth itself." The particular issue being contemplated in Vendler's exemplary passage—the same question about the potential of truth-making we have been investigating—makes it especially easy to appreciate the importance of recognizing its speaker's optimistic shade of gray.

Vendler's pessimistic interpretation of Stevens's "must," shared by Frank Lentricchia,[78] is paralleled by the more widespread misreading of one of his signature auxiliaries: the "as if." A great number of Stevens's critics have interpreted his "as if" clauses as conscious fictions. In doing so they have a powerful precedent in the philosopher of "as if" himself. In his analysis of the term, Vaihinger specifies clearly that it signals a proposition "whose impossibility and unreality is at the same time admitted." The "as if" is a synonym for the "consciously-false"; the "'[a]s if' world" is "the world of the unreal." Vaihinger justifies his characterization of "as if" phrases by analyzing them into their component parts: the metaphor-making "as" and the conditional phrase "if it were." Although the "as" posits a likeness between reality and the specified condition, he says, the form of the conditional "affirms that the [posited] condition *is an unreal or impossible one.*"[79] If we regard Vaihinger's stipulations as normative, and then appreciate the extraordinary frequency with which "as if" appears in Stevens's poetry, we find ourselves forced to concede that Stevens's work is primarily escapist in nature, composed in defiance or despair of the truth. But there are good reasons for questioning the assumption that Vaihinger's code must serve as our guide. First, Stevens gives no indication that he uses the term according to Vaihinger's specifications (or even that he knew exactly what those specifications were).[80] Second, and more importantly, the "as if" is not restricted to such an epistemologically pessimistic meaning in common usage. According to Fowler, for example, the use of "it were" after "as if" is common and proper but is required in *all* cases, even in those in which "the clause gives a supposed actual fact";[81] thus it does not *necessarily* signal a consciously false proposition. For an instance where a speaker shows great faith in his "as if" proposition, consider the following example from James:

> I thus disclaim openly on the threshold of all pretension to prove to you that the freedom of the will is true. The most I hope is to induce some of you to following my own example in assuming it true, and acting as if it were true. (WB 115)

Here it is quite clear from the context that "as if" introduces a hypothesis in the purest sense: a proposition about the freedom of the will that James believes to be true (and is prepared to test) even if he suspects its truth cannot be proven beyond a shadow of a doubt. It would be a serious mistake to contend that James denies free will, just because he cannot be dogmatic about it. Indeed, as James makes clear in *The Varieties of Religious Experience*, the "as if" signifies an open-mindedness toward the propositions it precedes, *both* because these may prove to be efficacious *and* because they may, after all, prove to be true:

> We can act *as if* there were a God; feel *as if* we were free; consider Nature *as if* she were full of special designs; lay plans *as if* we were to be immortal; and we find then that these words do make a genuine difference in our moral life. Our faith *that* these unintelligible objects actually exist proves thus to be a full equivalent in *praktischer Hinsicht,* as Kant calls it, or from the point of view of our action, for a knowledge of *what* they might be, in case we were permitted positively to conceive them. (VRE 55)

It is equally clear, on reflection, that many of Stevens's "as if" propositions are uttered in a similar spirit of hope. A case in point would be his Nietzschean critique of an "over-human god," in "Esthétique du Mal":

> If only he would not pity us so much,
> Weaken our fate, relieve us of woe both great
> And small, a constant fellow of destiny,
>
> A too, too human god, self-pity's kin
> And uncourageous genesis . . . It seems
> As if the health of the world might be enough.
>
> It seems as if the honey of common summer
> Might be enough, as if the golden combs
> Were part of a substance itself enough,
>
> As if hell, so modified, had disappeared,
> As if pain, no longer satanic mimicry,
> Could be borne, as if we were sure to find our way.

(CP 315–16)

The sequence of "as if" propositions here, like the "must" propositions Vendler describes, displace what the speaker believes to be unbearable alternatives. But it is also evident that those alternatives strike the speaker as having little credibility and that the happier propositions seem to him to be the ones most acceptable to common sense. The very least thing that must be said in response to those who would regard these and many other "as if" propositions in Stevens's poetry as conscious fictions is that they are not assuredly false but rest on what Brogan has called the "precarious threshold" between possibility and impossibility.[82] The stronger response would be that their speakers dream hopefully of a place for them (and for the must that has inspired them) beyond that threshold, in the realm of the unequivocably true.

As I have suggested, the epistemological optimism with which Stevens's speakers regard their qualified propositions also informs a dutiful effort to test those propositions against the evidence of the "actual world." There are many instances in the poetry, that is, where the tensionality of utterances is not simply the consequence of a war between arbitrary impulses toward belief and doubt but a more pointed struggle between what James called the "theoretic need" and the "impulse to be *acquainted* with the parts rather than to comprehend the whole" (WB 58–59). I have already observed that the tensionality of Stevens's utterances is in some instances a function of sequential revisions and in others a function of simultaneous ones and that his equivocating speakers sometimes "move to and fro" between belief and doubt, and sometimes display "both / At once" (CP 396). The same distinction holds among those cases where he qualifies abstract propositions by positing empirical counterevidence. We can appreciate the depth of Stevens's commitment to the "struggle with fact" by considering each kind in turn.

The first type of empirical testing found in Stevens's poetry, the kind in which a proposition is asserted, then followed by discordant evidence, is the easiest to spot and hence the most accessible proof of Stevens's conviction that imagination is susceptible to the pressure of reality. I am thinking of the kind of qualification we find in "Les Plus Belles Pages":

> Nothing exists by itself.
> The moonlight seemed to.

> (CP 244)

Or in the pairs of generalizations and contrary particulars with which Stevens considers the inadequacy of a "World Without Peculiarity":

> The day is great and strong—
> But his father was strong, that lies now
> In the poverty of dirt.

Nothing could be more hushed than the way
The moon moves toward the night.
But what his mother was returns and cries on his
    breast.

(CP 453)

In these examples Stevens challenges the authority of general propositions by following them with statements of the "peculiar" facts they leave out. He compels the speakers of both poems to descend from their theoretical flights and to consider the validity of the insights attained there in the actual world. Reflecting on a similar pair of abstract assertions and empirical counterevidence in "A Primitive Like an Orb," Stevens speaks openly about the contrast he wishes to establish:

> Here, then, is an abstraction given head,
> A giant on the horizon, given arms,
> A massive body and long legs, stretched out,
> A definition with an illustration. . . .

(CP 443; my italics)

Earlier in the poem, Stevens describes the moment of undoing of imaginings that for a while "need[ed] no proof." The moment of disintegration is marked by the sudden intervention of "sharp informations, sharp, / Free knowledges," all of which had been suppressed as the imaginings were sustained. He is determined, in other words, to confront abstract propositions with the reality they purport to represent. Like the linguistic banners Fenollosa celebrated, his abstractions are to be "blooded" (CP 385), assaulted with the unassimilable differences on whose forgetting they depend.

If these sequential moves "from the abstract to the real, to and fro"[83] (*Letters* 434) resemble a "luminous flittering" (CP 396), in which bits of empirical counterevidence serve as an "after-shining flicks" (CP 46), there is another kind of tensional utterance in the poetry whose manner of reconciling the abstract and the concrete more closely recalls "the concentration of a cloudy day" (CP 396). This second kind of empirical testing is one in which the faith inspired by a proposition, and the doubt introduced by concrete counterexamples, occur simultaneously. Louise Brogan has called this important practice "simile"; I would call it Stevens's commitment to the form of expression Pound called "interpretive metaphor." It may seem strange to seek evidence of Stevens's respect for empirical reality in the act of metaphor-making, an act he frequently characterizes as an "evasion" of such reality (CP 373, 396, 486). Within the realm of epochal thinking, however, where unequivocal statements are ruled out, certain kinds of figurative language can be seen to signify greater deference to this reality than others. The use of symbol, for example, represents the culmination of

a process of abstraction, a point at which a writer treats the identity between two (or more) objects as a fait accompli; one object serves as substitute for the other(s), whose phenomenality has been annihilated. On the
other hand, as we have seen, the "interpretive metaphor" is a device that
arrests the evasive process of theory-making at its initial, and by no means
victorious, stage, inviting the reader to consider a similarity between entities
whose particularity remains accessible. Stevens's respect for the kind of
figurative device favored by Hulme and Pound is apparent in several medi-
tations on the expressive power of "resemblances" or "relations." In the
1947 essay "Three Academic Pieces," he notices a correlation between the
"ambiguity that is so favorable to the poetic mind" and the detection of
"resemblances" (NA 79). More significantly, he specifies that the precise
correlate of the kind of ambiguity he is talking about is "[t]he point at
which [the process of abstraction] *begins*" (NA 78; my italics): the point
when a resemblance between two things lends significance to both, sacrificing neither. In a late poem with the pointed title "Thinking of a Relation
Between the Images of Metaphors," Stevens captures the tension involved
in the state of apprehending phenomenal particulars and incipient categories at once:

> . . . The fisherman is all
> One eye, in which the dove resembles the dove.
>
> There is one dove, one bass, one fisherman.
> Yet coo becomes rou-cou, rou-coo. . . .
>
> State the disclosure. In that one eye the dove
> Might spring to sight and yet remain a dove.
>
> The fisherman might be the single man
> In whose breast, the dove, alighting, would grow still.
>
> (CP 357; my italics)

Sensing the inadequacy of theories that would reduce the multiplicity of
particulars to a single concept, Stevens proposes a simultaneous acknowl-
edgment of sense data and concept as a compromise. A bundle of sense
data "Might spring to sight" yet still remain a "dove"; something energetic
and unique may survive the process of being "stilled" by its resemblance
to other creatures. Like the ideal poet imagined in "Notes," the fisherman
"stop[s] to watch / A definition growing certain and / . . . Wait[s] within
that certainty" (CP 386); he remains intensely aware of the cindery thing
that is unlike anything else that shares its definition. As Brogan has pointed
out, Stevens works in many of his poems to establish precisely this "Relation between the Images of Metaphors." His figures of choice, like those

of the Imagists, are those that hint at resemblances without annihilating any of the phenomena involved.

Although it would be inaccurate to say that Stevens is never a symbolist (my reading of much of his doctrine depends to some extent, for instance, on a theory about his private symbolism of birds and houses), his figurative strategies, first developed in *Harmonium,* have much more in common with Imagism and Vorticism. Working either by simple juxtaposition or with the aid of the gentle comparatives "like" and "as," he invites his reader to detect and to contemplate the "shadow[s] that look[] regular" in the cinders (Hulme, CW 18). (Stevens's version of Hulme's metaphor appears in "The Connoisseur of Chaos": acknowledging the elusiveness to theory of the world's "squamous facts," he nonetheless witnesses how "relation appears, / A small relation expanding like the shade / Of a cloud on sand, a shape on the side of a hill" (CP 215)). Some of his juxtapositions recall those of Pound and H.D., in inviting the reader to consider the affinity between human and natural things. There is the portrait, for example, of the old Chinese philosopher in "Six Significant Landscapes":

> His beard moves in the wind.
> The pine tree moves in the wind.
>
> (CP 73)

There is also the provocative, because apparently mysogynistic, comparison in "Depression Before Spring":

> The hair of my blonde
> Is dazzling,
> As the spittle of cows
> Threading the wind.
>
> (CP 63)

Most intriguing of all, however, are numerous juxtapositions that recall Hulme's efforts to draw attention to the homelier side of entities the Symbolists imbued with transcendental light. The humbled stars I have already mentioned (whose fate resembles that of the stars in Hulme's "Autumn") have company in the shrouded moon in "Of the Surface of Things" (whose fate recalls that of the moon in Hulme's "Above the Dock"):

> The singer has pulled his cloak over his head.
> The moon is in the folds of the cloak.
>
> (CP 57)

Stevens encourages his reader to consider the resemblance between beard and pine tree, between hair and spittle, between the mysterious moon and a human head. But by preserving both objects in each comparison he ensures that the force of the similarity meets resistance in empirical difference: whatever the generalization suggested by the suggested likeness, the reader can see that "the mask is strange, however like" (CP 181). Stevens demonstrates the kind of balanced speculation he intends his figures to encourage in the third of his "Six Significant Landscapes," where the implied principle at stake is once again the affinity between humans and natural objects. The speaker acknowledges the limitation, as well as the validity, of the comparison, reaching no final conclusion about the naturalist philosophy:

> I measure myself
> Against a tall tree.
> I find that I am much taller,
> For I reach right up to the sun,
> With my eye;
> And I reach to the shore of the sea
> With my ear.
> Nevertheless, I dislike
> The way the ants crawl
> In and out of my shadow.
>
> (CP 74)

As Wyndham Lewis would put it, in this poem a perceptual comparison enables the speaker to contemplate an abstract principle but not to "settle down and snooze" on its assuredness.[84] Indeed when Stevens proselytizes for this mode of figuration in the last of the "Six Significant Landscapes," his description of it leaves no doubt about his philosophical and aesthetic affinity with Lewis and the rest of the Vorticist artists:

> Rationalists, wearing square hats,
> Think, in square rooms,
> Looking at the floor,
> Looking at the ceiling.
> They confine themselves
> To right-angled triangles.
> If they tried rhomboids,
> Cones, waving lines, ellipses—
> As, for example, the ellipse of the half-
> moon—
> Rationalists would wear sombreros.
>
> (CP 75)

Their deductive methods, Stevens suggests, may lead rationalists to dogma, but they cut them off from life. Were they to enrich their abstractions with vital, material shapes—like the rhomboids and wavy lines of Bomberg's

"Jiu-Jitsu" or Gaudier-Brzeska's "Red Stone Dancer"—they would find themselves rescued from intellectual torpor. They would find themselves ready for an exhilarating game of truth-making, a dance at once ordered and sensual.

If Stevens's analogies and juxtapositions resemble Imagist and Vorticist ones in their tensional structure, they also resemble them in being conceived as "possibly really true guides" to reality—not mere fancies.[85] The prevailing view of Stevens's concept of metaphor reinforces his reputation as a Nietzschean fiction-maker; Frank Lentricchia, for example, has said that for Stevens "metaphor is a self-satisfying method of ordering reality by the making of pleasing resemblances *which do not exist outside the mind.*"[86] But like most judgments about Stevens's radical skepticism, the one proposing he regards metaphor as an illusion depends on ignoring the ways in which Stevens *undercuts* his pessimistic statements. Stevens is as careful to qualify his statements about the illusory nature of resemblances as he is to problematize all expressions of epistemological and ontological pessimism. Notice the qualifications, for example, in a passage from Stevens's seminal essay on metaphor, "Three Academic Pieces" (1947)—a passage Lentricchia cites as evidence of Stevens's conviction that the perception of an ordered world is part of an "adult make-believe":[87]

> One may find intimations of immortality in an object on the mantelpiece; and these intimations are as real in the mind in which they occur as the mantelpiece itself. *Even if* they are only a part of an adult make-believe, the whole point is that the structure of reality because of the range of resemblances that it contains is measurably an adult make-believe. (NA 74; my italics)

The most obvious qualifier here, of course, is the auxiliary "even if," which turns the proposition that the ornament's participation in universal order is an illusion into a hypothesis (and not a particularly likely one, at that). But the pessimistic proposition is also undercut by Stevens's statement that "adult make-believe" and "reality" are identical, an ambiguous assertion that at least partly suggests that what is desired *may actually be what is.* The logic here is made more explicit later in the essay, where Stevens, describing the "ambiguity" of any theory arrested at the point where an analogy is perceived, conveys the nature of that ambiguity by juxtaposing two opposing statements:

> In this ambiguity, the intensification of reality by resemblance increases realization and this increased realization is pleasurable.

> Here what matters is that the intensification of the sense of reality creates a resemblance: that reality of its own is a reality. (NA 79)

The statements differ in what they imply about the origin of the sense that one is apprehending the structure of reality. In the first a (constructed) analogy creates the increased sense of reality. In the second the increased sense of reality "creates a resemblance." The first implies that we *construct* analogy to make our experience of the world more pleasurable. The second implies that analogy *emerges* as the sense of reality improves. Stevens describes the effect of the two propositions as one of "going round a circle, first clockwise, then anti-clockwise" (NA 79). The point of the exercise (as of an analogous exercise in "The Connoisseur of Chaos") is to underscore the fact that the desirable proposition is as possible as the undesirable one. As Stevens emphasizes in another essay using similar strategies, "The Effects of Analogy" (1948), an analogy may "not [be] enough to *establish* a principle. But [it is] enough to suggest the *possibility* of a principle" (NA 128; my italics). Stevens's sense of this possibility motivates him, as it did Pound, to specify that the poet choose those analogies that will communicate not only pleasure but a sentiment of their rationality:

> Poetry is a satisfying of the desire for resemblance. As the mere satisfying of a desire, it is pleasurable. But poetry if it did nothing but satisfy a desire would not rise above the level of many lesser things. Its singularity is that in the act of satisfying the desire for resemblance it touches the sense of reality, it enhances the sense of reality, heightens it, intensifies it. (NA 77)

Like Pound's "interpretive metaphor," Stevens's ideal trope is the one that will communicate to its readers a sense, not just of play, but of discovery. As he emphasizes in a disparaging note on the figures in surrealist painting: "The essential fault of surrealism is that it invents without discovering. To make a clam play an accordian is to invent not to discover" (OP 203).[88]

Stevens's cautious optimism about analogy and his conception of its purpose suggest that it is fair to apply the same hermeneutic principles to the analogies and similes we find in his poetry as I have applied to those in Hulme and Pound. That is, we should allow it to launch an ongoing effort to to find a relation, hence a principle, that *works*. An analogy may prove inadequate because of perceptible difference, but the sense of promise inspired by the analogy should spur us on, encourage us to consider some other incipient principle, which will give a more adequate accounting of empirical fact. Consider, for example, the analogy that concludes "The Death of a Soldier":

> Death is absolute and without memorial,
> As in a season of autumn,
> When the wind stops,

When the wind stops and, over the heavens,
The clouds go, nevertheless,
In their direction.

(CP 97)

Stevens invites us to consider the analogy between death and autumn, or, more specifically, between the death of a soldier and a moment in autumn when the wind suddenly stops. In this case he helps us on our way by articulating the first proposition suggested by the analogy that death brings an absolute end to things, as does the disappearance of the wind to the motion of the clouds. It is not long, however, before the proposition fails to satisfy, as the objects begin to resist the claim about their likeness. Again Stevens nudges us toward this perception of difference. The autumnal scene differs from death, in that the dying of the wind does not put an end to the motion of the clouds; Stevens paints the familiar picture of clouds moving steadily across the sky, despite the apparent stillness of the atmosphere. But contemplating this difference does not put an end to the appeal of the analogy we have been asked to consider. Instead, a revised proposition springs to mind. Perhaps the soldier's death, too, is only an ending of something irrelevant to the continuation of something else. Perhaps the soldier, motionless on earth, goes on living somewhere "over the heavens." Perhaps this is what empirical evidence will teach us if we go on searching. Like James in his tracts on human immortality,[89] Stevens offers his own provisional thesis on the subject only as a way of challenging his reader to consider the question for himself or herself, with all the philosophic and distinguishing powers at his or her disposal. His similes, like Pound's Images, do not tell the reader what is true, so much as they encourage him or her to make a pragmatic decision about the matter at hand, on the basis of empirical evidence. As he makes clear in another Image on the same subject, "Of Heaven Considered as a Tomb," the way to resolving the question is by assessing whatever "word" his "interpreters" have received from "men / Who in the tomb of heaven walk by night" (CP 56). Or as he puts it in "Gubbinal," a poem offering an array of potential analogies for the sun and therefore an array of different incipient theories about the disposition of nature, the sun "Is just what you say. / *Have it your way*" (CP 85; my italics).

A final example will confirm how Stevens uses analogies to leave metaphysical decisions, including those about the relations inhering in the universe, up to his readers. The poem is called "Tattoo"; the analogy it invites us to consider is one about the systems of relations we perceive in things:

The light is like a spider.
It crawls over the water.
It crawls over the edges of the snow.

It crawls under your eyelids
And spreads its webs there—
Its two webs.

The webs of your eyes
Are fastened
To the flesh and bones of you
As to rafters or grass.
There are filaments of your eyes
On the surface of the water
And in the edges of the snow.

(CP 81)

The central "interpretive metaphor" in the poem invites us to consider the
likeness between a spider and a source of light. As the spider spins its web,
the light creates those regular patterns we detect in the world—on water,
on snow, on the inside (perhaps both literally and metaphorically) of our
eyelids. In suggesting that we may find ourselves meditating on an objective
spider's web of relations, Stevens employs a figure with deep roots in the
transcendentalist tradition. Both Mallarmé and Whitman used the image
of the spider's web to represent a system of foreordained synaesthetic correspondences, to which a poet might become apprised in a moment of mystical illumination.[90] The second stanza of the poem, however, helps us to
articulate an objection to the suggested analogy. The difference between
light infiltrating from some mystical realm of Ideas and a spiderweb is that
the spiderweb is something constructed, not preexistent. We are forced to
revise our mystical proposition: perhaps the truth is that we are the spi-
derlike makers of all of those regular patterns detectable in the cinders,
that the patterns do not impose themselves on us, so much as we spin them
out of ourselves. The poem's balance is such, however, that neither option
subsumes the other—like all Hulme's efforts to call the status of symbolist
icons into question, it leaves the matter unresolved.[91]

It is a commonplace in criticism of Stevens that there is an absolute
discontinuity between the poetics of *Harmonium* and those of *Ideas of
Order* and beyond.[92] In fact there is perfect continuity between the two.
For one thing Stevens reiterates the doctrine of analogy that guides his
early practice in later poems like "Thinking of a Relation Between the
Images of Metaphors" and "Three Academic Pieces." More significantly
the qualified propositions that distinguish the later poetry establish the
same kind of noncoercive, encouraging relationship with the reader: modal
auxiliaries like "must" and "as if" transform otherwise dogmatic propositions into suggestions she can accept or reject at will. Realizing this
is crucial to appreciating the pervasiveness of Stevens's optimistic, Jamesian
rhetoric. There is, in particular, a direct continuity between the Imagist

poems that juxtapose earthly and transcendental images and those poems, like "Credences of Summer," "To an Old Philosopher in Rome," or "Study of Images, II," that offer qualified statements about revelation. Like the witness to the dying Santayana, that is, the reader of "The Death of a Soldier," "Gubbinal," or "Tattoo" must consider both a doubt about the possibility of mystical insight and its converse, both the possibility that a "human end" may be at work in what seem be experiences of revelation, and the possibility that such experiences are what they seem to be. Both types of poem, in other words, fulfill James's stipulations for the proselytizing mystic in the age of the new psychology. They are noncoercive hypotheses that problematize, but do not discount, the possibility that the mind may transcend the textual universe and look out on "a more extensive and inclusive world" (James, VRE 428).[93] To put it another way, they offer incipient theories that trace, if not certainly, possibly, a "*final* relation" (CP 465; my italics).

Stevens's philosophical and rhetorical optimism leads us inevitably to further questions. Does he every lay claim to having actually reached such a "point of termination"? Do his hypotheses, finally corroborated, ever give way to unqualified assertions? There are, to my knowledge, no moments in Stevens where he makes a generalization he does not qualify. The strongest theoretical statements in the poetry are all checked in some way, whether it be by images of circumscribed spaces, or deferred destinations, or by the most inobtrusive of grammatical qualifiers. That being said, however, there are moments when certain incontrovertible particulars enter the poetry and put an end to equivocation, profoundly disrupting the carefully balanced *epoche* Stevens otherwise works so hard to preserve. Stevens describes such an event in a poem from *The Rock* titled "The Green Plant." Beginning with the familiar assertion that we dwell in a "constant secondariness," an epochal space where the intellect, like a bird defeated by its quest, "turn[s] down toward finality," the poem's speaker startles the reader accustomed to the inviolable character of such spaces by abruptly acknowledging an exception to the rule. We know, he contends, that there is no perception not half-created by the mind,

> *Except* that a green plant glares, as you look
> At the legend of the maroon and olive forest,
> Glares, outside of the legend, with the barbarous green
> Of the harsh reality of which it is part.
>
> (CP 506; my italics)

The plant's intrusion into consciousness from a place "outside of the legend," puts an end to the speaker's perhaps too comfortable conviction that nothing can be known for certain. His dedication to epistemological uncertainty notwithstanding, he is confronted by a "harsh reality" whose objectivity will not be compromised. If his relation-seeking intellect has been unable to penetrate the walls of the *epoche* from within, these walls have been shattered by a force from without; an objective world forces itself on him, willy-nilly.

The event Stevens describes in "The Green Plant" is fully dramatized in two earlier poems: "Extracts from Addresses to the Academy of Fine Ideas" (1940) and "The Bouquet" (1948). In both cases the "harsh reality" that intrudes on the equivocating consciousness is the incontrovertible horror of war. As its title suggests, "Extracts" is a kind of philosophical credo, an address outlining a series of policy statements on epistemological and moral issues. Its dominant message is identical to the one initially proposed in "The Green Plant": the speaker assures his audience that "It is an artificial world" (CP 252) and that it is "What / One believes" and not what one knows that "matters" (CP 258). Lest the audience conclude too readily from this, however, that "it is enough / To believe in the weather and in the things and men / Of the weather and in one's self, as part of that / And nothing more" (CP 258), the speaker closes his speech with a bald statement of fact, an "extract" from actuality whose *kern* is inalterable:

> Behold the men in helmets borne on steel,
> Discolored, how they are going to defeat.
>
> (CP 259)

Whatever imaginative force one exerts against it, whatever uncertainty charges the hypotheses one constructs to comprehend it, these efforts will be insufficient to ward off the dark reality of a soldier's life. Had the speaker been intending to claim immunity to the call of actuality on the grounds of a theory that nothing can be known for certain, the end of the poem puts an abrupt end to that possibility.

There is no more complete testimony to the vulnerability of the *epoche,* however, than "The Bouquet," a poem that also establishes more clearly than any other the conditions that prevail in an epochal "dwelling-place" left undisturbed. In other poems depicting such a space—the equivalent of Crispin's "Nice Shady Home" (CP 40)—any disruption of domestic peace by the forces of actuality remains at the level of a threat; in "Contrary Theses," for example, the speaker's enjoyment of his summer home is strained but not destroyed by the "acid sunlight" (CP 267) streaming through the windows, by the ominous figure of a soldier stalking back and forth outside the door.[94] Here, however, the domestic peace of the "home" is definitively shattered, as the soldier leaves propriety behind and actually crosses the threshold. The first four cantos of the poem describe a place in which the speaker, like Stevens himself, or like some painter of expressionist still lifes, has been peacefully making a record of this "consciousness of" (CP 450) a bouquet of flowers. The terms of the description are unmistakably phenomenological: "The rose, the delphinium, the red, the blue" are to him simply *"questions of the looks they get,"* objects "queered by lavishings of [the] will to see" (CP 451; my italics). Most importantly the speaker emphasizes that the life he enjoys in these private surroundings is one in which he has indulged in a "dithering" (CP 452); he has been one of those jaunty, ironic philosophers, whose accessories—"chains of blue-green glitterings" and "hats of angular flick and fleck" (CP 449)—suggest a propensity for vacillation. The particular question he has been relieved from resolving is the same question that drove Crispin to take refuge in his cabin, that is, the question of the validity, or ultimate "origin" (CP 451) of the contents of his consciousness. There has been no need to classify the bouquet's "eccentric twistings" either as revelations or projections; so far as he has been concerned, they have been just "flatly there" (CP 452). With the events of Canto V, however, this luxurious practice of conflating the real and the imaginary, of denying certain knowledge of any reality, must come to an end, as a visitor breaks into the epochal space—a visitor whose origin in the world beyond the threshold renders him unequivocably real:

> A car drives up. A soldier, an officer,
> Steps out. He rings and knocks. The door is not locked.
> He enters the room and calls. No one is there.
>
> He bumps the table. The bouquet falls on its side.
> He walks through the house, looks round him and then leaves.
> The bouquet has slopped over the edge and lies on the floor.
>
> (CP 452–53)

The simple, declarative statements here reflect the new, distinctive status of the events they describe. If the previous stanzas were pure Woolf or Joyce, these words are pure Hemingway; the metaphorical style and dubious contents of a stream of consciousness narrative have given way to the simple clarity and nonnegotiable facts of realism. Stevens underscores the soldier's impact on the epochal space by having him violate not just one, but two, enclosures. There is the house, abruptly deserted by its fearful inhabitant, and there is the vase—or jar—knocked over, its contents spilled unceremoniously over the floor. At the beginning of the poem, Stevens implies that the jar performs the same function in relation to its contents as the house to its, reducing them to "metaphor, . . . a growth / Of the reality of the eye, an artifice, / Nothing much" (CP 448). Now both containers fail, shattered by the appearance of something about which there can be no further equivocation.

I emphasize these violations of epochal space—the most extreme exam-

ples of epistemological optimism and realism in Stevens's rhetorical arse-
nal—because they are of vital importance to the final issue I would like to
consider: the politics informing his poetic practice. As I have indicated, the
greatest danger in mistaking hypotheses for fictions is that it leaves the
hypothesis-maker open to unjust accusations about his indifference to the
actual world and his failure to respect the claims of what is decidedly
"other." In attempting to demonstrate Stevens's specifically Jamesian brand
of truth-making, whose epistemological optimism and realism firmly distinguishes it from that of Santayana, I have been preparing to correct just
such a misunderstanding. And nothing will be more important to that effort
than the fact that Stevens represents the *epoche* as sometimes being shattered from without: his conviction, as he articulates it in "Man Carrying
Thing," that an indulgence in uncertainty can last only "until / The bright
obvious stands motionless in cold" (CP 351).

THE POLITICS OF THE JAR

The features of Stevens's epistemology I have been noting—his dedication to the *epoche,* his optimism about the ends of theory making, and his
respect for the power of actuality to shatter both comforting hypotheses
and the *epoche* itself—are of considerable significance for discussions of
his politics. Although it is not feasible to argue that his kind of pragmatism
is the exclusive province of either left or right (James himself anticipated
that his position would "develop both right-wing and left-wing interpreters" [MT 72]), it helps us to see that Stevens was far more sympathetic to
the concerns of the left than either his left-wing detractors or his right-
wing champions have allowed. As Alan Filreis's groundbreaking account
of Stevens's reception in the 1940s and 1950s—*Wallace Stevens and the
Actual World* (1991)—demonstrates, the contrasting attitudes conservative
and marxist critics have adopted toward Stevens's work have invariably
turned on a shared perception of him as a pessimistic, if playful, maker of
fictions, who abdicates all responsibility for representing things as they
are. In the debate between the American New Critics and their left-wing
opponents in the early 1940s, for example, about the merits of literary
realism at a time of crisis, Stevens was praised by one camp and derided
by the other for what both perceived to be his unabashed formalism. Although John Crowe Ransom, Yvor Winters, and Alan Tate praised Stevens's refusal to corrupt his hermetic poems with direct references to world
events or exhortations to a nation at war, Alfred Kazin, Howard Mumford
Jones, and others on the left had little patience with Stevens's "polished
littlenesses,"[95] with what they saw as closed systems of reference, impervious to the harsh realities of their time. A similar polarization in the opinions

about Stevens's work occurred during the postwar era of American expansionism in Europe and has continued in contemporary discussions of the implicit "colonialisms" in his poetry. Whereas the right has embraced Stevens for his inspiring insights into the power of imagination to transform reality, the left has derided him for the apparent bracketing of actuality that was the cost of that celebration.[96] Henry Kissinger and Fredric Jameson alike have detected in Stevens "a valorization of the supreme power of the poetic imagination over the 'reality' it produces,"[97] but where that perception once led Kissinger to invite Stevens to participate in a seminar defending American expansionism, it has inspired Jameson (and Frank Lentricchia as well) to indict Stevens's practice as an "*analogon* of the imperialist world system," in which autonomous countries are reduced to mere ideas in the mind of a dominant culture.[98] I hope that I have already established that Stevens was not the idealist these discussions make him out to be.

Filreis's *Wallace Stevens and the Actual World,* with James Longenbach's *Wallace Stevens: The Plain Sense of Things* (1991), has done much to correct the misconception of Stevens's work on which judgments of his politics have depended.[99] But even this tide-turning work makes some common hermeneutic errors worth examining closely both because they are reminiscent of James's misinterpreters and because they are to be avoided if Stevens's pragmatist commitment to actuality is to be appreciated fully. Following the rare example of Roy Harvey Pearce, Filreis argues that Stevens underwent a sudden change in his attitude toward the relative importance of imagination and reality late in his career.[100] Discussing Stevens's position in the wartime debate between isolationist New Critics and left-wing nationalists, he claims that Stevens suddenly abandoned the formalist and isolationist principles of his early work after the Japanese bombing of Pearl Harbor in 1941. After that incident, he says, and under the influence of grim stories told by exiled Europeans, Stevens developed a sober respect for the dark actualities of a world at war and a profound sense of his responsibility, as a poet, to contribute what he could to alleviate the situation. One reason for Filreis's decision to situate Stevens's conversion at so precise (and late) a moment is what he sees as the unmitigated formalism of his April 1941 lecture, "The Noble Rider and the Sound of Words." It is not hard to see why Filreis would regard that lecture as articulating a position from which Stevens, if he was to be redeemed in the eyes of the left, had to be converted. Critics from Alan Tate to Marjorie Perloff have read it as a paean to modernist irresponsibility, a manifesto championing art's resistance to what James called the "circumpressure of experience" (MT 47).[101] They have pointed especially to its claim that "the poetic process is essentially an *escapist* process" (NA 30) and to its suggestion that poetry originates in an imagination that "press[es] back against the pressure of reality" (NA 36). They have cited remarks like the following to demonstrate that this propensity for uninterrupted fiction-making goes hand-in-hand with a complete denial of any social responsibilities:

> In this area of my subject I might be expected to speak of the social, that is to say sociological or political, obligation of the poet. He has none. . . .

> I do not think that a poet owes any more as a social obligation than he owes as a moral obligation, and if there is anything concerning poetry about which people agree, it is that the role of the poet is not to be found in morals.

> The truth is that the social obligation so closely urged is a phase of the pressure of reality which a poet . . . is bound to resist or evade today. (NA 27–28)

In accepting this common reading of "The Noble Rider," however, and situating Stevens's conversion to empirical responsibility at a later date, Filreis underestimates the longevity and strength of the poet's commitment to actuality. The powerful statements of formalist principles found in the essay are not, in fact, uncompromised; Filreis's mistake, as Tate's and Perloff's, lies in overlooking both the rhetorical strategies and the strategies of qualification—the "grammar of hypothesis"—in Stevens's prose.

Viewed in context, the contentious statements from the "Noble Rider" are clearly not to be taken at face value but rather meant as corrective overstatements. Consider, for example, the statements celebrating imagination's power to resist the "circumpressure" of experience. Stevens makes them only after he has made it clear that he believes actuality has achieved a *definitive victory* over imagination in his time and that this extreme situation has been "inimical to poetry" (NA 15). Speculation about God has given way to an obsession with the facts of a hostile world and contemplation of all kinds to the pressures of making a living; it is therefore necessary to stress the "affirmative" power of imagination in order to revive some hope for poetry.[102] The strong statements denying the poet's social obligation perform a similar, qualificatory function. Stevens is reacting against what he perceives as an oppressive dogmatism in literary circles in the late thirties and early forties, a doctrinaire insistence on a poetics of "commitment." The thrust of Stevens's own dogmatic statements on behalf of "escapist" poetry—rather like that of comparable statements made at the same time by George Orwell[103]—is not that the poet has no social role to play but rather that he should resist playing it at the bidding of his literary contemporaries.

Recognizing the polemical nature of these statements about the poet's freedom from the demands of actuality is the first step toward reading them fairly. The second is to notice that Stevens also *qualifies* these statements, and that he does so with such strength that they come to signify almost the opposite of what they literally say. If initially he frees the poet from actuality, ultimately he represents him as being deeply, inevitably, responsive to it. This becomes apparent when we turn back to the analysis of the charioteer passage in the *Phaedrus* with which the "Noble Rider" essay (and my own discussion of Stevens) begins. Had Stevens genuinely believed in the autonomy of imagination, he would have done nothing to interfere with the charioteer's flight. As it is, however, he not only halts the ascent but does so for *empirical* reasons: the problem with Plato's vision is that it "adheres [only] to what is *unreal*" (NA 7; my italics), whereas an ideal poetry will not stray from "the reality on which the lovers of truth insist" (NA 23). In a similar way and with the result, once again, of belying the formalist program assigned to him, Stevens qualifies his claim about the poet's autonomy from social obligations. Although maintaining that no outside forces have the right to speak of a poet's *obligation* to attend to social reality, he goes on to assert that the poet *will attend to that reality nonetheless,* because a desire to do so (the equivalent of James's persistent "sister passion") is innate and inevitable:

> Yes: the all-communing subject-matter of poetry is life, the never-ceasing source. But it is not a social obligation. One goes back out of a suasion not to be denied. (NA 28)

Stevens uniformly qualifies his "seraphic proclamations" (CP 45) about imaginative freedom and political autonomy, in other words, by "after-shining flicks" (CP 46). Critics who fail to credit such qualifications and who see Stevens as a single-minded champion of formalist lyricism practice the same kind of binary thinking that blinded James's critics to *his* commitment to actuality. Perloff's unwillingness to do so accounts for her extraordinary reading of the following passage from the "Noble Rider":

> We are confronting, therefore, a set of events, not only beyond our power to tranquillize them in the mind, beyond our power to reduce them and metamorphose them, but events that stir the emotions to violence, that engage us in what is direct and immediate and real, and events that involve the concepts and sanctions that are the order of our lives and may involve our very lives; and these events are occurring persistently with increasing omen, in what may be called our presence. (NA 22)

It is hard to imagine a stronger statement of the necessity of responding to actuality's "bright obvious," yet Perloff reads the passage as further evidence of Stevens's willingness to withdraw into imagination. She says, "It is difficult to conceive of Wordsworth," with whom Stevens is commonly compared, "*retreating from engagement* in this way."[104]

Two more examples from Filreis's reading of Stevens will illustrate the

apparent difficulty, and yet the necessity, of detecting a Jamesian sense of
responsibility in Stevens's equivocations. In the first case, Filreis clearly
lapses into binary thinking and so fails to see that Stevens's moment of
"conversion" to actuality should be pushed further back in time. In arguing
that the pivotal moment occurred at Pearl Harbor, he cites two documents
of 1939 to illustrate poetic and political isolationism in Stevens's work of
that period. These are the poem "Variations on a Summer's Day," written
in 1939 but published in the Winter 1940 issue of *The Kenyon Review,*
and an enigmatic letter to Hi Simons pertaining to it, dated December 29,
1939. The relevant part of the letter, which pits the options of confronting
reality against the practice of indulging pleasurable fictions, requires quoting at length:

> Of course, what one is after in all of these things is the discovery of a value that
> really suffices. Only last night I saw an expression in a French paper which is in
> point. It was something like this: "the primordial importance of spiritual values
> in time of war". [*sic*] The ordinary, everyday search of the romantic mind is
> rewarded perhaps rather too lightly by the satisfaction that it finds in what it
> calls reality. But if one happened to be playing checkers somewhere under the
> Maginot Line, subject to a call at any moment to do some job that might be
> one's last job, one would spend a great deal of time thinking in order to make
> the situation seem reasonable, inevitable, and free from question.
>
> I suppose that, in the last analysis, my own main objective is to do that kind
> of thinking. On the other hand, the sort of poem that I have in the winter number
> of *The Kenyon Review,* from which every bit of anything of that sort has been
> excluded, also has its justifications. In a world permanently enigmatical, to see
> and hear agreeable things involves something more than mere imagism. One
> might do it deliberately and in that particular poem I did it deliberately.[105]

Filreis concludes that this letter and the poem it discusses endorse the practice of evading reality through imagination. The poem, he says, in making
what the letter praises as a "deliberate" effort to evade reality by focusing
on "agreeable things," affirms "what is in effect an isolationist's ideal position." Even when the poem comes close to acknowledging the reality of
war, Filreis finds it "unable finally to resist aestheticizing" it (and likewise
unable to resist assimilating the British soldiers currently marching to their
deaths to those British soldiers of another era who were decidedly not
American allies):

> Everywhere the spruce trees bury soldiers:
> Hugh March, a sergeant, a redcoat killed,
> With his men, beyond the barbican.
> Everywhere spruce trees bury spruce trees.

(CP 234)

In Filreis's view the poem rationalizes its unwillingness to face the reality, finally, by dwelling on the undecidability of moral and epistemological questions. The most notable of its emblems of uncertainty is its descendental transformation of the image of a guiding star:

> Star over Monhegan, Atlantic star,
> Lantern without a bearer, you drift,
> You, too, are drifting, in spite of your course . . .

> (CP 232)

The unmoored star has the effect of "deny[ing] the validity of reference generally" and so of liberating the poet of any duties to attend to anything other than the most desirable of fancies.[106] Thus, both letter and poem endorse the Santayanan (and formalist) practice of unrestrained fiction-making, the poetic equivalent of isolationism in politics.

The problem with reading the 1939 letter and poem this way is that it ignores what is really another affirmation about the importance of both imagination and reality. In admitting only one side of this affirmation, Filreis joins those critics of Stevens who mistake signs of uncertainty for darkly pessimistic denials of the real, for rationalizations of complacency and inaction. But the truth of the matter is that Stevens's respect for the demands of actuality is, if anything, more powerful than his respect for the imagination. It is crucial to note that the rhetorical structure of Stevens's letter is identical to that of the "Noble Rider" essay. Here, once again, Stevens *accepts it as a given* that actuality impinges on the poet; his *"main* objective," he stresses, is to think with the soldier under the Maginot line, for whom the impending horrors can scarcely be wished away. His claim that a poetry that omits "anything of that sort . . . *also* has its justifications" is, then, like those overstated affirmations of imagination in the "Noble Rider": it is an attempt to preserve *some* role for the imagination in a frightening world but hardly an appeal to it as a viable alternative to facing realities. This is not a "choice . . . between," but a both-and assertion.

That Stevens is far from wholeheartedly endorsing the unrestrained transformation of reality by imagination is made more than apparent, too, by several stanzas in "Variations on a Summer Day," which is far more than just a poem of "agreeable things." Although many of the poem's images reinforce the picture of a world in which all has been reduced to uncertainty—the wandering star in stanza IV, the metamorphosed reality in stanza XII, the intermingling of sea-surface and sky in stanzas XV and XVI, the musical message, neither subjective nor objective, in stanza II—it also contains several expressions of frustration with that uncertainty and with both the doxic and practical stasis it entails. One such example is the speaker's exhortation to himself in stanza XVII, which reveals a determination to shatter the epochal walls reducing all within to uncertainty: a desire to "*Pass through* the door and through the walls, / Those bearing balsam, its field fragrance, / Pine-figures bringing sleep to sleep" (CP 235). The "pine-figures" the speaker wills to transcend are the poem's many evasive metamorphoses of trees: the obfuscating spruce trees of stanza XII, the "Arachne integument of dead trees" in stanza XIV. The impulse here is the same as the nostalgic longing for the "father" tree in stanza V: the wistful desire for an object *not* transformed by imagination (CP 233). While on the one hand appearing to revel, then, in the evasiveness induced by metaphor, Stevens is, on the other, deeply impatient with the sense of inevitable metaphoricity that justifies his "dithering" (CP 234). When he thinks approvingly of the alternative, in stanza X—a commitment to social action that pierces through uncertainty like a boat cutting through the epochal water of "Sea Surface Full of Clouds"—his terms are reminiscent of Marx:

> To change nature, not merely to change ideas.
> To escape from the body, so to feel
> Those feelings that the body balks.
> The feelings of the natures round us here:
> As a boat feels when it cuts blue water.
>
> (CP 234)[107]

I am not suggesting that merely toying with commitment can be adequate atonement for inaction; Stevens vacillates then concludes that "it was not yet the hour to be dauntlessly leaping" (CP 236). But it is important to recognize that "Variations on a Summer Day" is a poem *about* dithering, and only secondarily itself a dithering. As his letter about the poem suggests, Stevens recognizes that the poem is vulnerable to its own charge. The semiquote from Marx is self-arraignment.

The failure of many of his contemporaries to acknowledge Stevens's respect for actuality left the poet with a strong desire to clarify it. The result was his most powerful statement about the pragmatic character of poetry, "The Figure of the Youth as Virile Poet." Addressing an audience of exiled European intellectuals, whose firsthand experience of war would have given them reason to doubt a man of his reputation, Stevens went to great lengths in this 1943 address to emphasize that a tolerance for "noble" imaginative affirmations (NA 35) need not mean indifference to the pressures of the actual world. This time his corrective overstatements serve the cause of *reality* rather than imagination:

> There is a difference between [philosophic truth and poetic truth] and it is the difference between logical and empirical knowledge. (NA 54)

If, for the poet, the imagination is paramount, and if he dwells apart in his imagination, as the philosopher dwells in his reason, and as the priest dwells in his belief, the masculine nature that we propose for one that must be the master of our lives will be lost. (NA 66)

It would not be surprising were Stevens's listeners dubious of these claims, given what he says elsewhere in his speech about the kind of "fact" for which poetry is accountable. A radical empiricist still, he observes that "fact includes poetic fact" and that an "indefinite number of actual things . . . are indistinguishable from objects of the imagination." (NA 62). But if his audience found themselves wary of a position that might confound Hitler's oppression with fanciful imaginings, they would have been wrong to interpret this apparent leveling of fact and fiction as a sign of political complacency. Stevens was fully apprised of what James sought so hard to demonstrate to his critics in *The Will to Believe* and *The Meaning of Truth*: that acknowledging an element of interpretation in fact need not entail giving up the "quest or hope of truth itself," the practice of "systematically continuing to roll up experiences and think." Ironically giving up on verification procedures is more likely to be the response of metaphysical philosophers bent on certainty. In accepting uncertainty Stevens's ideal poet never becomes disillusioned but continues to seek that "agreement with reality" (NA 54) on which society, and his own "masculine nature," depend.[108] "Poetic truth is the truth of *credible* things," not fanciful ones (NA 53; my italics). Stevens's commitment to this position is still apparent in 1955 in a disquisition on the attitudes that make a "Whole Man": "The great modern faith," he says there, "is faith in the truth and particularly in the idea that the truth is attainable, and that a free civilization based on the truth . . . is no less attainable" (OP 288).

The second criticism of Stevens from the left to be addressed is the perception of an analogy between Stevens's strategy of representation and the blinkered vision of American imperialism. This attack fuses something like Lukács's objection to the "attenuation of actuality" or "negation of history" in the modern novel with Edward Said's powerful insights into imperialist discourse. In essence the argument is that Stevens reduces all that is genuinely "other" to something identical with the perceiver's consciousness of it and that he happily "disinvolves . . . impressions from their material grounds." "Little by little," in Stevens's poetry, writes Fredric Jameson, "images of things and their 'ideas' begin to be substituted for the things themselves," until the expanding mind has dissolved and redefined the whole of the actual world.[109] Although Jameson and Lentricchia are particularly critical of Stevens's appropriation of "Third World" locations and commodities, his cognitive imperialism is for them more thoroughgoing than these examples would indicate. *All* of his acts of "making interior" are problematic in their presumptuous elevation of the power of an individual consciousness over the force of material circumstances. Lentricchia points out the likeness between Stevens's indulgent explorations of the poetry of the subject and the "commodity fetishism" of a capitalistic consumer. Like such a consumer, Stevens detaches his objects of desire from the social context that produced them; like a consumer, too, his main object is to enjoy the feeling of desire, to defer the satisfaction that complete possession of such objects will bring. This interpretation of Stevens explicitly links his dubious politics with his habit of retreating into epochal domiciles. Consumption, says Lentricchia, "is radical metaphor for nourishing empty interior spaces—a taking into the home, 'my room,' the mind, spirit, heart."[110]

This critique of Stevens's imperialist vision is particularly enlightening when we recall that one of Stevens's first endorsements of such interiorization in poetry came at the end of a chronicle relating the failure of an imperialist venture. Crispin becomes a poet of Being, "magister" of a "single room" (CP 42), once he finds that he has no authority to impose his vision on whole continents. Lentricchia's and Jameson's analyses of his poetry of Being are sharp reminders that imperialism may persist even when absolutist confidence has been shaken. They show that a perceiver may comply with the designs of an imperialist culture simply in becoming an "indulgent fatalist" (CP 44) and in resigning knowledge of any experience but his own. Thus, they show that Stevens's renunciation of the authoritarianism of the "old" masculinity is no cause, in itself, for celebration. The self-sufficient sphere of his "new" virility—the sphere of *"my own speech and the strength of it, this only"* (NA 60)—can exert its own kind of violence on the world.

But this critique of Stevens holds only so long as his "landscape of the mind" remains inviolate. To return to Lukács, the Marxist's problem with modernist writing is that in it the "rift" between stream of consciousness and objective world is complete:

> First, the hero is strictly confined within the limits of his own experience. There is not for him—and apparently not for his creator—any preexistent reality beyond his own self, acting upon him or being acted upon by him. Secondly, the hero himself is without personal history. He is "thrown-into-the-world": meaninglessly, unfathomably. He does not develop through contact with the world; he neither forms nor is formed by it.[111]

Although this may accurately describe the impervious consciousness of the Santayanan fiction-maker, or that of Said's orientalist, for whom empirical data is irrelevant to the perpetuation of his theories,[112] it is clearly not identical to the mind whose struggle with reality I have been tracing through Stevens's poetry. Stevens's initial renunciation of metaphysics may seem to be an effort to create a garrison out of just this kind of hermetic space, because of its disavowal of certain knowledge of reality's "plum." But this disavowal does not amount to a denial of intractable "facts" nor to an unwillingness to seek the best version of those facts available. As we have seen, over the course of his career Stevens both pursues the correctives offered by empirical data and gives in to violent actualities crashing into the epochal "home" from the outside. He recognizes that there is a distinction between the "stream of consciousness," which is "individual," and the "stream of life," which is "total" and impossible to ignore (OP 184). No argument about his disengagement from actuality, marxist or otherwise, will be complete until it has acknowledged these aspects of his work and consciously sought to avoid "throwing out the baby with the bathwater" in interpreting his pragmatist uncertainty.

Despite Filreis's intention in *Wallace Stevens and the Actual World* to demonstrate that Stevens's later poetry makes significant concessions to actuality, many of his close analyses of key texts support the view of him as a poet of consciousness exclusively—and thus an "imperialist" in the sense explained by Jameson and Lentricchia. Like his reading of "The Noble Rider and the Sound of Words," these analyses reflect a failure to respect the ways in which Stevens *qualifies* his enthusiasm for imaginative transformation and a damaging kind of binary thinking, *acknowledging only the pessimistic side* of Stevens's "blue-green glitterings" (CP 449). One such example is his reading of "Description Without Place," a poem that on the surface of things epitomizes the Crispinlike retreat into the "landscape of the mind." Stevens delivered the poem as part of the Phi Beta Kappa proceedings at Harvard in June 1945; his partner on the platform was Sumner Welles, former undersecretary of state and powerful advocate of American efforts at reconstruction in Europe. In an April 1945 letter to Henry Church, Stevens describes the poem's informing concept as "the idea that we live in the description of a place and not in the place itself."[113] The message of the poem, for Filreis (and other critics), is that we *inevitably* live in a mental landscape, rather than a real one, and that there is *no way* of transcending epochal space and confronting things as they really are.[114] Filreis supports his view of the poem's thesis by citing a line that describes all that "seems" as but "a knowledge / Incognito."[115] He might as well have cited, as straightforward assertion, Stevens's statement that "seeming . . . / Is description without place" (CP 343). In his view, moreover, the poem itself perfectly exemplifies the condition it describes in effacing present and historical realities with fanciful imaginings. It substitutes theoretical speculation for references to postwar reality, fanciful transformations of Nietzsche and Lenin and others for historical fact (CP 342–43). Filreis concludes that the poem attests to the morality and the efficacy of transforming reality through imagination; Stevens's "conception of place" is thus the equivalent of the imperialistic "assimilation of place" that his fellow panelist Welles was advocating in Europe.[116]

Where this reading of "Description without Place" goes awry is in taking Stevens's assertion that seeming is "description without place" both as an absolute assertion and a contented one. It ignores the fact, first of all, that this assertion comes in the form not of a dogmatic statement but of a *hypothesis*. Stevens does not simply contend that "seeming *is* description without place"; he observes that "*if* seeming is description without place" (CP 343; my italics), we will have to accept the consequences, including a denial of the accuracy even of those perceptions which seem most certain. *If* this, "*then* . . . Even the seeming of a summer's day, / Is description without place" (CP 343; my italics). This hypothesis is, furthermore, only one of two provisional theories offered in the poem about the significance of what seems: Stevens also speculates ("it is possible . . .") that there may be moments when "to seem—it is to be," for example, when what fills our consciousness is something from the outside, something "actual" (CP 339). It is by no means self-evident to Stevens, in other words, that we *must* dwell in an epochal space that is perennially uncertain or that we are justified, therefore, in being satisfied with whatever seems to us to be the truth. One thing that is clear, however, is that Stevens is conscious of the practical importance of *how we decide among such hypotheses*. It is "the theory of description," he says, that "matters most" (CP 345). And the theory that the inner landscape is all that we can hope to know, a theory that frees us to engage in cavalier acts of inventing "nation[s] in a phrase," will have consequences, not necessarily positive, for how we proceed in the world. "It matters," Stevens says, because it will determine how we read "everything we say / Of the past" (CP 345). It will determine whether we regard historical descriptions with optimism, believing that they *can* contain a grain of truth, or whether we dismiss them all as inadequate. Insofar as the poem's own descriptions willfully efface history, they are illustrations of a "theory of description" that the text itself acknowledges is both provisional and problematic.

Two final examples from Filreis's record of Stevens's imperialist gestures demonstrate that his tendency to ignore the qualifiers to his pessimistic assertions is not accidental but part of a pattern. One of his most powerful pieces of evidence for Stevens's faith in the transformative power of imagination is a comment in a 16 May 1945 letter to Leonard Geyzel, where Stevens attempts to outline his recent thoughts concerning the place of poetry in society. At one point in the letter, Stevens asserts that for him the "most important thing" is to realize "the desire *to contain the world wholly within one's own perception of it* . . . within perceptions that include perceptions that are pleasant." Filreis takes this as an unqualified statement of support for the practice of defining the world in one's own terms: in political language the equivalent of the endeavor to establish a new American hegemony. In doing so, however, he ignores several other remarks in the letter emphasizing the *limits* a poet must impose on such a practice. Stevens comments, for example, that a poetry "limited to the vaticinations of the imagination . . . soon becomes worthless"; it must be counterbalanced by "the consciousness of reality." Responding to a rumor that Hemingway is writing poetry, he endorses what he expects will be the novelist's scrupulous attention to reality. And he closes the letter with a statement that strongly undercuts any suggestion that it is desirable or even possible for a mind to continue in pleasurable meditation, resistant to evidence of the horrors of the actual world. "At the moment," he suddenly remarks, "the war is shifting from Europe to Asia, and *why one should be writing about poetry at all is hard to understand.* The war against Japan is likely to be a prodigious affair before long, and I am afraid that, with some of the things that may develop, we may not have reached an end, but merely a beginning."[117]

Filreis also neglects Stevens's vacillations on the subject of imaginative imperialism in a reading of a key passage in "Notes Toward a Supreme Fiction." The portrait of the young poet in the first section of the poem seems to him to endorse the particular mode of imperialism to which Lentricchia and Jameson object: the fanciful idealization of Third World locations. After giving a relatively accurate description of the fierce beasts that occupy these faraway places, Stevens describes the ephebe's tendency, in his imaginings, to subdue them:

> But you, ephebe, look from your attic window,
> Your mansard with a rented piano. You lie
>
> In silence upon your bed. You clutch the corner
>
> Of the pillow in your hand. You writhe and press
> A bitter utterance from your writhing, dumb,
>
> Yet voluble dumb violence. You look
> Across the roofs as sigil and as ward
> And in your centre mark them and are cowed . . .
>
> These are the heroic children whom time breeds
> Against the first idea—to lash the lion,
> Caparison elephants, teach bears to juggle.
>
> (CP 384–85)

Filreis is right in asserting that this passage is about the imagination's power (and inclination) to tame all that is foreign and frightening, to construct fictions "sufficient for making existence pleasurable."[118] But he is wrong in implying that Stevens simply assents to the practice. In fact this portrait merely constitutes evidence for the first thrust in a tensional assertion about the construction of supreme fictions: "It Must be Abstract." The counter-thrust, of course, comes in the second section of the poem, "It Must Change." The young poet huddling in his garret has a counterpart in this alternative story: the Crispinlike planter, now dead, whose house has disintegrated in the face of the jungle's "garbled green" (CP 393). As we have seen, the lesson of this landscape is that no imaginative domicile will be strong enough to prevent the world subdued by the imagination from reasserting itself. And the imperative in the section's title clearly underscores Stevens's conviction that this disruption of the imagination's aspirations is every bit as necessary as the one it serves to dismantle. The complacent ephebe, in short, whom Filreis views as Stevens's role model, is no ideal; Stevens condemns the "voluble, dumb violence" of his representations.[119]

Filreis expresses surprise at finding in Stevens's letters an occasional criticism of the ethnocentric enterprises of U.S. business and government.[120] But these overt criticisms seem surprising only if, like Filreis, Jameson, and Lentricchia, we ignore the many instances, from *Harmonium* onwards, where Stevens *himself* critiques the kind of mind that acknowledges the validity of only its own interpretations. In "Cuisine Bourgeoise" (CP 227), for example, we find Stevens attacking something very close to what Lentricchia calls fetishistic "gourmandizing," both as literal activity and as metaphor for phenomenological reduction.[121] Stevens asks a rhetorical question about bourgeois consumers in which he clearly equates their pleasure with a kind of cognitive solipsism:

> Is the table a mirror in which they sit and look?
> Are they men eating reflections of themselves?
>
> (CP 228)

What Stevens sees here, but the consumers do not, is that they feast on a plate of "human heads" (CP 227–28): real lives made miserable for their pleasure. Stevens shows similar contempt for the hotel guest in "Arrival at the Waldorf," who cossets himself in that bourgeois palace in an attempt to ignore an "alien, point-blank, green and actual Guatemala" (CP 241). In both cases Stevens satirizes the retreat into interiority that he himself has undertaken, suggesting that the cost of that activity has been a regrettable disregard for the actual world. The richest of these satirical portraits is found in "Extracts from the Academy of Fine Ideas" (the poem, we'll remember, where a theory about the sufficiency of believing what we want to believe is confronted with a bald description of the horrors that such beliefs cannot successfully keep at bay). Notice, once again, how Stevens likens the activity to one of relishing a culinary delicacy:

> The eye believes and its communion takes.
> The spirit laughs to see the eye believe
> And its communion take. And now of that.
> Let the Secretary for Porcelain observe
> That evil made magic, as in catastrophe,
> If neatly glazed, becomes the same as the fruit
> Of an emperor, the egg-plant of a prince.
> The good is evil's last invention. Thus
> The maker of catastrophe invents the eye
> And through the eye equates ten thousand deaths
> With a single well-tempered apricot, or, say,
> An egg-plant of good air.

(CP 253)

Stevens is more than gently satirical in representing the kind of mind that will translate "ten thousand deaths" into the simple pleasure of "a single, well-tempered apricot." This example of what Lentricchia calls the disinvolvement of impression from actuality is, for the poet who has been accused of it himself, "evil's last invention," the crime of a complacent "emperor"; we have moved beyond the realm of the slightly ridiculous to a case where the bracketing of actuality amounts to a criminal abuse of power.

That Stevens appreciated the political dangers of a phenomenological poetry becomes even clearer when we explore the course of one of his most memorable metaphors for the *epoche*. There is nothing accidental, of course, in his appointment of the grandly titled "Secretary for Porcelain" to oversee the emperor's gourmandizing in the "Extracts." With the title he gives to this functionary, he alerts us to the double significance of the poem's figure for imperial oppression: "neatly glazed," the emperor's fetishes resemble not just candied fruits but also those hermetically sealed pots, bottles, and jars Stevens identifies with the space of phenomenological reduction. The passage quoted, then, directly *indicts* the activity of retreating into the self-contained "vessel" of consciousness, equating it with the oblivious cruelties of imperial rule. And it is only one of several such indictments to be found in Stevens's poetry, all of which attest to his profound understanding of the political evil involved in translating all the world into a hazy good.[122]

Stevens's most powerful indictment of cognitive imperialism, however, is found in the much earlier "Anecdote of the Jar":

I placed a jar in Tennessee,
And round it was, upon a hill.
It made the slovenly wilderness
Surround that hill.

The wilderness rose up to it,
And sprawled around, no longer wild.
The jar was round upon the ground
And tall and of a port in air.

It took dominion everywhere.
The jar was gray and bare.
It did not give of bird or bush,
Like nothing else in Tennessee.

(CP 76)

In his long meditation on this poem in the opening chapter of *Ariel and the Police*, Lentricchia observes that the jar's subordination of the wilderness resembles an act of colonization and that the poem, in being profoundly critical of the act of jar-placing, has a place in "a tradition of American anti–imperialist writing." Despite this valuable observation, however, Lentricchia fails to entertain the possibility that the poem might be a sign of Stevens's own awareness of the political problematics of his emerging aesthetic—a criticism remarkably similar to the one Jameson and Lentricchia himself level against it. Lentricchia's failure to make the connection between the anti–imperialist statement he finds in the poem and his own anti–imperialist reading of Stevens, some chapters later, may have something to do with his working definition of the jar's imperialism. He identifies the vessel exclusively with "various forms and effects of systematic endeavour; all the creation of structure, systems, reasons; all effects . . . of abstraction."[123] The jar's domination of the wilderness, in other words, is for Lentricchia identical to the imposition of dogmatic theories, like those emerging from the "categorical gut" of Crispin's banjo, which have been hypostatized and imposed on the world. Yet a reading more faithful to the totality of Stevens's writings would suggest that that the jar is the equivalent of the hermitage devised in Crispin's recoil from such metaphysical endeavors and that what Stevens is really doing is issuing a warning that, even within his more "condign" rounds, a Crispin will remain an "Effective colonizer" (CP 44). In a poem published alongside "Anecdote" in a 1919 issue of *Poetry* titled "The Indigo Glass in the Grass," Stevens uses a vessel to represent a mental landscape, inadequate, despite all efforts, to "contain the world" (OP 43). On this evidence it seems reasonable to suggest that the steadily expanding wall of the jar in "Anecdote" is a prototype for those impenetrable, because all-assimilating, cognitive boundaries Stevens describes in the later poetry: the eggshell enveloping the speaker in "Things of August" (CP 490), the skin of the "egg-plant" of "good air" in "Extracts" (CP 253). It defines a mind content with "merely circulating," like a pot on a wheel, a mind content with neutralizing the frightening otherness of the wilderness by denying the necessity of distinguishing between playful imaginings and facts.[124] The barren space it creates anticipates the "colony" of imagination Stevens describes, many years later, in "An Ordinary Evening at New Haven": a place where "public green" turns "private gray" (CP 479) and where the imagination holds the green world of actuality "Prostrate below the singleness of its will" (CP 478).

It can be argued, then, that Stevens's imperial jar is the earliest of the poet's many comments on the political dangers of a poetry that celebrates phenomenological reduction without simultaneously seeking to check its representations of reality against the best facts available. Although the speaker in "Anecdote of the Jar" does not overtly condemn the practice of cognitive imperialism (his attitude toward the progress of the jar is less hostile than awestruck), two details in the poem suggest a certain reservation about its blind expansion. The jar is not as impermeable as the poem's penultimate line suggests: it is "of a port" (a place of entry and departure) "in air." And Stevens's decision to set the drama in what Filreis would call the "geopolitically precise" location of Tennessee,[125] disrupts attempts to read the poem as a formalist icon: a written equivalent of the hermetic, purely self-referential vessel. With these gestures Stevens leaves open the "fissures" that his campaign against metaphysics might otherwise seem to close, and he calls attention to the way the "barbarous green" of actuality encroaches (or rises up to meet) the epochal space from the outside. This is not the Stevens, confident in the supreme power of imagination over reality, that Tate and Kissinger celebrated and Lentricchia and Jameson condemn. It is Stevens the Jamesian pragmatist, who is certain of the autonomy of the material world and of the power it can and must wield over the potentially imperialistic constructs of consciousness—positions far more favorable to a committed materialist aesthetic than set against it.

I shall leave Stevens by calling attention to the lesson to be learned from one of his last poems, "The Course of a Particular" (1950). The poem demonstrates once again what I have been arguing in stressing Stevens's likeness to James: the rejection of metaphysics and the retreat into the chronically uncertain *epoche* are for him merely steps on the way to a renewed faith in the importance of heeding at least some of his perceptions. Before penning a final description of an epiphanic experience—the perception of a "cry" coming from dead leaves at autumn's end—Stevens rejects both a mystical and a dogmatically skeptical account of his experience: "It is not a cry of divine attention, / Nor the smoke-drift of puffed-out heroes, nor human cry" (OP 123). The previous stanzas explain his rejection of the latter. Like James he has grown weary of the skeptic's insistence that everything is projection. Effort is involved in remembering "that one is part of everything." "Being part," he says, "is an exertion that declines." And as the will to sustain the *epoche* weakens, he says, one begins to feel "the life of that which gives life as it is" or to acknowledge the bright obvious as being exactly what it seems. Hence the final, acceptable description—a description decidedly with, not without, "place":

> It is the cry of leaves that do not transcend themselves,
> In the absence of fantasia, without meaning more
>
> Than they are in the final finding of the ear, in the thing
> Itself. . . .
>
> (OP 123–24)

In the process of defining his "practical muse" in his early poetry, Stevens held out hope that she might be not only useful but also reliable. Rationalizing his continuing courtship of her in "Le Monocle de Mon Oncle," for example, he reminded himself of the possibility that she might yet turn out to be "A damsel heightened by eternal bloom" (CP 15). Or as the Crispin-like cabindweller is promised in "Hymn from a Watermelon Pavilion":

> A feme may come, leaf-green,
> Whose coming may give revel
> Beyond revelries of sleep. . . .
>
> (CP 89)

By the last years of his life, Stevens has realized that believing such a muse has arrived, as well as coming to terms with the harsh "green" actuality she conveys, is a psychological, ethical, and political necessity.

5

"Both Sides of the Line":
Pragmatist Poetry and Critical Debate

> But it was not a choice
> Between excluding things. It was not a choice
>
> Between, but of. He chose to include the things
> That in each other are included, the whole,
> The complicate, the amassing harmony.
>
> —Wallace Stevens, CP

JAMES conceived pragmatism, above all else, as a mediator. Personified it is a woman, called in to resolve disputes between male philosophers trapped in binary thinking.[1] The conflicts to be resolved reflect the philosophers' commitment to one or the other of two habits of mind they regard as irreconcilable but which pragmatism knows should be blended and generally are. These are the "two tendencies" James identified in "The Sentiment of Rationality" and which he detailed in *Pragmatism* as the "tender-minded" and "tough-minded" dispositions:

THE TENDER-MINDED	THE TOUGH-MINDED
Rationalistic (going by "principles"),	Empiricist (going by "facts"),
Intellectualistic,	Sensationalistic,
Idealistic,	Materialistic,
Optimistic,	Pessimistic,
Religious,	Irreligious,
Free-willist,	Fatalistic,
Monistic,	Pluralistic,
Dogmatical.	Sceptical.

(P 13)

Unlike the male philosophers who stubbornly defend positions fulfilling one or the other temperament, pragmatism understands that "[m]ost of us

217

have a hankering for the good things on both sides of the line" (P 14). Her program is aimed to "satisfy both kinds of demand. It can remain religious like the rationalisms, but at the same time, like the empiricisms, it can preserve the richest intimacy with facts" (P 23).

This study has demonstrated how Hulme, Pound, and Stevens emulate pragmatism's strategies, reconciling tender-mindedness and tough-mindedness in their conceptions of inspiration and in their views about how the content of inspiration should be expressed. Recognizing the degree to which these poets follow James's program should enable us, furthermore, to engage in our own acts of mediation, as we consider many of the critical debates about them: debates defined by a firm commitment to preserving James's set of antinomies. In what follows, I shall review how the pragmatist conception of these poets' writings resolves some of the problems set by their critics. Viewed through the pragmatist lens, their work is not as inconsistent as it is often deemed to be, and it invites reconciliation among those critics who have stressed its exclusive commitment to one or the other "side of the line," developing, like James's male philosophers, "antipathies of the most pungent character" toward "those who lay the emphasis differ-ently" (P 12). Finally, these Jamesian poetics resist efforts to assimilate them to another position going by the name of "pragmatism," popularized in the 1980s by Richard Rorty. This avant-garde pragmatism differs from Hulme's, Pound's, and Stevens's because it abandons James's program of reconciliation. It not only reinforces the divide between the "two tenden-cies" but also bifurcates dispositions on the right side of the line by insisting that there there can be no cooperation between skeptical and empiricist habits of mind. Rorty has encouraged critics to view modernist writing as his pragmatism's literary counterpart.[2] The modernist writers I have considered stand with James, not Rorty, affirming that poetry is never to be "a choice / Between excluding things" but always a choice of things— an "amassing harmony."

My account of Hulme's "new classicism" has shown how Hulme blends attributes from both of James's columns. More precisely it represents Hulme's ideal as combining a "religious" and "free-willist" attitude, with a scientific commitment to "going by 'facts.'" Hulme's position reflects his antipathy toward two different kinds of "romanticism" or *hubris* about human capacities: the arrogance of nineteenth-century scientism, which had sacrificed human freedom for the supremacy of the intellect, and Ideal-ist metaphysics, which had taken the opposite tack and exalted intuition as a means of gaining access to the "Infinite." Like James's account of religious experience, it endorses intuition and free will[3] while rejecting metaphysical speculation; it rejects science's intellectualism and determin-ism while adopting its empiricist discourse. This balance of concerns shapes the practice of the "new classical" poet, which is to write poems that are nondiscursive and uncalculated but that avoid the presumptious obscurities of Symbolism. By respecting Hulme's own definition of the "romanticism" he opposes—a concern with the overestimation of human capacities on two fronts—we have been able to dispense with one of the major premises behind the popular view of him as a muddled thinker: the view, proposed by Kermode, Krieger, and others that it is inconsistent to oppose Romanticism and at the same time to be an intuitionist and organicist.[4]

Acknowledging Hulme's affinity with James also enables the resolution of another apparent inconsistency in his work, one that has received more attention of late than the question of his relationship to Romanticism. This is the seeming contradiction between his attraction both to skepticism and to absolutism—a set of allegiances that becomes incomprehensible only if we insist on bifurcating doubt and faith. Michael Roberts first identified this problem in 1938, citing the following statements as evidence of the inconsistency:

> . . . [T]here is no such thing as an absolute truth to be discovered. All general statements about truth, etc., are in the end only amplifications of man's appetites. (Hulme, CW 8)

> I hold the religious conception of ultimate values to be right. . . . From the nature of things, these categories are not inevitable, like the categories of time and space, but are *equally objective*. In speaking of religion, it is to this level of abstraction that I wish to refer. (CW 455)[5]

The most recent efforts to come to terms with the contradiction between these skeptical and absolutist positions have been Michael Levenson's and Karen Csengeri's. Both argue that the inconsistency can be explained by recognizing something obscured by Herbert Read's arrangement of the materials in *Speculations*. Hulme's thought went through a radical change, sometime around late 1911 (Csengeri) or early 1913 (Levenson).[6] Hulme's poetics, they explain, belong to the early, skeptical, or "subjectivist" phase of his thought, shaped by Bergsonian nominalism. His Imagist poetry is to reflect the arbitrariness and inadequacy of ideas and thus "to avoid pursuit of the epic, the absolute and the permanent."[7] But subsequently whether because he disliked some of Bergson's followers, or because he discovered the more compelling arguments of Frege, G. E. Moore, and Wilhelm Worringer, he abandoned Bergson and embraced a new, absolutist way of thinking. This is why he was able, in the essay that appeared in *Speculations* as "Humanism and the Religious Attitude," originally published in 1915–16 as "A Notebook," to insist on "the religious conception of ultimate values" and why he was able to argue in the last two years of his life for an art of pure, geometric abstraction, which rejected all allusions to life and change.

The Jamesian model enables us, however, to see an alternative way of accounting for Hulme's ethics and visual aesthetics—one that does not require the drastic (and unconvincing) measure of claiming that he suddenly repudiated Bergsonism, and its antimetaphysical way of thinking altogether.[8] In my account of Hulme, I have endeavored to show that Hulme's determination to take the "Infinite" out of the intuitive moment is not thoroughgoing and that it is ultimately only an effort to suspend judgment about its ultimate significance. And just as the "early" phase of Hulme's thought is not as dogmatically skeptical as Csengeri and Levenson suggest, so the "late" phase is not as dogmatically absolutist. Read's editorial decisions in *Speculations* have obscured the pragmatist context for Hulme's statement that the "religious conception of ultimate values [is] . . . right," making it seem more categorical than it actually is. In essays and notes written prior to "A Notebook," Hulme writes frequently, and often autobiographically, of the psychological appeal of absolute ethical values, particularly in a climate where scepticism prevails. Citing James's accounts of conversion experiences in both *The Will to Believe* and *The Varieties of Religious Experience,* he also repeatedly emphasizes that philosophical decisions are inevitably made at the level of emotion, rather than logic, and that there is nothing suspect, therefore, about consciously following the directives of feeling, or need, in making them.[9] When we look at the first installment of "A Notebook," which Read left out of *Speculations,* it becomes clear that Hulme is still thinking of these things when he makes his assertions about the rightness of the "religious conception" of ethics. Writing in early December 1915, while recovering from wounds acquired at the front, he introduces his discussion of ethics by "admit[ting] as fact" that "individuals in a condition of danger, when . . . pseudo-absolutes melt away into a flux, require once more a real absolute, to enable them to live." Failing to believe in absolute values and taking the relativist position espoused by the pacifists will mean certain defeat. Hulme's repeated claims that an unwavering ethics is what is required by the "verifiable facts of the European situation"[10] strongly recall James's justifications for maintaining religious faith in times of crisis, that is, his claims that to be lost in the woods, or caught in a snowstorm, and to be without it, is to perish.

That Hulme frames his defense of absolutist ethics in an argument about their usefulness is easy to miss, because in the same installment he speaks out strongly against something he describes as the pacifists' "relativist utilitarian ethics." On close examination, however, his opposition to the pacifists is not so much an attack on the admission of *any* degree of subjectivity into ethical matters as it is an attack on the presumption that dogmatic skepticism is the *only* viable position to which such an admission leads. The pacifists are guilty of displaying an "inane confidence" in the skeptical position, of forgetting that all things, including their own relativism, "are *constructions,* full of risk and not *inevitable.*" Hulme's discomfort with their confidence is in part motivated by something like James's "ethics of optimism": a sense that it is necessary to fight the perverse habit, particularly prevalent in a skeptical era, of automatically discrediting any account of things that corresponds to desire. The pacifists, he believes, are guilty of assuming that the efficacy of the view that the English have something timeless and eternal to fight for is enough to "explain it away" as a fiction.[11] They have got it into their heads that religious belief requires a "deadening" of our "*natural acuteness,*" where surely the will to believe is as viable a candidate for respect as the will to doubt.[12] Carefully considered, then, Hulme's position seems more a Jamesian defense of the religious attitude than an unequivocal assertion about the purity of ethical values. Lest his readers miss the fact that he does not mean simply to counter the pacifists with dogmatism of the opposite kind, he emphasizes that he presents the religious view "not as *true*" but only "as a passage from a false to a true *opinion.*"[13] Levenson and others are simply wrong, then, when they represent "A Notebook" as an essay where Hulme "insist[s] that questions of ultimate value [have] nothing to do with subjectivity."[14]

If commentators have gone too far in expunging doubt from Hulme's ethics, they have exaggerated his taste in visual art in the same way. According to Levenson and others, Hulme's assumption of a religious attitude on moral issues corresponded to his renunciation of Impressionism in visual art, to his endorsement of the new art of pure, geometric abstraction.[15] That the two moves might be related is suggested by the account of abstraction given by Worringer in *Abstraktion und Einfühlung* (1908) and paraphrased at length by Hulme in a January 1914 lecture on "Modern Art and Its Philosophy." A taste for abstract art reflects on this view a desire for stability in a world "whose lack of order and seeming arbitrariness" inspires fear (CW 273). "The geometrical line," like the absolute ethical principle, "is something absolutely distinct from the messiness, the confusion, and the accidental details of existing things" (CW 274). For the critics, Hulme's renunciation of the "subjective, tentative and relativist" techniques of Impressionism is as wholehearted as his rejection of any subjectivist tendencies in ethics. But the truth of the matter, once again, is that he won't allow the flight into the absolute to go unchecked. His celebration of the new art is tempered by a sense that it should never leave the empirical world behind and that its regular lines and geometric forms always be accompanied by references to particular, changing things. "However strong the desire for abstraction," he argues,

it cannot be satisfied with the reproduction of merely inorganic forms. A perfect cube looks stable in comparison with the flux of appearance, but *one might be pardoned if one felt no particular interest in the eternity of a cube;* but if you can put *man* into some geometrical shape which lifts him out of the transience of the organic, then the matter is different. (CW 283; my italics)[16]

The contemporary works Hulme most admires are those in which recognizably human and vital forms aspire to the condition of geometry: Cézanne's triangular "Women Bathing" (CW 281), Epstein's cuboid mothers with children (CW 283–84), Lewis's machinelike men and women (CW 283). His taste is epitomized by a sculpture on display at the Alpine Gallery at the same time he delivered his lecture, which he knew well—Gaudier-Brzeska's "Red Stone Dancer." Hulme's tender-minded attraction to abstraction, in other words, was tempered by a tough-minded dedication to its opposite: in Worringer's terms, the urge to "empathize" with lines evocative of life.[17] His views on art corresponded to the pragmatist aesthetic of Vorticism and may, indeed, have done something to help sharpen it. Pound, Lewis, and Gaudier-Brzeska attended Hulme's weekly salons, at the London home of Ethel Kibblewhite, between 1912 and 1914, and the venue for his January 1914 lecture was the Quest Society, with both Lewis and Pound in attendance.

Appreciating the pragmatist character of Pound's Vorticist art—both in the "interpretive metaphor" of his Imagisme and the "ideogramic method" of *The Cantos*—also enables us to mediate between two competing schools of thought in Pound criticism. I have already noted the suggestions of Longenbach and others that Pound was a dogmatic mystic, who viewed the poet's task as one of embodying the "transcendental Image." The mystical reading of Pound also surfaces in claims that he admired and emulated the transcendentalist Symbolism of Swedenborg, Mallarmé, and Emerson and that his *Cantos* represent the culmination of his quest to reveal a timeless system of identities. Andrzej Sosnowski, for example, has cited apparent allusions to Swedenborg in Pound's manifestos to support the claim that he upholds a "mystical epistemology," according to which we live "in a world of correspondences."[18] Another indirect suggestion about Pound's Symbolist affinities has been made by Marjorie Perloff, Michael Harper, and other critics who view his endorsement of "objectivity" through a post-Saussurean lens.[19] On this view Pound's interest in using words that "stick close to things"[20] is evidence of his faith in an indelible union between signifier and signified and thus in a universe of fixed identities. The opposing view of Pound's poetics, most thoroughly expounded by Joseph Riddel but also espoused by Kathryne Lindberg and Anthony Easthope, has taken Pound's objections to spiritualism and symbolism very seriously, implying his dogmatic disbelief in any kind of transcendental order.[21] For Riddel (who was inspired by Derrida's appropriation of Pound for postmetaphysical writing in *Of Grammatology* and by Deleuze's description of Pound's technique as "anti-logos," in *Proust and Signs*), the "interpretive metaphor" becomes a "decentered image," and the juxtaposed fragments in *The Cantos* becomes a no-holds-barred attack on "the dream of the Book, of totalization or closure."[22] The visions of order the Vorticist poet experiences and translates are entirely the products of desire, illusions projected by a sublimated sex-drive; the model of creative experience Pound invokes is the materialist one expounded in Nietzsche's *Will to Power* and Remy de Gourmont's *Physique de l'Amour*.[23] This epistemological pessimism motivates what Riddel, after Derrida, calls an "irreducibly graphic poetics," in which Pound is constantly emphasizing "that poetic language *cannot* be idealized as natural and immediate." Riddel offered his account of the Nietzschean Pound to dispute the more common view of him as an objective or historical writer, firmly committed to the Imagiste precept to avoid the falsifications of "rhetoric."[24] This is significant because, like the critics who point to Pound's mystical allegiances and who are inspired by a need to dispute the common critical practice of distinguishing Pound's skepticism from Yeats's credulity, as well as by the need to contest accounts of the "postmodernist" Pound like Riddel's own,[25] it assumes an extreme position about Pound's doxic attitudes, for the sake of strong argument.

But the fact is, of course, that Pound, like James, lies somewhere between faith and doubt—both in his expectations for unity in the world and in his hopes for language. The "cluster" of ideas that inspires the Vorticist poet, the "Image," is neither the "transcendental" entity Longenbach identifies nor the illusion proposed by Riddel, but something that could be *either:* perhaps a "mirage of the senses," perhaps an "effect of the theos." The verbal "arrangement" in which the poet renders the "Image," similarly, neither presumes a natural affinity with things, nor precludes that possibility; it reflects what is "*not necessarily* belief in a permanent world, but . . . a belief *in that direction*."[26] Both sides in the debate over Pound's beliefs would benefit, then, by conceding something to the other. Longenbach, Surette, and Sosnowski should heed the qualifiers with which Pound frequently undermines his mystical pronouncements, to his efforts to neutralize, if not entirely to undermine, Swedenborgian talk about poetry's "angelic language."[27] Critics following the line of Riddel and Easthope must confront more directly the hopes for apprehending a coherent universe that pervade both Pound's accounts of creativity and *The Cantos:* his commitment to metaphors corroborated by experience; his expectation that they will serve as "doors into eternity"; and his considered guess, near the end of his fragmentary epic, that the world "coheres all right / even if my notes do not."[28] The Jamesian Pound is one who embodies a reluctance to claim "a metaphysical anchoring point" and a continuing fascination with the possibility of a transcendental world. He is one who has doubts about whether the world is a complex of fixed identities, and who communicates these doubts not only by using the noncoercive tropes of juxtaposition and simile but also through various methods of foregrounding the materiality of the signifier, like typographical experimentation and sonic play.[29] But he is also one who retains some hope that language might successfully communicate its signifieds, if it only avoids more than inevitable abstraction—hence the concrete diction of Imagiste poetry and the "luminous" historical details of *The Cantos*.

Although neither the argument for the "mystical" Pound nor that for the radical skeptical or "neo-Nietzschean" one is entirely right, the latter view is perhaps the hardest one to defend. It is more difficult to find statements in Pound about the world's chaos than it is to find expressions of hope in its order. When roses appear in the steel dust, the drama is never wholly subjective.[30] And the array of often ugly, historical information amassed in *The Cantos* clearly belies any account of Pound as a complacent fictionalist—of the sort Stevens, for example, is often accused of being. The poem's wealth of historical references is overwhelming testimony of his faith in the educative value of empirical data and of his hope that language might successfully communicate it. This is true even as the poem experiments with typography and demands the participation of the reader in any move beyond "fact" to theory. Though Riddel seeks to undermine the simple view of the objective and historical Pound and overstates his case to that end, in his best moments he reveals his own discomfort with the effort to make the poet too radically skeptical. He concedes that Pound, though knowing a "natural" or "primordial" language cannot be taken for granted, shows every sign of "hoping to recuperate" such a language; this is why the poet idealizes the Chinese ideogram, a mark he regards as material and transparent.[31] As Perloff has observed in a similar moment of self-correction, *The Cantos* "occupies a middle space between the mimetic on the one hand and the non-objective or 'abstract' on the other."[32] Pound's commitment to leaning forward into experience he knows is mediated, and his invitation to readers to do the same, is an effort reflecting James's conviction that giving up "the doctrine of objective certitude" does not mean giving up "the quest or hope of truth itself" and that we gain a "better position" toward truth "by systematically continuing to roll up experiences and think" (WB 24). Marjorie Levinson and others are discovering that this makes his practice a potential model for the projects of contemporary new historicist critics, who share the double desire to acknowledge that all knowledge is mediated, and yet to uncover, and learn from, the "facts."[33]

If Pound's critics must come to terms with the way he balances both tender-mindedness and tough-mindedness and with the cooperation of skeptical and empiricist tendencies represented by the latter, the same is true of critics of Stevens. Almost from their inception, writings about Stevens have been informed by an assumption about the incompatibility of the attributes on either side of James's dividing line. The most accurate way of representing their informing premise, perhaps, is as an opposition of "optimistic" and "pessimistic" habits of mind or a bifurcation of affirmation and negation, belief and doubt. The first influential characterization of the poet, by Conrad Aiken, was part of a battle between two antagonistic ideologies in early twentieth-century criticism: the "humanist" position, exemplified by Louis Untermeyer, and the "aesthetic" position, championed by Aiken.[34] When Untermeyer excluded Stevens's poetry from his 1919 anthology *The New Era in American Poetry*, he did so because he regarded it as too pessimistic, as affirming neither "God" nor the "divinity of man," nor the "rightness of democracy," nor the "beauty and immortality of life." In his view "no major art has ever existed and, with a few brilliant exceptions, no art-work has survived *that has not been built on faith*." In protesting Untermeyer's dismissal of Stevens, Aiken did not dispute the judgment that he is a poet of doubt, or negation, but only celebrated the sense of freedom and the willingness to indulge a taste for imaginative and linguistic beauty that he saw coming with Stevens's renunciation of epistemological and ontological hope.[35]

Most commentators since have agreed that Stevens's poetry is based on "pessimistic" premises, either epistemological or ontological or both.[36] Early appreciators of *Harmonium*'s gay, exotic language assumed it to represent an escape from "time and space and . . . all the other ills to which the flesh is heir," or to regard it as a "silvery music signifying nothing."[37] Although some New Critical readers in the 1940s detected both a hope for humankind and for an ordered universe in Stevens's poetry, the long-term effect of the New Criticism was to perpetuate "pessimistic" readings; as the maker of autotelic poems, Stevens remained the fictionalist, unconcerned with history either because it was impossible or unbearable to know. Finally, of course, there has been the deconstructionist appropriation of Stevens, initiated by J. Hillis Miller.[38] The retreating horizons faced by Stevens's questers and his self-undermining language have been viewed as anticipating Derridean deferrals and decenterings. Many who read Stevens as deconstructor, including Miller and Paul Bové, have coupled his radically skeptical epistemology with a profoundly negative ontology. The world his birds cannot reach has become an abyss, a "universal nothing": godless, chaotic, violent, even, in the extremest versions, altogether unreal.[39] Frank Lentricchia's account of how Stevens enabled the growth of a "conservative fictionalism" in criticism, beginning with Frank Kermode's influential *The Sense of an Ending* and reaching its second wave with the deconstructionist readings, has done much to consolidate the reading of Stevens as "pessimist" and exemplar of a regressive, because escapist, politics. Outside Stevens criticism, particularly in general studies of postmodernism, the name

"Wallace Stevens" has become synonymous with a radical fictionalism, incompatible with the values of progressive, materialist readers.

Lentricchia's acceptance of the conservative fictionalist reading of Stevens is surprising, because it is a misreading analogous to the popular misreading of Derrida he took pains to correct in *After the New Criticism*. His arguments that Derrida is not to be read as an "up-dated Sartre," that it is wrong to read "il n'y a pas de hors-texte" as positing "an ontological 'nothing' outside the text," as signifying "our freedom from the tyrannizing presence of the . . . world of objects," are volleys that might equally well have been directed against "pessimistic" readings of Stevens, including Lentricchia's own.[40] Like Lentricchia's Derrida, Stevens "is no ontologist of *le néant* because he is no ontologist."[41] He is as prepared to undermine pessimistic assertions about the nature of reality as "optimistic" ones, as suspicious of nihilism as of theism. It is vital that we reinstate the qualifiers and the counterstatements that accompany many of his darkest pronouncements about reality and humankind, turning those pronouncements into perverse maxims "found in the handbook of heartbreak" (CP 507). It is a mistake for Miller, for example, to ignore the fact that Stevens's description of reality as "the dominant blank, the unapproachable" is something the poet *undermines*—an imaginary or "Blue" proposition that is *made* real or "verdured" (CP 477).[42] It is wrong to regard as doctrine the Canon Aspirin's thought that "nothingness was a nakedness" when that thought is only one the Canon is free to choose, and the one Stevens represents as the least useful option at that—"a point / Beyond which thoughts could not progress as thought"(CP 403). Stevens may sometimes appear to endorse Sartre's position that "the real is never beautiful" and that beauty "is a valuable applicable only to the imaginary," but it is important to remember that he also sometimes contradicts Sartre directly, proclaiming that the "most beautiful . . . thing in the world is, of course, the world itself" (OP 193) and that the beautiful imaginary and the real may be "one" (OP 192). Lentricchia's statement that the "constant and wearisome message" of Stevens's poetry is "the futility of all human effort" is as incomplete a representation of the "amassing harmony" of Stevens's work as Miller's.[43] Just as we mustn't forget the Stevens who won't rule out a beautiful reality, so we mustn't forget the poet who maintains some hope for human endeavors, that is, the poet who thinks it possible the "fictive hero" might be a forerunner of the "real" (CP 408).

The best defense against reading Stevens too pessimistically is to remember that virtually everything we find in his poetry, from his floating women, to his hopeful birds, to his various propositions about the world, is suspended within the liminal space defined and endorsed by James. Whether it takes the form of images like the jar or of grammatical qualifiers, this enclosure has the effect not of rendering its contents invalid but only of

declaring them to be of uncertain provenance: perhaps the 「
desire, perhaps reflections of the way things are. To the recog
the "light-bound space of the mind" (CP 436) is an ambigu
rather than a purely subjective one, we must add an appreciat
other Jamesian refrain running through the poetry: its constant ⸺
that the happiest, most comforting propositions about the world need not
be false—that the oriole, too, may be a realist. Recognizing the potential
for truthfulness in Stevens's "fictions"—the potential that properly makes
them hypotheses—reopens several doors that the poststructuralist appro-
priations of Stevens have kept closed. It enables us, first of all, to dispute
the view of Stevens as atheist, perpetuated by Miller and others. Although
Stevens sees God as a "being of the mind" or a "child of the desire that is
the will" (CP 436), and although it appears to him "as if" Santayana's
Catholic dreams are realized in death (CP 511), these do not amount to
dogmatic claims that God is an illusion. Indeed for every time Stevens
entertains a proposition about the death of God, there is another when he
considers the alternative possibility, such as when he contemplates the
double-barreled hypothesis that "God is Good" and "it is a beautiful
Night" (CP 285).[44] Similarly if Stevens recognizes that the metaphors and
theories that speak of the world's order are as "pleasant as port" (CP 215),
his perception of their pleasure is not tantamount to an admission that they
lie. Every proposition commonly quoted to demonstrate Stevens's belief in
the essential disorder of the world can be seen to be counterbalanced by
another, equally respected hypothesis about its underlying order,[45] and
many poems emphasize that there is nothing necessarily illusory about the
perception of a "universe without life's limp and lack," the "Philosophers'
end" (OP 119). Finally, the recognition that Stevens did not give up hope
of the truthfulness of metaphors and theories leads us to challenge the
popular image of him as an aesthete, engaged in making fictions accountable to nothing but pleasure. It alerts us to evidence that he was, in fact,
contemptuous of art committed wholly to "invention," rather than "discovery"—that he took no pleasure, for example, in surrealist art depicting
accordian-playing clams (OP 203). For him, as for James, the lingering
sense that that the mind's constructs have some hope of being true informs
a commitment to dismantling the imagination's constructions when they
come into conflict with empirical counterevidence. This means remaining
alert to the "squirming facts" that exceed the constructs of the "squamous"
mind (CP 215) and incorporating them into revised versions of the same.
It means not allowing the desiring imagination to hold those facts and
persons that resist happy, or easily ethnocentric, interpretation "prostrate
below the singleness of its will" (CP 478).

Since Margaret Peterson first explored the James-Stevens connection seriously in 1983,[46] an increasing number of Stevens's critics have been pre-

pared to declare him a pragmatist. By and large, however, these claims have either ignored, or seriously underestimated, how his pragmatism is at odds with his reputation as ontological and epistemological "pessimist," as a complacent aesthete, disinclined to look into the facts. One reason for this missed opportunity, undoubtedly, has been the fact that, for many critics, pragmatism has come to be identified with the deeply skeptical, and finally conservative, positions of Richard Rorty and Stanley Fish.[47] Rorty especially has done much to obscure the optimistic and politically progressive elements in the work of the early American pragmatists, Dewey as well as James, recruiting their names in support of a program to which they no doubt would strenuously have objected. At least three characteristics of what Cornel West calls Rorty's "avant-garde" pragmatism make it an uncomfortable fit with James's "moderate" pragmatism, which is also Stevens's.[48] First, the "de-divinization" of the world Rorty imagines is thoroughgoing; his "liberal utopia" will be one having no more use for the notion that "finite, mortal, contingently existing human beings might derive the meanings of their lives from anything except other finite, mortal, contingently existing human beings."[49] Second, Rorty regards the contingency of language, and therefore of all perceptions, as sufficient reason to release theory-making from all restraints and regulations. In his view no account of reality can ever claim superiority over another on the grounds that it more accurately "fits the facts."[50] Generally, this means giving up all questions about the accuracy of the propositions we live by. For the artist it means renouncing all efforts to "represent human emotions or situations 'correctly'" and all efforts to seek metaphors that communicate what is true, rather than merely fanciful.[51] The ideal citizen, in Rorty's utopia, will be the "ironist," who, recognizing the contingency of everything, will play freely with whatever vocabularies answer his desires.[52] Finally, though Rorty is at pains to emphasize that a culture of ironists can still be a "liberal" one—one committed to the principle that "cruelty is the worst thing we can do"—he is also adamant that the postmetaphysical thinker has no meaningful public role.[53] His justification for keeping the doubting intellectual out of politics is the example of Nietzsche and Heidegger, whose lessons in soul-building furthered the cause of Nazism.

Several scholars have taken Rorty to task for appropriating James and Dewey for the cause of "liberal ironism." Cornel West, Robert Westbrook, Thomas McCarthy, Richard Bernstein, and Charlene Haddock Seigfried have argued convincingly that the key elements of Rortyan pragmatism I have outlined are out of step with the tenets of the early American pragmatists and have urged readers to return to James and Dewey for a way out of the disheartening impasse to which Rorty's relentless skepticism leads.[54] West invokes James as the model for a "prophetic pragmatism," an optimistic quest for social change that, while rejecting metaphysics, does not rule out either the usefulness of the idea of God or the possibility that God really exists. Seigfried has given a detailed account of the strenuous verification processes James outlined for the pragmatist, in an effort to discredit Rorty's portrait of him as an advocate of "floating, ungrounded conversations."[55] Westbrook, McCarthy, and Bernstein have joined West in emphasizing the disjunction between Rorty's cynicism about the public role of the postmetaphysical intellectual and the social activism recommended by the classical pragmatists—primarily by Dewey but also by James. All these arguments serve as useful warnings to Stevens scholars too eager to read his pragmatism as being incompatible with any degree or kind of faith.[56]

The most striking difference between Rorty and Stevens is how seriously they take the potential for cruelty in unimpeded fiction-making. The dangers of imposing no restraints on one's descriptions of the world are greatest when one describes other people, particularly those from cultures whose vocabularies for self-description are different from one's own and particularly when the describer is in a position of power over the person described. As Rorty himself acknowledges, the ironist has the capacity to "humiliate" the objects of his descriptions, by threatening their ability to make sense of themselves in their own terms;[57] there is an apparent conflict, in other words, between the commitment to irony and the liberal principle that causing pain is the worst thing one can do. Rorty's solution to this problem is to say that in his "liberal utopia" the ironist will become educated in the literature of people different from himself. This literature will teach him to empathize with the suffering of others and thus to avoid causing such suffering with his own descriptions. Like Shelley he believes that an education in literature helps develop a skill for "imaginative identification" and from there a commitment to avoiding cruelty that need not involve a commitment to absolute ethical values or any other vestiges of metaphysical nostalgia.[58] But his invocation of literature's humanizing capacity is unconvincing in the context of his repeated claims about the futility of any efforts to gain greater access to the truth. For what else do efforts at "imaginative identification" require but a willingness to believe one can have better knowledge of others? How likely will the reader be, who has given up all hope of disinterestedness, to allow his or her fictions to be changed by the situations literature dramatizes? And how fit can a literature be to accomplish this task if it makes no effort to render those situations accurately? Despite his own appreciation for what a book like Nabokov's *Lolita* teaches about the cruelty of "incuriosity,"[59] Rorty glosses over the fact that the only way the ironist can avoid cruelty is by abandoning the dogmatically pessimistic epistemology that makes him an ironist. If he is committed to avoid humiliating others, he will also have to be prepared to regard her fictions as hypotheses, as descriptions that may, indeed, be better or worse than others in representing the facts: prepared, in other words, to embrace something like the kind of moderately hopeful truth-making James and Stevens recommend.[60]

Although it is impossible to hold up the author of "Like Decorations in a Nigger Cemetary" and "A High-Toned Old Christian Woman" as an exemplary describer of others, it is also wrong to ignore the powerful critique of the cruelties of fiction-making found in his work—as apt a criticism of Rorty's ironism as it is of the more complacent, and undeniably offensive, moments in Stevens himself. Despite its title, which seems to promise an endorsement of fictionalism, the poem "Description Without Place" is one of many showing Stevens's awareness that there is more than one option facing the postmetaphysical poet, more than one "theory of description" (CP 345) to be put to work in the world. It points to many other poems and essays of the 1940s and 1950s that measure these options: "Variations on a Summer Day," "The Bouquet," "Extracts from Addresses to the Academy of Fine Ideas," "Man Carrying Thing," "The Noble Rider and the Sound of Words," "The Figure of the Youth as Virile Poet," "On Receiving an Honorary Degree from Bard College." As I have shown, although these works have often been used to support the view of Stevens as escapist, concerned only with the poet's right to keep pushing back the "violence" (NA 36) of reality, they are all in fact sharply critical of the "theory of description" that honors no retraints. They all concede that no perception of the facts will be uncontaminated, but then they proceed to endorse the Jamesian view that theories must, nonetheless, be driven forward into experience, checked against the best evidence available and revised accordingly. Unlike Rorty, in other words, Stevens *does* hold some descriptions and perceptions to be better than others because they account more perfectly for reality as it is experienced by the poet and by his ever-widening community. This respect for the importance of verification, however imperfect one's evidence may be, is what we hear when Stevens remarks, in "The Figure of the Youth as Virile Poet," that "the incredible is not a part of poetic truth," that "what concerns us in poetry, as in everything else, is the belief of credible people in credible things" (NA 53). It is what we hear in "Extracts from Addresses to the Academy of Fine Ideas," when Stevens "laughs" (CP 253) at the person too ready to live with self-interested descriptions and elevates the one who manages to "feel curious" (CP 254–55) in the face of a world of difference. The latter poem is Stevens's most extensive critique of the kind of thinking Rorty encourages, indicating the position that there is no reason to seek "the real wall behind the painted ones"[61]—the "land beyond" the "artificial" ones (CP 252)— on moral grounds. In its scathing portrait of the fictionalist as emperor, freely translating deaths into apricots, it underscores the connection between fiction-making and imperialism evident in Stevens's earliest work, with its portraits of the "Emperor of Ice-Cream," whipping his concupiscent descriptions, and of the mind as dominion jar, giving in to none of the empirical facts of Tennessee. Where Rorty suggests that the imperialism of the ironist can be defended on the grounds it is no greater than that of the absolutist, and better, because it has no pretensions to truth,[62] Stevens points to a genuine alternative to these imperialisms, both perpetrated by Crispin: a policy of deferring to what one's best investigations suggest are the irreducible realities of other worlds and other persons. In this he again demonstrates his affinity with James, whose emphasis on the importance of verification in *Pragmatism* and *Essays on Radical Empiricism* was integrally related to his opposition to American policy in the Philippines in the wake of the Spanish American War. James's letters to the editor on the subject of American imperialism demonstrate that his pragmatism's commitment to a relentless process of dipping theory into facts was at least partially motivated by a sense that to theorize freely is to colonize brutally. "What worse enemy for a situation of need can there be," he writes, "than dim, foggy, abstract good will, backed by energetic officiousness and unillumined by any accurate perception of the concrete wants and possibilities of a case?" The evils of imperialism are for him epitomized by the mind in which "empty abstractions [have] the unrestricted right of way," oblivious to the minds and bodies they flatten and destroy.[63]

The view of Stevens I am proposing is compatible with that of Alan Filreis and other scholars who have been writing recently about Stevens's very real interest in public events and causes and documenting how his poetry engages with them.[64] The reading closest to my own, however, and intriguing for what it promises about Stevens's relevance for the more progressive forms of pragmatism being discussed today, is David Bromwich's, in an article exploring the conflict between Nietzschean and Jamesian attitudes in *Parts of a World*. Although I am less convinced than Bromwich that reaching this conclusion required an intense struggle, I agree with his contention that the Jamesian Stevens wins and that he ultimately proposes an alternative to a community of private fiction-makers. What I have been calling Stevens's critique of fictionalist cruelty, Bromwich identifies as his resistance to "the hero of the Nietzschean sublime, the extra-moral agent who looks on the general life as *materia poetica* for his own creations." What I have been calling the cautiously "optimistic" or "hypothetical" attitude in Stevens's qualifiers is what he describes as "a 'supposing' frame of mind": one in which Stevens invites his readers to imagine the best for humankind in the expectation that believing might help it to be so.[65]

In calling for renewed attention to the "public speech" in Stevens's corpus, particularly to the critically neglected "Examination of the Hero in a Time of War," Bromwich enables us to detect not only a critique of Rorty in Stevens ("Can we live on dry descriptions. . . . And nourish ourselves on crumbs of whimsy?" [CP 278]) but also a version of the more promising pragmatisms being championed today by opponents of Rorty, like Cornel West. Thinking of Dewey, and perhaps of the James of "The Moral Philosopher and the Moral Life" (1891), West envisions a pragmatism in which the postmetaphysical intellectual engages in an empathetic and cooperative relationship with others, balancing a profound sense of the irreducible evil in the world with a hope for incremental improvements in sites of suffering. The intellectual who shrinks from totalizing theories can contribute importantly to this process through genealogical analyses of specific social practices, analyses undertaken in the light of the "best available" historiographical insights.[66]

It is not difficult to find all the key elements of West's program in Stevens. His "virile poet" remembers that his insights must be weighed against those articulated by others and that he is both to "suppose" and to "receive what others [have] supposed" (NA 63; CP 242). His sense of the world's "harsh reality," of the "ferocities" in Russia (CP 224) or the "dogs and dung" in the villages of indigenes (CP 198), is counterbalanced by suppositions that autumn need not be the "veritable season," nor "familiar man" the "veritable man" (CP 281). In other words, one's hopes for the world may be as viable as its atrocities. Finally West's expectations for the new historicist, continuing to seek better, even if inevitably mediated, knowledge of historical situations, are echoed in the many poems and essays I have listed that stress the continuing importance of discovery in an elusive world. Stevens's 1951 address "On Receiving an Honorary Degree from Bard College" is perhaps his most straightforward expression of a cautious but determined historicism. Having acknowledged that looking into history is inevitably a "poetic act," in which "the real is constantly being engulfed in the unreal" (OP 256, 255), Stevens has no doubt of the promise that remains in the strenuous investigation of "particulars." His praise for such an effort is worth quoting at length, because the voice is one so long ignored:

The poet finds that as between these two sources: the imagination and reality, the imagination is false, whatever else may be said of it, and reality is true; and being concerned that poetry should be a thing of vital and virile importance, he commits himself to reality, which then becomes his inescapable and ever-present difficulty and inamorata. In any event, he has lost nothing; for the imagination, while it might have led him to purities beyond definition, never yet progressed except by particulars. Having gained the world, the imaginative remains available to him in respect to all the particulars of the world. Instead of having lost anything, he has gained a sense of direction and a certainty of understanding. He has strengthened himself to resist the bogus. He has become like a man who can see what he wants to see and touch what he wants to touch. In all his poems with all their enchantments for the poet himself, there is the final enchantment that they are true. The significance of the poetic act then is that it is evidence. It

is instance and illustration. It is an illumination of a surface, the n
self in the rock. Above all it is a new engagement with life. (OP 2

Of all the reconciliations the Jamesian pragmatist concep
poets' effects perhaps the most significant is its bridging of what numerou
commentators have seen as an unbridgeable "schism" or "gap" between
Pound and Stevens as definers of modernism.[67] Pound, it is said, is the
open-minded historian, the "encyclopaedic" poet who knows there have
been other times, other places, and other people. Stevens, by contrast, is
the lyric poet who effaces history, oblivious to everything but his own
desires. Pound is the poet who simply presents images, having nothing to
say about them; Stevens is the writer with the "rage for order," coercing
the world into satisfying analogies, metaphors, fictions.[68] Tracing the two
writers' affinities with James, however, has made it clear that this division is
unnecessary. Both writers face a muse of uncertain authority who demands
nonetheless to be made useful. Under the influence of this "Image" or
"Sister of the Minotaur," both writers presume they have something, however provisional, to say. And both articulate their insights in hypothetical
structures, the "interpretive metaphor" and ideogram, the epochal landscape and "as if" clause, that make the same promise to the reader willing
to continue the pragmatist practice of unrolling the coil and ball of truth:
at the least a more manageable world; at the most a world yielding both
history and design.

The three case studies I have offered only begin the process of demonstrating that there is a philosophical solidarity between modernist literature
and Jamesian pragmatism. Recent work on the writers who came into
James's orbit at Harvard—Robert Frost, T. S. Eliot, and Gertrude Stein—
and of that exemplary modernist novelist, James's brother Henry, indicate
that the project is gathering strength.[69] There is some indication, however,
that the James being introduced into modernist literary studies is Rorty's—
the de facto radical skeptic and fictionalist. In fact, it will only be by re-
turning to a Jamesian conception of pragmatism unmediated by Rorty, a
Jamesian pragmatism scrupulously careful to preserve the epistemological
and ontological possibilities Rorty rejects, that James's importance for literary modernism will be fully understood. Where using Rorty's pragmatism
as a paradigm will teach us to look at well-established clichés about modernism—that it is dogmatically pessimistic about knowledge, order, and
human communion and that its only affirmation is in Nietzschean play—
using James's will bring into focus its reserves of epistemological, ontological, and social optimism and its concomitant sense of empirical
responsibility.

Notes

PREFACE

1. See especially Richard Poirier, *Poetry and Pragmatism* (Cambridge, Mass.: Harvard University Press, 1992) and *The Renewal of Literature* (New York: Random House, 1987); Frank Lentricchia, *Ariel and the Police: Michel Foucault, William James, Wallace Stevens* (Madison: University of Wisconsin Press, 1988), and *Modernist Quartet* (Cambridge: Cambridge University Press, 1994). An earlier version of the seminal essay in *Modernist Quartet,* "Philosophers of Modernism at Harvard, Circa 1900," was published as "On the Ideologies of Poetic Modernism, 1890–1913: The Example of William James," in Sacvan Bercovitch, ed., *Reconstructing American Literary History* (Cambridge, Mass.: Harvard University Press, 1986), 220–49. I am deeply indebted to Lentricchia's insight into the affinity between modernist poetry and the essays of the Harvard philosophers (including, in addition to James, Santayana, and Royce) and also to Sanford Schwartz's comments on James and modernism in *The Matrix of Modernism: Pound, Eliot and Early 20th-Century Thought* (Princeton: Princeton University Press, 1985). Richard Shusterman develops a pragmatist aesthetics from a Deweyan perspective in *Pragmatist Aesthetics: Living Beauty, Rethinking Art* (Oxford: Basil Blackwell, 1992). Shusterman offers a pragmatist defense against the charge that "art is necessarily a conservative force of social oppression and class privilege" and finds a modernist case study in T. S. Eliot's "Portrait of a Lady"; in its approach to Stevens, in particular, this study shares Shusterman's conviction that we "need a greater openness to the ways high art can further a progressive ethical and socio-political agenda through greater critical attention to the ethical and social dimensions of its works, many of which embody their own potent critique of high art's ethical limitations and sociocultural dangers" (140).

For more author-specific studies of pragmatism and poetry, see Thomas C. Grey, *The Wallace Stevens Case* (Cambridge, Mass.: Harvard University Press, 1991); David M. LaGuardia, *Advance on Chaos: The Sanctifying Imagination of Wallace Stevens* (Hanover: University Press of New England, 1983); Donald J. Childs, "Risking Enchantment: The Middle Way Between Mysticism and Pragmatism in Four Quartets," *Words in Time: New Essays on Eliot's Four Quartets,* ed. Edward Lobb (London: Athlone, 1993), 107–30; Manju Jain, *T. S. Eliot and American Philosophy* (Cambridge: Cambridge University Press, 1992); David W. Shaw, "The Poetics of Pragmatism: Robert Frost and William James," *New England Quarterly* 59 (January 1986): 159–88; Lisa Ruddick, "Fluid Symbols in American Modernism," *Allegory, Myth and Symbol,* ed. Morton W. Bloomfield (Cambridge: Harvard University Press, 1981: 335–53); and *Reading Stein Reading* (Ithaca: Cornell University Press, 1991).

2. Richard Rorty, *Consequences of Pragmatism* (Minneapolis: University of

Minnesota Press, 1982), 153. See also *Contingency, Irony, and Solidarity* (Cambridge: Cambridge University Press, 1989), 39, where Rorty cites Proust as exemplary modernist. Of the authors listed in note 1, Shusterman and Poirier are the exceptions in explicitly distinguishing Jamesian pragmatism from Rortyan pragmatism and in seeing the relevance of the former, specifically, for modernist poetry. Poirier, however, is primarily concerned with demonstrating the "alliance of pragmatism with the workings of language in literature" (*Renewal of Literature* 13); he does not consider, as I do, the theories of creative inspiration to which these correspond. See also *Poetry and Pragmatism,* 97.

3. I draw the term partly from James's discussion of "tender-minded" and "tough-minded" attributes, in *Pragmatism,* ed. Frederick H. Burkhardt, Fredson Bowers, and Ignas K. Skrupskelis (Cambridge: Harvard University Press, 1975). Further references will appear in the text with the abbreviation P. Here James aligns an "optimistic" attitude with a "religious" and "dogmatical" one. Although in general he aligns an "empiricist" attitude (or a propensity to "go by 'facts'") with a "pessimistic" one, he would have regarded a *faith in the potential accuracy* of human truths as "optimistic" in the sense that it allows for the possibility the will-to-knowledge may be satisfied. In the latter sense, James applies what Gerald Myers has called an "ethics of optimism" to epistemological matters. See note 9 below. James also equates "optimistic" thinking with "hypothetic" thinking in "German Pessimism," a scathing review of Edmund Pfleiderer's *Der moderne Pessimismus* and the Schopenhaurian school it exemplifies. See William James, *Essays, Comments and Reviews* (Cambridge, Mass.: Harvard University Press, 1987), 313. As I shall show, the "hypothetic" thinking of James is to be distinguished from the "fictionalist" thinking of Rorty.

4. Rorty, *Consequences of Pragmatism,* 153. For Rorty's appropriation of James, see especially *Consequences of Pragmatism,* xviii, 152, 155–56, and 162.

5. James endorses the "reflex-action" model of psychology in *The Principles of Psychology* (1890) and two seminal essays reprinted in *The Will to Believe* (1897): "The Sentiment of Rationality" (1879) and "Reflex-action and Theism" (1881). I discuss the relevance of the model for poetic theory and its affinity with the "sincerity-criterion" in modernist poetics at length in my Introduction.

6. Graham Hough, *Image and Experience* (London: Duckworth, 1960), 33.

7. Wallace Stevens, *Opus Posthumous,* ed. Milton J. Bates (Revised, enlarged, and corrected edition, New York: Knopf, 1989), 253. Subsequent references to this volume will appear in the text with the abbreviation OP.

8. For LaGuardia and Grey, see note 1. For an excellent overview of critical perceptions of Stevens, see Melita Schaum, *Wallace Stevens and the Critical Schools* (Tuscaloosa: University of Alabama Press, 1988).

9. Gerald Myers, *William James: His Life and Thought* (New Haven: Yale University Press, 1986), 404–14.

10. Alan Filreis, *Wallace Stevens and the Actual World* (Princeton: Princeton University Press, 1991), and *Modernism from Right to Left* (Cambridge: Cambridge University Press, 1994); James Longenbach, *Wallace Stevens: The Plain Sense of Things* (Oxford: Oxford University Press, 1991). I argue in chapter 4 that Filreis, in particular, undermines his own argument by ignoring how the poet qualifies several statements about poetry's value as a means of escape.

11. Ezra Pound, "Vorticism," in *Gaudier-Brzeska* (New York: New Directions, 1970), 84. Subsequent references to this volume will appear with the abbreviation GB.

12. Marjorie Perloff, *The Dance of the Intellect* (Cambridge: Cambridge University Press, 1985), 2.

INTRODUCTION: INSPIRATION, REFLEX-ACTION, AND PRAGMATISM

1. See Myers, *William James,* 19–20, 493–94.

2. For a discussion of this problem in James criticism, see Charlene Haddock Seigfried, *William James's Radical Reconstruction of Philosophy* (Albany: SUNY Press, 1990), 21, 399n.

3. James, "Reflex-Action and Theism," WB, 98.

4. See vol. 2, chapter 21 of *The Principles of Psychology,* particularly the section "Belief in Objects of Theory" in William James, *The Principles of Psychology,* 2 vols. (1890; reprint, New York: Dover, 1950), pp. 311–20). Further references to *The Principles of Psychology,* vols. 1 and 2, will appear in the text with the abbreviation PP 1, 2. Hans Vaihinger, another philosopher important to modernism, was also interested in this theory; see *The Philosophy of "As if",* trans. C. K. Ogden (London: Kegan Paul, Trench, Trubner, 1924), xxxi.

5. James, "Reflex Action and Theism," WB 91. For an account of the physiological principle and its importance for psychology, see Edwin G. Boring, *A History of Experimental Psychology* (New York: Meredith, 1957), 29ff. and 35–39.

6. James, "Reflex Action and Theism," 92 (italics mine) and "The Sentiment of Rationality," 72.

7. James, "Reflex Action and Theism," 98 (italics mine).

8. James comments that the reflex action theory of mind commits those who accept it "to regarding the mind as an essentially teleological mechanism. I mean by this that the conceiving or theorizing faculty—the mind's middle department— *functions exclusively for the sake of ends* that do not exist at all in the world of impressions we receive by way of our senses, but are set by our emotional and practical subjectivity altogether" ("Reflex Action and Theism," 94–95).

9. Ibid., 107, 97.

10. That James might have thought it appropriate to use the reflex-action model to describe his own, interrelated philosophical concerns is suggested by his comment that the endeavor to interpret or define a divine "presence" (without question his own concern in *The Varieties of Religious Experience*) belongs to "Department two" of a reflex action ("Reflex Action and Theism," 107).

11. James, *The Varieties of Religious Experience* (Harmondsworth: Penguin, 1982), 25. Further references to this volume will appear in the text with the abbreviation VRE.

12. Judith Ryan, *The Vanishing Subject: Early Psychology and Literary Modernism* (Chicago: University of Chicago Press, 1991), 2.

13. See also 58. For a general discussion of James's contribution to the development of phenomenology, and especially of his influence on Husserl, see James M. Edie, *William James and Phenomenology* (Bloomington: Indiana University Press, 1987). For Edie the key phenomenological texts in James's *corpus* are "The Sentiment of Rationality" and *The Varieties of Religious Experience.*

14. See *The Varieties of Religious Experience,* 510–11.

15. Ibid., 380–81.

16. James, "The Sentiment of Rationality," WB 19.

17. For evidence that James made a conscious effort to devise an appropriate

response to this question, see VRE 422–29. James's concern in this section is to "inquire whether we can invoke [the mystical state] as authoritative" (VRE 422). The methods he recommends for dealing with the state correspond to the methods outlined in *Pragmatism*. For further evidence of the pragmatic method in VRE, see 455–56.

18. On p. 33, James cites Fitz James Stephen, *Liberty, Equality, Fraternity* 2d ed. (London: n.p., 1874), 353.

19. James, "Reflex-action and Theism," WB 112.

20. James, "The Sentiment of Rationality," WB 86.

21. James Leuba, *A Psychological Study of Religion, Its Origin, Function and Future* (New York: Macmillan, 1912). For an account of the development of empirical theology in America, see Nancy Frankenberry, *Religion and Radical Empiricism* (Albany: SUNY Press, 1987), 1–35. Following Bernard M. Loomer, Frankenberry defines empirical theology as "a methodology which accepts the general empirical axiom that all ideas are reflections of concrete experience, either actual or possible. All propositional or conceptual knowledge originates from and is confirmable by physical experience. The limits of knowledge are defined by the limits of the experienceable, by the limits of relationship. Reason functions in the service of concrete fact and experience" (*Religion and Radical Empiricism* 2–3).

22. Ibid., 111, 99, 39, 13.

23. Ibid., 13, 112.

24. For a fuller account of how James insists on verification without falling back on the "correspondence" theory, see Seigfried, *William James's Radical Reconstruction of Philosophy*, 292–94.

25. For James's fullest account of the problematics of fact, see *Essays in Radical Empiricism*, eds. Frederick H. Burkhardt, Fredson Bowers, and Ignas K. Skrupselis (Cambridge: Harvard University Press, 1976), passim. Further references to this volume will appear in the text with the abbreviation ERE. I discuss the relationship between James's anti–imperialism and the pragmatist's duty to attend to fact in chapter 5 of this study.

26. James, "Reflex Action and Theism," WB 33; my italics.

27. *William James on Exceptional Mental States: The 1896 Lowell Lectures*, ed. Eugene Taylor (Amherst: University of Massachusetts Press, 1984), 150. James draws from the work of psychologists who equate genius with degenerative insanity: L. F. Lelut, Jacques-Joseph Moreau, John F. Nisbet, and Césare Lombroso. For an account of these psychologists and their work, see 203.

28. "Reflex Action and Theism," WB 103.

29. James, "Philosophical Conceptions and Practical Results," in *Writings 1878–1899*, ed. Gerald E. Myers (New York: Library of America, 1992), 1078.

30. See for example *Pragmatism*, 44, 144.

31. James, "Philosophical Conceptions and Practical Results," 1079.

32. Compare James's remark that the writings of the philosopher "must more and more ally themselves with a literature which is confessedly tentative and suggestive rather than dogmatic." See "The Moral Philosopher and the Moral Life," WB 159.

33. Plato, *Phaedrus*, trans. and ed. R. Hackworth (Cambridge: Cambridge University Press, 1952), 58.

34. For a description of the German Idealists' efforts in this area, and the tendency of their contemporaries to ignore them, see David Simpson, *The Origins of Modern Critical Thought* (Cambridge: Cambridge University Press, 1988), 14–16. For more about the variety of epistemological claims made by self-described

Idealists and the inherent contradictions in the subjectivist version of Idealism's subjectivist version that makes it easily, though mistakenly, assimilated to Plato, see Ralph Barton Perry, *Present Philosophical Tendencies* (New York: George Braziller, 1955), 113–93. The modernist poets I consider appear to have read the Romantics and Symbolists as espousing what Perry calls "Absolute Idealism": a form of Idealism that incorporates the "terms of a devotional mysticism—Spirit, Perfection, Eternity, Infinity—[into the] . . . very letter of its discourse" (164).

35. For an account of the Symbolists' tendency to do this, see A. G. Lehmann, *The Symbolist Aesthetic in France 1885–1895* (Oxford: Blackwell, 1968), 38, 42.

36. Lehmann, *The Symbolist Aesthetic in France*, 57.

37. Arthur Schopenhauer, *The World as Will and Representation*, trans. E. F. J. Payne (New York: Dover, 1969), vol. 1 of 2: 144, 235. That Schopenhauer understood the "Idea" to constitute a form of universal, absolute knowledge is suggested by his remarks in the same volume, 250–53.

38. Ibid., 234–35.

39. See Immanuel Kant, *The Critique of Judgment*, trans. J. H. Bernard (New York: Hafner, 1951), 157ff.

40. Schopenhauer, *The World as Will and Representation*, 1: 235. For Kant's description of the organic process and its product, see *Critique of Judgement*, 19–24. Schopenhauer comments that "the transition from the Idea to the concept" that takes place in translation "is always a descent." *The World as Will and Representation*, 1: 238.

41. Ibid., 239.

42. Albert Mockel, *Propos de littérature* (1894), in Guy Michaud, *Message poétique du symbolisme* (Paris: Librairie Nizet, 1947), 752. The translation is mine.

43. For examples of absolute Idealism in Moréas and Gide, see Michaud, *Message poétique du symbolisme*, 725, 731. See also Stéphane Mallarmé, *Oeuvres complètes*, ed. Henri Mondor and G. Jean-Aubry (Paris: Gallimard, 1945), 378, and Charles Baudelaire, *Oeuvres complètes*, vol. 1 of 2 vols., ed. Charles Pichois (Paris: Gallimard, 1975), 11.

44. Stéphane Mallarmé, letter to Théodore Aubanel, 28 July 1866, in *Correspondance complète 1862–1871*, ed. Bertrand Marchal (Paris: Gallimard, 1959), 315–16.

45. Arthur Rimbaud, *Oeuvres complètes*, ed. Rolland de Renéville and Jules Mouquet (Paris: Gallimard, 1946), 255. Generally the Symbolists' renunciation of any control over inspiration, their habit of attributing it to the intervention of some higher power, extended to the whole process of committing that inspiration to words. Mallarmé, for example, represented the process of articulation as one in which a transcendental *Geist* worked out its intentions. See Robert Gibson, *Modern French Poets on Poetry* (Cambridge: Cambridge University Press, 1961), 85. The Symbolists' commitment to representing the poetic process as an instinctive, organic one, also manifested itself in numerous claims about the identity of form and content. The Symbolist poet claimed never to know what he was to say before he has said it and after he said it that he could never say it again in any other way.

46. See Michaud, *Message poétique du symbolisme*, 731.

47. Baudelaire, *Oeuvres complètes*, 1: 127, 2: 334.

48. Mallarmé said that the poet's aim ought to be to evoke "l'objet tu, par des mots allusifs, jamais directs" (*Oeuvres complètes*, 400). For examples of his use of synecdoche and negation, see the poems "Sainte," "Ses purs ongles . . . ," and "Prose: pour des Esseintes," in *Oeuvres complètes*, ed. Henri Mondor and G. Jean-Aubry (Paris: Gallimard, 1945), 53, 68, 55–57.

49. See Rimbaud, "Le Bateau ivre," *Oeuvres complètes,* 66–69. For prose poems that demonstrate this practice, see "Après le déluge," "Enfance," and "Ornières," *Illuminations,* in *Oeuvres complètes,* 121–22, 122–23, 135.

50. Over the course of several poems, for example, women are juxtaposed with roses, and roses with diamonds, and diamonds with ice, and ice with virgins; when we then see a woman juxtaposed with an image of a weeping diamond, we may (or may not) intuit the point that the loss of virginity is a cause for sadness. For this repeated cluster of images, see the poems "Surgi de la croupe et du bonde," "Dame," "O si chère de loin . . . ," and "Hérodiade" in *Oeuvres complètes,* 74, 61, 41–49.

51. Baudelaire, *Oeuvres complètes,* 2: 133.

52. Ibid.

53. W. B. Yeats, *Essays and Introductions* (London: Macmillan, 1961), 147.

54. Northrop Frye discusses the "anagogic" metaphor in *Anatomy of Criticism: Four Essays* (Princeton: Princeton University Press, 1957), 124. Frye says that when metaphor reaches the anagogic level, the "literary universe . . . is a universe in which everything is potentially identical with everything else" and that "there is no metaphor, not even 'black is white,' which a reader has any right to quarrel with in advance." For examples of claims about the "intrinsic" rather than "extrinsic" significance of symbols, see Mockel, above, and Thomas Carlyle, *Sartor Resartus* (London: Chapman and Hall, 1885), 168–69. Rimbaud's and Mallarmé's faith in the intrinsic power of symbols led them to experiment with what they believed to be the intrinsic power of individual letters. See Rimbaud, "Voyelles" (*Oeuvres complètes,* 53) and Mallarmé, "Un Coup de dés" (*Oeuvres complètes,* 457).

55. T. E. Hulme, "A Lecture on Modern Poetry," in *The Collected Writings of T. E. Hulme,* ed. Karen Csengeri (Oxford: Oxford University Press, 1994), 51. Subsequent references to this volume will appear in the text with the abbreviation CW.

56. Hulme, "Notes on Language and Style," CW 44–45.

57. For Hulme's disgust with Yeats's efforts to "ennoble" the poetic vocation and other comments against the concept of poetry's "nobility," see Hulme, "Notes on Language and Style," CW 43 and 38. For Stevens's critique of "the fortunes of the idea of nobility as a characteristic of the imagination," see "The Noble Rider and the Sound of Words," in *The Necessary Angel* (London: Faber and Faber, 1960), 7. Subsequent references to this volume will use the abbreviation NA. Read only in excerpts, the "Noble Rider" essay might be mistaken for a straightforward *defense* of the nobility of poetry, but its main point is that a kind of nobility in poetry that does not acknowledge concrete realities is unacceptable. A fuller account of the essay and of how its argument can be misconstrued is found in chapter 4 of this study.

58. See Hulme's comment that "people anxious to be poets think there is no work, just as haymaking. . . . [They are c]oncerned in the field with ecstasy, but the pains of birth and parturition are sheets and sheets of paper." See also his comment that poetry's "intensity of meaning" is the product of "agony and bloody sweat." "Notes on Language and Style," CW 43, 36. I discuss Stevens's concern that poetry performs useful work in the world at length in chapter 4 of this study. For an account of how pragmatist poets tend to associate poetry making with physical labor, see Richard Poirier, *Poetry and Pragmatism,* 79.

59. Hulme, "Romanticism and Classicism," and "A Lecture on Modern Poetry," CW 66, 51; Stevens, "The Figure of the Youth as Virile Poet," NA 30.

60. Suzanne Clark explores this issue and surveys the criticism of it in *Sentimen-*

tal Modernism (Bloomington: Indiana University Press, 1991). She notes the irony in the modernists' conflation of romanticism and femininity, because romanticism has been regarded by some critics (and in some ways by itself) as an aesthetic that renounced feminine values (27–28).

61. See Frank Kermode, *Romantic Image* (London: Routledge and Kegan Paul, 1957). I discuss Kermode's argument at length in chapter 1 of this study. The position that Hulme's "new classicism" was muddled, because it is based largely on Romantic tenets, is also espoused by Alun R. Jones, *The Life and Opinions of T. E. Hulme* (London: Victor Gollancz, 1960), 57; Murray Krieger, *The New Apologists for Poetry* (Minneapolis: University of Minnesota Press, 1956), 35; Graham Hough, *Image and Experience* (London: Duckworth, 1960), 30.

62. Kermode, *Romantic Image*, 130.

63. Judith Ryan, *The Vanishing Subject*, 219. Ryan defines "Daylight mysticism" as a representation of mystical experience that "divest[s] mystical experience of its mystery" (223). Where Ryan's recent study is mainly concerned with the representations of epiphany in literary texts—especially in the fiction of Proust, Musil, Woolf, Joyce and others—my study focuses on the examples of "daylight mysticism" in modernist manifestos. In my argument the carefully demystified accounts of epiphany found in Hulme's, Pound's, and Stevens's poetry are measures taken to coordinate poetic style with the redescriptions of inspiration in the manifestos.

64. For the full range of Bergson's psychological sources, see Ben-Ami Scharfstein, *Roots of Bergson's Philosophy* (New York: Columbia University Press, 1943), 32ff and 59ff. Bergson had tremendous respect for the work of James and corresponded with him regularly after the turn of the century. Despite the strong resemblance between his conception of pure mental experience as *durée réelle* and James's conception of the "stream of consciousness," Bergson denied that James was in any way responsible for his own views (Scharfstein, 30–31).

65. Théodule Ribot, *Essai sur l'imagination créatrice* (Paris: Félix Alcan, 1921), 67. I discuss Ribot's and Bergson's accounts of the *conception idéale* in chapter 1 of this study. For a comparable notion in James, see PP 1: 269–71; 2: 1168–69.

66. Henri Bergson, *La Pensée et le mouvant* (Paris: Presses Universitaires de France, 1938), 119, 130. Translations from Bergson, *The Creative Mind*, trans. Mabelle L. Andison (Westport, Conn.: Greenwood, 1968), 128, 139.

67. Hulme, "A Lecture on Modern Poetry," and "Notes on Language and Style," CW 49, 34, 26, 25. Hulme alludes to *L'Evolution créatrice* in "The Philosophy of Intensive Manifolds," CW 189. Paraphrasing Bergson, Hulme emphasizes that the idea that governs the process of expression is not to be confused with Schopenhauer's Idea ("Bergson's Theory of Art," CW 194).

68. Pound, "Vortex. Pound," in *Blast*, ed. Wyndham Lewis (1914; reprint. Santa Barbara: Black Sparrow Press, 1981), 154; Stevens, *The Collected Poems of Wallace Stevens* (New York: Knopf, 1954), 381; Stevens, *Opus Posthumous*, 253; Stevens, *Collected Poems*, 381; Stevens, "The Figure of the Youth as Virile Poet," NA 60; Hulme, "Bergson's Theory of Art," CW 194. Subsequent references to Stevens's *Collected Poems* will appear in the text with the abbreviation CP. For evidence that Pound and Stevens agree with Hulme's desire to eliminate "metaphysical baggage," see Pound's insistence that his claims about the "Image" do not entail any presumption about the poet's apprehension of a "deathless light" or about his insights into a "permanent world" ("Vorticism," GB 86). Stevens stresses that he makes no claims for the mystical origins either of the "first idea" or of the "companion of the conscience." He refuses to trace the idea back to any "voluminous master

folded in his fire" (CP 381), and, as I explain in chapter 3, he pulls his muses back from the Beyond onto the threshold of the self, a move similar to James's treatment of his deflated "divinities" in *The Varieties of Religious Experience.*

69. Throughout this study, I shall use the term *epoche* as Husserl used it: to denote the condition of being detached from all consideration of origins or of being subjected to phenomenological reduction. See Edmund Husserl, *Ideas: General Introduction to Pure Phenomenology,* trans. W. R. Boyce Gibson (New York: Collier-Macmillan, 1962), 99–100.

70. Pound, "Vorticism," GB 86.

71. One of the best-known expressions of this commitment is Pound's statement in "Vorticism," where he describes the "image" (in the second sense of the term) as a type of poem: "The 'image' is the furthest possible remove from rhetoric. Rhetoric is the art of dressing up some important matter so as to fool the audience for the time being. . . . Even Aristotle distinguishes between rhetoric, 'which is persuasion,' and the *analytical examination of truth*" (GB 83; my italics). Pound also describes serious art as "sincere self-expression" and twice cites Remy de Gourmont's statement of the principle (GB 85; SP 386; LE 349). Hulme's call for sincerity is implicit in his concern that the extravagant claims of Symbolists and Romantics did not reflect the truth about the creative experience and in his repeated injunctions against the use of cliché. See, for example, "Notes on Language and Style," CW 55–56. In "Bergson's Theory of Art," he insists that the poet should make an extraordinary effort to bend the "curves" of language, so as to represent himself truthfully; in the best poet, he says, there is "a passionate desire for accuracy" (CW 200). Stevens distinguishes the "poetry of experience," which he endorses, from the "poetry of rhetoric" (OP 187), which he does not. His values are apparent in his explanation for citing "The Emperor of Ice-Cream" as his favorite poem: the poem, he says, "represented what was in my mind at the moment, with the least possible manipulation" (OP 212). The poets' concern with sincerity is the hallmark of their expressive poetics and a reflection of their concession that truth in the absolute sense may not be a standard the poet can realistically be expected to meet. See I. A. Richards's distinction between "scientific" truth and the truth of "Sincerity" in poetry, *Principles of Literary Criticism* (London: Routledge and Kegan Paul, 1967), 212–14.

72. The Impressionist painters and poets like Wilde and Symons aimed above all to capture the particularity of things—to avoid what Walter Pater called the "roughness of the eye that makes any two persons, things, situations, seem alike." *Walter Pater: Essays on Literature and Art,* ed. Jennifer Uglow (London: Dent, 1973), 40–41. The impulse was to resist any device that would translate things into *types:* it included a resistance to metaphor (more successful, inevitably, in painting than in poetry). Pound excoriated the tentativeness of such art, calling it "flaccid" ("Vortex. Pound," 153) and emphasized that Imagisme was not Impressionism.

73. The picture of a cindery chaos, probably derived from Bergson, is the central image in Hulme's intriguing notebook fragments, both those collected under the title "Notes on Language and Style" and those called "Cinders" (CW 7–45). Pound uses a similar image to describe empirical data in one of his best-known metaphors for the organizational principle in art: the "rose in the steel dust." *The Cantos* (London: Faber and Faber, 1975), 449. Stevens also represents experience as a gritty flux awaiting and resisting theoretical organization. See CP 412, 529.

74. Frank Kermode, *The Sense of an Ending* (Oxford: Oxford University Press, 1966), 49.

75. See Pound, LE 162, and Ernest Fenollosa, *The Chinese Written Character as a Medium for Poetry*, ed. Ezra Pound (San Francisco: City Lights, 1936), 23n.

76. Frye, *Anatomy of Criticism*, 123.

77. Or from what Gelpi has called the "type": "A type [is] an inherently significant and signifying symbol, a manifestation of spiritual truth in material form, to be communicated verbally, whereas a trope [is] itself figurative language, a metaphorical invention." Albert Gelpi, *A Coherent Splendour: The American Poetic Renaissance, 1910–1950* (Cambridge: Cambridge University Press, 1987), 68.

78. Sanford Schwartz, *The Matrix of Modernism: Pound, Eliot and Early 20th-Century Thought* (Princeton: Princeton University Press, 1985), 62, 75. In describing the Image this way, I agree with Schwartz's representation of Pound's metaphor: "Pound's interpretive metaphor . . . is neither fact nor fiction but a construct that bridges the distinction between them. It transcends fiction in that it discloses reality exactly as it appears in a special state of mind . . . Pound avoids both Nietzsche's fictionalism and Fenollosa's realism: the interpretive metaphor enables us to view the world 'as if' it possesses certain forms, but it projects these forms as experiential rather than factual, as 'interpretation' rather than explanation" (95). Schwartz's use of Stevens's favorite qualifier, "as if," points to one of my major points in this study: Pound and Stevens were more alike than they were different, and what united them was a commitment to a particular kind of provisional expression, incorporating the principles of phenomenological reduction.

79. Hulme, CW 22; Pound, "The Wisdom of Poetry," SP 332.

CHAPTER 1. PRAGMATISM AND IMAGISM

1. Pound denies Hulme's influence in "This Hulme Business," *Townsman* 2 (January 1939): 15. His position is accepted as fact by Herbert N. Schneidau, in *Ezra Pound: The Image and the Real* (Baton Rouge: Louisiana State University Press, 1967), among others.

2. See Herbert Read, Introduction to T. E. Hulme, *Speculations: Essays on Humanism and the Philosophy of Art* (London: Routledge and Kegan Paul, 1936), xiii.

3. See "The Plan for a Book on Modern Theories of Art," *Speculations*, 261–64. In it Hulme proposes to discusses the work of Ribot and Bergson, among other French and German psychologists of art. He views the major accomplishment of these psychologists as their advance beyond the "merely literary method" of discussing both "a specifically aesthetic emotion" and the "state of mind characterised as creative imagination."

4. See Csengeri, introduction to CW, ix–xxxvi. Csengeri makes the point in arguing for the importance of the new edition of Hulme's works, which reproduces all of his writings in chronological order. She contends that the perception of a contradiction between Hulme's skepticism and absolutism has been the result of the inverted chronological order of the writings in *Speculations*, with the 1915 "Humanism and the Religious Attitude" appearing first and the 1906–8 "Cinders" appearing last. The argument for absolute ethical values in "Humanism and the Religious Attitude," therefore, has seemed primary and contradicted by the endorsement of Bergsonian nominalism in subsequent pieces. Csengeri argues that Hulme's support for Bergson can be confined to the years 1909–12, after his interest in poetry wained and before his discovery of Lasserre, Maurras, and Sorel. For Levenson's similar view of the stages in Hulme's career, see *A Genealogy of Modernism: A*

Study of English Literary Doctrine 1908–1922 (Cambridge: Cambridge University Press, 1984), 94ff.

5. For my discussion of an apparent contradiction between skepticism and absolutism in Hulme's work, see chapter 5 of this study, pp. 219–22.

6. Hulme's first published article ("The New Philosophy," *New Age* 5 [1 July 1909]), was a review of James's *A Pluralistic Universe* (1909). He also refers to *The Principles of Psychology* in that article (CW 85). Elsewhere in his work, he employs some of the central concepts developed in *Principles of Psychology;* note, for example, his references to the "stream of conscious life" and to James's concept of the peripheral "fringe" of awareness in "Notes on Bergson," CW 148, 147. Note also what may be an allusion to the opening chapter of *Principles of Psychology,* in Hulme's comment that "most of our life is spent in buttoning and unbuttoning" ("Cinders," CW 11). James uses "buttoning and unbuttoning" as examples of automatic reflex actions in *Principles of Psychology,* I: 19. Hulme refers to *The Will to Believe* in "A Note on the Art of Political Conversion," CW 207. I have not been able to find any explicit references to *Pragmatism* in Hulme's writings, but Hulme uses many of the same metaphors as James in outlining what I shall argue is a pragmatic approach to theory-making. He also refers explicitly to "pragmatism" as a concept. See, for example, "Searchers after Reality I: Bax," and "The New Philosophy," CW 89, 85.

7. "Romanticism and Classicism," CW 66.

8. Murray Krieger, *The New Apologists for Poetry,* 35; Alun R. Jones, *The Life and Opinions of T. E. Hulme* (London: Victor Gollancz, 1960), 38. Cf. Graham Hough, *Image and Experience* (London: Duckworth, 1960), 30.

9. *The New Apologists for Poetry,* 37. See also Jones's comment that through Bergson Hulme was simply "led back to what amounts to a re-statement of the romantic theory of poetry and to a re-affirmation of romantic Platonism" (*The Life and Opinions of T. E. Hulme,* 46). For further skeptical treatments of Hulme's antiromanticism, see J. B. Harmer, *Victory in Limbo: Imagism 1908–1917* (London: Secker and Warburg, 1975); John Bayley, *The Romantic Survival: A Study in Poetic Evolution* (London: Constable, 1957); Ronald Primeau, "On the Discrimination of Hulme's: Toward a Theory of the Anti-Romantic Romanticism of Modern Poetry," *Journal of Modern Literature* 3 (1974): 1104–22, and Kermode, *Romantic Image.*

10. Prior to its reproduction in Csengeri's *The Collected Writings of T. E. Hulme,* "A Tory Philosophy" was reprinted only in Jones, *The Life and Opinions of T. E. Hulme.*

11. Hulme, "A Tory Philosophy," CW 234.

12. Harmer wrongly states that Hulme denounced "romanticism at large" (*Victory in Limbo,* 176). Jones refers to Hulme's "whole-hearted rejection of Romanticism in all its manifestations" (*The Life and Opinions of T. E. Hulme,* 63).

13. Kermode, *Romantic Image,* 43.

14. Hulme, "Romanticism and Classicism," CW 59.

15. Excerpts from "A Notebook" appeared in *Speculations* under the title "Humanism and the Religious Attitude." The complete essay appeared in seven installments in *The New Age:* 18 (2 December 1915), 112–13; 18 (9 December 1915), 137–38; 18 (16 December 1915), 158–60; 18 (23 December 1915), 186–88; 18 (6 January 1916), 234–35; 18 (27 January 1916), 305–7; and 18 (10 February 1916), 353–54.

16. Richards develops the distinction between the attitude expressed by a statement (its "emotive" aspect) and the statement's referential meaning (its "scientific"

aspect) in *The Principles of Literary Criticism* (London: Routledge and Kegan Paul, 1967), 211–12. Like Hulme he is especially interested in examining the emotive force of romantic texts, particularly those which manifest what he calls "revelation theories" (*Principles of Literary Criticism*, 200ff.). Husserl discusses the distinction between the attitude informing theories and the referential import of such theories in "Philosophy as Rigorous Science," *Phenomenology and the Crisis of Philosophy*, trans. Quentin Lauer (New York: Harper and Row, 1965), 77. Hulme refers to this discussion in "A Notebook," CW 430, 435.

17. Hulme, "A Notebook," CW 433; "Romanticism and Classicism," CW 61; "A Notebook," CW 427. Also note Hulme's definition of romantic thinkers as "all who do not believe in the Fall of Man," in his introduction to George Sorel's *Reflections on Violence* (CW 250). Pierre Lasserre, one of the major spokesmen for the French right-wing political group, *L'Action Française*, stipulated the same definition in a work Hulme discusses in that introduction. See Lasserre, *Le Romantisme français* (Paris: Mercure de France, 1907), 16.

18. For Hulme's association of romanticism with the notion that man is "essentially good" and that he will flourish if institutions of "oppressive" social order are eliminated, see "Romanticism and Classicism," 116.

19. Hulme, "A Tory Philosophy," CW 235.

20. Hulme, "Romanticism and Classicism," CW 67. Note also his comment that "the romantic, because he thinks man infinite, must always be talking about the infinite." Hulme may have derived his sense that romanticism entailed an obsession with the "infinite" from Lasserre. The French writer maintains that the "sentiment romantique de la nature" had its first exponent in Rousseau and cites one of Rousseau's letters, to M. de Malesherbes, to illustrate the phenomenon:

"L'esprit perdu dans cette immensité, je ne pensais pas, je ne raisonnais pas, je ne philosophais pas, je me sentais avec une sorte de volupté, accablé du poids de cet univers, je me livrais avec ravissement à la confusion de ces grandes idées, j'aimais à me perdre en imagination dans l'espace, mon coeur resserré dans les bornes des êtres s'y trouvait trop a l'étroit; j'étouffais dans l'univers; j'aurais voulu m'élancer dans l'infini."

[My mind lost in that immensity, I wasn't thinking, I wasn't reasoning, I wasn't philosophizing. I felt, with a kind of voluptuous pleasure, overcome by the weight of this universe, I surrendered with rapture to the confusion of these great ideas, in my imagination I loved to lose myself in space; my constricted heart found itself too confined within the bounds of beings, I was suffocating in the world; I would have liked to throw myself into infinity.] (*Le Romantisme français*, 50–51)

21. Hulme, "Romanticism and Classicism," CW 68.

22. Ibid., 62.

23. Hulme, "Bergson's Theory of Art," CW 194. Hulme would have been aware of the French Symbolists' appeals to the "infinite." His friend F. S. Flint wrote enthusiastically about Mallarmé's transcendentalist aspirations: "Mallarmé dreamed the superhuman dream of *putting the reader in direct contact with the infinite,* by the choice of words which could give the sensation thereof, and in such a way that the poem would convey simultaneously the divination of musical, plastic, philosophical and emotion analogies." He went on to celebrate the power of Symbolist verse to "*set vibrating the infinity* within us, by the exquisite juxtaposition of images" and to refer to the *infinity* that has its "culminating point" in inspiration (355, 357; my italics). F. S. Flint, "Contemporary French Poetry," *Poetry Review* 1 (August 1912): 356; italics mine. For Schopenhauer's importance for French Symbolism, see A. G. Lehmann, *The Symbolist Aesthetic in France*, 2nd ed. (Ox-

ford: Basil Blackwell, 1968), 55–67. For the Symbolist longing to transcend the world of time and fly into mystical regions, see Mallarmé's "Les Fenêtres," *Oeuvres complètes,* 33. Compare Yeats's "The White Birds," *Collected Poems,* ed. Richard J. Finneran (New York: MacMillan, 1983), 41.

24. Hulme, "Bergson's Theory of Art," CW 194.

25. Hulme, "Notes on Language and Style," CW 43. See also Hulme's disparagement of a journalist's recent description of poetry as "the means by which the soul soared into higher regions, and as a means of expression by which it became merged into a higher kind of reality" ("A Lecture on Modern Poetry," CW 67).

26. Hulme, "Bergson's Theory of Art," CW 193.

27. Hulme, "A Notebook," CW 424–25.

28. Hulme, "Notes on Bergson," CW 141.

29. Karl Shapiro has claimed that a hostility to mysticism was an essential part of Hulme's antiromanticism, observing that "Hulme formulated for Eliot the attack on Romanticism and the attack on mysticism (for the Romantic and the mystical are always related)." Karl Shapiro, *In Defense of Ignorance* (New York: Random House, 1952), 58.

30. Hulme, "Romanticism and Classicism," CW 68, 66.

31. For other accounts of Hulme's use of French sources, see Wallace Martin, "The Sources of the Imagist Aesthetic," *PMLA* 85 (1970): 196–204, and Karen Csengeri, "T. E. Hulme's Borrowings from the French," *Comparative Literature* 34 (Winter 1982): 16–27.

32. Ribot, *La Psychologie anglaise contemporaine* (Paris: Félix Alcan, 1896), 22, 34.

33. Ibid., 17. Trans. from Ribot, *English Psychology,* trans. unknown (London: Henry S. King, 1873), 11. See also 28, where Ribot describes the turn towards metaphysics as a move towards "questions vaines, factices."

34. I borrow this term from I. A. Richards, *Poetries and Sciences: A Reissue of Science and Poetry (1926, 1935) with Commentary* (London: Routledge and Kegan Paul, 1970), 67. The term is preferable to "demystification" in that it captures the equivocation on epistemological matters of thinkers who psychologize moments of "knowing." Such thinkers relinquish the right to make final judgments about the truth or falsity of the knowledge attained in such moments; they remain "neutral" on the subject.

35. Ribot, *La Psychologie anglaise contemporaine,* 28.

36. Albert H. N. Baron, preface to Théodule Ribot, *Essay on the Creative Imagination,* trans. Albert H. N. Baron (London: Kegan Paul, 1906), v. In likening Ribot to Prometheus, Baron also comments that Ribot's work serves to dispel the notion that the imagination is "an entity *sui generis . . .* a lofty something found only on long-haired, wild-eyed 'geniuses.'" Hulme probably read this translation of Ribot's work.

37. See Ribot, *La Psychologie des sentiments* (Paris: Félix Alcan, 1939), 328, 307, 309, 95. Translation from Ribot, *Psychology of Emotions,* trans. unknown (London: Walter Scott, 1911). In the last citation, Ribot refers to what became known as the James-Lange theory of emotions. The theory is discussed in James, *Principles of Psychology* 2: 1058.

38. Ribot, *La Psychologie des sentiments,* 328, 37.

39. Ribot, like James, implies that the responses a person has to the impressions bombarding consciousness are inextricable from his or her motor tendencies. For a discussion of James's account, see my introduction, p. 26.

40. Ribot, *La Psychologie des sentiments*, 366; *Essai sur l'imagination créatrice*, 67, 31, 165, 22, 153.

41. For a discussion of Ribot's *Schopenhauer* (1874), see Lehmann, *The Symbolist Aesthetic in France*, 40.

42. Ribot, *Essai sur l'imagination créatrice*, 68.

43. Ibid., 43.

44. Ibid., 133. The intuitive process Ribot describes is one that moves from an apprehension of its informing idea to the gradual recognition of particulars that will articulate it: "de l'unité aux détails." The *unité* is changed through the process of discovering the *détails*. He opposes this process to the one typical of building a mosaic or a jigsaw puzzle, which he associates with the operation of the *imagination combinatrice*. In the latter process, the artist moves "des détails à l'unité," and the shape of the unité is predetermined. See 132.

45. Ribot, *Essai sur l'imagination créatrice*, 45.

46. Compare James's parallel discussion of inspiring divinities in *The Varieties of Religious Experience* discussed in chapters 2 and 3 of this study, pp. 81–83 and 114–19.

47. Ribot, *Essai sur l'imagination créatrice*, 186, 187, 91, 191, 188.

48. Ribot, *La Psychologie anglaise contemporaine*, 14.

49. For a discussion of Ribot's plans for the journal, see G. Lamarque, *Théodule Ribot* (Paris: Rasmussen, 1928), 14.

50. Bergson, "Introduction à la métaphysique," *La Pensée et le mouvant*, 206. Translation from *The Creative Mind*, 216.

51. Bergson was especially interested in Ribot's writings on the unconscious mind; see Scharfstein, *Roots of Bergson's Philosophy*, 63–66. Bergson's other psychological sources included Binet, Paulhan, and James. He argued his antimaterialist and antideterminist metaphysics in the *Essai sur les données immédiates de la conscience* (1889) and *Matière et mémoire* (1896).

52. Hulme's review of Visan's *L'Attitude du lyrisme contemporain* appeared in *New Age 9* (24 August 1911): 400–401. See CW 57–58.

53. Tancrède de Visan, *L'Attitude du lyrisme contemporain* (Paris: Mercure de France, 1911), 425.

54. The dates I have listed for *La Pensée et le mouvant* indicate the original dates of publication, or in some cases verbal delivery, of the essays included in that volume. The volume was published in 1938.

55. This characterization of Bergson is shared by many later critics. See, for example, E. Fiser, *Le Symbole littéraire* (Paris: Librairie Jose Corti, 1941), 10, and Enid Starkie, "Bergson and Literature," in *The Bergsonian Heritage*, ed. Thomas Hanna (New York: Columbia University Press, 1962), 79.

56. For accounts of the transcendental experience in Symbolist writings, see Baudelaire, *Oeuvres complètes* 1: 419, 659; 2: 596; and Mallarmé, letter to Cazalis, 14 May 1867, in Gibson, *Modern French Poets on Poetry*, 85.

57. Not in his early writings on the subject at least. By the time of his final work, *Les Deux sources de la morale et religion* (1932), Bergson had left the restrictions of psychological discourse behind and embraced a form of mysticism. *L'Évolution créatrice* would seem to pose as problem for this claim, asserting as it does the existence of a universal force, *l'élan vital*. But in that text Bergson generally uses *l'élan vital* and its operation as a *model* for the *moi fondamentale*, not as something continuous with it. For exceptions, see Bergson, *L'Évolution créatrice* (Paris: Félix Alcan, 1908), 240, 261–62, 264, 267.

58. Bergson, *La Pensée et le mouvant*, 25–26. Translation from *The Creative Mind*, 34.

59. For Schopenhauer's account of the artist's intuitive communion with objects, an experience he represents as involving the apprehension of a divine essence or Idea, see *The World as Will and Representation*, 1: 178–79, 182. For Bergson's description of the experience, see "Introduction à la métaphysique," 181.

60. Bergson, "Introduction à la métaphysique," 179–80.

61. Hulme, "Bergson's Theory of Art," CW 194.

62. Bergson, "Introduction à la métaphysique," 181. Translation from *The Creative Mind*, 190–91. As I have suggested (see note 56, above), in his early career, at least, Bergson claims no continuity between this flux and any transcendental Spirit. In saying that the poet contacts this self (Bergson, *Le Rire* [Paris: Presses Universitaires de France, 1964], 123), a self that provides him with unexpected insights and leads him to say unexpected things, he provides a neutral alternative to Symbolist claims about the artist's connection with a higher mind. That is, the *moi fondamentale* enables Bergson to redescribe the heuristic process in which the poet heeds an unpredictable series of *états d'âme* within him. See Visan's discussion of this aspect of Bergson's thought in *L'Attitude du lyrisme contemporain*, 119, 270, 272–73, 276, 442. This process is the same one Mallarmé explained by calling himself "une aptitude qu'a l'Univers Spirituel à se voir et à se développer" and of his poetry as "l'image de ce développement." See Mallarmé's letter to Henri Cazalis, 14 May 1867, in Gibson, *Modern French Poets on Poetry*, 85. Rimbaud wrote of the unsought appearance of images flowing, *de là-bas*, through his soul. See Rimbaud's letter to Demeny, 15 May 1871, in Rimbaud, *Oeuvres complètes*, 127. Bergson's account of the *moi fondamental* may have been influenced by Ribot's and Binet's accounts of the unconscious and possibly by James's account of the "stream of consciousness." See Scharfstein, *Roots of Bergson's Philosophy*, 61–67.

63. See Bergson, *Essai sur les données immédiates de la conscience* (Paris: Félix Alcan, 1908), 97, 119–22, 124–27.

64. Ibid., 95, 127. People who operate this way are prisoners of *actions réflexes* (182).

65. Bergson describes the process by which the artist recovers his freedom in *L'Évolution créatrice* (202). See also "Introduction à la métaphysique," 213 and *La Pensée et le mouvant*, 103.

66. Bergson, "L'Effort intellectuel," *Oeuvres*, ed. Andre Robinet and Henri Gouhier (Paris: Presses Universitaires de France, 1963), 942–43. Bergson cites Robertson's article "Reflex Speech," published in the *Journal of Mental Science*, April 1888, and Feré, "Le langage réflexe," *Revue philosophique*, January 1896. Hulme cites Robertson in "Romanticism and Classicism," CW 64.

67. Bergson paraphrases Ribot's account at some length in "L'Effort intellectuel," 946–48.

68. Bergson, "L'Effort intellectuel," 941.

69. See note 43.

70. Instead of working with a schema "aux formes immobiles et raides, dont on se donne tout de suite la conception distincte," the poet works with "un schéma élastique ou mouvant, dont l'esprit se refuse à arrêter les contours, parce qu'il attend sa décision des images mêmes que le schéma doit attirer pour se donner un corps." [An elastic and moving schema whose outlines the mind refuses to arrest because it awaits the decision of the same images that the schema must attract in order to give itself a body.] Like Mallarmé and other Symbolist theorists, Bergson likens the process to dancing. Dancing, he observes, begins with the appearance of

a similar mental schema: a sketch of movements that the individual then attempts to objectify in certain physical gestures. This schema is modified as it is subjected to the test of performance: the act of objectifying it results in the "adaptations des images au schéma et du schéma aux images" (Bergson, "L'Effort intellectuel," 948, 952). For a discussion of the Symbolists' version of this notion, see Lehmann, *The Symbolist Aesthetic in France*, 63, and Kermode, *Romantic Image*, 49–91.

71. *La Pensée et le mouvant*, 119. Translation from *The Creative Mind*, 128.

72. Bergson, *L'Évolution créatrice*, 259. Bergson emphasizes the contrast between evolutionary process and the activity of putting together a jigsaw puzzle, an activity where the end result is entirely predictable, and the speed of execution makes no difference to the product. Like the final details of a poem or a painting, the precise character of an evolving species cannot be known until it has been completely made. Like the final constitution of poetry or painting, too, the nature of a species will reflect the speed and duration of the process. Ultimately, then, the notion of the organically developing *schéma* is the basis for an antimechanistic account of natural evolution (*Évolution créatrice* 6, 339–40).

73. Bergson, *L'Évolution créatrice*, 251.

74. See Bergson, *Creative Evolution*, trans. Arthur Mitchell (London: Macmillan, 1911).

75. See Hulme, "The Plan for a Book on Modern Theories of Art," 263. Jones provides convincing evidence that Hulme read Ribot before November 1912. See *The Life and Opinions of T. E. Hulme*, 209. Hulme's interest in Bergson is well documented. He wrote many articles on the philosopher for *The New Age* between 1909 and 1912, and in 1912 published an English translation of Bergson's "Introduction à la métaphysique." He gave a series of lectures on Bergson's work in London and Cambridge in 1911 and 1912, later collected by Herbert Read and published in *Speculations* as "The Philosophy of Intensive Manifolds."

76. Hulme, "The Plan for a Book on Modern Theories of Art," 263.

77. Hulme, "Romanticism and Classicism," CW 66; "Cinders," CW 15; "Bergson's Theory of Art," 193.

78. See *The Life and Opinions of T. E. Hulme*, 46. Cf. Hough, *Image and Experience*, 30.

79. Hulme, "The Philosophy of Intensive Manifolds," CW 174, 177, 176, 175.

80. Ibid., 173; Hulme, "Bergson's Theory of Art," CW 200. For further evidence of Hulme's conviction that the states the poet apprehends are unique, see also "Notes on Language and Style," CW 91.

81. Ibid., 194.

82. Hulme, "Notes on Language and Style," CW 34, 25, 26.

83. See Hulme, "Notes on Language and Style," 44, 24, 29, 36–38.

84. Hulme, "Notes on Language and Style," 34. My italics.

85. Ibid., 29.

86. Hulme, "The Philosophy of Intensive Manifolds," CW 189; "Notes on Language and Style," CW 26, 40.

87. Hulme, "The Philosophy of Intensive Manifolds," CW 178–82.

88. See Hulme, "The Plan for a Book on Modern Theories of Art," 263.

89. Hulme, "The Philosophy of Intensive Manifolds," CW 178; "Romanticism and Classicism," CW 64; "Bergson's Theory of Art," CW 200.

90. For another description of automatic speech, which Hulme likens to "reflex action in the body," see "A Lecture on Modern Poetry," CW 55. Hulme identifies such speech with the use of cliché ("A Lecture on Modern Poetry," 55; "Theory and Practice," 388). Another account of automatic speech that may have influenced

Hulme's was Remy de Gourmont's. In a book Hulme read, Gourmont distinguishes the *idéo-émotif* writer, who uses expressions "sans aucune intervention de conscience et de la sensibilite" from the poet, who pays attention to the images attached to his words and invents new expressions. The *idéo-émotif* writer deals in *mots-sentiments*, while the poet deals in *mots-images*. Using a metaphor employed by both Ribot and James and used subsequently by Hulme, Gourmont describes the *mot-sentiment* or cliché as "une monnaie jetée dans la circulation," and the poet's original expression as "le premier exemplaire de cette monnaie" (*Problème du style*, 37, 81, 93). For a full account of the contrast between the two ways of speaking and, inevitably, thinking, see *Problème du style*, 69–70.

91. "The Philosophy of Intensive Manifolds," CW 170, 184; "Notes on Language and Style," CW 26, 42. For more examples of Hulme's Bergsonian use of the "cinders" metaphor, see "Cinders," CW 9, 12.

92. Hulme, "Notes on Language and Style," CW 88.

93. James develops his arguments for free will in the essay "The Dilemma of Determinism" (in *The Will to Believe*) and in *The Principles of Psychology*. For an excellent summary of these arguments, see Myers, *William James*, 206–9, 391–95.

94. Hulme refers to Schiller and "the much advertised English pragmatic movement" at the beginning of his first published article, "The New Philosophy," in 1909 (CW 85). James outlines and defends Schiller's humanist philosophy in *Pragmatism* (116ff.) and recommends the English philosopher's work in his preface to that volume (3). Hulme cites Le Roy, another French pragmatic thinker whose work James endorses in his preface, in "Searchers after Reality III: Jules de Gaultier" (CW 99).

95. Gaultier's works, in addition to *Le Bovarysme*, include *De Kant à Nietzsche* (1900), *La Fiction universelle* (1903), *Nietzsche et la Réforme philosophique, Les Raisons de l'Idéalisme* (1906), *La dépendance de la Morale et l'Indépendance des Moeurs* (1907).

96. Gaultier, "Pragmatisme," *Mercure de France* 77 (1909): 422.

97. Gaultier, *Le Bovarysme* (Paris: Mercure de France, 1922), 26.

98. Ibid., 58, 182, 52, 59, 60. When Gaultier describes the bovaric "notion" in a related article, "De la Nature des vérités," he explicitly identifies it with Ribot's *conception idéale*. See "De la Nature des vérités," 566.

99. Gaultier, *Le Bovarysme*, 223, 182.

100. Ibid., 174–75.

101. Ibid., 113.

102. See especially, "Does Consciousness Exist" (1904), ERE 3–19. For a fuller account of James's recognition of the problem and his proposed solution, see chapter 3 of this study, pp. 113–14.

103. Gaultier, *Le Bovarysme*, 207. Cf. "De la Nature des vérités," 563.

104. Gaultier, *Le Bovarysme*, 217. Translation from Gaultier, *Bovarysm*, trans. Gerald M. Spring (N.Y.: Philosophical Library, 1970), 22.

105. Ibid., 245. Translation from *Bovarysm*, 137.

106. Ibid., 260, 265; "De la Nature des vérités," 589; *Le Bovarysme*, 284–85, 208.

107. Gaultier, *Le Bovarysme*, 268.

108. This is how I interpret Gaultier's description of the tendency to regard reality as an *objet* and the countertendency to attribute it to a *subjet*. See *Le Bovarysme*, 261.

109. A tendency to indulge the *principe d'arrêt* exclusively, Gaultier argues, leads to the hypostatization of man-made concepts. This is what happens when Christians

ignore the original function of their dogma as a tranquillizer for a barbaric world, and Kantians ignore the *interêt étranger* in their categorical imperatives; it is also the flaw of empire builders (*Le Bovarysme,* 114, 121, 137–38, 112).

110. Gaultier, "De la Nature des vérités," 592. Gaultier also identifies the two impulses as tendencies toward "association" and "dissociation," by which he means the impulses to group particulars into concepts, or concepts into larger theories, and to distinguish particular from particular, concept from concept (*Le Bovarysme,* 272). This version of the opposition derives from the work of Remy de Gourmont, particularly *La Culture des idées* (1900). In that work, which was known to both Gaultier and Hulme, Gourmont attempts to "dissociate" the particulars and concepts clustered together in a series of notions from "decadence" to "love." Garnet Rees has traced Gourmont's technique of dissociating ideas to a clinical practice of Théodule Ribot's. See *Remy de Gourmont* (Paris: Boivin, 1939), 157.

111. Gaultier, "De la Nature des vérités," 587.

112. Gaultier, "Pragmatisme," 425; interview with Wilmot E. Ellis, *Bovarysm: The Art Philosophy of Jules de Gaultier* (Seattle: University of Washington Press, 1928), 35. For more on the distinction between Gaultier's *intellectualisme esthétique* and its relation to American pragmatism, see Georges Palante, introduction to Jules de Gaultier, *La Philosophie du Bovarysme* (Paris: Mercure de France, 1912): 74.

113. Hulme, "Searchers after Reality III. Jules De Gaultier," CW 130.

114. Hulme, "Notes on the Bologna Congress," CW 106.

115. The dating of the "Cinders" is Csengeri's; see CW 7.

116. Hulme, "Cinders," CW 12, 15, 20, 15; "War Notes," CW 396. Like Gaultier, too, Hulme likens these illusions to projections on a "stage" (CW 15).

117. Hulme, "Cinders," CW 14, 19.

118. Ibid., 15–16.

119. Ibid., 15, 18.

120. Ibid., 12, 44, 13, 22.

121. Hulme thinks, for example, of the debate between those who believe in the primacy of "mind" or "matter" ("Cinders," CW 17). Hulme is probably referring here to contemporary debates between Idealists and realists. Bergson discusses these debates and proposes a resolution to them in *Matière et mémoire,* a book Hulme knew.

122. Hulme, "Cinders," CW 19.

123. See, for example, the enthusiasm Hulme expresses in his review of Gaultier for the notion that philosophy need only paint a "good picture" to be acceptable ("Searchers after Reality III. Jules De Gaultier," 103). Note also his implied comparison between a simplifying theory and London at night, made "pretty" by the fact that "for the general cindery chaos there is substituted a simple ordered arrangement of a finite number of lights" ("Cinders," 10).

124. Hulme, "Cinders," CW 16. Cf. "Cinders," CW 12, where Hulme describes the objects one sees when looking through a microscope as "[t]hings revealed, not created, but there before."

125. Ibid., 13, 21, 12.

126. Note also Hulme's description of the empirical preoccupations of his hypothetical poet "Aphra," "Cinders," CW 236–37:

Aphra's Finger.
There are moments when the tip of one's finger seems raw. In the contact of it and the world there seems a strange difference. The spirit lives on that tip and is thrown on the rough cinders of the world. All philosophy depends on that—the state of the tip of the finger.
When Aphra had touched, even lightly, the rough wood, this wood seemed to cling to

his finger, to draw itself backward and forward along it. The spirit returned again and again, as though fascinated, to the luxurious torture of the finger.

Notice, too, the contrast Hulme sets up between "the Persian Gulf on a map" and what it looks like in real life; he recommends travel, an "education in cinders," as a corrective to abstract theorizing ("Cinders," CW 245).

127. Hulme, "Notes on Language and Style," CW 41, 46. Cf. 35 and "Cinders," CW 13.

128. Hulme, "Romanticism and Classicism," CW 63.

129. Ibid., 62.

130. Hulme, "Cinders," CW 13. For further evidence of Hulme's conviction about the interestedness of theories, note his criticism of the metaphysician ("Cinders," 19):

The metaphysician imagines that he surveys the world as with an eagle's eye. And the farther he flies, the "purer" his knowledge becomes.
Hence we can see the world as pure geometry, and can make out its dividing lines.
But the eye is in the mud, the eye *is* mud.
Pure seeing of the whole process is impossible. Little fancies help us along, but we never get pure disinterested intellect.

131. Hulme, "Romanticism and Classicism," CW 68.

132. Hulme, "Notes on Language and Style," CW 23–24.

133. Hulme, "Romanticism and Classicism," 69; "Notes on Language and Style," CW 25; "Romanticism and Classicism," CW 70. "Prose," Hulme says, is "a train which delivers you at a destination" and poetry "a pedestrian taking you over the ground" ("Romanticism and Classicism," CW 135). Hulme would have encountered the view that certain words were more likely than others to evoke images in Ribot. In *L'Évolution des idées générales,* Ribot hierarchizes words according to their capacity to evoke images. The more obscure the resemblances between the things a word stands for, he says, the more likely a reader or listener will be conscious of nothing but the word itself, that is, the more obvious the likenesses, the more likely the word to evoke images. Ribot even backs up his findings by recounting a laboratory experiment, in which subjects were asked to describe their responses to a long series of words. Théodule Ribot, *L'Évolution des idées générales* (Paris: Ancienne Libraire Germer Baillière, 1897), 129–45, 124. If Hulme had not read *L'Évolution des idées générales,* he may have encountered Remy de Gourmont's account of Ribot's experiment in *La Culture des idées.* See Remy de Gourmont, *La Culture des idées* (Paris: Mercure de France, 1926), 90.

134. See Bergson, "L'Effort intellectuel," 942–43.

135. Hulme, "Theory and Practice," CW 226; "Notes on Language and Style," CW 24. Cf. "Notes on Language and Style," CW 25, where Hulme says that in "Visual Poetry" "each *word* must be an image *seen,* not a counter." Ribot and Remy de Gourmont are two other possible sources for Hulme's economic metaphor. Ribot says that "les termes généraux couvrent un savoir organisé, latent, qui est le capital caché sans lequel nous serions en état de banqueroute, manipulant de la fausse monnaie ou du papier sans valeur" (*Essai sur l'imagination créatrice,* 149). See also 124–25. Like Hulme he prefers concrete terms, which he likens to real commodities.

136. Hulme, "Romanticism and Classicism," CW 68. An unpublished poem depicts the poet at work with these "stone images":

Over a large table, smooth, he leaned in ecstasies,
In a dream.
He had been to woods, and talked and walked with trees
Had left the world
And brought back round globes and stone images
Of gems, colours, hard and definite.
With these he played, in a dream,
On the smooth table.

("Notes on Language and Style," CW 34)

137. Hulme, "Notes on Language and Style," CW 24.
138. Hulme, "Cinders," CW 16.
139. Ibid., 16.
140. Ibid., 19.
141. See James, *A Pluralistic Universe, Essays in Radical Empiricism and A Pluralistic Universe,* ed. Ralph Barton Perry (New York: E. P. Dutton, 1971), 63–82. Further references to *A Pluralistic Universe* will appear in the text with the abbreviation PU.
142. Ribot, *L'Évolution des idées générales,* 30–33, 45, 34.
143. Hulme, "Cinders," CW 14. In his notebooks Hulme resembles Ribot in associating prelinguistic thinking—which he says consists in "the simulaneous presentation to the mind of two different images"—with animals: "Animals are in the same state that men were before symbolic language was invented" ("Notes on Language and Style," CW 29). Of abstract philosophical debate, he asks, "What would an intelligent animal (without the language disease) or a carter in the Leek road, think of it all?" ("Cinders," CW 8). In the latter note, animals take their place alongside the ordinary man who has no time for metaphysical speculation; the "carter in the road" is Hulme's Jamesian appelation for the man who has time only for practical concerns—unlike "spectacled anaemics" who manipulate their counters and do nothing of use in the world ("Cinders," CW 21).
144. Hulme, "Cinders," CW 18.
145. Hulme, "A Lecture on Modern Poetry," CW 54; "Cinders," CW 17, 10, 17.
146. James was fascinated by the poet whose mind is "fertile in . . . analogies, but, at the same time, keenly interested in the particulars of each suggested image." See James, *Essays in Psychology,* ed. Frederick H. Burkhardt, Fredson Bowers, and Ignas K. Skrupselis (Cambridge: Harvard University Press, 1983), 30. For detailed discussions of James's own metaphorical style, see Seigfried, *William James's Radical Reconstruction of Philosophy,* and David Heddendorf, "Filling Out the What: William James, Josiah Royce and Metaphor." *American Transcendental Quarterly* 2 (1988): 125–38.
147. See also Hulme's reference to the "fringe," or "penumbra of instinct," in "Searchers After Reality I. Bax," 91, and note 7. For further discussion of James's theory of analogy, see chapter 2 of this study, pp. 91–93. Hulme also knew Fechner; he planned to discuss his work in his book on modern art.
148. Hulme, CW 3.
149. Ribot, *Essai sur l'imagination créatrice,* 162. Hulme uses the term "Plastic Imagination" to head a description of the ideal poetic process in "Notes on Language and Style," CW 28.
150. Hulme, CW 3.
151. Geoffrey Hartman, *The Fate of Reading and Other Essays* (Chicago: University of Chicago Press, 1975), 152, 154, 160, 176.
152. Hulme, "Cinders," CW 18.

153. Hulme, CW 4.

154. Compare the exchange between earth and sky in "Susan Ann and Immortality" with that in Stevens's "Sea Surface Full of Clouds," which I discuss at length in chapter 3 of this study. The comparison between Susan Ann's equivocal vision and that of a "rabbit" foreshadows Stevens's depiction of the rabbit in "A Rabbit as King of the Ghosts"; see p. 154. In comparing Susan Ann to a rabbit, Hulme may be attributing to her that nonmetaphysical "logique des images" he believes characteristic of animals.

CHAPTER 2. THE "IMAGE" AND THE CHESS-GAME

1. Ezra Pound, letter to Harriet Monroe (10 April 1915), in K. K. Ruthven, *A Guide to Ezra Pound's Personae* (Berkeley: University of California Press, 1976), 75.

2. Pound, "Dogmatic Statement on the Game and Play of Chess," *Blast II*, ed. Wyndham Lewis (1915; reprint, Santa Barbara, Calif.: Black Sparrow Press, 1981), 19. This poem was subsequently published in *Lustra* (1916) under the title "The Game of Chess."

3. The image of the theoretical chessboard recurs throughout T. E. Hulme's essays and notebooks. Note, for example, his description of phenomenal and intellectual realities in his review of Bergson's *L'Évolution créatrice* and James's *A Pluralistic Universe*:

> On the one hand the complicated, intertwined, inextricable flux of reality, on the other the constructions of the logical intellect, having all the clearness and 'thinness' of a geometrical diagram. To use another metaphor, on the one hand a kind of chaotic cinder-heap, on the other a chessboard. In the latter, movement is always from one square to another, always just so; in the other it is indefinite. The first is an analogy for the world of sensation—the many: the other for the constructs of the intellect. ("The New Philosophy," 198).

See also CW 9, 30–31. For Fenollosa's use of the chessboard, see *The Chinese Written Character as a Medium for Poetry*, 12. Pound became executor for Fenollosa's manuscripts in 1913.

4. I use the word "counter" in Hulme's sense, to designate the abstractions used in symbolic reasoning. See, for example, "Cinders," CW 218: "Symbols are picked out and believed to be realities. People imagine that all the complicated structure of the world can be woven out of 'good' and 'beauty.' These words are merely counters representing vague groups of things, to be moved about on a board for the convenience of the players."

5. I borrow this term from Sanford Schwartz, *The Matrix of Modernism*, 85.

6. See for example Timothy Materer, *Vortex: Eliot, Pound and Lewis* (Ithaca: Cornell University Press, 1979); William Wees, *Vorticism and the English Avant-garde* (Toronto: University of Toronto Press, 1972); and Richard Cork, *Vorticism and Abstract Art in the First Machine Age*, 2 vols. (Berkeley and Los Angeles: University of California Press), 1969. One of the difficulties these critics have in seeing any common purpose between Pound's poetic Vorticism and Vorticist painting has stemmed from the mistaken perception of the latter as an art "of total abstraction" (Materer, 87; cf. Cork 1: xxiii; and Wees, 151). It has proven difficult to see the affinity between such an art and a poetry that would *"go in fear of abstractions"* (Pound, "A Retrospect," LE 5). As Reed Way Dasenbrock notes, "to stress the abstractness of Vorticism" is to "distort the movement and to deny it what originality it did possess." *The Literary Vorticism of Ezra Pound and Wynd-*

ham Lewis (Baltimore: Johns Hopkins University Press, 1985), 63. For a fuller account of the problem with reading Vorticist art in this way and for an alternative reading, see below, pp. 99–103.

7. Pound explicitly identified Imagisme with poetic Vorticism, and so I shall use the terms interchangeably. See "Vorticism," GB 82. I use the word also to distinguish Pound's program from Hulme's Imagism. Pound's major objection to the Imagism of Hulme and his circle was that it failed to incorporate *moving* images. See Pound, *ABC of Reading* (London: Faber and Faber, 1951), 52. My point in this chapter is not, however, to emphasize the differences between the two but to call attention to their similarities as tensional, or hypothetical, poetics.

8. Pound, "Vorticism," GB 82.

9. For these artists' conception of the expressive purpose of their art, see James McNeill Whistler, *The Gentle Art of Making Enemies* (New York: Dover, 1962), 42–43; and Wassily Kandinsky, *Concerning the Spiritual in Art,* trans. M. T. H. Sadler (New York: Dover, 1973), 34–35. Pound cites both Whistler and Kandinsky as advocating expressionist principles compatible with his own. See "Vorticism," GB 81–82, 86–87; and "Vortex. Pound," 154. For a comprehensive account of expressionism in Post-Impressionist art, and of its roots in German Idealist theory, see August K. Wiedmann, *Romantic Roots in Modern Art* (Old Woking, Surrey: Gresham, 1979).

10. Pound, "Vorticism," GB 85; "Affirmations: Vorticism," *Ezra Pound and the Visual Arts,* ed. Harriet Zinnes (New York: New Directions, 1980), 9, 8. On the quest for "arrangements," see "Affirmations: Vorticism," 6; "Vorticism," 81; and "Affirmations: Gaudier-Brzeska," 22. See also Wyndham Lewis, "A Review of Contemporary Art," *Blast II* (1915; reprint, Santa Barbara, Calif.: Black Sparrow Press, 1981), 39.

11. See, for example, Leon Surette, *The Birth of Modernism: Ezra Pound, T. S. Eliot, W. B. Yeats, and the Occult* (Kingston: McGill-Queen's University Press, 1993); and Demetres P. Tryphonopoulos, *The Celestial Tradition: A Study of Ezra Pound's* The Cantos (Waterloo: Wilfred Laurier Press, 1992). Surette reads Pound's associations with occultists and his borrowings from the occult writings as evidence of absolute faith in the supernatural. He argues further that the evidence he provides of Pound's occultism should dispel the notion that Pound was one of many early twentieth-century writers who eschewed occultism for science, and the growing view that modernism was thus "a precursor—rather than the antagonist—of post-modern cognitive relativism and scepticism" (*The Birth of Modernism,* 6). Trypho-nopoulos is more careful in describing Pound's attitudes toward the occult, saying that he regarded it with a sort of "playful skepticism" (*The Celestial Tradition,* 83).

12. James Longenbach, *Stone Cottage: Pound, Yeats & Modernism* (Oxford: Oxford University Press, 1988), 80; my italics.

13. See Andrzej Sosnowski, "Pound's Imagism and Emanuel Swedenborg," *Paideuma* 20 (1991): 36, and Surette, *The Birth of Modernism,* passim, and note 11 above. For other works emphasizing the mysticism implicit in Pound's Imagisme, see Schneidau, *Ezra Pound: The Image and the Real;* Ian F. A. Bell, *Critic as Scientist: The Modernist Poetics of Ezra Pound* (London: Methuen, 1981); Walter Baumann, "Ezra Pound and Magic: Old World Tricks in a New World Poem," *Paideuma* 10 (1981): 209–24; and Angela Elliott, "The Word Comprehensive: Gnostic Light in the *Cantos,*" *Paideuma* 18 (1989): 7–57. Although Bell discusses Pound's practice of couching his mysticism in the language of science, he continues to maintain that Pound upholds a "transcendentalist" epistemology and ideology (3). His position is similar to Baumann's, when Baumann claims that "behind

[Pound's] formidable 'scientific' vocabulary the same magic continued" (210), and to Kermode's in his claim that Imagism was merely Symbolism "given a new philosophical suit" (*Romantic Image,* 130). As in my accounts of Hulme and Stevens, I shall argue that the scientific vocabulary with which Pound described moments of enlightenment was more than simply window dressing—something having a profound influence on Imagiste modes of expression.

For a discussion of the critical tradition regarding Pound as a skeptic, and an explanation of how aligning Pound with James enables mediation between the opposing interpretations, see chapter 5 of this study, pp. 222–24. The early view that Pound was defiantly *anti*mystical was inspired by Pound's own attempts to distance himself from Yeats. See Colin McDowell and Timothy Materer, "Gyre and Vortex: W. B. Yeats and Ezra Pound," *Twentieth Century Literature* 31 (1985): 343–67.

14. Walter Sutton, "Coherence in Pound's *Cantos* and William James's Pluralistic Universe," *Paideuma* 15 (1986): 7–21; Cary Wolfe, *The Limits of American Literary Ideology in Pound and Emerson* (Cambridge: Cambridge University Press, 1993), 31–32, 77–79. For Lentricchia's account of these attributes in James, see *Ariel and the Police,* 104–33. Lentricchia emphasizes Pound's and James's shared hostility to abstraction in *Modernist Quartet,* 31. Ian F. A. Bell anticipates the connection I shall be exploring between Pound's and James's representations of mystical experience by including *The Varieties of Religious Experience* in a list of turn-of-the-century books dedicated to scientific descriptions of religious experience. See *Critic as Scientist,* 76.

15. Sutton, "Coherence in Pound's *Cantos* and William James's Pluralistic Universe," 11.

16. For Pound's association with Hulme, see Noel Stock, *The Life of Ezra Pound* (San Francisco: North Point Press, 1982), 104; for his association with Yeats, see Longenbach, *Stone Cottage,* 224–25.

17. Surette, *The Birth of Modernism,* 34.

18. The Society for Psychical Research was founded in England in 1882 by Henry Sidgwick, Edmund Gurney, and F. W. H. Myers. The American branch was established in 1884; James served as vice president and then president over the next twelve years.

19. See PP 1: 6, where James writes that the psychologist is to avoid "explaining our phenomenally given thoughts as products of deeper-lying entities," whether these entities be named "'Soul,' 'Transcendental Ego,' 'Ideas,' or 'Elementary Units of Consciousness.'" In an unpublished note on metaphysics at the Houghton Library, James says, "I call essentially metaphysical, every affirmation of a *transcendency* on the part of any discriminable thing, idea, or representation. . . . [This] leads in its different applications to the categories of *cause, meaning, purpose, Substance* (both in the noumenal and in the phenomenal sense,) *nature, Essence* and *objective* reality. . . . Ordinary usage also classes as metaphysical, notions of the *absolute,* the *infinite,* and the *noumenon*" (MS. 4464, folder 4).

20. James, *The Letters of William James,* 2 vols., ed. Henry James (London: Longman's, Green, 1920), 1: 250.

21. Ralph Barton Perry, *The Thought and Character of William James,* 2 vols. (Boston: Little, Brown, 1935), 2: 161. This approach to psychic phenomena is identical to the one he was to outline for psychologists in *Psychology: The Briefer Course.* There he says that the psychologist is to collect evidence of noetic experiences and describe them accurately, leaving decisions about their "ulterior significance and truth" to "more developed parts of Philosophy." William James,

Psychology: The Briefer Course, ed. Frederick H. Burkhardt, Fredson Bowers, and Ignas K. Skrupselis (Cambridge: Harvard University Press, 1984), 10. For other examples of James's insistence that spiritualists should pay attention only to the "facts" of experience, see "What Psychical Resesarch Has Accomplished" (WB 240), and James's 13 December 1890 letter to Thomas Davidson: "The only Society worth lifting one's finger for must be one for *investigation of cases,* not for theoretic discussion—for *facts,* and not yet for *philosophy*" (Perry, *Thought and Character,* 2: 161).

22. James, "What Psychical Research Has Accomplished," WB 236.

23. James, "The Confidences of a Psychic Researcher," *Essays in Psychical Research,* ed. Frederick H. Burkhardt, Fredson Bowers, and Ignas H. Skrupselis (Cambridge: Harvard University Press, 1986), 366; and "What Psychical Research Has Accomplished" (WB 236).

24. James, "Mrs. Piper's Hodgson-Control," *Essays in Psychical Research,* 284.

25. James, "The Confidences of a Psychic Researcher," 366. James's cautious optimism about the spiritualist hypothesis is also evident when he emphasizes that although he awaits "knock-down proof" of the existence of ghosts, the evidence to date is "compatible" with that proposition ("Mrs. Piper's Hodgson-Control," 139–41, 146).

26. James defines "mystical" moments as all those that are "transient," "passive," "noetic," and "ineffable" (VRE 380–81).

27. For Ribot's account of the subconscious origin of the *conception idéale,* see above, p. 55. See also James's discussion of the role of the "subconscious" or "subliminal" self, VRE 511. James attributes his own appreciation for this concept to his friend F. W. H. Myers, whose book on the subject, *Human Personality and Its Survival of Bodily Death,* was to be published posthumously in 1903. For a fuller discussion of the significance of James's attribution of "divinities" to the subconscious mind, see chapter 3 of this study, pp. 115–17.

28. When Surette cites Pound's involvement with the Quest Society as evidence of his dogmatic spiritualism, he seems to imply that members of the Quest Society and contributors to *The Quest* were unanimous in their faith in the existence of higher spiritual realms. He notes that contributors differed about the nature of supernatural powers—that occultists like Mead, for example, differed from Christian mystics like Underhill—but he does not acknowledge the suspension of judgment about such powers characterizing many of the essays. See *The Birth of Modernism,* 132–33. Although Tryphonopoulos suggests that Pound was both interested in and skeptical about Mead's work, he doesn't take advantage of the context for Pound's work provided by the scientific strain in the journal. An example of the bifurcation of science and mysticism is Levenson's remark that when Pound compares poetry to a science, "the pursuit of transcendence is thus summarily abandoned" (*A Genealogy of Modernism,* 110). The assumption that an interest in science and an interest in mysticism were incompatible also shapes Surette's discussion when he presents as proof of the mystical thinking prevalent in the early twentieth century the fact that "literary and artistic circles . . . were not all that devoted to materialism, empiricism, or scepticism" (*The Birth of Modernism,* 80; see also 94).

29. Walter Walsh, "Trespassers on the Mystic Way," *Quest* 5 (1914), 501–2. Walsh includes the *anti-scientist* among his "Trespassers on the Mystic Way." Karl Joel was another contributor to *Quest* who excoriates the "modern bureaucrats of thought" and who divide religion and science; see "The Romanticism of the First Thinkers of Hellas," *Quest* 3 (1912): 639. Joel notes that a failure to recognize

the potential for their cooperation is responsible for another false opposition: the opposition of romantic (or Idealist) thinkers against classical (or materialist) ones. It might be argued that the persistence of the latter opposition has been what has made many critics regard Hulme's (and Bergson's) intuitionist "classicism" as inconsistent.

30. F. Aveling, "Psychology with and Without a Soul," *Quest* 6 (1915–16): 451; my italics.

31. Readers of *Quest* had many opportunities both to acquaint themselves with the parameters of scientific discourse and to listen to arguments about its usefulness to the spiritualist cause. Among the many essays in the journal to outline its discursive limits was an anonymous review appearing in the same issue as Pound's "Psychology and Troubadours": Review of J. Arthur Thompson, *Introduction to Science*, *Quest* 4 (1912–13): 187–88. The reviewer cites Thompson to emphasize that scientists are barred from making claims about primary causes:

> It is absurd to expect from Science an explanation of the "why" of things; its proper function is the description of the "how" in the simplest terms. "The aim of Science," Professor Thompson writes, "is to describe the impersonal facts of experiences in verifiable terms as exactly as possible, as simply as possible, and as completely as possible. It is an intellectual construction,—a working thought-model of the world. In its "universe of discourse" it keeps always to experiential terms or verifiable derivatives of these. . . . The causes that Science seeks after are secondary causes, not ultimate causes; effective causes, not final causes. (187)

The journal also delineated how these discursive limits applied to psychology in particular. Rev. Cobb, for example, contrasts the language in which the psychologist describes apparently transcendental experiences with the metaphysical language used by Christians, Hindus, and American Transcendentalists. Whereas the latter describe elevated states of mind as moments of contact with an "Infinite Spirit," the psychologist simply treats them as "objects for analysis and description," offering no account of their origin. Rev. W. F. Cobb, "The Nature of Culture," *Quest* 1 (1909–10): 209. Lest readers conclude that the spiritualist has nothing to learn from psychology, however, Cobb dedicates a subsequent article to elaborating the gains to be made by heeding both its discoveries and its methodology. He points out that the psychologist's records of nonrational experiences present sufficient evidence to keep the spiritualist hypothesis alive. More importantly he joins Walsh and, ultimately, James, in suggesting that those not wishing spiritualism to be discounted will succeed best if their writings emulate psychology's restraint. "[D]irectly we leave the solid ground of experience," he writes, "and begin to treat the airy fields of metaphysical speculation about the nature of God and the mysteries of His being, about the hypostatic union, about the great hereafter, and the 'laws' of spiritual working, we abandon religion for fancy and overstep the just boundaries of our own capacities." Rev. W. F. Cobb, "Culture and the Church," *Quest* 1 (1909–10), 512. Aveling's warnings about how a dedicated materialist might exploit the practice notwithstanding, Cobb insists that the most responsible discussions of mystical phenomena will be those that stick to experience, claiming nothing for which there is no evidence. The position was echoed by other contributors who made their affinity with James overt, by citing his example and by characterizing their approach as a form of "radical empiricism." For references to "radical empiricism," see Edward Douglas Fawcett, "Bergson's 'Time and Free Will,'" *Quest* 2 (1910–11): 500; G. R. S. Mead, "The Philosophy of the As-if: A Radical Criticism of Human Knowledge," *Quest* 4 (1912–13), 460 and 470, and anonymous, Review of Emile Boutroux, *William James, Quest* 3 (1912); 787.

32. See my introduction, p. 26.

33. W. R. Boyce Gibson, "The Intuitionism of Henri Bergson," *Quest* 2 (1910–11): 213, 212. Cf. Emile Boutroux, "Certitude and Truth," *Quest* 7 (1916): 586.

34. Boutroux, "Certitude and Truth," 586–88; Gibson, "The Intuitionism of Henri Bergson," 212. Boutroux characterizes romantic individualism as the consequence of overstepping these boundaries; see "Certitude and Truth," 586–88. Cf. Wilhelm Windelband, "Present-Day Mysticism," *Quest* 4 (1912–13): 206. For Gibson the works by Bergson that leave this impression are "Introduction à la metaphysique" and *L'Évolution créatrice*. For a study of epistemological feeling indebted to Ribot, see William Brown, "The Logic of the Emotions," *Quest* 3 (1912): 601–15.

35. See Joel's paraphrase of what he regards as the prevailing view of the Romantic poets ("The Romanticism of the First Thinkers of Hellas," 636) and Ward's and Redgrove's representations of Wordsworth (A. H. Ward, "The Power of Imagination" *Quest* 1 (1909): 62; H. Stanley Redgrove, "The Sight of the Soul: An Essay in Christian Mysticism," *Quest* 3 (1912): 502.

36. See, for example, Alun Jones's contention that in adopting Bergson Hulme was "led back to what amounts to a re-statement of the romantic theory of poetry," a statement at odds with Hulme's claims to be championing a form of "classicism" (*The Life and Opinions of T. E. Hulme*, 46). See also Krieger, *The New Apologists for Poetry*, 37. Evelyn Underhill appropriates Bergson for a transcendentalist metaphysics in "The Mystic as Creative Artist," *Quest* 4 (1912–13): 631.

37. Cobb, "Culture and the Church," 511 (my italics); Anonymous, Review of Thompson, *Introduction to Science*, 188; J. Arthur Hill, "The Inspiration of Genius," *Quest* 5 (1914): 538; Boutroux, "Certitude and Truth," 3, 5.

38. Evelyn Underhill, "A Note upon Mysticism," *Quest* 1 (1909–10): 743; "The Mystic as Creative Artist," 630.

39. For Ward the artist recovers this "central idea" or "ideal" from a Platonic Oversoul (or from what Wordsworth, whom he cites, calls the "eternal sea"); the process of articulation is one in which the mind's eye turns towards concrete things and away "from *heaven where the ideals abide*" ("The Power of Imagination," 70, 62, 63; my italics). In Underhill's account the construct takes the form of a set of "symbolic pictures," suddenly descending from the "supersensual" world:

> These pictures are seen by the mystic—sometimes, as he says, within the mind, sometimes as projections in space—always in sharp definition, lit by that strong light which is peculiar to visionary states. They are not produced by any voluntary process of composition; but loom up, as do the best creations of other artists, from his deeper mind, bringing with them an intense conviction of reality. ("The Mystic as Creative Artist," 643)

Compare Mallarmé's account of being inspired by the Idea in a letter to Henri Cazalis, 14 May 1867, cited by Gibson, *Modern French Poets on Poetry*, 85. Also note Mallarmé's descriptions of the ideas captured in verse in "Variations sur un suject," *Oeuvres complètes* 368, 400. See also Albert Mockel's "Propos de littérature," in Michaud, *Message poétique du symbolisme*, 752.

40. Émile Boutroux, "The Subliminal Self Philosophically Considered," *Quest* 6 (1914–15): 19. Cf. Hill, "The Inspiration of Genius," 538.

41. Underhill, "The Mystic as Creative Artist," 634; Redgrove, "The Sight of the Soul," 502.

42. F. S. Flint's phrase. See Longenbach, *Stone Cottage*, 31. For convincing

evidence that Pound was a regular reader of *Quest,* see Tryphonopoulos, *The Celestial Tradition,* 97–98.

43. Pound, "Psychology and Troubadours," *Quest* 4 (1912–13): 47, 50, 44; "Vortex. Pound," 154. For James's definition of the "mystical" moment, see note 26.

44. Pound, "Art Notes," *Ezra Pound and the Visual Arts,* ed. Harriet Zinnes, 124. In this respect, the Image differs from what first appears before the mind of the writer of "LITERATURE": "FORMED WORDS" ("Vortex. Pound," 154). The distinction reinforces the parallel between Imagisme and *Symbolisme,* in recalling the distinction between symbolic processes and allegorical ones. For the suspension of the action, will, and intellect in the appearance of the Image, see "Vorticism," GB 91.

45. Pound, "Vorticism," GB 91; see also "A Retrospect," LE 4.

46. Pound, "Vorticism," GB 92. As I have discussed in my Introduction, the Symbolists, after Schopenhauer, had frequently invoked the transcendental Idea not only to make the poet's mind a locus for truths from beyond himself but also to account for a process of articulation that was intuitive and exploratory. Saying that the creative process begins with the apprehension of the Idea enabled them to explain the series of unanticipated utterances flowing from the poet's pen as the Idea's endlessly generated particulars. As Schopenhauer phrases it, the Idea that "floats before [the artist's] mind" resembles "a living organism, developing itself and possessed of the power of reproduction, which brings forth what was not put into it" (*The World as Will and Representation* 1: 302–4). The organic process governed by the Idea was what distinguished symbol from allegory. For example, see Michaud, *Message poetique du symbolisme,* 750–52. Also note Yeats, "William Blake and His Illustrations to the Divine Comedy," *Essays and Introductions,* 116. Pound also distinguishes his Imagisme from allegory and attacks certain Symbolists for allowing their Symbols to degenerate into allegories. In contrast to those Symbolists whose Symbols "have a fixed value," he says, "The imagiste's images have a variable significance, like the signs *a, b,* and *x* in algebra" ("Vorticism," GB 84). In what follows I shall argue that although Pound shared many Symbolist's enthusiasm for verse that was endlessly suggestive, his understanding of the *cause* of the ongoing generation of meaning was quite different.

47. Pound, *Guide to Kulchur* (New York: New Directions, 1970), 73–74, my italics.

48. Pound, "Psychology and Troubadours," 44. Note also how Pound translates claims about the appearance of gods into feeling-claims. The gods are "explications of *mood*"; moments of revelation moments occur when an individual "*feels* his immortality upon him" ("Psychology and Troubadours," 47; my italics). Or as he puts in elsewhere, a god amounts to an "eternal *state of mind,*" an entity whose status is no different from the "taste of a lemon, or the fragrance of violets, or the aroma of dung-hills, or the feel of a stone or of tree-bark, or any other direct perception" ("A Retrospect," LE 47; "Axiomata," SP 50).

49. Pound, "A Retrospect," LE 4; "Vorticism," GB 86.

50. Pound, "Affirmations: As for Imagisme," SP 345–46. It is possible that Hulme also used the term. According to F. S. Flint among the group of poets with whom Hulme and Pound met in 1909, there was "a lot of talk and practice" about "what we called the 'Image'" ("History of Imagisme," *Egoist* 2 [1 May 1915]: 70–71).

51. Pound, "A Retrospect," LE 4.

52. Bernard Hart, "The Conception of the Subconscious," in Morton Prince,

ed., *Subconscious Phenomena* (London: Rebman, 1910), 129–30; my italics. See the review of this volume in *Quest* 2 (1911–12): 389–92. Munsterberg was a colleague of James's at Harvard. His volume contains essays on the subconscious by Hugo Munsterberg, Théodule Ribot, Pierre Janet, Joseph Jastrow, Morton Prince, as well as by Hart. The anonymous reviewer, however, focuses on Hart's essay. For Pound on the subconscious, see *Ezra Pound and the Visual Arts*, 214.

53. Pound, "Axiomata," SP 50.

54. Pound, "Psychology and Troubadours," 41.

55. Kevin Oderman, *Ezra Pound and the Erotic Medium* (Durham: Duke University Press, 1986), 22.

56. Pound, "Coitus," in *Collected Shorter Poems* (London: Faber and Faber, 1952), 120.

57. G. R. S. Mead, "On the Nature of the Quest," *Quest* 1 (1909–10): 36, my italics.

58. Walsh, "Trespassers on the Mystic Way," 493.

59. See, for example, Walter Walsh's recommendation that the expression be used for representing the "results of . . . meditative, inspirational, or ecstatic conditions." "[T]he refusal to submit to tests," he writes, "cannot but excite grave suspicion, and is one of the dangers which beset the pilgrims of the mystic way" ("Trespassers on the Mystic Way," 496).

60. Mead, "The Philosophy of the As-if," 476. For further discussion of Vaihinger's distinction and of its relevance for Wallace Stevens, see chapter 4 of this study, pp. 172–73.

61. Walsh cites this chapter of *The Varieties of Religious Experience* in "Trespassers on the Mystic Way," 497.

62. James, "The Sentiment of Rationality," WB 59. The impulses are James's versions of Jules de Gaultier's "pouvoir d'arrêt" and "principe de mouvement" (*Le Bovarysme*, 268). The difference is that James's "passion for distinguishing" dismantles theories on the grounds of empirical differences; it makes James's provisional truth a "hypothesis," where Gaultier's is a "fiction."

63. Ibid., 61.

64. The program for pragmatic truth-making James outlines in *Pragmatism* has its roots in James's perception of these psychological needs. In "The Sentiment of Rationality," he observes that no philosophy has ever survived that has failed to balance these needs: neither a dogmatic rationalism, with its "barren union of all things," nor a skeptical empiricism, with its discomfiting "uncertainty," have been sufficient to endure for any length of time (WB 60, 70). The pragmatic method of truth-making, accordingly, is meant to be at once "dogmatical" and "skeptical," "rationalistic" and "empiricist," "religious" and "irreligious," "romantic" and "scientific" (P 13, 17). The pragmatist's tentative "truth" is, like the mystic's, a form of hypothesis: an abstraction "emerging from facts" but always "dipping" back into them, in order to "create or reveal new truth . . . and so on indefinitely" (P 13, 17, 108).

65. James's father, Henry James, Sr., maintained a strong interest in Swedenborg. See Myers, *William James*, 17–18.

66. Pound, "The Serious Artist," LE 46; "Wisdom of Poetry," SP 331. Pound's instructions to the poet to avoid philosophy mirror James's instructions to the psychologist in *The Principles of Psychology and Psychology: The Briefer Course*. They are part of an effort to reverse Sidney's conception of poetry as rhetoric; "The Serious Artist," the essay where the parallel between poet and scientist is

developed most extensively, is a conscious revision of Sidney's *Defence of Poetry*. See especially LE 46.

67. "Vorticism," GB 86, my italics; "A Retrospect," LE 3. "Perceived" and "conceived" are equivalents in Pound for "objective" and "subjective"; see "Vortex. Pound," 153; and "Vorticism," GB, 90.

68. A comparable example of the use of hypothesis to express a spiritualist claim is found in the 1913 prose poem "Ikon":

> It is in art the highest business to create the beautiful image; to create order and profusion of images that we may furnish the life of our minds with a noble surrounding.
>
> *And if*—as some say, the soul survives the body; *if* our consciousness is not an intermittent melody of strings that relapse between whiles into silence, then more than ever should we put forth the images of beauty, that going out into tenantless spaces we have with us all that is needful—an abundance of souls and patters to entertain us in that long dreaming; to strew our path to Valhalla to give rich gifts by the way.

Ezra Pound and Dorothy Shakespear: Their Letters: 1909–1914, ed. Omar Pound and A. Walton Litz (New York: New Directions, 1984), 277–78. Longenbach cites this passage as evidence of the "visionary" character of Pound's "Doctrine of the Image" but in doing so ignores the qualifiers "and if" and "if" (*Stone Cottage,* 31). In fact the passage supports my thesis that Pound conceived the Imagiste's utterances as provisional gestures made in the likelihood that the consciousness moves in "tenantless spaces." Another crucial "if" is found in a passage from Canto 74, in which Pound remembers Mead's cautious attitude toward ghosts:

> "ghosts move about me" "patched with histories"
> > but as Mead said: *if* they were,
> *what have* they done in the interval,
> > eh, to arrive by metempsychosis at.... ?
> and there are also the conjectures of the Fortean Society
> Beauty is difficult.

> (*Cantos* 446; first italics mine)

The Fortean Society, organized in 1931, was a society dedicated to the study of Charles Fort, an American journalist interested in documenting unexplained natural phenomena; its conjectures would have been the kind of qualified speculation about spiritualist hypotheses recommended by James to psychic researchers.

69. Longenbach, *Stone Cottage,* 194ff.; Daniel Pearlman, *The Barb of Time: On the Unity of Ezra Pound's Cantos* (New York: Oxford University Press, 1969), 43–45, 284.

70. Walter Sutton has rightly noted the likeness between *The Cantos* and *The Varieties of Religious Experience,* in that both are records of apparently mystical experiences. He is, however, both imprecise and self-contradictory in his description of the positions James and Pound take toward the kind of experience they record, saying at one point that these are experiences of "genuine transcendence" and at another that they are records of "subliminal powers of the self or psyche," which are not, therefore "literally superhuman or supernatural" ("Coherence in Pound's *Cantos* and William James's Pluralistic Universe," *Paideuma* 15 [1986]: 15). My point is that James and Pound both regard their works as records of "subliminal powers" and that this does not preclude the possibility that they are records of the "literally superhuman or supernatural." For an account of *The Cantos* as a phenomenology of religious experience, see Martin A. Kayman, *The Modernism of Ezra Pound: The Science of Poetry* (London: MacMillan, 1986), 131.

71. Gelpi, *A Coherent Splendour*, 233.

72. Pound, *Cantos*, 483. There may be a link, too, between the Princess Ra-Set, who joins the "gods" moving in the "protection of crystal" in Canto 81 (*Cantos* 611), and the "fat girl" of Stevens's "Notes Toward a Supreme Fiction," revolving in a "crystal" that is the equivalent of the phenomenal consciousness (CP 406–7). Whatever its metaphysical associations may be, Pound's crystal is always only a formation "seen under water": an image suspended in a "liquid" (*Cantos* 119, 449). (Carroll Terrell, for example, identifies it with the great "acorn of light" in Groseteste's *de Luce*, the equivalent of platonism's and neoplatonism's primal creative force [*A Companion to the Cantos of Ezra Pound* (Berkeley: University of California Press, 1980; 1984], 548). Pound identifies the "liquid" with a "property of the mind" (*Cantos* 449). Notice also that, in "Cavalcanti," to be "under water" is to be "untouched" by the "Hebrew" and "Hindoo" diseases—to be free, in other words, from metaphysical speculations, as any perception placed under phenomenological reduction (LE 154). Pound provides a vivid image of the liquid world of religious experience in the 1912 poem "Sub Mare" (CSP 82). For a discussion of the workings and significance of a comparable liquid world in Stevens, see chapter 4 of this study.

73. For the "interpretive" or "absolute" metaphor, see GB 88 and *The Chinese Written Character as a Medium for Poetry*, 23.

74. Pound, "I Gather the Limbs of Osiris," SP 28. Cf. "Psychology and Troubadours," 46: "I have no dogma but the figures may serve as an assistance to thought."

75. Pound, "Psychology and Troubadours," 48.

76. Pound, "Axiomata," SP 51.

77. Pound, "The Wisdom of Poetry," SP 332; and "I Gather the Limbs of Osiris," SP 25.

78. Pound, "Axiomata," SP 52; and "Vortex. Pound," 153. In his translation of Remy de Gourmont, Pound characterizes the philosophical tendency as an activity of "charging, head-on, the female chaos." Gourmont, *The Natural Philosophy of Love*, trans. Ezra Pound (New York: Rarity Press, 1931), 170.

79. Pound, *ABC of Reading*, 25. I agree with Schwartz's assessment that the interpretive metaphor and the ideogram are structurally identical in their dedication to maintaining a tension between sensory particulars and incipient categories (*The Matrix of Modernism*, 95).

80. Pound, *The Chinese Written Character as a Medium for Poetry*, 25.

81. Pound, "Vorticism," GB 89.

82. Pound, *ABC of Reading*, 17.

83. Pound, "I Gather the Limbs of Osiris," 25.

84. Paul Ricoeur, "The Metaphorical Process as Cognition, Imagination, and Feeling," *On Metaphor*, ed. Sheldon Sacks (Chicago: University of Chicago Press, 1979).

85. Baudelaire, *Oeuvres complètes* 2: 329; André Gide, from *Le Traité du Narcisse*, cited by Michaud, 731. Yeats describes the experience of encountering a symbol as one in which "[w]e feel our minds expand convulsively or spread out slowly like some moon-brightened image-crowded sea" (*Essays and Introductions*, 245).

86. For the "ptyx," see Mallarmé's "Ses purs ongles" in *Oeuvres complètes*, 68. This poem presents an extreme example of pressure to look beyond the natural object for its equivalents, in that there is no such thing as a "ptyx." For Mallarmé's use of synecdoche, see especially "Le Tombeau de Charles Baudelaire" (*Oeuvres complètes*, 70). For Yeats a symbol's meaning—the product either of divine ordina-

tion or of decisions made by the poet's ancestors and stored in the Universal Memory—will be available to the reader's "instinct" (*Essays and Introductions,* 147).

87. For a detailed account of Pound's debts to Symbolism, see Scott Hamilton, *Ezra Pound and the Symbolist Inheritance* (Princeton: Princeton University Press), 1992. For Pound's objections, see "A Retrospect," LE 7, 9; and letter to Harriet Monroe, 5 January 1915, cited by Longenbach, *Stone Cottage,* 136. The term "anagogic metaphor" is Northrop Frye's; he views it as a trope assuming a monistic universe, characterized primarily by unity or identity:

> In the anagogic aspect of meaning, the radical form of metaphor, "A is B," comes into its own. Here we are dealing with poetry in its totality, in which the formula "A is B" may be hypothetically applied to anything, for there is no metaphor, not even "black is white," which a reader has any right to quarrel with in advance. The literary universe, therefore, is a universe in which everything is potentially identical with everything else. This does not mean that any two things in it are separate and very similar, like peas in a pod, or in the slangy and erroneous sense of the word in which we speak of identical twins. If twins were really identical they would be the same person. On the other hand, a grown man feels identical with himself at the age of seven, although the two manifestations of this identity, the man and the boy, have very little in common as regards similarity or likeness. In form, matter, personality, time, and space, man and boy are quite unlike. This is the only type of image I can think of that illustrates the process of identifying two independent forms. All poetry, then, proceeds as though all poetic images were contained within a single universal body. Identity is the opposite of similarity or likeness, and total identity is not uniformity, still less monotony, but a unity of various things.

Anatomy of Criticism (Princeton: Princeton University Press, 1957), 124–25.

88. Pound, "Psychology and Troubadours," 37–38; my italics. Pound makes the same point by saying that the interpretive metaphor is one that seems to involve the reader in a process of discovery or exploration. See "Vorticism," GB 88.

89. Mead, "Philosophy of the as-if," 481.

90. Pound praises Cavalcanti's use of metaphor for its "accuracy," situating it within a project of seeking "proof by experience" ("Cavalcanti," LE 162, 158). Later in *ABC of Reading,* he notes that although one can "*prove* nothing by analogy," a "dozen rough analogies may flash before the quick mind, as so many *rough tests* which eliminate grossly unfit matter or structure" (*ABC of Reading* 84; my italics).

91. Pound, "Vorticism," GB 84, my italics; "The Wisdom of Poetry," SP 333.

92. This reading challenges Longenbach's contention that the passage is evidence of the elitism of Pound's "Doctrine of the 'Image,'" that is, evidence of Pound's intention to cater only to the interests of an occult brotherhood (*Stone Cottage,* 92–93). Although Pound clearly acknowledges such a brotherhood, he is a long way from suggesting that he need cater only to the already enlightened. For the claim that Pound's occultism is essentially elitist, see also Surette, *The Birth of Modernism,* 14.

93. Materer, *Vortex: Pound, Eliot, and Lewis* (Ithaca: Cornell University Press, 1979) 87. See also Wees, *Vorticism and the English Avant-garde,* 151; and Cork, *Vorticism and Abstract Art in the First Machine Age,* 1: xxiii. For an illuminating analysis of the cause of this misrepresentation, see Dasenbrock, *The Literary Vorticism of Ezra Pound and Wyndham Lewis,* 63.

94. Longenbach, *Stone Cottage,* 239.

95. For another example of this phenomenon, see Wilhelm Worringer, *Abstraction and Empathy,* trans. Michael Bullock (New York: International Universities Press, 1953), 19–21. Worringer discusses the history of art in terms of two impulses

that correspond closely to James's two tendencies: the "urge for abstraction" and the "urge for empathy." In summarizing Worringer's position in his January, 1914, lecture to the Quest Society, "Modern Art and Its Philosophy," Hulme notes that "the first gods were always pure abstractions without any resemblance to life. Any weakening of these abstract forms and approximation to reality would have let in change and life and so would have done what it was desired to avoid—it would have taken the thing out of eternity and put it into time" (CW 89–90). For other examples of the identification of abstract form with noumenal or mystical truth, see *Cubism,* ed. Edward F. Fry (London: Thames and Hudson, 1966), 65, 152–53; and *Theories of Modern Art,* ed. Herschel B. Chipp (Berkeley: University of California Press, 1968), 227–28.

96. Wyndham Lewis, "A Review of Contemporary Art," 40, 43. Kandinsky outlines the correspondences between color and phenomena from the other categories of sense in *Concerning the Spiritual in Art,* trans. M. T. H. Sadler (New York: Dover, 1973), 36–45. In the same work, an excerpt of which appeared in *Blast,* he calls for an art that will eschew natural images in favor of the *eternal truth* of the spirit world explored by Madam Blavatsky and her Theosophical Society (13). Despite this, however, Kandinsky shared Lewis's view that the artist cheated himself if he aimed to deny all representation; see 32.

97. Pound, "Affirmations: Vorticism," 7, "Affirmations: Gaudier-Brzeska," 18; Lewis, "A Review of Contemporary Art," 40. Cf. Henri Gaudier-Brzeska's remarks in "Vortex: Gaudier-Brzeska," *Blast,* 158.

98. Lewis, "A Review of Contemporary Art," 44.

99. Lewis's classification. See "A Review of Contemporary Art," 37.

100. Jules Laforgue, "Impressionism: The Eye and the Poet," trans. Linda Nochlin, in Nochlin, ed., *Impressionism and Post-Impressionism 1874–1904* (Englewood Cliffs, N.J.: Prentice-Hall, 1966), 18; Lewis, "A Review of Contemporary Art," 45. Laforgue summarizes Impressionism's relativism and pluralism thus:

Each man is, according to his moment in time, his racial milieu and social situation, his moment of individual evolution, a kind of keyboard on which the exterior world plays in a certain way. My own keyboard is perpetually changing, and there is no other like it. All keyboards are legitimate. (18–19)

For the Impressionist's obligation to avoid regularity, see Nochlin, 35–36, 44–51. Cf. Walter Pater's instruction to the artist to avoid giving in to "the roughness of the eye that makes any two persons, things, situations, seem alike" (*Walter Pater: Essays on Literature and Art,* 197).

101. Lewis, "A Review of Contemporary Art," 42; "Our Vortex," *Blast 2,* 148–49. Lewis's view of the dithering, disempowered Impressionist is consistent with many unsympathetic critiques of Impressionism in the Post-Impressionist era. Compare Ford Madox Ford's portrayal of John Dowell, whom he identifies as an Impressionist, in *The Good Soldier* (1915). An excerpt of that novel was published under the title "The Saddest Story" in *Blast.*

102. Lewis, "Futurism, Magic and Life," *Blast,* 134; "A Review of Contemporary Art," 40.

103. Lewis, "Wyndham Lewis Vortex No. 1" *Blast,* 2. The "tensional" condition I have identified here corresponds to the "dynamic formism" that Dasenbrock sees as essential to Vorticist art (*The Literary Vorticism of Ezra Pound and Wyndham Lewis,* 36).

104. Lewis, "Review of Contemporary Art," 40, 44. Lewis does not, for example, deny the possibility that red is the color of "exasperation"—any more than

Pound would deny the hawk its association with "war"—but he is concerned that the artist (and his audience) never forget it is first and foremost the color of blood.

105. Ibid., 40; my italics.

106. Lewis, *Wyndham Lewis on Art*, ed. Walter Michel and C. J. Fox (New York: Funk and Wagnall's, 1969), 330; Pound, GB 138. See also Lewis's call for "LIVING plastic geometry" ("Relativism and Picasso's Latest Work," *Blast*, 140) and his assertion in "The London Group" that "in Vorticism the direct and hot impressions of life are mated with Abstraction, or the combinations of the Will" (*Blast II*, 79).

107. The view that curved lines are "organic," where straight lines are "nonvital" or "mechanical," is implicit in Hulme's "Modern Art and Its Philosophy," 82. Pound describes "animated" abstractions in GB 138.

108. Pound called the spherical triangle the "central life-form" (GB 137) in the work of Lewis as well as Gaudier-Brzeska; he also encountered many examples of it in the sculpture of Brancusi. For another example in Gaudier-Brzeska, see "Mother and Child" (1913–15). For Brancusi's use of the form, see "Mlle. Pogany" (1913), "La Muse Endormie" (1909–10), "Danaïde" (1918) and "Le Commencement du Monde" (1924).

109. This is evident in the studies for the painting. See Cork, 1: 80–81.

110. A parallel might also be drawn between Wadsworth's "Slack Bottom"(1914) and the image of the chessboard in Hulme's notes. The image presented by the former is of a chessboard sagging at its center. It recalls Hulme's comparison of theories to chessboards, perched atop the "cinder-heap" of the phenomenal world, momentarily order it, but then quickly collapsing back into it, only to be reconstructed. See note 3, above.

111. James, letter to Charles A. Strong, 9 April 1907, in *Letters of William James*, 2: 269.

112. Martin Heidegger, *Poetry, Language, Thought*, trans. Albert Hofstadter (New York: Harper & Row, 1971), 55, 71.

Chapter 3. Effacing the Muse

1. Stevens, "The Noble Rider and the Sound of Words," NA 3, 6, 4; I. A. Richards, *Principles of Literary Criticism* (London: Routledge and Kegan Paul, 1967), 211. Stevens consulted Richards's *Coleridge on Imagination* before composing "The Noble Rider and the Sound of Words." See Alan Filreis, *Wallace Stevens and the Actual World* (Princeton: Princeton University Press, 1991), 89; and Milton Bates, *Wallace Stevens: Mythology of Self* (Berkeley: University of California Press, 1985), 259.

2. See chapter 1, p. 50.

3. Hulme, "A Lecture on Modern Poetry," CW 49, "Romanticism and Classicism," CW 62, my italics.

4. Stevens, "The Noble Rider and the Sound of Words," NA 23.

5. Stevens, "The Irrational Element in Poetry," OP 228, 230.

6. Stevens, "The Noble Rider and the Sound of Words," NA 35; "The Figure of the Youth as Virile Poet," NA 53, 60, 66.

7. Stevens, "The Irrational Element in Poetry," OP 231.

8. In taking care here, and throughout his poetry and criticism, to substitute the discourse of "belief" for the discourse of "knowledge," Stevens follows C. S. Peirce's instructions to the pragmatist:

You only puzzle yourself by talking of this metaphysical "truth" and metaphysical "falsity," that you know nothing about. All you have any dealings with are your doubts and beliefs, with the course of life that forces new beliefs upon you and gives you power to doubt old beliefs. If your terms "truth" and "falsity" are taken in such senses as to be definable in terms of doubt and belief and the course of experience (as for example they would be if you were to define the "truth" as that . . . [to] which belief would tend if it were to tend indefinitely toward absolute fixity), well and good: in that case, you are only talking about doubt and belief. But if by truth and falsity you mean something not definable in terms of doubt and belief in any way, then you are talking of entities of whose existence you can know nothing, and which Ockham's razor would clean shave off. Your problems would be greatly simplified if, instead of saying that you want to know the "Truth," you were simply to say that you want to attain a state of belief unassailable by doubt.

C. S. Peirce, "What Pragmatism Is," *Charles S. Peirce: Selected Writings*, ed. Philip P. Wiener (New York: Dover, 1958), 189; my italics. In Stevens compare the "affirmation free from doubt" experienced by the "Woman Looking at a Vase of Flowers," CP 247.

9. Stevens, "Imagination as Value," NA 136.

10. Ibid., 137–39.

11. *The Letters of Wallace Stevens*, ed. Holly Stevens (New York: Knopf, 1966), 631, 696.

12. Stevens, "The Effects of Analogy," NA 115. Margaret Peterson cites this passage to make a similar point. See *Wallace Stevens and the Idealist Tradition* (Ann Arbor, Mich.: UMI Research Press, 1983), 43.

13. Stevens, "Imagination as Value," NA 139.

14. Stevens, "The Figure of the Youth as Virile Poet," NA 58.

15. Stevens, *Letters*, 23. See Frank Lentricchia, *Ariel and the Police*, 104–24, and an earlier version, "Patriarchy Against Itself—The Young Manhood of Wallace Stevens," *Critical Inquiry* 13 (Summer 1987). The latter prompted a hostile response from Sandra Gilbert and Susan Gubar, and the Wallace Stevens Journal published a special issue dedicated to the debate over Stevens's treatment of women in its fall 1988 issue. Alan Filreis and Milton Bates have also discussed Stevens's concern with the relationship between poetry and manliness. See Filreis, "Wallace Stevens and the Strength of the Harvard Reaction," *New England Quarterly* 58 (1985): 27–45; and Bates, *Wallace Stevens*, 32–48.

16. Stevens, *Souvenirs and Prophecies: The Young Wallace Stevens*, ed. Holly Stevens (New York: Knopf, 1966), 40. Hulme complains about imitative, post-Romantic verse on the grounds that it "becomes the expression of sentimentality rather than of virile thought" ("A Lecture on Modern Poetry," CW 69).

17. *Ariel and the Police*, 160: Stevens refers to Stedman in Letters, 41–42.

18. E. C. Stedman, *The Nature and Elements of Poetry* (Boston: Houghton, Mifflin, 1892), 46, 127–28; Stevens, "The Figure of the Youth as Virile Poet," 66.

19. Stevens, "The Figure of the Youth as Virile Poet," 59.

20. Although Stevens never took any of Santayana's courses and never heard him lecture, he came to know him through one of his first-year instructors, Pierre LaRose. By mid-March 1899 the two had exchanged sonnets, and by 1900 they were sharing dinner table conversation. See Joan Richardson, *Wallace Stevens: The Early Years 1879–1923* (New York: Beech Tree, 1986), 61; and Bates, *Wallace Stevens*, 25.

21. See Bates, *Wallace Stevens*, 34; and Filreis, "Wallace Stevens and the Strength of the Harvard Reaction," 29. Stevens said of his visits with Santayana that he "always came away from my visits to him feeling that he made up in the

most genuine way for many things that I needed." See letter to José Rodríguez Feo, 4 January 1945 (*Letters*, 482).

22. See Stevens's letters to Henry Church, 8 December 1942, and to Gilbert Montague, 22 March 1943 (*Letters*, 430, 443).

23. Bloom observes that "a Stevensian denial of influence . . . is merely a confirmation of how unconvincing Stevensian notions of influence are" (*Wallace Stevens: Poems of Our Climate* (Ithaca: Cornell University Press, 1977), 189).

24. Samuel French Morse says that Stevens was very likely the author of an anonymous review of Santayana's *Interpretations of Poetry and Religion*, printed in the Harvard Advocate when Stevens was its editor. See *Wallace Stevens: Poetry as Life* (New York: Pegasus, 1970), 54–55. In a journal entry of 13 June 1900, Stevens records listening to his friend Warwick Green reading notes for Santayana's course in aesthetics—the course that culminated in *The Sense of Beauty* (*Souvenirs and Prophecies*, 71). Milton Bates notes that at his death Stevens's library contained Santayana's *The Hermit of Carmel and Other Poems, Sonnets and Other Verses, Lucifer,* and three volumes of Santayana's autobiography, *Persons and Places.* See "Stevens's Books at the Huntington: An Annotated Checklist," *Wallace Stevens Journal* 2 (1978): 52, 60. Stevens cites a letter from William James to Bergson, dated 13 June 1907, in "The Figure of the Youth as Virile Poet" (NA 40), as well as another (unidentified) passage concerning virility and General Sherman (NA 58–59).

25. See, for example, Santayana's letter to James, Easter 1900 (*The Letters of George Santayana,* ed. Daniel Cory [New York: Scribner's, 1955], 61–62) and James's letter to Santayana, 2 May 1905 (James, *Letters,* 2: 229).

26. Santayana, "A Brief History of My Opinions," *The Philosophy of Santayana,* ed. Irwin Edman (New York: Scribner's, 1936), 13–15; James, letter to George H. Palmer, 2 April 1900 (*Letters,* 122). In a letter of Easter 1900, James points out that the affinity between the philosophers exists "in spite of such divergence" in their opinions (*Letters,* 229).

27. Stevens, "The Figure of the Youth as Virile Poet," NA 58.

28. *Essays on Radical Empiricism* was published posthumously. The essays it contains, however, had previously been published in 1904 and 1905.

29. The original, from a 30 April 1905 address in French to the Congrès International de Psychologie, reads as follows:

L'externe et l'interne, l'étendu et l'inétendu, se fusionnent et font un marriage indissoluble. Cela rappelle ces panoramas circulaires, où des objets réels, rochers, herbe, chariots brisés, etc., qui occupent l'avant-plan, sont si ingénieusement reliés à la toile qui fait le fond, et qui représente une bataille ou un vaste paysage, que l'on ne sait plus distinguer ce qui est objet de ce qui est peinture. Les coutures et les joints sont imperceptibles. (ERE 110)

Cf. ERE 113–14.

30. For a full description of the "stream of consciousness," see James, PP 1: 262–69. A. N. Whitehead provides a lucid account of the epistemological problem posed by dualism and of James's solution to it in *Science and the Modern World,* 142–45. Compare Husserl's account of the dualist dilemma and his attempt to bypass the problem by introducing the doctrine of "intentionality" in the 1911 essay "Philosophy as Rigorous Science" (*Phenomenology and the Crisis of Philosophy,* 88–89). For a discussion of how James's "Stream of Consciousness" chapter anticipates Husserl's doctrine of intentionality, see Edie, *William James and Phenomenology,* 25.

31. Compare VRE 380–81.

32. This definition and James's methods of investigation in *Varieties* has led Edie to describe it as "the only phenomenology of religious experience to have been written up to now." See *William James and Phenomenology*, vii.

33. For Husserl's distinction between *noesis* and *noema*, see *Ideas*, 235–59.

34. Compare Rudolph Otto's remarks that one of the essential qualities of a mysterious divinity is its quality of seeming "wholly other." "Taken in the religious sense," he says, "that which is 'mysterious' is . . . quite beyond the sphere of the usual, the intelligible, and the familiar, which therefore falls quite outside the limits of the 'canny', and is contrasted with it, filling the mind with blank wonder and astonishment." *The Idea of the Holy*, trans. John W. Harvey (Oxford: Oxford University Press, 1950), 26.

35. Yeats, *Poems*, 215. Cf. James VRE 419: "This overcoming of all the usual barriers between the individual and the Absolute is the great mystic achievement. In mystic states we both become one with the Absolute and we become aware of our oneness." On VRE 380 James discusses the "noetic quality" of such states, by which he means their quality of seeming also to be "states of knowledge."

36. See chapter 2 of this study for James's refusal to commit himself on the matter of whether or not the moment of enchantment is a "gift of our organism" or a gift of (a genuine)"God's grace" (VRE 47), and his refusal to ally himself with either materialist or spiritualist philosophers, who speak confidently of the divinity's "pathological" or "supernatural" origins (VRE 19).

37. Compare Ribot's equivocal position on the status of the subconscious mind, discussed in chapter 1 of this study, p. 55.

38. For further evidence of James's willingness to entertain the possibility that there is a god, or a single being that unifies the world, note P 79:

> Pragmatism, pending the final empirical ascertainment of just what the balance of union and disunion among things may be, must obviously range herself upon the pluralistic side. Some day, she admits, even total union, with one knower, one origin, and a universe consolidated in every conceivable way, may turn out to be the most acceptable of all hypotheses.

39. Compare VRE 34:

> The sort of appeal that Emersonian optimism, on the one hand, and Buddhistic pessimism, on the other, make to the individual and the sort of response which he makes to them in his life are in fact indistinguishable from, and in many respects identical with, the best Christian appeal and response. We must therefore, from the experiential point of view, call these godless or quasi-godless creeds "religions"; and accordingly when in our definition of religion we speak of the individual's relation to "what he considers the divine," we must interpret the term "divine" very broadly, as denoting any object that is godlike, whether it be a concrete deity or not.

40. See ERE 99 for James's conviction that radical empiricism "by refusing to entertain the hypothesis of transempirical reality at all," gets rid of "the whole agnostic controversy." Agnosticism, as Huxley defined it, asserted that persons are unjustified in believing in anything that cannot be proven. Attacking this position was also the central purpose of the essay "The Will to Believe" (1896).

41. William James, *The Meaning of Truth*, ed. Frederick H. Burkhardt, Fredson Bowers, and Ignas K. Skrupselis (Cambridge: Harvard University Press, 1975), 105; my italics. Further references will appear in the text with the abbreviation MT.

42. In *The Varieties of Religious Experience*, James links the dogmatism that tends to ensue from mystical experiences with imperialism, commenting that "the

unhesitating and unreasoning way in which we feel that we must inflict our civilization upon 'lower' races, by means of Hotchkiss guns, etc., reminds one of nothing
so much as of the early spirit of Islam spreading its religion by the sword" (77).
The argument that ensues—that mystics have a right to entertain their insights but
no right to be dogmatic about them—is therefore indirectly an argument against
imperialism. For accounts of James's efforts to fight American imperialism in the
Phillipines, including his membership in the New England Anti–Imperialist League,
see Santayana's reminiscence in *Persons and Places, The Works of George Santayana,* ed. William G. Holzberger and Herman J. Saatkamp, Jr., vol. 1 (Cambridge:
MIT Press, 1987), 402–3; Lentricchia, *Ariel and the Police,* 111, 122–23, 251 n.,
and *Modernist Quartet,* 19, 22–25; Wolfe, *The Limits of American Literary Ideology in Pound and Emerson, 31;* and George F. Cotkin, *William James: Public
Philosopher* (Baltimore: Johns Hopkins University Press, 1990), 154–63. Cotkin's
study is particularly useful for its account of how James's anti–imperialism was
overlooked by his contemporaries—an analogous phenomenon, perhaps, to the
minimal critical response to Stevens's anti–imperialism.

43. Santayana, *Interpretations of Poetry and Religion* (New York: Harper &
Brothers), 1957.

44. Ibid., 12.

45. Ibid., 14, 12, 20. The worry introduced by dualism, Santayana says, is that
imagination may turn out to be confined within the "prison . . . of science and
history" and that therefore "everything in the real world may turn out to be disposed otherwise than as it would wish" (*Interpretations of Poetry and Religion,*
21, 10).

46. Cf. James's criteria for "mystical" moments as outlined in VRE 380–82.
Note that Santayana describes the moment of inspiration as one of complete peace,
in which the mystic declares, "It is attained" (*The Sense of Beauty,* [New York:
Dover, 1955], 160).

47. Santayana, *Interpretations of Poetry and Religion,* 47; my italics.

48. Santayana, *The Sense of Beauty,* 160–61, 112, 9, 98. For further examples
of Santayana's suspicion of accounts that translate this feeling into claims about
contact with eternity, see his discussion of Michael Angelo on beauty and of Plato
on love (*Interpretations of Poetry and Religion,* 143, 137).

49. Santayana, *The Sense of Beauty,* 7, 31, 162, 163, my italics. Note that
Santayana, like James and Bergson, represents consciousness thus delimited as a
"fluid," in which one state flows imperceptibly into another; see *The Sense of
Beauty,* 162. It is interesting to note that he uses the image of the chessboard to
demonstrate the inability of the intellect to fully account for this flux. See also
Interpretations of Poetry and Religion, 261.

50. See *The Sense of Beauty,* 160.

51. Ibid., 116.

52. I use the words "nothing but" here in the spirit of James Edie's comment
that James's phenomenology must be distinguished from that of philosophers like
Mach on the grounds that the latter regards the physical world as "nothing but"
our consciousness of it. See *William James and Phenomenology,* 70.

53. Santayana, *The Sense of Beauty,* 116; my italics. Cf. the picture of Christ
in *Interpretations of Poetry and Religion,* 92–93: "Let not the reader fancy that in
Christianity everything was settled by records and traditions. The idea of Christ
himself had to be constructed by the imagination in response to moral demands,
tradition giving only the barest external points of attachment. The facts were noth-

ing until they became symbols; and nothing could turn them into symbols except an eager imagination on the watch for all that might embody its dreams."

54. Santayana, *Letters*, 82.

55. Santayana, *The Sense of Beauty*, 74.

56. Ibid., 74, 80, 75. For further evidence of the subjective or relative status of ideals in Santayana, see "Walt Whitman: A Dialogue" (1890) and "What Is Aesthetics?" (1904).

57. Santayana, *Letters*, 76.

58. Santayana, *The Sense of Beauty*, 6.

59. Ibid., 82. Santayana's remarks here anticipate Hulme's claim about the importance of attending to the "*fringe of cinders* which bounds every ecstasy" (CW 17). Both Hulme and Santayana may have had in mind James's discussion of the "fringe" of consciousness in *The Principles of Psychology* (PP 1: 249ff.).

60. Santayana, *The Sense of Beauty*, 92, 102–3.

61. Santayana, *Interpretations of Poetry and Religion*, 218. Emerson's essay "The Poet" provides an excellent example of the phenomenon Santayana describes. After making a series of claims about the mystical powers of the poet, Emerson claims that "I look in vain for the poet whom I describe." In the same essay, Emerson anticipates Stevens's image for the process of transcendentalist enthusiasm and disillusionment; see Ralph Waldo Emerson, *Essays and Lectures* (New York: Library of America, 1983), 465, 451–52.

62. Santayana, *Interpretations of Poetry and Religion*, 219.

63. For a summary of the characteristics of Santayana's "essence," as he describes it in *Realms of Being* (1927–40), see Peterson, *Wallace Stevens and the Idealist Tradition*, 92.

64. Santayana, *Realms of Being* (New York: Cooper Square, 1972), xiii.

65. Santayana, *Interpretations of Poetry and Religion*, 270, 263, 272. Santayana's lack of concern with the empirical accuracy of poetic propositions is apparent in a comment on the "poetry" of Christianity: "The other circumstance that ennobled the Christian system was that all its parts had some significant and poetic truth, although they contained, or needed to contain, nothing empirically real" (*Interpretations of Poetry and Religion*, 88–89).

66. Santayana, *Interpretations of Poetry and Religion*, 270, 277. For the aesthetic considerations that Santayana believes should guide our choice of theories, see *The Sense of Beauty*, 87. For poetry's freedom from concerns about "practical efficacy" and its distinction from religion and understanding, see *Interpretations of Poetry and Religion* 289, 5. Peterson gives a vivid description of the realm of undirected daydreaming inhabited by Santayana's poet:

One is given a realm of spiritual aspiration but of aspiration toward no end; complete freedom, but no principle of selection. In the world of essences no values inhere, in the world of spirit no obligations. One is afloat in a sea of infinite possibilities, where to sink or to swim are equally meaningless alternatives. The world of spirit is, for Santayana, a world of "post-rational detachment," where neither emotion nor thought are efficacious. It represents, in fact, the full fruition of the skepticism and astheticism so characteristic of its author. (*Wallace Stevens and the Idealist Tradition*, 82)

67. For an account of the critics' misreadings of James, see chapter 4 of this study, pp. 173–74.

68. James, *Letters* 2: 122–24; Santayana, *Letters*, 80. My account of Santayana's attitudes toward truth-making is based on the writings roughly contemporaneous with Stevens's time at Harvard. Later in his career, he became a supporter of

"critical realism," a position more respectful of the role an objective "reality" should play in verification processes. For an account of the latter position, see Bruce Kuklick, *The Rise of American Philosophy* (New Haven: Yale University Press, 1977), 362–65.

69. At the beginning of the poem, Crispin asserts that "man is the intelligence of his soil" (CP 27); by the time he proposes his colony, he has reversed the assertion, saying that "his soil is man's intelligence" (CP 36). The reversal suggests a move from the Idealist faith in the power of the mind to create reality to the materialist faith that it is material reality that determines mind.

70. Richard P. Adams, "'The Comedian as the Letter C': A Somewhat Literal Reading,'" *Tulane Studies in English* 18 (1970): 107. Harold Bloom has invited the same reading of Crispin, in reading "Comedian" as a Romantic crisis-poem, and Crispin's retirement as Stevens's own "farewell to poetry" (*Poems of Our Climate*, 70).

71. Adams, 107.

72. John Crowe Ransom and R. P. Blackmur, for example, both regarded the poem as a perfect example of "pure" poetry—poetry without a message. See John Pauker, "A Discussion of Sea Surface Full of Clouds," *Furioso* 5 (1950): 36.

73. Lisa Ruddick argues that the images of fluidity in "The Comedian as the Letter C" might have been inspired by comparable images in Santayana's *Interpretations of Poetry and Religion*; see "Fluid Symbols in American Modernism," *Allegory, Myth and Symbol*, ed. Morton W. Bloomfield (Cambridge: Harvard University Press, 1981), 351 ff. She reads Santayana as endorsing the testing of propositions against empirical experience and sees Crispin's seafaring as an effort to do the same, His retirement is a disillusionment with the process. Although I support her view of the significance of Crispin's efforts at sea, I disagree with her reading of Santayana and with her view of Crispin's retirement.

74. Stevens was to problematize the sun in a similar way, with a similar purpose, throughout his career. See chapter 4 of this study, p. 159.

75. For evidence that James's endorsement of radical empiricism amounted to a support for pathetic fallacy, see ERE 110–11. For a comparable position in Santayana, see *Interpretations of Poetry and Religion*, 266.

76. This reading is supported by Stevens's suggestion, in a 1909 letter to his future wife, that the "mind" might be envisioned as "a motionless sea" (*Letters*, 118–19).

77. J. Hillis Miller anticipates this allegorical reading of "Sea Surface," commenting that the "marriage of sea and sky is an analogy for the relation of mind and world" ("Wallace Stevens's 'Poetry of Being'" in *The Act of the Mind: Essays on the Poetry of Wallace Stevens*, ed. J. Hillis Miller and Roy Harvey Pearce [Baltimore: Johns Hopkins University Press, 1965], 240). See also Dorothy Emerson, "Wallace Stevens's Sky That Thinks," *Wallace Stevens Journal* 9 (1985): 71–84.

78. That one does not have to seek certainty to be allowed to retain belief is, as I have suggested, the central thesis of "The Will to Believe." The principle that mystical experiences can be appreciated without being validated, of course, governs both James's own scientific practice and the advice he gives to the mystic in *The Varieties of Religious Experience*.

79. Dorothy Emerson, "Wallace Stevens's Sky That Thinks," 77–79.

80. See, for example, George McFadden, "Probings for an Integration: Color Symbolism in Wallace Stevens," *Modern Philology* 58 (1961): 187; Michel Benamou, *Wallace Stevens and the Symbolist Imagination* (Princeton: Princeton Univer-

sity Press, 1972), 19; and Frank Doggett, *Stevens's Poetry of Thought* (Baltimore: Johns Hopkins University Press, 1966), 101.

81. Compare Stevens's descriptions of the role played by Elsie Moll in his letters to her. See especially the letters of 10 March 1907 and 15 February 1909 (*Letters,* 95–96, 131–32).

82. See, for example, the portrait of Nanzia Nunzio in "Notes Toward a Supreme Fiction" (CP 395–96), the appeal to the bride in "Ghosts as Cocoons," and Stevens's claim that a "bride with her gauze and glitter" is the "genius of poetry," in an address on receiving the gold medal from the Poetry Society of America (OP 252–53). Stevens's bride-muse has an ancestor in the medieval Irish muse St. Brigit. See Robert Graves, *The White Goddess* (London: Faber and Faber, 1961), 394. For the tradition of representing inspiration as coitus, see Mary K. DeShazer, *Inspiring Women* (New York: Pergamon, 1986), 2.

83. See note 36 above.

84. For a discussion of the significance of Stevens's "middle spaces," see chapter 4 of this study.

85. For another instance of Stevens's refusal to commit himself about the objectivity of his muses, see Mary Nyquist's discussion of his treatment of Susanna in "Peter Quince at the Clavier" and "Musing on Susanna's Music," *Lyric Poetry: Beyond New Criticism,* ed. Chaviva Hosek and Patricia Parker (Ithaca: Cornell University Press, 1985), 324.

86. Graves, *The White Goddess,* 448.

87. See, for example, Matisse's *On the Sofa* (date unknown), *Goldfish and Sculpture* (1911), *Woman at the Fountain* (1917), *Woman with a Green Parasol on a Balcony* (1918), and *Dancer and Armchair, Black Background* (1942).

88. "So-and-So" has a counterpart in the "naked, nameless dame" in "The Hand as a Being" (CP 271). Note also that the "sister of the Minotaur" is faceless: she remains an "enigma and mask" to the male poet who communes with her (NA 67). Another muse is enjoyed while being "free from images" is the woman in "Romance for a Demoiselle Lying in the Grass." The speaker of that poem tells her that he willfully invokes an image of "monotony" to conceal "[a]ll [her] characters / And their desires" (OP 23). Stevens's characterization of the muses might be compared with his characterization of the idea of the hero in "Examination of the Hero in a Time of War." See especially canto XII (CP 278–79).

89. See chapter 4, pp. 154–55.

90. The speaker summarizes this by likening the inspired poet lovers to barbers, who have attempted to impose order on nature, such as a fancy coiffure on a wild head of hair. "Have all the barbers lived in vain," he asks "that not one curl in nature has survived?" Compare Crispin's career in barbering, CP 27.

91. The reasoning in "Monocle de Mon Oncle" resembles that in another poem in Harmonium titled "Homonculus et la Belle Etoile." There Stevens considers the case of the "mistress" who inspires both philosopher and poet, likening her to the "evening star." While being unable to determine for certain who or what this being truly is, he notices that she is both a generator of speech (she is "Fecund") and also that she does something to tranquilize "confusion." And he concludes that these benefits are all that really matter and that they are sufficient, despite all unanswerable questions, to make the muse a "good light," worth cultivating (CP 25–27).

92. Stevens, *Letters,* 538; my italics.

93. See Sandra Gilbert and Susan Gubar, *The Madwoman in the Attic* (New Haven: Yale University Press, 1979), 43–44.

94. From an untitled poem by Anne Finch; cited in *The Madwoman in the Attic*, 8–9.

95. Jacqueline·Vaught Brogan, "'Sister of the Minotaur': Sexism and Stevens," *Wallace Stevens and the Feminine*, ed. Melita Schaum (Tuscaloosa: University of Alabama Press, 1993), 3–22. See pp. 12–13. Mary Nyquist, "Musing on Susanna's Music," *Lyric Poetry: Beyond New Criticism*, ed. Chaviva Hosek and Patricia Parker (Ithaca: Cornell University Press, 1985): 310–27. See p. 313. Mary B. Arensberg makes the same point about the interior paramour in "Notes toward a Supreme Fiction"; see "'A Curable Separation': Stevens and the Mythology of Gender," *Wallace Stevens and the Feminine*, 23–45; 36. Sandra Gilbert and Susan Gubar, "The Man on the Dump versus the United Dames of America; or, What Does Frank Lentricchia Want?", *Critical Inquiry* 14 (Winter, 1988) 386–407. See p. 392. Gilbert and Gubar's phrase is originally Lentricchia's ("Patriarchy Against Itself" 744).

96. Mary B. Arensberg, "Wallace Stevens's Interior Paramour," *Wallace Stevens Journal* 3 (1979): 3–7. See p. 6.

97. Friedrich Nietzsche, *The Gay Science*, trans. Walter Kaufmann (New York: Vintage, 1974), 124. For a detailed discussion of Nietzsche's ambivalent attitude toward femininity, see Jean Graybeal, *Language and "the Feminine" in Nietzsche and Heidegger* (Bloomington: Indiana University Press, 1990), pp. 27–93.

98. Compare the philosophical debate outlined in "Life on a Battleship" with the one James discusses in Lecture IV of *Pragmatism*, "The One and the Many."

99. Hélène Cixous, "The Laugh of the Medusa," trans. Keith Cohen and Paula Cohen, *Signs* 1 (Summer 1976): 875–93. See p. 883.

100. Julia Kristeva, "Oscillation Between Power and Denial," trans. Marilyn August, in *New French Feminisms*, eds. Elaine Marks and Isabelle de Courtivron (Boston: University of Massachusetts Press, 1980), 165–67. See p. 166. Madeleine Gagnon, "Body I," trans. Isabelle de Courtivron, *New French Feminisms*, 179–80. See p. 180.

101. Notice also that the feminine principle in "Of Hartford in a Purple Light" is again identified with the sea. See CP 227.

102. Springer has sensed Stevens's affinity with Cixous and commented on the extent to which the feminine impulse he celebrates in his theory is allowed to flourish in his practice. "Stevens's whole figurative and expressive mode," she asserts, "as well as his thought . . . seems to me related to what Cixous has dubbed 'l'écriture féminine,' a mode increasingly understood not to be limited to women." See Mary Doyle Springer, "The Feminine Principle in Stevens's Poetry: 'Esthétique du Mal,'" *Wallace Stevens Journal* 12 (1988): 119–37, 125.

103. Cixous, "Laugh of the Medusa," 889.

104. Ibid., 887.

105. For a discussion of the seasons in Stevens's poetry, see chapter 4, p. 159.

106. James, *Pragmatism*, 43–44. James resumes his discussion of pragmatism's likeness to a woman in *Pragmatism*, 78, where he attributes the notion that pragmatism "unstiffens" theory to the Italian pragmatist G. Papini.

107. Jacques Derrida, *Spurs: Nietzsche's Styles*, trans. Barbara Harlow (Chicago: University of Chicago Press), 1978.

108. For Nietzsche's expressed opposition to feminism, see Derrida, *Spurs*, 65. Derrida comments that, for Nietzsche, "a woman's scepticism knows no bounds," and further that "the truth . . . does not concern her in the least" (*Spurs*, 63). Nietzsche's conception of feminine subversiveness differs from James's in emphasizing its indifference to the truth. In James, of course, the process of "unstiffening"

theories is at last partly motivated by a perception of a discrepancy between theory and empirical fact; it is part of an open-minded quest for the truth. The question of whether the femininity that Stevens celebrates more closely resembles James's or Nietzsche's is the subject of chapter 4 of this study.

109. Derrida, *Spurs,* 104.

110. Ibid., 39.

111. Jacques Derrida, *Positions,* trans. Alan Bass (Chicago: University of Chicago Press, 1981), 6; my italics.

112. In Freudian terms, we might call Stevens's aggressive, virile gestures examples of a "reaction formation," which Bloom describes as "a defensive movement of the spirit that is opposed to a repressed desire and so manifests itself as a reaction against that desire" (*Poems of our Climate,* 376).

113. James, "Philosophical Conceptions and Practical Results," 1078; Pound, "Vorticism," GB 86.

114. For a more detailed discussion of Stevens's dissatisfied birds and their significance, see chapter 4 of this study, pp. 161–63.

115. Compare James, *Pragmatism,* 119–20:

> When we talk of reality "independent" of human thinking, then, it seems a thing very hard to find. It reduces to the notion of what is just entering into experience and yet to be named, or else to some imagined aboriginal presence in experience, before any belief about the presence had arisen, before any human conception had been applied. It is what is absolutely dumb and evanescent, the merely ideal limit of our minds. We may glimpse it, but we never grasp it; what we grasp is always some substitute for it which previous human thinking has peptonized and cooked for our consumption. (My italics)

116. And which in Stevens's language of colors signifies the power to make bold assertions. See CP 243–44 and Helen Vendler's comments in *On Extended Wings: Wallace Stevens's Longer Poems* (Cambridge: Harvard University Press, 1969), 105–6.

Chapter 4. Stevens's Pragmatism

1. Pound, "The Wisdom of Poetry," SP 331. See chapter 2 of this study, pp. 86ff.

2. Gaston Bachelard, *The Poetics of Space,* trans. Maria Jolas (Boston: Beacon, 1969), xxxi.

3. This sense of the function of the whole is suggested also by Stevens's description of the function of a part: in this "simplified geography," he says, the "rising sun comes up like news from Africa" (CP 334).

4. Santayana, *Interpretations of Poetry and Religion,* 274; my italics.

5. See Stevens's expression of admiration for Cézanne's "psychological landscapes" (NA 46).

6. Mircea Eliade, *Patterns in Comparative Religion* (London: Sheed and Ward, 1958), 39; my italics.

7. Santayana, *The Sense of Beauty,* 90.

8. Hartman, *The Fate of Reading and Other Essays,* 152, 154, 160, 176. See above, p. 76. James's comment on comparable efforts to demystify the stars may have had some influence on Hulme's and Stevens's efforts. In *Pragmatism* he comments on the name "Big Dipper," saying that "my friend Frederick Myers was

humorously indignant that that prodigious star-group should remind us Americans of nothing but a culinary utensil" (P 121–22).

9. For further affirmation that Stevens grants the stars a place within the world of time, rather than beyond it, cf. "Martial Cadenza," CP 238.

10. Cf. Hulme's descendental metaphors in "Autumn" (CW 3). Cf. also the descendental moves in Stevens's "Evening Without Angels" (CP 137–38).

11. See, for example, "Forces, the Will & the Weather," "Variations on a Summer Day," and "A Lot of People Bathing in a Stream" (CP 229, 233, 371). Frank Doggett has found another method of synthesizing subject and object in Stevens's frequent use of the color purple (*Stevens's Poetry of Thought*, 28). Purple, of course, is a synthesis of red and blue, generally regarded as Stevens's colors for reality and imagination, respectively. A significant example of this may occur in "Large Red Man Reading," where the large red man reads "the outlines of being and its expressings" from out of the "purple tabulae" (CP 424). Although I sympathize with Doggett's reading, I would also reiterate that the color blue is itself sufficient to denote an ambiguity about subjectivity or objectivity. See the analysis of "Sea Surface," chapter 3, p. 129–32.

12. James also writes that "the theoretic faculty lives between two fires which never give her rest, and make her incessantly revise her formulations" (WB 102). Stevens refers to the "two poles" in "The Man with the Blue Guitar," calling them "The imagined and the real, thought / And the truth, Dichtung und Wahrheit" (CP 177). Helen Vendler comments that "Stevens is not a poet of antinomies, but a poet of the midworld between them, a world not of infinite Miltonic dimensions but of limited space." Stevens's most characteristic mode, she remarks, "is a tentative, diffident, and reluctant search for a middle form between ecstasy and apathy, a sensible ecstasy of pauvred color, to use Stevens's own phrase." *On Extended Wings: Wallace Stevens's Longer Poems* (Cambridge: Harvard University Press, 1969), 47, 13. See also Eleanor Cook's discussion of "acrossness" in Stevens's poetry, particularly in "An Ordinary Evening in New Haven," in *Poetry, Word-Play, and Word-War in Wallace Stevens* (Princeton: Princeton University Press, 1988), 306–7.

13. As an account of perception, this poem clearly underscores what Husserl called the "intentional" aspect of that experience. See *Ideas*, 107–9. In the rabbit's mind, all objects exist "for me" (CP 209).

14. Husserl, *Ideas*, 139.

15. See also "The Bouquet," where the speaker apprehends "the rudiments in the jar" (CP 452), the object-turned-jar in "Someone Puts a Pineapple Together" (NA 83), and the "bowl" of "cold porcelain, low and round," in "The Poems of Our Climate" (CP 193). Thomas J. Hines has also suggested that Stevens's vessels effect the first phase of phenomenological reduction. *The Later Poetry of Wallace Stevens: Phenomenological Parallels with Husserl and Heidegger* (Lewisburg: Bucknell University Press, 1976), 91–92, 97.

16. In both German and English. See Martin Heidegger, *Being and Time*, trans. John Macquarrie and Edward Robinson (Oxford: Blackwell, 1962), 80; and "Letter on Humanism," and "Building, Dwelling, Thinking" in (*Basic Writings*, ed. David Farrell Krell (New York: Harper and Row, 1977), 236–37, 320–39.

17. Heidegger, Martin. *Basic Writings*. Edited by David Farrell Krell (New York: Harper and Row, 1977), p. 236.

18. The earliest of the very few references to Heidegger in Stevens's published work is in a letter to Paule Vidale on 29 July 1952, where he asks for a copy of Heidegger's "little work dealing with the poetry of the German poet, Hölderlin"

(*Letters*, 758). Because Hölderlin did much to inspire Heidegger's discussion of the likeness between being and dwelling and because Stevens indicates a familiarity with Hölderlin as early as 1948 (*Letters*, 576), it is possible that the German poet inspired the philosopher and the poet to similar ends. For further discussion of Heidegger, Hölderlin, and the concept of "dwelling" in Stevens, see Frank Kermode, "Dwelling Poetically in Connecticut," *Wallace Stevens: A Celebration*, ed. Frank Doggett and Robert Buttel (Princeton: Princeton University Press, 1980), 256–73.

19. Compare the states enjoyed by Crispin, "dwelling" in his newly circumscribed "home" (CP 40) and by the "one dwelling in a seed" in "Description Without Place" (CP 341).

20. Bloom, *Poems of Our Climate*, 331.

21. Bachelard, *The Poetics of Space*, 8.

22. Heidegger, *Basic Writings*, 327. Bachelard says, "From the phenomenologist's viewpoint," "life begins well, it begins enclosed, protected, all warm in the bosom of the house." Anxiety, in the form of "conscious metaphysics," starts "from the moment when the being is 'cast into the world'" (*The Poetics of Space*, 8). The parallel between Heidegger's and Stevens's representations of the dwelling-places of *Dasein* may be confirmed further by noting the ways in which Heidegger emphasises the "between-ness" of that space, the way it brings about an interpenetration of earth and sky, man and god. See, for example, "Poetically Man Dwells," *Poetry, Language, Thought*, 220; and "Building, Dwelling, Thinking," *Basic Writings*, 328.

23. Heidegger, *Basic Writings*, 332.

24. Husserl, *Ideas*, 275.

25. Stevens's distinction between the "true subject" and the "poetry of the subject" is a distinction between the idea or perception to which a poem refers and the "attitude" or "bearing" (OP 227) the writer assumes toward it. It corresponds precisely to Husserl's distinction between the "subject matter" of consciousness, "pure and simple," and the "appreciating" directed toward that subject-matter (*Ideas*, 110)—a distinction that Husserl may well first have encountered in James (PP 2: 917). The "doxic modalities" Husserl identifies are particular types of appreciation.

26. Husserl, *Ideas*, 274.

27. In "Ode: Intimations of Immortality from Recollections of Early Childhood," Wordsworth regrets the passage from childhood that sees the fading of platonic light into "the light of common day" (l. 76). The movement represents a loss of absolute knowledge and a move into a state of uncertainty, a state in which the child's ability to know is impeded by a conceptual "prison-house" (l. 7). In "Elegiac Stanzas," Wordsworth laments the effect such a loss has had on his creative powers, the impossibility of adding to his perceptions "the gleam, / The light that never was, on sea or land" (l. 15). See *The Poetical Works of William Wordsworth*, ed. E. de Selincourt and Helen Darbishire, vol. 5 (Oxford: Clarendon, 1947), 28, 279, and 259.

28. Heidegger, *Being and Time*, 51. Cf. Heidegger, "The End of Philosophy and the Task of Thinking" (*Basic Writings*, 383–84).

29. As in the following lines from "Adonais":

> The One remains, the many change and pass;
> Heaven's light forever shines, Earth's shadows fly;
> Life, like a dome of many-coloured glass,
> Stains the white radiance of Eternity. . . .

The Complete Poetical Works of Percy Bysshe Shelley, ed. Thomas Hutchinson

(Oxford: Oxford University Press, 1923), 438. In "William Blake and His Illustrations to the Divine Comedy," Yeats comments that the symbol is "the only possible expression of some invisible essence, a transparent lamp about a spiritual flame" (*Essays and Introductions*, 116).

30. Husserl, *Ideas*, 248.

31. See Richard Macksey's comment, "As the sun warms the earth of Crispin's tropics or Florida's 'venereal soil,' the earth proliferates its imagery and the imagination discovers resemblances and correspondences" ("The Climates of Wallace Stevens," in *The Act of the Mind: Essays on the Poetry of Wallace Stevens*, ed. Roy Harvey Pearce and J. Hillis Miller (Baltimore: Johns Hopkins University Press, 1965), 189).

32. Given Stevens's representation of summer as the moment of most intense belief, it is appropriate that he also sees it as the time for the appearance of what James called the "perfect object of belief": God (PP 2: 317). The religious rituals at the end of "Sunday Morning" take place on a "summer morn" (CP 70); summer is the time when the mind intuits an "inhuman author" for all it sees (CP 377), when it constructs a "statue of Jove among the boomy clouds" (CP 482).

33. Note that the sun is identified here with the questing bird. Stevens is coordinating his doxic codes.

34. Stevens underscores the pragmatic nature of the "freed man's" attitude with his repeated use of the word "how." Instead of examining the sun as a "what," he emphasizes that it is "how" something is made possible for the freed man. It is not a thing of any discernible nature, but an enabling experience. Compare the "latest freed man's" state of mind with the state desired in "Extracts from Addresses to the Academy of Fine Ideas" (257).

35. An analogous image is found in "Hibiscus on the Sleeping Shores." There the roaming moth is the roaming "mind" (CP 22).

36. Note also James's comment that "what characterizes both consent and belief is the cessation of theoretic agitation, through the advent of an idea which is inwardly stable, and fills the mind solidly to the exclusion of contradictory ideas" (PP 2: 913–14).

37. Another description of a bird incapable of transcending epochal space is found in "Thirteen Ways of Looking at a Blackbird":

> When the blackbird flew out of sight,
> It marked the edge
> Of one of many circles.
>
> (CP 94)

The "circles" referred to here could be Emerson's (see note 41 below). Note also the "blue pigeon," enjoying the pleasures of merely circulating in "Le Monocle de Mon Oncle" (CP 17); its motion signifies the happy acceptance of confinement within epochal space.

38. Heidegger, *Basic Writings* 236; my italics.

39. For Santayana's description of the poet's obligation to be a builder of comforting shelters in the midst of chaos, see *Interpretations of Poetry and Religion*, 270. James may have been inspired to use architectural metaphors by C. S. Peirce's 1891 essay "The Architecture of Theories," *Charles S. Peirce: Selected Writings*, ed. Philip P. Wiener (New York: Dover, 1958), 142–59; note especially 144–45.

40. Compare Hulme: "A house built is then a symbol, a Roman Viaduct; but the walk there and the dirt—this must jump right into the mind also" (CW 18). Also compare Stevens's picture of the planter's collapsed home in "Notes," overcome by

tropical vegetation ("garbled green" (CP 393). Other striking images of crumbling theoretical buildings are found in "Add This to Rhetoric" (CP 198) and "Blue Buildings in the Summer Air" (CP 217).

41. In view of the audience's prescription, it is interesting to note that in both of the ideal (but unattainable) constructions cited above, the resting place is a place filled with a transcendental light. In the example from "Credences" (CP 373), the column is a place where the sun rests; in the lofty structure in "Architecture," the interior is "pierced" with "pouring shafts" (OP 38). Another indirect statement about the futility of acts of theoretical building, about their failure to pierce a fissure through to transcendental truth, is found in "Six Significant Landscapes" (CP 74–75).

42. Compare Emerson's account of the questing mind, for which certainty is endlessly deferred, in "Circles":

> The life of man is a self-evolving circle, which, from a ring imperceptibly snall, rushes on all sides outwards to new and larger circles, and that without end. The extent to which this generation of circles, wheel without wheel, will go, depends on the force or truth of the individual soul. For it is the inert effort of each thought, having formed itself into a circular wave of circumstance,—as, for instance, an empire, rules of an art, a local usage, a religious rite,—to heap itself on that ridge, and to solidify and hem in the life. But if the soul is quick and strong, it bursts over that boundary on all sides, and expands another orbit on the great deep, which also runs up into a high wave, with attempt again to stop and to bind. But the heart refuses to be imprisoned; in its first and narrowest impulses, it already tends outward with a vast force, and to immense and innumerable expansions.

Ralph Waldo Emerson, *Essays and Lectures* (New York: Library of America, 1983), 404–5.

43. Bachelard, *The Poetics of Space,* 183.

44. For a general account of philosophical discussion about "mirror-space," see Ryan, *The Vanishing Subject,* 188. For an account of Edwin Bissell Holt's use of the figure, see Kuklick, *The Rise of American Philosophy,* 345. Holt discusses the phenomenon in *The Concept of Consciousness* (New York: Macmillan, 1914).

45. Bachelard's example of a topoanalytical inversion is from a poem by Tristan Tzara:

> Le marche du soleil est entre dans la chambre
> Et la chambre dans la tete bourdonnante.
>
> [The progress of the sun has come into my room
> And the room into my buzzing head.]
>
> (*The Poetics of Space,* 226)

46. Another example of the phenomenon of "intimate immensity" in Stevens is found in "Less and Less Human, O Savage Spirit." There Stevens folds God into Being, figuring it as a "god in the house" (CP 327–28).

47. *Poems of Our Climate,* 359.

48. See, for example, Kermode, *The Sense of an Ending,* 37; and Doggett, *Stevens's Poetry of Thought,* 105–6, 109.

49. The sixth edition of *Philosophie des Als Ob* was translated as *The Philosophy of "As If"* (1924). For what Pound would have learned from Mead, see chapter 2 of this study, pp. 90.

50. Vaihinger, *The Philosophy of "As If,"* xli, 268.

51. See Ibid., 89.

52. See Ibid., 49, 71, 74, 77. Vaihinger also notes that theorists subject fictions to a wrongful criterion when they try to demonstrate their logical consistency. Although the failure to be logically consistent is another reason to discard a hypothesis, it is no reason, in Vaihinger's opinion, to discard a fiction. This distinction anticipates I. A. Richards's distinction between the expectations justified for scientific and emotive language (*Principles of Literary Criticism,* 211–12).

53. Sir Philip Sidney, *Defense of Poetry,* ed. Lewis Soens (Lincoln: University of Nebraska Press, 1970), 35.

54. Others who interpreted pragmatism to entail an indifference to fact included G. E. Moore, "William James' 'Pragmatism,'" in *Philosophical Studies* (London: Routledge, 1922), 97–146, see esp. 127; Bertrand Russell, "William James's Conception of Truth," in *Philosophical Essays* (London: Longmans, Green, 1910), 127–49, see esp. 141; Alfred Edward Taylor, "Truth and Practice," *Philosophical Review* 14 (1905): 265–89; and James Bissett Pratt, "Truth and Its Verification," *Journal of Philosophy, Psychology and Scientific Method,* 4 (1908): 320–24. See also James's objections to this interpretation of pragmatism in WB 143, 208.

55. For a direct response to the accusation that his philosophy "denied reality's existence," see James's response to Marcel Hébert, MT 130–32.

56. For Doggett's failure to acknowledge the distinction and Kermode's failure to give sufficient weight to it, see note 47 above. Doggett and A. Walton Litz effectively collapse the distinction when they make the mistake of asserting Stevens's affinity with Nietzsche and Vaihinger rather than James. See Doggett, *Stevens's Poetry of Thought,* 105–6 and 109; and Litz, *Introspective Voyageur: The Poetic Development of Wallace Stevens* (New York: Oxford University Press, 1972), vi. Also note Doggett's entirely pessimistic reading of what Stevens means by enclosure in a "room" (in his view, it is simply to become a "skeptic," to be definitively excluded from "actuality") and his equation of Stevens's notion of the textuality of the world with Santayana's (146–47). His conviction that Stevens is a dogmatic skeptic is summed up by his claim that "the notion that to know is merely to regard one's own idea, . . . that an idea is always and inherently fictive [,] permeates all of the poetry of Stevens" (148–49).

Unduly pessimistic readings of Stevens's qualifiers by Helen Vendler, Joseph Riddel, and Helen Regueiro are discussed below. Milton Bates, one of the few critics to respect the distinction between hypothesis and fiction, argues that Stevens preserved a Jamesian optimism until 1940 but was a thoroughgoing Santayanan from then on (*Wallace Stevens,* 207–10). His evidence for the shift is unconvincing. My account is based on a conviction about the essential continuity of Stevens's thought; the evidence I provide from the later poetry should be sufficient to dispel the notion that Stevens becomes an epistemological pessimist after 1940. Indeed the evidence shows that if he shifted, it was in the direction of greater epistemological optimism.

57. James, *Letters,* 2: 269.

58. Heidegger, "The End of Philosophy and the Task of Thinking," *Basic Writings,* 375.

59. Bates, *Wallace Stevens,* 209.

60. Other passages that suggest that a skeptical view of truth is just one theory among many, subject to questioning for its lack of foundation, can be found in both "Notes Toward a Supreme Fiction" and "The Auroras of Autumn." In the "It Must Change" section of "Notes," for example, the "necessity" of the "freshness of transformation" we demand of our imaginative constructions is represented as something we project: one of the "rubbings of a glass in which we peer" (CP 398). Later in the poem, Stevens includes the image of "Cinderella fulfilling herself be-

neath the roof" (CP 405) in a list of notions willed and projected into the world. This image seems an appropriate one for the kind of masturbatory, self-fulfilling truth-making imagined by the skeptic; in being included in a list of arbitrary notions, it is itself brought into question. In "Auroras," Stevens represents skepticism as a transitory notion like any other, which must inevitably be critiqued and revised:

> It must change from destiny to slight caprice.
> And thus its jetted tragedy, its stele
> And shape and mournful making move to find
> What must unmake it and, at last, what can,
> Say, a flippant communication under the moon.
>
> (CP 417–18)

61. Kermode cites the statement that "final belief must be belief in a fiction" as support for Stevens's sympathy with a Santayanan fictionalism (*The Sense of an Ending*, 36, 64). See also Litz, *Introspective Voyageur*, 271. Compare Hillis Miller's citation of a passage from Stevens's "Two or Three Ideas" (OP 260) as evidence for a claim about Stevens's dogmatic atheism ("Wallace Stevens's Poetry of Being," Pearce and Miller, *The Act of the Mind*, 145). His reading ignores the qualifiers that render the passage a *description of the experience* of losing faith, rather than a statement of doctrine.

62. Stevens also suggests the connection between the crystal and epochal equivocation earlier in "Notes" when he represents the "major man" MacCullough as an "expedient . . . crystal hypothesis" (CP 387). For another metaphor equating the mind and a crystal, see "The Sail of Ulysses" (OP 129). The attempt to qualify the victory over the fat girl in "Notes" is matched by the debate over the "nakedness" of Nanzia Nunzo in Canto VIII. If Nanzia's self-described status of being "stripped more nakedly / Than nakedness" (CP 396) is a condition implying her authority as a muse, Ozymandias is still trying to subordinate the muse to his will when he counters that "the bride / Is never naked," but covered "always" with a "fictive covering" (CP 396). It is crucial to note, however, that Stevens leaves Ozymandias's claim as part of a dialogue. There is nothing to say that Nanzia's self-description is not equally liable to be true.

63. Bloom, *Poems of Our Climate*, 329.

64. Canto XXX is particularly intriguing in this regard. Stevens offers an unqualified description of a revelatory moment, in which what is only "imagined" has been "washed away." Its final stanza employs the figure of a synopticon to suggest the transcendental nature of the vision.

65. The color green frequently denotes objective reality in Stevens. Compare the "alien, point-blank, green and actual Guatemala" in "Arrival at the Waldorf" (CP 241).

66. Stevens echoes this passage in "The Planet on the Table," a poem from *The Rock* in which the degree of genuine truth captured in his poetry is a source of satisfaction to him as he looks over his career (CP 532).

67. For an extended discussion of Stevens's Jamesian conception of heroism, see David Bromwich, "Stevens and the Idea of the Hero," *Raritan* 7 (1987): 1-27. Bromwich notes the theme of the self-fulfilling prophecy in the poem "Gigantomachia," among others.

68. See Filreis, *Wallace Stevens and the Actual World*, and Longenbach, *Wallace Stevens: The Plain Sense of Things*. For the sake of emphasizing the distinction between irresponsible "fictions" and responsible "hypotheses," throughout the sub-

sequent discussion I regard empirical evidence and actuality as commensurate. This equivalence is of couse disputable, but not on grounds relevant to my argument.

69. Cf. James's remark that the conditions of phenomenological reduction do not prevent the radical empiricist from believing in an "existing beyond" (ERE 43). Also note his hostility to the idealist position that positing "independence of being from being known" would "disintegrate the universe beyond all hope of mending" (PU 33).

70. For this motion and its significance, see note 37 above. Stevens also suggests the relationship between mere circulation and a willingness to respect epochal limits in "Notes Toward a Supreme Fiction" where "merely going round" is the activity of a bird who stops "just short" of singing a dogmatic song (CP 405).

71. For the significance of green in Stevens, see note 65 above.

72. See Helen Vendler, "The Qualified Assertions of Wallace Stevens," *The Act of the Mind,* ed. Pearce and Miller, 163–78.

73. Stevens, *Souvenirs and Prophecies,* 165.

74. Michel Benamou, for example, sees the "as if" as a device by which Stevens reminds himself "that symbols are not to be confused with things as they are" (*Wallace Stevens and the Symbolist Imagination,* xv). Paul Bové reads "as if" in a similar way in his reading of "As You Leave the Room," *Destructive Poetics* (New York: Columbia University Press, 1980). I dispute this reading in what follows. Comparable epistemological negativism—or the critical error of "throwing away of the baby with the bathwater"—in interpreting Stevens's qualifiers can be found in readings of his qualifying "blue" of imagination, his qualifying "interior" or epochal spaces, and the qualifier "seems." The phenomenon also occurs when critics read his pragmatist statements about the correlation between "truth" and "desire"; see my discussion of this tendency in "Cannon Aspirin: Wallace Stevens's Defense of Pleasure," forthcoming, *Analecta Husserliana.*

75. Alan Tate on Stevens in 1971; cited in Filreis 64.

76. Vendler, "The Qualified Assertions of Wallace Stevens," 168.

77. Ibid., 169.

78. See Frank Lentricchia, *The Gaiety of Language: An Essay on the Radical Poetics of W. B. Yeats and Wallace Stevens* (Berkeley: University of California Press, 1968), 165. Harold Bloom initially described the passage as an example of Stevens's "faithless faith." ("Notes Toward a Supreme Fiction: A Commentary," *Wallace Stevens: A Collection of Critical Essays.* Twentieth Century Views, ed. Marie Borroff (Englewood Cliffs, N.J.: Prentice-Hall, 1963), 76–95.) But he retracts this reading in *Poems of Our Climate,* reading the passage more positively (211).

79. Vaihinger, The Philosophy of "As If," 93, xli, vii, 258; my italics.

80. Brogan suggests that Stevens may not have known Vaihinger's work directly but only secondhand through Santayana (127). Poirier also believes that Stevens's "as if" owes nothing to Vaihinger, pointing out that *Philosophie des Als Ob* was not available in English until 1924, after Stevens had begun using the expression in his poetry. See *Poetry and Pragmatism,* 154.

81. H. W. Fowler, *A Dictionary of Modern English Usage* (Oxford: Oxford University Press, 1926), 32.

82. Louise Brogan, *Stevens and Simile* (Princeton: Princeton University Press, 1986), 133.

83. Stevens, *Letters,* 434.

84. Wyndham Lewis, "Wyndham Lewis Vortex No. 1," 91.

85. See James, MT 105.

86. Lentricchia, *The Gaiety of Language,* 145; my italics.

87. Ibid., 75.

88. See Pound's specifications about metaphor, chapter 3, pp. 93–99. In *Stevens and Simile,* Louise Brogan has described Stevens's method of figuration as an effort to balance the impulse toward "metaphor" and the impulse toward "fragmentation" or the "unitive" and the "disjunctive" processes of language. By uniting these impulses in a single trope, she observes, Stevens protects his poetry "from becoming either too dogmatic or too disillusioned" (170); the "threshold" in "To an Old Philosopher in Rome," she remarks, is an appropriate "image for language itself" (136). Most important, however, is the significance of this view of simile for correcting misconceptions about Stevens's skepticism. Where deconstructionist critics like Joseph Riddel, she insists, have regarded Stevens's extensive use of simile as an admission of what language cannot do, of its inadequacy in accounting for the world (154, 166, 183), those apprised of the balance the simile achieves will appreciate that the difference to which it attests disrupts, but does not destroy, its gestures toward unification. "Although the simile may well undercut the possibility of oneness . . . it is also the means of positing [its] possibility" (154).

89. "What Psychical Research Has Accomplished," in *The Will to Believe* (1897) and *Human Immortality* (1898).

90. See Mallarmé, letter to Aubanel, 28 July 1866, *Correspondance complète 1862–1871,* 315–16; and Whitman, "A Noiseless Patient Spider," *Complete Poetry and Collected Prose,* ed. Justin Kaplan (New York: Library of America, 1982), 564–65. These examples present the dogmatic extremes between which Stevens's poem mediates. In Mallarmé the poet-spider discovers the synaesthetic relations; in Whitman he creates them.

91. Compare the effect of another poem about "correspondences" in the world: "Domination of Black." In particular note the analogy Stevens highlights between the planets and fragile autumn leaves (CP 9). Also compare the analogy between the mind's aspirations and the limited flights of a moth in "Hibiscus on the Sleeping Shores" (CP 22). In both cases, again, the force of the similarity meets resistance in empirical difference, leaving the more optimistic conclusions (that the planets are part of a celestial system, that the mind's capacities are greater than those of the moth) within the realm of the possible.

92. Lentricchia summarizes the "standard generalization" about Stevens's poetic development: "[A]s he grew older he put on the vocal weight which enabled him to transcend the more aesthetic perfections of his earlier poems—so sensuously full, so exquisitely achieved, so intellectually empty" (*Ariel and the Police,* 206). A typical claim for the discontinuity can be found in Litz, *Introspective Voyageur,* v–vii.

93. See James, VRE 428.

94. Compare the effect of the thunder in another poem from *Parts of a World,* "The Girl in a Nightgown" (CP 214). See Filreis, *Wallace Stevens and the Actual World,* 63.

95. Howard Mumford Jones, "An Outpouring of Americana," *Saturday Review of Literature* 25, 43 (24 October 1942): 17. Cited by Filreis, *Wallace Stevens and the Actual World,* 75.

96. Similar political differences separated Lentricchia (who denounced Stevens's "fictionalism" (*After the New Criticism,* 30–35) and Stevens's deconstructionist champions, such as Riddel. For a more detailed account of Lentricchia's position, see chapter 5, pp. 225–26.

97. Fredric Jameson, "Periodizing the 60s," *The Ideologies of Theory: Essays 1971–1986,* vol. 2 of 2, ed. Neil Larsen (Minneapolis: University of Minnesota

Press, 1988), 198; see also Jameson, "Wallace Stevens," *New Orleans Review* 2 (Spring 1984): 10–19. For an account of the Kissinger/Stevens correspondence, see Filreis, *Wallace Stevens and the Actual World*, 243–44.

98. Jameson, "Periodizing the 60s," 199.

99. Filreis has developed its argument in an equally important study, *Modernism from Right to Left: Wallace Stevens, the Thirties, & Literary Radicalism* (Cambridge: Cambridge University Press, 1994). The later book somewhat undermines the thesis of the earlier one, in pointing to Stevens's sympathies with leftist thinkers and particularly with their concern that literature engage with the actual world, *prior* to Pearl Harbor. It uses Stevens's example to support the contention that that the traditional critical opposition between rightist modernism and leftist radicalism must be collapsed: an argument with which I would concur. See also James Longenbach's *Wallace Stevens: The Plain Sense of Things*, and the essays published in special issue of *Wallace Stevens Journal* 13 (Fall 1989) on Stevens and politics. Longenbach's close readings are, on the whole, more sensitive to Stevens's qualifying language than Filreis's, but he somewhat undermines his argument on behalf of Stevens's attentiveness to the actual world by reading Stevens's "fictions" in the Vaihingerian vein and also by missing the crucial hypothesis in "Description Without Place" (287–92). Of the essays collected in the special issue, the one most compatible with my argument, in proposing a kind of tensional or hypothetical aesthetic for Stevens, is Robert Emmett Monroe's "Figuration and Society in 'Owl's Clover,'" *Wallace Stevens Journal* 13 (Fall 1989): 127–49.

100. See Roy Harvey Pearce, "Wallace Stevens: The Life of the Imagination," *PMLA* 66 (September 1951): 561–82. Reprinted in *Wallace Stevens: A Collection of Critical Essays*, ed. Marie Borroff (Englewood Cliffs, N.J.: Prentice-Hall, 1963), 111–32.

101. Marjorie Perloff says that Stevens "seems . . . to be obsessed by what he calls in 'The Noble Rider' 'the pressure of reality,' even as be abjures that reality as alien to the purity of art." "Revolving in Crystal: The Supreme Fiction and the Impasse of Modernist Lyric," *Wallace Stevens: The Poetics of Modernism*, ed. Albert Gelpi (Cambridge: Cambridge University Press, 1985), 46.

102. See NA 15, 19, 35, 17.

103. For Orwell's argument—an analogous one from a committed socialist writer—see "Inside the Whale," *An Age Like This*, vol. 1 of *The Collected Essays, Journalism and Letters of George Orwell* (New York: Harcourt Brace Jovanovich, 1968), 493–527.

104. Perloff, "Revolving in Crystal," 50; my italics.

105. Stevens, *Letters*, 345–45.

106. Filreis, *Wallace Stevens and the Actual World*, 23.

107. Cf. the eleventh of Marx's "Theses on Feuerbach": "The philosophers have only interpreted the world, in various ways; the point, however, is to change it." "Theses on Feuerbach," in *The Marx-Engels Reader*, ed. Robert C. Tucker (New York: W. W. Norton, 1978), 145.

108. Compare the masculine nature of James's empiricists, the "Rocky Mountain toughs" (P 14). Note James's identification of masculine and feminine principles. Elsewhere, as we have seen, he equates the same kind of empiricism with the "unstiffening" of abstract propositions (P 43).

109. Georg Lukács, *The Meaning of Contemporary Realism*, trans. John and Necke Mander (London: Merlin, 1963), 25, 21; Lentricchia, *Ariel and the Police*, 232; Jameson, "Wallace Stevens," 198. Lentricchia supports his claim about the abundance of disinvolved impressions in Stevens's work by pointing to Stevens's

claim, in the "Noble Rider" essay, that psychologically the poetic process is an "escapist" process (*Ariel and the Police*, 232; NA 30). In doing so and throughout his discussion of the similarity between the disinvolvement of impressions and imperialism (232–39), he ignores the important qualification Stevens makes immediately afterward:

> Escapism has a pejorative sense, which it cannot be supposed that I include in the sense in which I use the word. The pejorative sense applies where the poet is not attached to reality, where the imagination does not adhere to reality, which, for my part, I regard as fundamental. (NA 30–31)

Said describes the discourse of Orientalism as a practice in which the Oriental is "contained and represented by dominating frameworks" in which it "seems to be, not an extension beyond the familiar European world, but rather a closed field, a theatrical stage affixed to Europe." *Orientalism* (New York: Vintage, 1979), 40, 63.

110. Lentricchia, *Ariel and the Police*, 232, 131, 238. Lentricchia's and Jameson's objection to Stevens's appropriation of Third World and other objects matches the feminist objection to his representations of women as *pour-soi*.

111. Lukács, *The Meaning of Contemporary Realism*, 21. For the "rift" between stream of consciousness and objective world, see 37.

112. With the aid of Isaiah Berlin, Said identifies a profoundly antiempirical attitude as one of the distinguishing characteristics of the Orientalist. The Orientalist attitude "shares with magic and with mythology the self-containing, self-reinforcing character of a closed system, in which objects are what they are because they are what they are, for once, for all time, for ontological reasons that no empirical material can either dislodge or alter." What the Orientalist does "is to confirm the Orient in his readers' eyes; he neither tries nor wants to unsettle already firm convictions" (*Orientalism*, 70, 65). This attitude is clearly at odds with Stevens's Jamesian propensity for dismantling theories in the face of contrary experience.

113. Stevens, *Letters*, 496.

114. For similar readings of "Description Without Place," see Bloom, *The Poems of Our Climate*, 239; Joseph N. Riddel, *The Clairvoyant Eye: The Poetry and Poetics of Wallace Stevens* (Baton Rouge: Louisiana State University Press, 1965), 199, 198; Vendler, *On Extended Wings*, 218, 219; and Michael T. Beehler, "Meteoric Poetry: Wallace Stevens's 'Description without Place,'" *Criticism* (Summer 1977): 241. Filreis cites these readings in support of his own. See *Wallace Stevens and the Actual World*, 155, 323.

115. Filreis, *Wallace Stevens and the Actual World*, 156; CP 343.

116. Ibid., 160; CP 154.

117. Stevens, *Letters*, 500–501; my italics. See Filreis, *Wallace Stevens and the Actual World*, 179.

118. Filreis, *Wallace Stevens and the Actual World*, 171.

119. Filreis misreads Canto xxviii of "An Ordinary Evening in New Haven" in a similar way, ignoring the force of the "if" that introduces the claim he criticizes. See *Wallace Stevens and the Actual World*, 226.

120. *Wallace Stevens and the Actual World*, 179.

121. Lentricchia, *Ariel and the Police*, 231.

122. Two poems from *Parts of a World*, "Man and Bottle" and "The Glass of Water," are both sharply critical of those surveyors of history who are satisfied with seeing everything in terms of their own privileged experience. Filreis has ably demonstrated how the former poem reveals Stevens's "awareness of [modernism's]

... insensitivity ... to real crises" (*Wallace Stevens and the Actual World*, 18), and I will do nothing more here than to recommend his reading, adding only that he might have explicitly added the *epoche* to his list of potential interpretations for the poem's oblivion-inducing "bottle." The case of "A Glass of Water" deserves more comment, insofar as it is a poem that sets the practice of vessel-dwelling into a specifically colonial context. Briefly, Stevens's point here is that to live in an epochal "glass," worrying only about "what stands ... in the centre" (CP 197), is to resemble an oblivious politician "playing cards" in the face of human despair. The arrogant colonist, paying a visit to "a village of the indigenes," sees there only his "ideas," and nothing at all of the "dogs / and dung" (CP 198) that constitute its irreducible actuality.

123. Lentricchia, *Ariel and the Police*, 21, 13.

124. The analogy between "merely circulating" and not caring about fact is apparent in the following passage (where the fact at stake is the nationality of Mrs. Anderson's baby):

> The garden flew round with the angel,
> The angel flew round with the clouds,
> And the clouds flew round and the clouds flew
>   round
> And the clouds flew round with the clouds.
>
> Is there any secret in skulls,
> The cattle skulls in the woods?
> Do the drummers in black hoods
> Rumble anything out of their drums?
>
> Mrs. Anderson's Swedish baby
> Might well have been German or Spanish,
> Yet that things go round and again go round
> Has rather a classical sound.

(CP 149–50)

125. *Wallace Stevens and the Actual World*, 154.

Chapter 5. "Both Sides of the Line"

1. For James's use of the female pronoun to describe pragmatism, see P 43–44. Contrast his use of the male pronoun to describe the philosophers, P 11–12. The contrast may also be implied by his statement that philosophy "bakes no bread" (P 10). James's association of the feminine with the power to collapse binary oppositions anticipates the work of Hélène Cixous.

2. Rorty has stated that "Pragmatism is the philosophical counterpart of literary modernism," because modernist writing is "the kind of literature which prides itself on its autonomy and novelty rather than its truthfulness to experience." He claims that the "moral of modernist literature" is realized in the hermeneutics of "strong textualism," that is, in a critical practice that aims not to decode texts but to construct playful, provocative readings that feel no need to be accountable to the facts of the text (*Consequences of Pragmatism*, 153). My reading of modernism maintains not only that it retains a concept of the necessity of "truthfulness to experience" but also that its "moral" is realized in an effort to "decode," however problematic the results.

3. For a brief discussion of James's Bergsonian argument for free will, see chapter 4, p. 187. For a detailed account of this aspect of his thought, see Myers, *William James,* 206–9, 390–95, and especially 364–7, where Myers discusses James's sense of the intimate relationship between freedom and effort—a sense compatible with Bergson's and Hulme's view that the way to freedom is through the effort to reverse the habits of the "superficial self."

4. It is necessary to acknowledge that my "pragmatist" reading of Hulme in no way puts to rest the question of whether he breaks with the "Romantic" tradition. Kermode's and Krieger's work on Hulme reflects a conception of English Romanticism that is now obsolete; more recent work, like that of David Simpson, has focused on Romanticism's use of qualified revelations and provisional, self-undermining utterances. See *Irony and Authority in Romantic Poetry* (Totowa, N.J.: Rowman & Littlefield, 1979). The question of the relationship between Romanticism and modernism generally awaits reconsideration, as we ask what pragmatist strategies are evident in both. For an account of the relationship between Jamesian pragmatism and Romanticism, see Kathleen Wheeler, *Romanticism, Pragmatism, and Deconstruction* (Cambridge University Press, 1993).

5. See Michael Roberts, *T. E. Hulme* (Manchester: Carcanet New Press, 1938; reprint. 1982, with Introduction by Anthony Quinton), 135.

6. See Csengeri, Introduction to Hulme, CW and Levenson, *A Genealogy of Modernism,* 89.

7. Levenson, *A Genealogy of Modernism,* 47.

8. The claims that Hulme left Bergson behind are unconvincing, because he continued to defend Bergson explicitly after writing what Levenson and Csengeri regard as the article marking his break with the philosopher ("Bergson Lecturing," *New Age* 10 [2 November 1911]: 15–16). For examples of this continuing defense, see the last installments of his "Notes on Bergson," *New Age* 10 (23 November 1911): 79–82; (30 November 1911): 110–12; (22 February 1912): 401–3; in CW 125–53. His continuing commitment to Bergson's ideas is also evident in his account of the different realms of knowledge corresponding in "A Notebook"; his distinction between the realms of psychology and physics demonstrates his continuing Bergsonian commitment to fighting intellectualism in psychology.

9. For Hulme's discussion of the emotional basis of conversion experiences, see "A Note on the Art of Political Conversion," CW 207–18. For evidence of his sense that it is acceptable to follow conversions based on feeling, see his account of how he embraces Bergson in order to escape from the "nightmare" of determinism. ("Notes on Bergson," CW 127.) A precedent for his observation about the pragmatic value of absolute ethical values is found in "Cinders":

> All is flux. The moralists, the capital letterists, attempt to find a framework outside the flux, a solid bank for the river, a pier rather than a raft. Truth is what helps a particular sect in the general flow. (CW 10).

10. Hulme, "A Notebook," CW 419; "War Notes," CW 391. Hulme published these commentaries on the First World War in seventeen installments in *New Age,* between on 11 November 1915 and concluding on 2 March 1916. "A Notebook" was published in the same journal in seven installments between 2 December 1915 and 10 February 1916. The "War Notes" are highly personal, emphasizing the importance of faith to a soldier at the front, whereas "A Notebook" contains no personal references, thus effacing the pragmatic rationale behind Hulme's decision to advertise an absolute ethics. A full appreciation of the pragmatic nature of Hulme's ethics requires both restoring the suppressed installment and reading seg-

ments of "A Notebook" with the "War Notes" with which they are interspersed. Csengeri's recently published *Collected Writings of T. E. Hulme,* which reproduces the complete text of "A Notebook" for the first time, will make such a reading possible.

11. Hulme, "A Notebook," CW 419.

12. A position Hulme also attributes to Pascal. See "A Notebook," CW 420.

13. Hulme, "A Notebook," CW 420.

14. Some readers might object to the reading of Hulme as pragmatist because he, in the same installment, explicitly rejects "pragmatism" ("A Notebook," CW 419). One explanation for his dismissal of a position he himself seems to espouse might be that he shared the common misperception that pragmatism was dogmatically skeptical—a position corroborated by the version of self-named "pragmatism" with which he was most familiar—Gaultier's. In other words Hulme may have made the same mistake as his interpreters and not realized how much of a Jamesian pragmatist he was. For Hulme's sense that pragmatism was a dogmatically skeptical position, see "A Notebook," CW 536, where he includes it in a list of positions that hold "that all the 'ideal' sciences, logic, mathematics, ethics, etc., could all have meaning and validity only in reference to the human mind." For another example of this view of pragmatism in Hulme's and James's period, a misreading that may inform Levenson's blindness to Hulme's Jamesian tendencies, see Levenson's discussion of Irving Babbitt, *A Genealogy of Modernism,* 81.

15. See Levenson, *A Genealogy of Modernism,* 94 ff. For other arguments that Hulme's art theory represented a departure from his Bergsonism, see Alun R. Jones, "T. E. Hulme, Wilhelm Worringer, and the Urge to Abstraction," *British Journal of Aesthetics* 1 (January 1960): 1–7; and Alan Robinson, *Poetry, Painting and Ideas 1885–1914* (London: Macmillan, 1985), 120.

16. For more evidence of Hulme's concern that abstract art retain references to the flux, see "Modern Art—III: The London Group," CW 294–98.

17. The notion that one "empathizes" with wavy lines is Theodor Lipps's, as discussed by Worringer. Lipps argued that the chief enjoyment to be gained in art was a kind of apperception or objectified self-enjoyment. The central argument of Worringer's *Abstraktion und Einfühlung* is that this is not the kind of enjoyment needed in a time, like the present, when viewers only wish to escape from a frightening world. There may be a connection between Hulme's continuing respect for "empathy" and his continuing adherence to Bergson, whose account of the "intuitive" experience of art is very close to Lipps'. For an account of the relationship between Bergsonian intuition and empathy, see Arthur Szathmary, *The Aesthetic Theory of Bergson* (Cambridge: Harvard University Press, 1937), 47–48.

18. Sosnowski, "Pound's Imagism and Emanuel Swedenborg," 34–36. For other claims that Pound endorses the theory of correspondences, see Hamilton, *Ezra Pound and the Symbolist Inheritance,* 156–57; Harold Bloom, *Figures of Capable Imagination* (New York: Seabury, 1976), 75; Ian F. A. Bell, *Critic as Scientist,* 129–35; and "Pound, Emerson and 'Subject-Rhyme,'" *Paideuma* 8 (1979): 237–42.

19. See Michael F. Harper, "The Revolution of the Word," *Ezra Pound and William Carlos Williams,* ed. Daniel Hoffman (Philadelphia: University of Pennsylvania Press, 1983), 88–106. In other words he contends that Pound believes in a "natural language" (90).

20. Pound, "I Gather the Limbs of Osiris," SP 41.

21. See Kathryne V. Lindberg, *Reading Pound Reading: Modernism after Nietzsche* (Oxford: Oxford University Press, 1988), 210. See Easthope's comment that The Cantos "are grounded in a decentered immanence," that in them "the

possibility of a metaphysical anchoring point [is] not envisaged at all." "Eliot, Pound, and the Subject of Postmodernism," *After the Future: Postmodern Times and Places,* ed. Gary Shapiro (Albany: SUNY Press, 1990), 58.

22. Joseph Riddel, "Pound and the Decentered Image," *Georgia Review* 29 (1975): 565, 588. See Jacques Derrida, *Of Grammatology,* trans. Gayatri Chakravorty Spivak (Baltimore: Johns Hopkins University Press, 1976), 92; and Gilles Deleuze, *Proust and Signs* (New York: George Braziller, 1972), 156–57. For the influence of Deleuze and Derrida on Riddel's conception of *The Cantos,* see Riddel, "Pound and the Decentered Image," 583; and "'Neo-Nietzschean Clatter,'" *Ezra Pound: Tactics for Reading,* ed. Ian F. A. Bell (London: Vision, 1982), 187–220, 191.

23. Pound published a translation of Gourmont's *Physique de l'Amour* in 1922 under the title *The Natural Philosophy of Love* and added a translator's "Postscript." The comment in the "Postscript" to which Riddel attaches the greatest importance is his remark that "it is more than likely" that "the brain itself is, in origin and development, only a sort of clot of genital fluid held in suspense or reserve.'" *Natural Philosophy of Love,* 295. See Riddel, "Pound and the Decentered Image," 566–67 and "'Neo-Nietzschean Clatter,'" 201.

24. Riddel, "'Neo-Nietzschean Clatter,'" 204; 200; 196.

25. For an example of an argument directed against the common practice of distinguishing Pound's and Yeats's attitudes toward mysticism and the occult, see McDowell and Materer, "Gyre and Vortex: W. B. Yeats and Ezra Pound," 344–45. For an objection to the "postmodern" appropriation of Pound, see Surette, *The Birth of Modernism,* 6.

26. Pound, "Axiomata," SP 50; and "Vorticism," GB 84; my italics.

27. Longenbach, for example, takes Pound's endorsement of "symbolism in the profounder sense" as an endorsement of a dogmatic, transcendentalist symbolism, ignoring Pound's warnings that the symbolism he is prepared to accept is "not necessarily" a belief in fixed correspondences but a belief "in that direction." See *Stone Cottage,* 78ff. Sosnowski supports his argument that Pound had a Swedenborgian faith in "correspondences" and in a symbolic language reflecting them, by referring to the following passage, from a letter Pound wrote to William Carlos Williams, 24 October 1907 (in the Beinecke Library, Yale University):

> Swedenborg has called a certain thing "the angelic language" by the way I will send you certain things out of Swedenborg that will save me much preface. It will take a week or two for me to get at them. This "angelic language" I choose to interpret into "artistic Utterance."

See Sosnowski, "Pound's Imagism and Emanuel Swedenborg," 131, and compare Surette, *The Birth of Modernism,* 130. I would argue that Pound's decision to "interpret" Swedenborg's transcendentalist claim into the phrase "artistic Utterance" is simply an attempt, compatible with many others in his work, to redescribe certain linguistic effects in terms purged of metaphysics. It is thus an effort to suspend judgment about the significance of these effects—not an expression of unequivocal support for a monistic ontology.

28. Pound, "The Wisdom of Poetry," SP 333; and *The Cantos,* 797.

29. Easthope, "Eliot, Pound, and the Subject of Postmodernism," 58. For discussions of Pound's efforts to foreground the signifier, see Hugh Kenner, *The Pound Era* (London: Faber, 1975), 187; Marjorie Perloff, *The Poetics of Indeterminacy* (Princeton: Princeton University Press, 1981), 195ff.; *Poetic License,* (Evanston:

Northwestern University Press, 1990), 137; and Riddel, "'Neo-Nietzschean Clatter,'" 196.

30. See *The Cantos* 449 and 430. For how the assertion "the drama is wholly subjective" is undermined by its context, see Gelpi, *A Coherent Splendour*, 237.

31. Riddel, "'Neo-Nietzschean Clatter,'" 204. Easthope is also uncomfortable with his categorical claim that in *The Cantos*, "the possibility of a metaphysical anchoring point [is] not envisaged at all." He also, inconsistently but more accurately, comments that "the poem does not assume meaning as an absolute point of origin; nor, for that matter does it admit, through negation, the positive absence of such a center" ("Eliot, Pound, and the Subject of Postmodernism," 58; my italics).

32. Perloff, *The Poetics of Indeterminacy*, 182. This is a self-correction in the sense that Perloff's expressed purpose in *The Poetics of Indeterminacy* is to call attention to the tradition of modernist writing in which the focus shifts "from signification to the play of signifiers" (23), a tradition in which she claims Pound is a central figure.

33. Marjorie Levinson has called for stylistic innovations in new historicist writing that mirror Pound's, in "Posthumous Critique," a paper delivered at Queen's University, March 1993. Sandra Bermann has made a similar point in "Juxtaposing Particulars: From Cultural Myth to Cultural Critique," a paper delivered at the University of Tulsa, March 1993.

34. See Schaum, *Wallace Stevens and the Critical Schools*, 36–37.

35. Conrad Aiken, "The Ivory Tower I," *New Republic* 10 (May 1919): 60; Louis Untermeyer, "The Ivory Tower II," *New Republic* 19 (10 May 1919): 61; my italics. Aiken celebrated the fact that Stevens felt free to produce "art for art's sake" ("The Ivory Tower I," 59).

36. Exceptions to the general practice of reading Stevens as an ontological pessimist are found in the 1940s in the work of Lloyd Frankenberg and Randall Jarrell, who argue both for his humanism and his faith in an ordered world. See Schaum, *Wallace Stevens and the Critical Schools*, 87, 89. The best known argument for his epistemological optimism is the one offered by Roy Harvey Pearce ("Toward Decreation: Stevens and the 'Theory of Poetry,'" *Wallace Stevens: A Celebration*, ed. Doggett and Buttell, 286–307) and Hines (*The Later Poetry of Wallace Stevens*) who call attention to his faith, particularly in the late poetry, in the essences to be attained through "decreation"—the equivalent of the second stage of phenomenological method, "eidetic" reduction.

37. Anon. review, *Bookman* (1923), cited by Schaum, *Wallace Stevens and the Critical Schools*, 44; Paul Rosenfeld, *Men Seen: Twenty-four Modern Authors* (New York: Dial Press, 1925), 157.

38. See J. Hillis Miller, "Wallace Stevens's 'Poetry of Being'" and "Theoretical and Atheoretical in Stevens," *Wallace Stevens: A Celebration*, 274–85. The essays were published in 1960 and 1980, respectively.

39. Miller, "Wallace Stevens's 'Poetry of Being,'" 157. For comparable claims, see Miller, "Theoretical and Atheoretical in Stevens," 277; and Paul Bové's readings of "The Snow Man" and "The Rock," *Destructive Poetics*, 191–93 and 209; Lentricchia, *After the New Criticism* (Chicago: University of Chicago Press, 1980), 32–33, 53–55. For an example of the claim that his world is godless, see Miller, "Wallace Stevens's 'Poetry of Being,'" 145.

40. Lentricchia, *After the New Criticism*, 163, 171, 181.

41. Ibid., 171.

42. I rely here on Stevens's color symbolism, which holds green ("vert") to

be the colour of reality; to be "verdured," therefore, is to be "made green" or "made real."

43. Lentricchia, *After the New Criticism*, 53, 33. Lentricchia cites Jean-Paul Sartre, *The Psychology of Imagination* (Secaucus, N.J.: Citadel Press, n.d.), 8.

44. See also Stevens's depiction of the ring of men worshipping the sun "as a god might be" (CP 70), a description more open to the possibility that a divinity exists than has generally been acknowledged. Also consider the hypothetical tone of Stevens's references to God, CP 187, 327. One factor contributing to the view that Stevens firmly rejected God is the critics' habit of ignoring the qualifiers modifying his atheistic assertions. Miller, for example, ignores the words and phrases I italicize in the following passage to use it as evidence of Stevens's dogmatic rejection of a divinity:

> To see the gods dispelled in mid-air and dissolve like clouds is one of the great human experiences. It is not as if they had gone over the horizon to disappear for a time; nor as if they had been overcome by other gods of greater power and profounder knowledge. It is simply that they came to nothing. Since we have always shared all things with them and have always had a part of their strength and, certainly, all of their knowledge, we shared likewise this experience of annihilation. It was their annihilation, not ours, and yet it left us feeling that in a measure, we, too, had been annihilated. It left us feeling dispossessed and alone in a solitude, like children without parents, in a home that seemed deserted, in which the amical rooms and halls had taken on a look of hardness and emptiness. What was most extraordinary is that they left no mementoes behind, no thrones, no mystic rings, no texts either of the soil or of the soul. It was as if they had never inhabited the earth. There was no crying out for their return. (OP 260)

See Miller, "Wallace Stevens's 'Poetry of Being,'" 145. Other statements frequently cited as evidence of Stevens's atheism are similarly qualified when viewed in context. Consider, for example, the often ignored context for the statement "God and the imagination are one": "We say God and the imagination are one" (CP 524; my italics). Or note how the context modifies the statement "The thinking of god is smoky dew":

> For a moment final, in the way
> The thinking of art seems final when
>
> The thinking of god is smoky dew.
>
> (CP 168)

45. See, for example, the carefully balanced statements about order and disorder in "Connoisseur of Chaos" (CP 215–16) and "Three Academic Pieces" (NA 79).

46. See Peterson, *Wallace Stevens and the Idealist Tradition.*

47. See Rorty, *Philosophy and the Mirror of Nature* (Princeton: Princeton University Press, 1979); *Consequences of Pragmatism* (1982); and *Contingency, irony, and solidarity* (1989); and Stanley Fish, *Doing What Comes Naturally* (Durham, N.C.: Duke University Press, 1989). For Rorty's support for Fish, see *Contingency, Irony, and Solidarity*, 59. For Fish's support for Rorty, see *Doing What Comes Naturally*, 28, 143, 339, 501–2.

48. See Cornel West, "Theory, Pragmatisms and Politics," *Consequences of Theory*, ed. Jonathan Arac and Barbara Johnson (Baltimore: Johns Hopkins University Press, 1991), 24.

49. Rorty, *Contingency, irony, and solidarity*, 61, 45.

50. Ibid., 20. He "gives up on the idea that there can be reasons for using

languages as well as reasons within languages for believing statements" (48). This renunciation forms part of Rorty's rejection of logical positivism. See Cornel West, *The American Evasion of Philosophy* (Madison: University of Wisconsin Press, 1989), 183.

51. Rorty, *Contingency, irony, and solidarity*, 167. Rorty derives his theory of metaphor from Donald Davidson. See 18–19. On 41 he describes this move as the "de-divinization" of poetry and praises the version of it he finds in the work of Harold Bloom.

52. See especially Rorty, *Contingency, irony, and solidarity*, 91.

53. Ibid., xv.

54. See, for example, West, *The American Evasion of Philosophy*; Seigfried, *William James's Radical Reconstruction of Philosophy*; Robert Westbrook, *John Dewey and American Democracy* (Ithaca: Cornell University Press, 1991); Thomas McCarthy, "Private Irony and Public Decency: Richard Rorty's New Pragmatism," *Critical Inquiry* 16 (Winter 1990): 355–70; Richard J. Bernstein, *Philosophical Profiles* (Philadelphia: University of Pennsylvania Press, 1986); George F. Cotkin, *William James: Public Philosopher*.

55. See West, *The American Evasion of Philosophy*, 233; and Seigfried, *William James's Radical Reconstruction of Philosophy*, 4, 304. Seigfried cites Rorty's *Consequences of Pragmatism*, 174.

56. The most prominent example of a critical work that suffers for aligning Stevens with Rorty and that in doing so conflates Rorty and James, James and Nietzsche is Thomas C. Grey's *The Wallace Stevens Case* (Cambridge, Mass.: Harvard University Press, 1991). For the most part, Grey's Stevens is an atheist, a fictionalist, and a poet committed to leaving public issues alone. For claims about Stevens's atheism, see 31, and about his Rortyan eschewal of public responsibilities, 32–34. For comments on Stevens's fictionalism and examples of Grey's equation of James and Nietzsche, fiction and hypothesis, see 76 and 84. David M. Laguardia also relies on Rorty for his definition of pragmatism. See *Advance on Chaos: The Sanctifying Imagination of Wallace Stevens* (Hanover: University Press of New England, 1983), x–xi.

Ihab Hassan has also discussed the question of the similarity between Stevens and James and Stevens and Rorty. Although he correctly distinguishes between James and Rorty on the matter of religious belief and acknowledges an element of religious hope evident in Stevens that makes a complete equation of Stevens and Rorty inadvisable, he nonetheless sees Stevens as a champion of "aesthetic fictions," rather than tough, Jamesian truths, accountable to "'Real possibilities, real indeterminations, real beginnings, real ends, real evil, real crises, catastrophes, and escapes'" "Imagination and Belief: Wallace Stevens and William James in Our Clime," *Wallace Stevens Journal* 10 (1986): 6–7; Hassan quotes James's *The Will to Believe*. This is, in effect, to equate Stevens with Rorty's private ironist.

An article that refers to Rorty's pragmatism, but that rightly distinguishes between Nietzsche and James and supports the view that Stevens's writing reflects a Jamesian optimism, is Lyall Bush's "'Satisfactions of Belief': Stevens's Poetry in a Pragmatic World," *Wallace Stevens Journal* 14 (Spring 1990): 13–20. Bush's mistake is in assimilating Rorty to James—that is, in making Rorty more optimistic about the possibilities of pragmatic truth-making than he in fact is.

57. Rorty, *Contingency, irony, and solidarity*, 90. Although Rorty habitually uses the feminine pronoun to describe the ironist, I substitute the masculine to foreground the dangers of ironism when the ironist occupies a dominant position with respect to the described.

58. Ibid., 93. Compare Shelley's hope for literature's power to develop an empathetic imagination in "A Defense of Poetry":

> The great secret of morals is love, or a going out of our own nature and an identification of ourselves with the beautiful which exists in thought, action, or person, not our own. A man, to be greatly good, must imagine intensely and comprehensively; he must put himself in the place of another and of many others; the pains and pleasures of his species must become his own. The great instrument of moral good is the imagination; and poetry administers to the effect by acting upon the cause.

Shelley's Prose, ed. David Lee Clark (London: Fourth Estate, 1988), 282–83.

59. Rorty, *Contingency, irony, and solidarity*, 158.

60. Another, related argument against Rorty's program is of course that the division between public and private life is never a clear one. This is a concern expressed by feminist theorists, especially. See, for example, Nancy Fraser, "Solidarity or Singularity? Richard Rorty Between Romanticism and Technocracy," *Consequences of Theory*, eds. Jonathan Arac and Barbara Johnson (Baltimore: Johns Hopkins University Press, 1991), 48–50.

61. Rorty, *Contingency, irony, and solidarity*, 53.

62. See Rorty, *Contingency, irony, and solidarity*, 90.

63. William James, "The Philippines Again," *Essays, Comments and Reviews*, 161, 165. For critiques of the ethnocentrism in Rorty's arguments, see West, *The American Evasion of Philosophy*, 205–7, and Clifford Geertz, "The Uses of Diversity," *Michigan Quarterly Review* 25 (1986): 105–23. See also Rorty's response to Geertz's criticisms and his defense of the position of "anti-anti-ethnocentrism" in "On ethnocentrism: A Reply to Clifford Geertz," *Objectivity, Relativism, and Truth* (Cambridge: Cambridge University Press, 1991), 203.

64. See also James Longenbach, *Wallace Stevens: The Plain Sense of Things* (Oxford: Oxford University Press, 1991); Paul Bauer, "The Politics of Reticence: Wallace Stevens in the Cold War Era," *Twentieth Century Literature* 39 (Spring 1993): 1–31; and the essays by Longenbach, Filreis, Harvey Teres, Jacqueline Vaught Brogan, Melita Schaum, and Paul Bauer in *The Wallace Stevens Journal* 13 (Fall 1989)—a special issue on "Stevens and Politics."

65. Bromwich, "Stevens and the Idea of the Hero," 66, 13.

66. West, *The American Evasion of Philosophy*, 209.

67. Gelpi, *A Coherent Splendour*, 79; Perloff, *The Dance of the Intellect* (Cambridge: Cambridge University Press, 1985), 2.

68. See Perloff's compilation of remarks by Denis Donoghue, *The Dance of the Intellect*, 18–19. For an example of the claim that Pound refrains from commentary while Stevens does not, note Perloff's comment that "Stevens's rage for order, his need to make analogies . . . is at odds with Pound's deployment of metonymic linkages, his creation of Cubist surfaces or aerial maps where images jostle one another" (17).

69. For examples of this practice in Stevens criticism, see note 56, above. For examples in Eliot criticism, see Donald J. Childs, "Risking Enchantment: The Middle Way between Mysticism and Pragmatism in Four Quartets," *Words in Time: New Essays on Eliot's Four Quartets*, ed. Edward Lobb (London: Athlone, 1993), 107–30; and Manju Jain, *T. S. Eliot and American Philosophy* (Cambridge: Cambridge University Press, 1992). Lisa Ruddick has studied the influence of Jamesian pragmatism on Gertrude Stein, in both "Fluid Symbols in American Modernism" and *Reading Stein Reading* (Ithaca: Cornell University Press, 1991). Although she does not name Rorty explicitly, her interpretation of James is Rortian; like Childs

she regards a sympathy for mysticism—such as we find in Stein's heroine Melanctha—as evidence of a hostility to pragmatism. A more accurate reading of James, which explicitly acknowledges his tolerance for tender-mindedness, is found in W. David Shaw's study of the "poetics of pragmatism" in Frost. Although Poirier openly repudiates Rorty's view of pragmatism (primarily because it ignores its roots in Emerson), he inadvertently reinforces it by ignoring its continuing commitment to verification.

Patricia Waugh equates James (as well as Stevens) with Nietzsche and Rorty to argue for a continuity between modernism and postmodernism. See *Practising Postmodernism Reading Modernism* (London: Edward Arnold, 1992), passim, and especially 11, 16, 20, 35. Discriminating James from these more profoundly skeptical thinkers and recognizing his affinity with modernist writers might therefore provide a means of upholding the modernism/postmodernism distinction.

For a useful study of the pragmatist elements in Henry James's narrative style—and particularly of his propensity for using hypothetical structures—see Ross Posnock, *The Trial of Curiosity: Henry James, William James, and the Challenge of Modernity* (New York: Oxford University Press, 1991).

Bibliography

Adams, Richard P. "'The Comedian as the Letter C': A Somewhat Literal Reading.'" *Tulane Studies in English* 18 (1970): 95–114.

Aiken, Conrad. "The Ivory Tower I." *New Republic* 10 (May 1919): 58–61.

Arensberg, Mary. "Wallace Stevens' Interior Paramour." *Wallace Stevens Journal* 3 (1979): 3–7.

———. "'A Curable Separation': Stevens and the Mythology of Gender," *Wallace Stevens and the Feminine,* ed. Melita Schaum (Tuscaloosa: University of Alabama Press, 1993): 23–45.

Aveling, F. "Psychology with and Without a Soul." *Quest* 6 (1915–16): 430–52.

Bachelard, Gaston. *The Poetics of Space.* Translated by Maria Jolas. Boston, Mass.: Beacon, 1969.

Baron, Albert H. N. Preface to Ribot, *Essay on the Creative Imagination.* Translated by Albert H. N. Baron. London: Kegan Paul, Trench, Trübner, 1906.

Bates, Milton J. "Stevens' Books at the Huntington: An Annotated Checklist." *Wallace Stevens Journal* 2 (1978): 45–61.

———. *Wallace Stevens: A Mythology of Self.* Berkeley and Los Angeles: University of California Press, 1985.

Baudelaire, Charles. *Oeuvres complètes.* 2 vols. Edited by Charles Pichois. Paris: Gallimard, 1961.

Baumann, Walter. "Ezra Pound and Magic: Old World Tricks in a New World Poem." *Paideuma* 10 (1981): 209–24.

Bayley, John. *The Romantic Survival: A Study in Poetic Evolution.* London: Constable, 1957.

Beauvoir, Simone. *The Second Sex.* Translated by H. M. Parshley. Harmondsworth, England: Penguin, 1972.

Beckett, Lucy. *Wallace Stevens.* Cambridge: Cambridge University Press, 1974.

Beehler, Michael. "Meteoric Poetry: Wallace Stevens' 'Description Without Place.'" *Criticism* 29 (1977): 241–59.

Bell, Ian F.A. "Pound, Emerson, and Subject-Rhyme." *Paideuma* 8 (1979): 237–42.

———. *Critic as Scientist: The Modernist Poetics of Ezra Pound.* London: Methuen, 1981.

Benamou, Michel. *Wallace Stevens and the Symbolist Imagination.* Princeton: Princeton University Press, 1972.

Bergson, Henri. *Essai sur les données immédiates de la conscience.* Paris: Félix Alcan, 1908.

———. *L'Évolution créatrice.* Paris: Félix Alcan, 1908.

———. *Creative Evolution.* Translated by Arthur Mitchell. London: Macmillan, 1911.

———. *La Pensée et le mouvant*. Paris: Presses Universitaires de France, 1938.

———. "L'Effort intellectuel." In *Oeuvres*. Edited by Andre Robinet and Henri Gouhier, 930–59. Paris: Presses Universitaires de France, 1963.

———. *Le Rire*. Paris: Presses Universitaires de France, 1964.

———. *The Creative Mind*, trans. Mabelle L. Andison. Westport, Conn.: Greenwood, 1968.

Bernard, Henry M. "Heaven, Hell, and the Present Environment." *Quest* 3 (1912): 648–64.

Bevis, William W. *Mind of Winter: Wallace Stevens, Meditation, and Literature*. Pittsburgh, Penn.: University of Pittsburgh Press, 1988.

Bloom, Harold. "Notes Toward a Supreme Fiction: A Commentary." In *Wallace Stevens: A Collection of Critical Essays*. Twentieth Century Views. Edited by Marie Borroff, 76–95. Englewood Cliffs, N.J.: Prentice-Hall, 1963.

———. *Figures of Capable Imagination*. New York: Seabury, 1976.

———. *Wallace Stevens: The Poems of Our Climate*. Ithaca: Cornell University Press, 1977.

Boring, Edwin G. *A History of Experimental Psychology*. New York: Meredith, 1957.

Boutroux, Emile. "The Subliminal Self Philosophically Considered." *The Quest* 6 (1914–15): 1–22.

———. "Certitude and Truth." *Quest* 7 (1916): 585–613.

Bové, Paul. *Destructive Poetics*. New York: Columbia University Press, 1980.

Bradley, F. H. "On the Ambiguity of Pragmatism." *Mind* 17 (1908): 226–37.

Brogan, Jacqueline Vaught. "'Sister of the Minotaur': Sexism and Stevens." In *Wallace Stevens and the Feminine*. Edited by Melita Schaum, 3–22. Tuscaloosa: University of Alabama Press, 1993.

Brogan, Louise. *Stevens and Simile*. Princeton: Princeton University Press, 1986.

Bromwich, David. "Stevens and the Idea of the Hero." *Raritan* 7 (1987): 1–27.

Brown, William. "The Logic of the Emotions." *Quest* 3 (1912): 601–15.

Bruneau, Charles. *La Langue et le style de l'école parnassienne*. Paris: Tournier et Constans, 1946.

Carlyle, Thomas. *Sartor Resartus*. London: Chapman and Hall, 1885.

Childs, Donald J. "Risking Enchantment: The Middle Way Between Mysticism and Pragmatism in Four Quartets." *Words in Time: New Essays on Eliot's Four Quartets*. Edited by Edward Lobb, 107–30. London: Athlone, 1993.

Chipp, Herschel B., ed. *Theories of Modern Art*. Berkeley: University of California Press, 1968.

Cixous, Hélène. "The Laugh of the Medusa." Translated by Keith Cohen and Paula Cohen. *Signs* 1 (Summer 1976): 875–93.

Clark, Suzanne. *Sentimental Modernism*. Bloomington: Indiana University Press, 1991.

Cobb, W. F. "Culture and the Church." *Quest* 1 (1909–10): 505–23.

———. "The Nature of Culture." *The Quest* 1 (1909–10): 201–15.

Cook, Eleanor. *Poetry, Word-Play, and Word-War in Wallace Stevens*. Princeton: Princeton University Press, 1988.

Cork, Richard. *Vorticism and Abstract Art in the First Machine Age*. 2 vols. Berkeley: University of California Press, 1969.

Csengeri, Karen, "T. E. Hulme's Borrowings from the French." *Comparative Literature* 34 (Winter 1982): 16–27.

Dasenbrock, Reed Way. *The Literary Vorticism of Ezra Pound and Wyndham Lewis.* Baltimore: Johns Hopkins University Press, 1985.

Deleuze, Gilles. *Proust and Signs.* New York: George Braziller, 1972.

Derrida, Jacques. *Of Grammatology.* Translated by Gayatri Chakravorty Spivak. Baltimore: The Johns Hopkins University Press, 1976.

———. *Spurs: Nietzsche's Styles.* Translated by Barbara Harlow. Chicago: University of Chicago Press, 1978.

———. *Writing and Difference.* Translated by Alan Bass. Chicago: University of Chicago Press, 1978.

———. *Positions.* Translated by Alan Bass. Chicago: University of Chicago Press, 1981.

DeShazer, Mary K. *Inspiring Women.* New York: Pergamon, 1986.

Doggett, Frank. *Stevens' Poetry of Thought.* Baltimore, Md.: Johns Hopkins University Press, 1966.

———. and Robert Buttell. *Wallace Stevens: A Celebration.* Princeton: Princeton University Press, 1980.

Donoghue, Denis. *Connoisseurs of Chaos.* New York: Columbia University Press, 1965.

Easthope, Antony. "Eliot, Pound, and the Subject of Postmodernism." In *After the Future: Postmodern Times and Places.* Edited by Gary Shapiro. Albany, N.Y.: SUNY Press, 1990.

Edie, James M. *William James and Phenomenology.* Bloomington: Indiana University Press, 1987.

Eliade, Mircea. *Patterns in Comparative Religion.* London: Sheed and Ward, 1958.

Elliott, Angela. "The Word Comprehensive: Gnostic Light in the Cantos." *Paideuma* 18 (1989): 7–57.

Ellis, Wilmot E. *Bovarysm: The Art Philosophy of Jules de Gaultier.* Seattle: University of Washington Press, 1928.

Emerson, Dorothy. "Wallace Stevens' Sky That Thinks." *Wallace Stevens Journal* 9 (1985): 71–84.

Emerson, Ralph Waldo. *Essays and Lectures.* New York: Library of America, 1983.

Fawcett, Edward Douglas. "Bergson's 'Time and Free Will.'" *Quest* 2 (1910–11): 492–506.

Fenollosa, Ernest. *The Chinese Written Character as a Medium for Poetry.* Edited by Ezra Pound. San Francisco, Calif.: City Lights, 1936.

Filreis, Alan. "Wallace Stevens and the Strength of the Harvard Reaction." *New England Quarterly* 58 (1985): 27–45.

———. *Wallace Stevens and the Actual World.* Princeton: Princeton University Press, 1991.

———. *Modernism from Right to Left.* Cambridge: Cambridge University Press, 1994.

Fiser, E. *Le Symbole littéraire.* Paris: Librairie Jose Corti, 1941.

Fish, Stanley. *Doing What Comes Naturally.* Durham, N.C.: Duke University Press, 1989.

Flint, F. S. "Contemporary French Poetry." *Poetry Review* 1 (August 1912): 356.
———. "History of Imagisme." *Egoist* 2 (1 May 1915): 70–71.
Foucault, Michel. *The History of Sexuality.* Volume 1. Translated by Robert Hurley. New York: Vintage, 1980.
Fowler, H. W. *A Dictionary of Modern English Usage.* Oxford: Oxford University Press, 1926.
Frankenberry, Nancy. *Religion and Radical Empiricism.* Albany, N.Y.: SUNY Press, 1987.
Fraser, Nancy. "Solidarity or Singularity?: Richard Rorty Between Romanticism and Technocracy." In *Consequences of Theory.* Edited by Jonathan Arac and Barbara Johnson, 39–62. Baltimore: Johns Hopkins University Press, 1991.
Fry, Edward F., ed. *Cubism.* London: Thames and Hudson, 1966.
Frye, Northrop. *Anatomy of Criticism: Four Essays.* Princeton: Princeton University Press, 1957.
Frost, Robert. *The Poetry of Robert Frost.* Edited by Edward Connery Lathem. London: Jonathan Cape, 1971.
Gagnon, Madeleine. "Body I." Translated by Isabelle de Courtivron. In *New French Feminisms.* Edited by Elaine Marks and Isabelle de Courtivron, 179–80. Boston: University of Massachusetts Press, 1980: 179–80.
Gaultier, Jules de. *Bovarysm.* Trans. Gerald M. Spring. N.Y.: Philosophical Library, 1970.
———. "De la Nature des vérités." *Mercure de France* 39 (1901): 561–95.
———. "Pragmatisme." *Mercure de France* 77 (1909): 408–28.
———. *Le Bovarysme.* Paris: Mercure de France, 1922.
Gelpi, Albert. *A Coherent Splendour: The American Poetic Renaissance, 1910–1950.* Cambridge: Cambridge University Press, 1987.
Gibson, Robert. *Modern French Poets on Poetry.* Cambridge: Cambridge University Press, 1961.
Gibson, W. R. Boyce. "The Intuitionism of Henri Bergson." *Quest* 2 (1910–11): 201–28.
———. "The Soul in Plato and Bergson." *Quest* 6 (1914–15): 49–68.
Gilbert, Sandra, and Susan Gubar. *The Madwoman in the Attic.* New Haven, Conn.: Yale University Press, 1979.
———. "The Man on the Dump Versus the United Dames of America; or, What Does Frank Lentricchia Want?" *Critical Inquiry* 14 (Winter 1988): 386–407.
Gourmont, Remy de. *Le Problème du style.* Paris: Société du Mercure de France, 1907.
———. *La Culture des idées.* Paris: Mercure de France, 1926.
———. *The Natural Philosophy of Love.* Translated by Ezra Pound. New York: Rarity Press, 1931.
Graves, Robert. *The White Goddess.* London: Faber and Faber, 1961.
Graybeal, Jean. *Language and 'the Feminine' in Nietzsche and Heidegger.* Bloomington: Indiana University Press, 1990.
Grey, Thomas C. *The Wallace Stevens Case.* Cambridge: Harvard University Press, 1991.
Hamilton, Scott. *Ezra Pound and the Symbolist Inheritance.* Princeton: Princeton University Press, 1992.

Harmer, J. B. *Victory in Limbo: Imagism 1908–1917*. London: Secker & Warburg, 1975.

Harper, Michael F. "The Revolution of the Word." *Ezra Pound and William Carlos Williams*. Edited by Daniel Hoffman, 79–106. Philadelphia: University of Pennsylvania Press, 1983.

Hart, Bernard. "The Conception of the Subconscious." In *Subconscious Phenomena*. Edited by Morton Prince. London: Rebman, 1910.

Hartman, Geoffrey. *The Fate of Reading and Other Essays*. Chicago: University of Chicago Press, 1975.

Hassan, Ihab. "Imagination and Belief: Wallace Stevens and William James in Our Clime." *Wallace Stevens Journal* 10 (1986): 3–8.

Heddendorf, David. "Filling Out the What: William James, Josiah Royce and Metaphor." *American Transcendental Quarterly* 2 (1988): 125–38.

Heidegger, Martin. *Being and Time*. Translated by John Macquarrie and Edward Robinson. Oxford: Basil Blackwell, 1962.

———. *Poetry, Language, Thought*. Translated by Albert Hofstadter. New York: Harper & Row, 1971.

———. *Basic Writings*. Edited by David Farrell Krell. New York: Harper and Row, 1977.

Hill, J. Arthur. "The Inspiration of Genius." *Quest* 5 (1914): 529–40.

Hines, Thomas J. *The Later Poetry of Wallace Stevens: Phenomenological Parallels with Husserl and Heidegger*. Lewisburg, PA: Bucknell University Press, 1976.

Hough, Graham. *Image and Experience*. London: Duckworth, 1960.

Hulme, T. E. *Speculations: Essays on Humanism and the Philosophy of Art*. Edited by Herbert Read. London: Routledge and Kegan Paul, 1936.

———. *The Collected Writings of T. E. Hulme*. Edited by Karen Csengeri. Oxford: Oxford University Press, 1994.

Husserl, Edmund. *Ideas: General Introduction to Pure Phenomenology*. Translated by W. R. Boyce Gibson. New York: Collier-Macmillan, 1962.

—-. *Phenomenology and the Crisis of Philosophy*. Translated by Quentin Lauer. New York: Harper and Row, 1965.

Hyslop, James H. "The Subconscious." *Quest* 5 (1914): 232–46.

Jain, Manju. *T. S. Eliot and American Philosophy*. Cambridge: Cambridge University Press, 1992.

James, William. *The Letters of William James*. 2 vols. Edited by Henry James. London: Longman's, Green, 1920.

———. *The Principles of Psychology*. 2 vols. 1890. Reprint, New York: Dover, 1950.

———. *Essays in Radical Empiricism and A Pluralistic Universe*. Edited by Ralph Barton Perry. New York: E. P. Dutton, 1971.

———. *Pragmatism*. Edited by Frederick H. Burkhardt, Fredson Bowers, and Ignas K. Skrupskelsis. Cambridge: Harvard University Press, 1975.

———. *The Will to Believe*. Edited by Frederick H. Burkhardt, Fredson Bowers, and Ignas K. Skrupskelsis. Cambridge: Harvard University Press, 1979.

———. *The Meaning of Truth: A Sequel to Pragmatism*. Edited by Frederick H. Burkhardt, Fredson Bowers, and Ignas K. Skrupskelsis. Cambridge: Harvard University Press, 1979.

———. *The Varieties of Religious Experience*. Edited by Martin E. Marty. Harmondsworth, England: Penguin, 1982.

———. *Essays in Psychology*. Edited by Frederick H. Burkhardt, Fredson Bowers, and Ignas K. Skrupskelsis. Cambridge: Harvard University Press, 1983.

———. *Psychology: The Briefer Course*. Edited Frederick H. Burkhardt, Fredson Bowers, and Ignas K. Skrupskelsis. Cambridge: Harvard University Press, 1984.

———. *William James on Exceptional Mental States: The 1896 Lowell Lectures*. Edited Eugene Taylor. Amherst: University of Massachusetts Press, 1984.

———. *Essays in Psychical Research*. Edited by Frederick H. Burkhardt, Fredson Bowers, and Ignas K. Skrupskelsis. Cambridge: Harvard University Press, 1986.

———. *Essays, Comments and Reviews*. Edited by Frederick H. Burkhardt, Fredson Bowers, and Ignas K. Skrupskelsis. Cambridge: Cambridge, Mass.: Harvard University Press, 1987.

———. *Writings 1902–1910*. Edited by Bruce Kuklick. New York, Library of America, 1987.

———. *Writings 1878–1899*. Edited by Gerald E. Myers. New York: Library of America, 1992.

Jameson, Fredric. "Wallace Stevens." *New Orleans Review* II (Spring 1984): 10–19.

———. "Periodizing the 60s." *The Ideologies of Theory: Essays 1971–1986*. Edited by Neil Larsen, 178–208. Vol. 2. Minneapolis: University of Minnesota Press, 1988.

Jeffares, A. Norman. *A New Commentary on the Poems of W. B. Yeats*. London: Macmillan, 1984.

Joel, Karl. "The Romanticism of the First Thinkers of Hellas." *Quest* 3 (1912): 634–47.

Jones, Alun R. *The Life and Opinions of T. E. Hulme*. London: Victor Gollancz, 1960.

———. "T. E. Hulme, Wilhelm Worringer, and the Urge to Abstraction." *British Journal of Aesthetics* 1 (January 1960): 1–7.

Kandinsky, Wassily. *Concerning the Spiritual in Art*. Translated by M. T. H. Sadler. New York: Dover, 1973.

Kant, Immanuel. *Critique of Judgment*. Translated by J. H. Bernard. New York: Hafner, 1951.

Kayman, Martin A. *The Modernism of Ezra Pound: The Science of Poetry*. London: MacMillan, 1986.

Kenner, Hugh. *The Pound Era*. London: Faber, 1975.

Kermode, Frank. *Romantic Image*. London: Routledge and Kegan Paul, 1957.

———. *The Sense of an Ending*. Oxford: Oxford University Press, 1966.

———. "Dwelling Poetically in Connecticut." *Wallace Stevens: A Celebration*. Edited by Frank Doggett and Robert Buttel, 256–73. Princeton: Princeton University Press, 1980.

Krieger, Murray. *The New Apologists for Poetry*. Minneapolis: University of Minnesota Press, 1956.

Kristeva, Julia. "Oscillation Between Power and Denial." Translated by Marilyn August. In *New French Feminisms*. Edited by Elaine Marks and Isabelle de Courtivron, 165–67. Boston: University of Massachusetts Press, 1980.

Kuklick, Bruce. *The Rise of American Philosophy.* New Haven, Conn.: Yale University Press, 1977.

Laforgue, Jules. "Impressionism: The Eye and the Poet." Translated by Linda Nochlin. In *Impressionism and Post-Impressionism 1874–1904.* Englewood Cliffs, N.J.: Prentice-Hall, 1966.

LaGuardia, David M. *Advance on Chaos: The Sanctifying Imagination of Wallace Stevens.* Hanover, NH: University Press of New England, 1983.

Lamarque, G. *Théodule Ribot.* Paris: Rasmussen, 1928.

Lasserre, Pierre. *Le Romantisme français.* Paris: Mercure de France, 1907.

Lehmann, A. G. *The Symbolist Aesthetic in France 1885–1895.* 2d ed. Oxford: Basil Blackwell, 1968.

Lentricchia, Frank. *The Gaiety of Language: An Essay on the Radical Poetics of W. B. Yeats and Wallace Stevens.* Berkeley: University of California Press, 1968.

———. *After the New Criticism.* Chicago: University of Chicago Press, 1980.

———. "Patriarchy Against Itself—The Young Manhood of Wallace Stevens." *Critical Inquiry* 13 (1987): 742–86.

———. *Ariel and the Police: Michel Foucault, William James, Wallace Stevens.* Madison: The University of Wisconsin Press, 1988.

Leuba, James. *A Psychological Study of Religion, Its Origin, Function and Future.* New York: Macmillan, 1912.

Levenson, Michael H. *A Genealogy of Modernism: A Study of English Literary Doctrine 1908–1922.* Cambridge: Cambridge University Press, 1984.

Lewis, Wyndham, ed. *Wyndham Lewis on Art.* Edited by Walter Michel and C. J. Fox. New York: Funk and Wagnall's, 1969.

———. *Blast.* 1914. Reprint, Santa Barbara, Calif.: Black Sparrow Press, 1981.

———, ed. *Blast II.* 1915. Reprint, Santa Barbara, Calif.: Black Sparrow Press, 1981.

Lindberg, Kathryne V. *Reading Pound Reading: Modernism after Nietzsche.* Oxford: Oxford University Press, 1987.

Litz, A. Walton. *Introspective Voyageur: The Poetic Development of Wallace Stevens.* New York: Oxford University Press, 1972.

Longenbach, James. *Stone Cottage: Pound, Yeats & Modernism.* Oxford: Oxford University Press, 1988.

———. *Wallace Stevens: The Plain Sense of Things.* Oxford: Oxford University Press, 1991.

Lukács, Georg. *The Meaning of Contemporary Realism.* Translated by John Mander and Necke Mander. London: Merlin, 1963.

Mallarmé, Stéphane. *Oeuvres complètes.* Edited by Henri Mondor and G. Jean-Aubry. Paris: Gallimard, 1945.

Martin, Wallace. "The Sources of the Imagist Aesthetic." *PMLA* 85 (1970): 196–204.

Marx, Karl. *The German Ideology.* Edited by C. J. Arthur. New York: International, 1970.

———. "Theses on Feuerbach." In *The Marx-Engels Reader.* Edited by Robert C. Tucker, 143–45. New York: W. W. Norton, 1978.

Materer, Timothy. *Vortex: Eliot, Pound and Lewis.* Ithaca: Cornell University Press, 1979.

Mauclair, Camille. *Eléusis*. Paris: Perrin, 1894.

McDowell, Colin, and Timothy Materer. "Gyre and Vortex: W. B. Yeats and Ezra Pound." *Twentieth Century Literature* 31 (1985): 343–67.

McFadden, George. "Probings for an Integration: Color Symbolism in Wallace Stevens." *Modern Philology* 58 (1961): 186–93.

McTaggart, J. Ellis. Review of *Pragmatism, A New Name for Some Old Ways of Thinking*. *Mind* 17 (1908): 104–9.

Mead, G. R. S. "On the Nature of the Quest." *Quest* 1 (1909–10): 29–43.

———. "The Philosophy of the As-if: A Radical Criticism of Human Knowledge." *Quest* 4 (1912–13): 459–83.

Michaud, Guy. *Message poétique du symbolisme*. Paris: Librairie Nizet, 1947.

Miller, J. Hillis. *Poets of Reality*. Cambridge: Harvard University Press, 1965.

———. "Wallace Stevens' 'Poetry of Being.'" In *The Act of the Mind: Essays on the Poetry of Wallace Stevens*. Edited by J. Hillis Miller and Roy Harvey Pearce, 143–62. Baltimore: The Johns Hopkins University Press, 1965.

———. "Theoretical and Atheoretical in Stevens." *Wallace Stevens: A Celebration*. Edited by Frank Doggett and Robert Buttel, 274–85. Princeton: Princeton University Press, 1980.

Moore, G. E. "William James' 'Pragmatism.'" In *Philosophical Studies*. London: Routledge, 1922.

Morse, Samuel French. *Wallace Stevens: Poetry as Life*. New York: Pegasus, 1970.

Myers, Gerald E. *William James: His Life and Thought*. New Haven: Yale University Press, 1986.

Nietzsche, Friedrich. *The Gay Science*. Translated by Walter Kaufmann. New York: Vintage, 1974.

———. *Philosophy and Truth: Selections from Nietzsche's Notebooks of the Early 1870's*. Edited and translated by Daniel Breazeale. Atlantic Highlands, N.J.: Humanities Press, 1979.

———. "On Truth and Lie in an Extra-Moral Sense." *The Portable Nietzsche*. Edited by Walter Kaufmann, 42–47. New York: Random House, 1980.

Nochlin, Linda, ed. *Impressionism and Post-Impressionism 1874–1904*. Englewood Cliffs, N.J.: Prentice-Hall, 1966.

Nyquist, Mary. "Musing on Susanna's Music." In *Lyric Poetry: Beyond New Criticism*. Edited by Chaviva Hösek and Patricia Parker, 310–27. Ithaca: Cornell University Press, 1985.

Oderman, Kevin. *Ezra Pound and the Erotic Medium*. Durham, N.C.: Duke University Press, 1986.

Orwell, George. *Nineteen Eighty-Four*. Harmondsworth, England: Penguin, 1954.

Otto, Rudolph. *The Idea of the Holy*. Translated by John W. Harvey. Oxford: Oxford University Press, 1950.

Palante, Georges. Introduction to *Jules de Gaultier, La Philosophie du Bovarysme*. Paris: Mercure de France, 1912.

Pater, Walter. *Walter Pater: Essays on Literature and Art*. Edited by Jennifer Uglow. London: Dent, 1973.

Pauker, John. "A Discussion of Sea Surface Full of Clouds." *Furioso* 5 (1950): 36–62.

Pearce, Roy Harvey. "Toward Decreation: Stevens and the 'Theory of Poetry.'" In

Wallace Stevens: A Celebration. Edited by Frank Doggett and Robert Buttel, 286–307. Princeton: Princeton University Press, 1980.

Pearce, Roy Harvey, and J. Hillis Miller, eds. *The Act of the Mind: Essays on the Poetry of Wallace Stevens.* Baltimore, Md.: The Johns Hopkins University Press, 1965.

Pearlman, Daniel. *The Barb of Time: On the Unity of Ezra Pound's Cantos.* New York: Oxford University Press, 1969.

Peirce, Charles S. *Charles S. Peirce: Selected Writings.* Edited by Philip P. Wiener. New York: Dover, 1958.

Perloff, Marjorie. *The Poetics of Indeterminacy.* Princeton: Princeton UP, 1981.

———. *The Dance of the Intellect.* Cambridge: Cambridge University Press, 1985.

———. "Revolving in Crystal: The Supreme Fiction and the Impasse of Modernist Lyric." *Wallace Stevens: The Poetics of Modernism.* Edited by Albert Gelpi, 41–64. Cambridge: Cambridge University Press, 1985.

———. *Poetic License.* Evanston, Ill.: Northwestern University Press, 1990.

Perry, Ralph Barton. *The Thought and Character of William James.* 2 vols. Boston: Little, Brown, 1935.

———. *Present Philosophical Tendencies.* New York: George Braziller, 1955.

Peterson, Margaret. *Wallace Stevens and the Idealist Tradition.* Ann Arbor, Mich.: UMI Research Press, 1983.

Plato. *Phaedrus.* Translated and edited by R. Hackworth. Cambridge: Cambridge University Press, 1952.

Poirier, Richard. *The Renewal of Literature.* New York: Random House, 1987.

———. *Poetry and Pragmatism.* Cambridge, Mass.: Harvard University Press, 1992.

Posnock, Ross. *The Trial of Curiosity: Henry James, William James, and the Challenge of Modernity.* New York: Oxford University Press, 1991.

Pound, Ezra. "Psychology and Troubadours." *Quest* 4 (1912–13): 37–53.

———. *ABC of Reading.* London: Faber and Faber, 1951.

———. *Collected Shorter Poems.* London: Faber and Faber, 1952.

———. "This Hulme Business." *Townsman* 2 (January 1939): 15.

———. *Literary Essays of Ezra Pound.* Edited by T. S. Eliot. London: Faber, 1960.

———. *Gaudier-Grzeska.* New York: New Directions, 1970.

———. *Guide to Kulchur.* New York: New Directions, 1970.

———. *Selected Prose: 1909–1965.* Edited by William Cookson. London: Faber and Faber, 1973.

———. *The Cantos.* London: Faber and Faber, 1975.

———. *Ezra Pound and the Visual Arts.* Edited by Harriet Zinnes. New York: New Directions, 1980.

———. *Ezra Pound and Dorothy Shakespear: Their Letters: 1909–1914.* Edited by Omar Pound and A. Walton Litz. New York: New Directions, 1984.

Pratt, James Bissett. "Truth and Its Verification." *Journal of Philosophy, Psychology and Scientific Method* 4 (1908): 320–24.

Primeau, Ronald. "On the Discrimination of Hulme's: Toward a Theory of the Anti-Romantic Romanticism of Modern Poetry." *Journal of Modern Literature* 3 (July 1974): 1104–22.

Redgrove, H. Stanley. "The Sight of the Soul: An Essay in Christian Mysticism." *Quest* 3 (1912): 496–515.

Rees, Garnet. *Remy de Gourmont*. Paris: Boivin, 1939.

Review as written by E.C.T., of Émile Boutroux, *William James*. *Quest* 3 (1912): 787–88.

Review as written by anon., of Morton Prince, ed., *Subconscious Phenomena*. *Quest* 2 (1911/–12): 389–92.

Review as written by anon., of J. Arthur Thompson, *Introduction to Science*. *Quest* 4 (1912–13): 187–88.

Ribot, Théodule. *La Psychologie anglaise contemporaine*. Paris: Félix Alcan, 1896.

———. *English Psychology*. Trans. unknown. London: Henry S. King, 1873.

———. *Psychology of Emotions*, trans. unknown. London: Walter Scott, 1911.

———. *L'Évolution des idées générales*. Paris: Ancienne Libraire Germer Baillière, 1897.

———. *Essay on the Creative Imagination*. Translated by Albert H. N. Baron. London: Kegan Paul, 1906.

———. *The Psychology of the Emotions*. Translated by W. Scott. New York: Scribner's, 1911.

———. *Essai sur l'imagination créatrice*. Paris: Félix Alcan, 1921.

———. *La Psychologie des sentiments*. Paris: Félix Alcan, 1939.

Richards, I. A. *Principles of Literary Criticism*. London: Routledge and Kegan Paul, 1967.

———. *Poetries and Sciences: A Reissue of Science and Poetry (1926, 1935) with Commentary*. London: Routledge and Kegan Paul, 1970.

Richardson, Joan. *Wallace Stevens: The Early Years 1879–1923*. New York: Beech Tree, 1986.

Ricoeur, Paul. "The Metaphorical Process as Cognition, Imagination, and Feeling." In *On Metaphor*. Edited by Sheldon Sacks, 141–57. Chicago: University of Chicago Press, 1979.

Riddel, Joseph N. *The Clairvoyant Eye: The Poetry and Poetics of Wallace Stevens*. Baton Rouge: Louisiana State University Press, 1965.

———. "The Contours of Stevens Criticism." *ELH* 31 (1964): 106–38.

———. *The Clairvoyant Eye: The Poetry and Poetics of Wallace Stevens*. Baton Rouge: Louisiana State University Press, 1965.

———. "Pound and the Decentered Image." *Georgia Review* 29 (1975): 565–91.

———. "Neo-Nietzschean Clatter." *Ezra Pound: Tactics for Reading*. Edited by Ian F. A. Bell, 187–220. London: Vision, 1982.

Rimbaud, Arthur. *Oeuvres complètes*. Edited by Rolland de Reneville and Jules Mouquet. Paris: Gallimard, 1946.

Roberts, Michael. *T. E. Hulme*. Manchester: Carcanet New Press, 1982.

Robinson, Alan. *Poetry, Painting and Ideas 1885–1914*. London: Macmillan, 1985.

Rorty, Richard. *Philosophy and the Mirror of Nature*. Princeton, Princeton University Press, 1979.

———. *Consequences of Pragmatism*. Minneapolis: University of Minnesota Press, 1982.

———. *Contingency, Irony, and Solidarity*. Cambridge: Cambridge University Press, 1989.

————. *Objectivity, Relativism, and Truth*. Cambridge: Cambridge University Press, 1991.

Rosenfeld, Paul. *Men Seen: Twenty-four Modern Authors*. New York: Dial Press, 1925.

Ruddick, Lisa. "Fluid Symbols in American Modernism." In *Allegory, Myth and Symbol*. Edited by Morton W. Bloomfield, 335–53. Cambridge: Harvard University Press, 1981.

————. *Reading Stein Reading*. Ithaca: Cornell University Press, 1991.

Russell, Bertrand. "William James's Conception of Truth." 127–49. In *Philosophical Essays*. London: Longmans, Green, 1910.

Ruthven, K. K. *A Guide to Ezra Pound's Personae*. Berkeley: University of California Press, 1976.

Ryan, Judith. *The Vanishing Subject: Early Psychology and Literary Modernism*. Chicago: University of Chicago Press, 1991.

Said, Edward W. *Orientalism*. New York: Vintage, 1979.

Santayana, George. "Walt Whitman: A Dialogue." *The Harvard Monthly* (May 1890): 85–92.

————. "What Is Aesthetics?" *Philosophical Review* 12 (1904): 320–27.

————. "A Brief History of My Opinions." In *The Philosophy of Santayana*. Edited by Irwin Edman. New York: Scribner's, 1936.

————. *The Letters of George Santayana*. Edited by Daniel Cory. New York: Scribner's, 1955.

————. *The Sense of Beauty*. New York: Dover, 1955.

————. *Interpretations of Poetry and Religion*. New York: Harper & Brothers, 1957.

————. *Realms of Being*. New York: Cooper Square, 1972.

————. *Persons and Places*. The Works of George Santayana. Vol. 1. Edited by William G. Holzberger and Herman J. Saatkamp, Jr. Cambridge: MIT Press, 1987.

Sartre, Jean-Paul. *The Psychology of Imagination*. Secaucus, N.J.: Citadel Press, n.d.

Scharfstein, Ben-Ami. *Roots of Bergson's Philosophy*. New York: Columbia University Press, 1943.

Schaum, Melita. *Wallace Stevens and the Critical Schools*. Tuscaloosa: University of Alabama Press, 1988.

————. *Wallace Stevens and the Feminine*. Tuscaloosa: University of Alabama Press, 1993.

Schneidau, Herbert N. *Ezra Pound: The Image and the Real*. Baton Rouge: Louisiana State University Press, 1967.

————. "Wisdom Past Metaphor: Another View of Pound, Fenollosa, and Objective Verse." *Paideuma* 5 (Spring 1976): 15–29.

Schopenhauer, Arthur. *The World as Will and Representation*. 2 vols. Translated by E. F. J. Payne. New York: Dover, 1969.

Schwartz, Sanford. *The Matrix of Modernism: Pound, Eliot and Early 20th-Century Thought*. Princeton: Princeton University Press, 1985.

Seigfried, Charlene Haddock. *William James's Radical Reconstruction of Philosophy*. Albany, N.Y.: SUNY Press, 1990.

Shapiro, Karl. *In Defense of Ignorance.* New York: Random House, 1952.

Shaw, W. David. "The Poetics of Pragmatism: Robert Frost and William James," *New England Quarterly* LIX (January 1986): 159–88.

Shelley, Percy Bysshe. *The Complete Poetical Works of Percy Bysshe Shelley.* Edited by Thomas Hutchinson. Oxford: Oxford University Press, 1923.

———. *Shelley's Prose.* Ed. David Lee Clark. London: Fourth Estate, 1988.

Shusterman, Richard. *Pragmatist Aesthetics: Living Beauty, Rethinking Art.* Oxford: Basil Blackwell, 1992.

Sidney, Sir Philip. *Defense of Poetry.* Edited by Lewis Soens. Lincoln: University of Nebraska Press, 1970.

Simpson, David, ed. *The Origins of Modern Critical Thought.* Cambridge: Cambridge University Press, 1988.

Singh, G. "Ezra Pound: A Commemorative Symposium." *Paideuma* 3 (1974): 158–61.

Sosnowski, Andrzej. "Pound's Imagism and Emanuel Swedenborg." *Paideuma* 20 (1991): 31–38.

Springer, Mary Doyle. "The Feminine Principle in Stevens' Poetry: 'Esthetique du Mal.'" *Wallace Stevens Journal* 12 (1988): 119–37.

Starkie, Enid. "Bergson and Literature." In *The Bergsonian Heritage.* Edited by Thomas Hanna. New York: Columbia University Press, 1962.

Stedman, E.C. *The Nature and Elements of Poetry.* Boston: Houghton, Mifflin, 1892.

Stevens, Wallace. *The Collected Poems of Wallace Stevens.* New York: Knopf, 1954.

———. *The Necessary Angel: Essays on Reality and the Imagination.* London: Faber, 1960.

———. *Souvenirs and Prophecies: The Young Wallace Stevens.* Edited by Holly Stevens. New York: Knopf, 1966.

———. *Letters of Wallace Stevens.* Ed. Holly Stevens. New York: Knopf, 1966.

———. *Opus Posthumous.* Edited by Milton J. Bates. Revised, enlarged, and corrected edition. New York: Knopf, 1989.

Stock, Noel. *The Life of Ezra Pound.* San Francisco, Calif.: North Point Press, 1982.

Surette, Leon. *The Birth of Modernism: Ezra Pound, T. S. Eliot, W. B. Yeats, and the Occult.* Kingston, England: McGill-Queen's University Press, 1993.

Sutton, Walter. "Coherence in Pound's Cantos and William James's Pluralistic Universe." *Paideuma* 15 (1986): 7–21.

Szathmary, Arthur. *The Aesthetic Theory of Bergson.* Cambridge: Harvard University Press, 1937.

Taylor, Alfred Edward. "Truth and Practice." *Philosophical Review* 14 (1905): 265–89.

Terrell, Carroll F. *A Companion to the Cantos of Ezra Pound.* Berkeley: University of California Press, 1980.

Tryphonopoulos, Demetres P. "Ezra Pound and Emanuel Swedenborg." *Paideuma* 20 (Winter 1991): 7–15.

———. *The Celestial Tradition: A Study of Ezra Pound's The Cantos.* Waterloo, Ontario: Wilfred Laurier Press, 1992.

Underhill, Evelyn. "A Note upon Mysticism." *Quest* 1 (1909–10): 742–52.

————. "The Mystic as Creative Artist." *Quest* 4 (1912–13): 629–52.

Untermeyer, Louis. "The Ivory Tower II." *New Republic* 19 (10 May 1919): 60–61.

Vaihinger, Hans. *The Philosophy of "As If."* Translated by C. K. Ogden. London: Kegan Paul, Trench, Trübner, 1924.

Vendler, Helen. *On Extended Wings: Wallace Stevens' Longer Poems*. Cambridge: Harvard University Press, 1969.

Visan, Tancrède de. *L'Attitude du lyrisme contemporain*. Paris: Mercure de France, 1911.

Walsh, Walter. "Trespassers on the Mystic Way." *Quest* 5 (1914): 492–504.

Ward, A. H. "The Power of Imagination." *Quest* 1 (1909): 61–75.

Waugh, Patricia. *Practising Postmodernism Reading Modernism*. London: Edward Arnold, 1992.

Wees, William. *Vorticism and the English Avant-garde*. Toronto: University of Toronto Press, 1972.

West, Cornel. *The American Evasion of Philosophy*. Madison: University of Wisconsin Press, 1989.

————. "Theory, Pragmatisms, and Politics." In *Consequences of Theory*. Edited by Jonathan Arac and Barbara Johnson, 22–37. Baltimore, Md: Johns Hopkins University Press, 1991.

Westbrook, Robert F. *John Dewey and American Democracy*. Ithaca: Cornell University Press, 1991.

Whistler, James McNeill. *The Gentle Art of Making Enemies*. New York: Dover, 1962.

Whitehead, A. N. *Science and the Modern World*. New York: Macmillan, 1925.

Whitman, Walt. *Complete Poetry and Collected Prose*. Edited by Justin Kaplan. New York: Library of America, 1982.

Wiedmann, August K. *Romantic Roots in Modern Art*. Old Woking, Surrey: Gresham, 1979.

Windelband, Wilhelm. "Present-Day Mysticism." *Quest* 4 (1912–13): 201–11.

Wordsworth, William. *The Poetical Works of William Wordsworth*. Vol. 5. Edited by E. de Selincourt and Helen Darbishire. Oxford: Clarendon, 1947.

Worringer, Wilhelm. *Abstraction and Empathy*. Translated by Michael Bullock. New York: International Universities Press, 1953.

Yeats, W. B. *Essays and Introductions*. London: MacMillan, 1961.

————. *Collected Poems*. Edited by Richard J. Finneran. New York: MacMillan, 1983.

Index